Phyllis Ford

RECREATION, PARK AND LEISURE SERVICES:

Foundations, Organization, Administration

GEOFFREY GODBEY

Recreation and Parks Program,
The Pennsylvania State University,
University Park, Pennsylvania

with the assistance of

DIANA DUNN
WILLIAM FAILOR
PATRICIA FARRELL
GORDON GODBEY
SARAH GODBEY
FRANK GUADAGNOLO
FRED HUMPHREY
KARL MUNSON
JERRY WETTSTONE

1978

W. B. SAUNDERS COMPANY / Philadelphia / London / Toronto

W. B. Saunders Company: West Washington Square
Philadelphia, PA 19105

1 St. Anne's Road
Eastbourne, East Sussex BN21 3UN, England

1 Goldthorne Avenue
Toronto, Ontario M8Z 5T9, Canada

Library of Congress Cataloging in Publication Data

Godbey, Geoffrey,

Recreation, park, and leisure services.

Includes index.

1. Recreation—United States. 2. Parks—United States.
3. Leisure—United States. I. Title.

GV53.G62 301.5′7 77-78570

ISBN 0-7216-4143-1

Cover photography of a Massachusetts Sunset, Eastern Point, near Gloucester, by Ed Cooper

Recreation, Park and Leisure Services: Foundations, Organization, Administration ISBN 0-7216-4143-1

Last digit is the print number: 9 8 7 6 5 4 3 2 1

ABOUT THE AUTHOR

Geoffrey Godbey is an Associate Professor in the Recreation and Parks Program at The Pennsylvania State University. Previously, he was Acting Chairman, Department of Recreation, University of Waterloo, Ontario, Canada, and prior to that initiated an associate degree curriculum in Recreation Leadership at the Ogontz campus of The Pennsylvania State University near Philadelphia. He has been a Research Trainee with the Philadelphia Department of Recreation, a Recreation Coordinator with the Greater Newark Recreation Association in Delaware, a tennis instructor, and a houseparent for juvenile delinquents at the George Junior Republic in Freeville, New York. His articles have appeared in a number of publications, including *The Community Development Journal, the Journal of Leisure Research, Parks and Recreation* and *Recreation Canada.* He is the coauthor, with Stanley Parker, of *Leisure Studies and Services: An Overview,* published by W. B. Saunders in 1976. Professor Godbey is an associate editor of *Leisure Sciences* and of the *Review of Sport and Leisure.* His poetry has appeared in a number of literary magazines, including *Northwest Review* and *The Malahat Review.* A book of his poetry, *The Midget On A Bicycle,* was published in 1968 by Mansfield Press. He is married to the former Bonnie Ganous and has two daughters, Cassandra and Tamara. His leisure interests include writing poetry, vegetable gardening and playing tennis.

PREFACE

This book was written to introduce the reader to the principal types of organizations that provide recreation, park and leisure services and their roles in modern society. Additionally, a number of issues are examined which affect the decision-making process of such agencies. Although the organizations discussed here have diverse purposes, clientele and methods of operation, it is believed that the features such organizations have in common outweigh those which make them different. These common features, in terms of agency goals, processes and the skills needed to implement them, form the basis of a profession which is steadily, if unsurely, emerging. This commonality has been the central assumption in the preparation of this text.

It has been the intent of the book's principal author to utilize the talents of several coauthors in writing chapters about specific types of recreation, park and leisure service agencies. These coauthors have not only studied such organizations in colleges and universities but have also been affiliated with them as recreation, park and leisure service professionals or as involved citizens. Thus, these chapters represent more than a library compilation of secondary sources concerning the respective topics. It is therefore understandable, even desirable, that the chapters reflect variation in terminology, style and outlook. Such diversity was assumed to be worthwhile, reflecting the differences in perspective between, for instance, state recreation services and those of the commercial sector. Thus, each contributing author was free to develop his or her chapter within minimum guidelines.

There are two sections to this book. The first, Functions of Recreation, Park and Leisure Services, is devoted primarily to the types of organizations that provide leisure services and the types of clientele for which the services are provided. These chapters inevitably will overlap somewhat, since leisure service organizations have not emerged historically in a neat, coordinated fashion. We have attempted, however, to make each chapter correspond to a type or types of organizations having a number of unique, identifiable features and often corresponding to what may be considered a specialized area of employment, such as therapeutic recreation. Special attention is devoted to providing a brief historical overview of each type of organization, discussing purposes, methods of operation and organizational framework, types of services provided, methods of finance and overall trends.

The second section, Processes of Recreation, Park and Leisure Services, seeks to identify and describe the processes by which such organizations make decisions and the types of information they utilize. Particular attention is given to the role of the citizen or client in this process.

I would like to express my thanks to Kitty Hall Lange, Stan Francis and Glen Smoot, who introduced me to the recreation and parks profession; to Gold Metcalf, Fred Coombs and Betty van der Smissen, who contributed greatly to my education; to Gerry Kenyon and Tony Mobley, who encouraged me to write; and to my parents and my wife Bonnie for more things than I know.

GEOFFREY C. GODBEY

CONTENTS

SECTION ONE—FUNCTIONS OF RECREATION, PARK AND LEISURE SERVICES

RECREATION, PARK AND LEISURE SERVICES

FOUNDATIONS, ORGANIZATION, ADMINISTRATION

Leisure may be defined as the state of being free of everyday necessity.
,U.S. Bureau of Outdoor Recreation.

chapter 1

RECREATION, PARK AND LEISURE SERVICES IN MODERN SOCIETY

In this chapter, we will examine different meanings of leisure and recreation, leisure trends during past centuries, and the emerging role of leisure service organizations.

CONCEPTUALIZING LEISURE AND RECREATION

Since this is a book about recreation and leisure, and the organizations which provide such services, it is essential that we come to some understanding about what these words mean. Although no single definition may be adequate for each term, by understanding the range of meanings more completely we can better determine which services would qualify as leisure and which as recreation.

DEFINITIONS OF LEISURE

The term "leisure" has been conceptualized in three basic contexts: "time, activities, or a state of mind."[1] Although the meanings of the words used to identify these three contexts often overlap, this classification is useful in determining which aspect of the word was emphasized in various definitions of the term.

Leisure Defined As Time

Aristotle used the term "leisure" in two senses. One meaning he ascribed to the word was available time.[2] This idea of available time was given a negative connotation by Veblen in 1899, who used the word leisure in the sense of unproductive consumption of time.[3] At the time of Veblen's statement, leisure was the prerogative of an elite, at least in the sense of active leisure.[4] For the industrial and rural population, leisure was synonymous with killing time or resting.[5]

In 1928, May and Petgen spoke of leisure as "the time surplus remaining after the practical necessities of life have been attended to."[6] *The Dictionary of Sociology,* in 1944, used a conceptualization of leisure which was "an arithmetic one of time devoted to work, sleep, and other necessities, subtracted from 24 hours—which gives the surplus time."[7]

Today leisure, defined as time, often connotes "The state of having time at one's own disposal; time which one can spend as he pleases; free or unoccupied time."[8] De Grazia believed: "The word leisure has turned into the phrase free time, and the two are now almost interchangeable."[2]

The term lesiure is used as an adjective to modify time and as such means "being unoccupied by practical necessities."[9] Moore spoke of leisure in one sense as the "optional use of time."[10] Weiss believed that "leisure time is that portion of the day not used for the exigencies of existence."[11] Soule broadened the concept of leisure in relation to time by considering leisure as all time which an individual did not sell.[12] Leisure was also defined in an economic sense by Dumazedier, who related it to time by saying that leisure was "the time freed from productive work, thanks to technical progress and social action, for man's pursuit of a non-productive activity before, during, or after the period of his productive occupation."[13]

Neumeyer and Neumeyer pointed out that one problem involved in conceptualizing leisure as free time is that "the line of demarcation between necessities and spare time is not rigid."[14] Therefore, there could be disagreement as to whether certain social conditions should be considered leisure. Heckscher, for instance, thought it was a mockery to speak of persons forcibly retired to idleness or the unemployed persons as men and women of leisure.[15] Nakhooda, however, believed unemployment provided leisure, although undesired.[9] Unemployment compensation, according to Suhm, Jorgensen and Jondahl, today gives unemployed people a genuine opportunity for meaningful leisure.[16] In discussing whether retirement could be considered leisure, Kaplan posed this question: "If leisure is looked upon as a contrast to work in its psychological perception, what if there is no juxtaposition?"[17] He believed the nature of the activity undertaken during retirement determined whether or not it was leisure.

De Grazia thought that "in changing from the term leisure to the term free time we had gone from a qualitative to a quantitative concept."[2] He did not personally equate leisure with free time, because of the personal nature of leisure.

The very idea of free time, Berger stated, belonged in a presociological age. "If sociology has taught us anything it has taught us that no time is free of normative constraints; what is work for some is leisure for others. . . ."[18]

A classification of the meanings of leisure compiled by Kaplan contained two concepts of leisure in a time context. First, Kaplan stated, leisure could be classified as "a bulk of quantitatively distinct time," and secondly, as "using the time of others to influence or win them over."[19]

Kaplan also identified five different kinds of free time: "permanent, voluntary leisure of the rich, temporary involuntary leisure of the unemployed, regularly allocated voluntary leisure of the employed on holidays or vacations, and the temporary incapacity of the employed, permanent incapacity of the disabled, and the voluntary retirement of the aged."[19] The fifth type of free time identified was the free time of unemployed old people and of the disabled.

Some authors have sought to relate the concept of leisure as time to the concept of leisure as a state. Said Recreation and Park Educator Charles Brightbill: "I see leisure as an opportunity; and there can be no choice, no judgment, no attitude, and hence no freedom without opportunity. Nor can there be opportunity without time, which to me is the overriding component of leisure."[20]

Fitzgerald also related leisure to a state of opportunity, stating that "Leisure represents time; time is opportunity. Leisure represents freedom; freedom allows for choice; and choice is opportunity."[21]

The meaning of leisure to the layman was defined by Nakhooda as "that part of the individual's daily life in which he finds himself free from the demands of his regular calling and able to enter upon any line of activity he may choose within his own interests—whether it be work or play or meditation."[9]

Leisure Defined As Activity

The ancient Greek word for leisure, "schole," meant "serious activity without the pressure of necessity."[22] This term did not imply a strict distinction from work, nor was it synonymous with the term "recreation," since the Greeks had another term meaning "playful amusement to pass the time."[22] The English word "school" is derived from the Greek word for leisure.[14] From this conception of leisure as activity, the term has often been referred to as a "cluster of activities."[8]

Four types of activities, which arise from leisure but represent some degree of obligation, were termed "semi-leisure" by Dumazedier and Latouche. These were classified as leisure activities of a semi-lucrative, semi-disinterested nature, such as participation in orchestras; domestic activities of a semi-utilitarian, semi-recreational nature, such as do-it-yourself projects; family activities of a semi-distractive, semi-educational nature, such as playing with children; and small, agreeable jobs, such as making models.[23]

Anderson stated that in activities which took place during leisure time there was "a sharp contrast to the external controls of time, space, and production imposed in the work situation."[24] Leisure as activity was conceptualized by Kaplan as activity which served as "an end, distinct from work as a means" and also as "a re-creation in order to prepare for better work; self-improvement; social control."[19]

A definition of leisure devised by the International Group of the Social Sciences of Leisure stated:

> **Leisure consists of a number of occupations in which the individual may indulge of his own free will—either to rest, to amuse himself, to add to his knowledge or improve his skills disinterestedly or to increase his voluntary participation in the life of the community after discharging his professional, family and social duties.[13]**

Smigel felt that often the term "leisure" was misused, and mentioned that when such words as "recreation," "amusement," "play" and "hobby" were used interchangeably, the confusion as to the true meaning of leisure was compounded.[25] Goodman added that discussion of mass leisure by sociologists did not center on serious activity at all.[22] Conversely, sociologist Riesman stated that "leisure is an occasional essay at refinement."[26] The nature of an activity, according to Larrabee and Meyersohn, could not serve as a specific guide to determining what was leisure, since any and all activities could provide leisure.[8]

In spite of the many meanings of leisure, Dempsey stated that students of leisure "are agreed that the test of leisure is that it should be an end in itself, and that it must represent an individual's own choice of activity."[27]

Leisure Defined as a State of Existence

The English word "leisure" originated from the Latin verb "licere," which meant "to be allowed."[2] Aristotle used the term "leisure" to mean the "absence of the necessity of being occupied."[2] In such ancient concepts of leisure, there was great emphasis on a state of freedom.[28]

Philosopher Joseph Pieper stressed this idea when he said:

> **Leisure, it must be understood, is a mental and spiritual attitude—it is not simply the result of external factors, it is not the inevitable result of spare time, a holiday, a weekend or a vacation. It is, in the first place, an attitude of the mind, a condition of the soul.**[29]

Pieper further stated that leisure could not be a means to an end, but rather must be an end in itself. A related concept of leisure was advanced by Brightbill, who described leisure as "a state of quiet contemplative dignity."[20] Kaplan believed that leisure could be classified as "freedom from activities which must be done," as "sets of motivations of attitudes," and as an "emotional or psychological necessity."[19] Larrabee and Meyersohn defined leisure in terms of a state of existence as "a mood of contemplation," and "an absence of obligations."[8] De Grazia said that the definition of leisure that "gave it its long life" was that "leisure is the state of being free of everyday necessity," but he also noted that "our own conception of leisure is mainly recreative."[2]

Summary

From the preceding, it is evident that while leisure is defined differently in different cultures, the notion of free choice at an individual level is usually central. Disagreements concerning definitions of leisure often center on the relationship of leisure to time, on what assumptions can be made about people's motivation for participation in an activity, and on what social, psychological and political conditions are likely to result in individual freedom.

DEFINITIONS OF RECREATION

Recreation has traditionally been defined as activity done in opposition to work which refreshed or restored the individual. Rainwater, in 1923, stated: "Recreation is re-creation or restoration of depleted motor power or emotional state."[30] May and Petgen similarily noted that "The word 'recreation' as used in America has often the limited connotation of play, and etymologically has the suggestion of rebuilding from a subnormal condition."[31] In Europe, however, adult education, cultural pursuits and even political study and activity were considered a recreational use of leisure.[31] Mead stated that the word recreation epitomized a "whole attitude of conditional joy in which the delights of both work and play are tied together in a tight sequence. Neither one may be considered by itself, but man must work, then weary and 'like some recreation' so he may work again."[32]

Some concepts of recreation have overlapped concepts of leisure. Both, for instance, have been defined as unobligated activity. Wrenn and Hardy defined recreation as follows: "Recreation is what a person finds pleasure in doing when he is not paid for it and does not feel any other kind of obligation to do it."[33] In 1944, the *Dictionary of Sociology* defined recreation as "any activity pursued during leisure, either individual or collective, that is free and pleasureful, having its own immediate appeal, not impelled by a delayed reward beyond itself."[34]

Many educators and practitioners in the recreation movement, both in the United States and in Canada, limited their definitions of recreation to activities that were morally sound or non-debilitating. Hutchinson, for example, defines recreation as "a worthwhile, socially acceptable leisure experience providing immediate, inherent satisfaction to the individual who voluntarily participates in activity."[35] Recreation, according to Doell and Fitzgerald, is leisure time activities that are "morally sound, mentally and physically upbuilding, respectful of the rights of others, voluntarily motivated, and (which) provide a sense of pleasure and achievement."[36] Romney stated: "recreation is not a matter of motions—but rather emotions. It is a personal response, a psychological reaction, an attitude, an approach, a way of life."[37] Some recent definitions of recreation, however, do not consider recreation to be in opposition to work or confined to activity which is morally sound. Avedon, for instance, says:

> **Recreation—a personal sensation of well-being experienced in the process of anticipating, recalling, or engaging in any activity. This sensation of well-being is a phenomenon in which physical, biological, psychological, and social components are integrated to form a functional unit. This functional unit has properties which are not derivable from its component parts.[38]**

The notion of recreation's providing personal well-being was further developed by Gray and Greben, who suggested that the recreation and park profession consider recreation to be "an emotional condition within an individual human being that flows from a feeling of well-being and self-satisfaction. It is characterized by feelings of mastery, achievement, exhilaration, acceptance, success, personal worth and pleasure. It reinforces a positive self-image. Recreation is a response to aesthetic experience, achievement of personal goals, or positive feedback from others. It is independent of activity, leisure or social acceptance.[39]

As may be observed, there are a number of disagreements and differences in conceptual emphasis in these definitions. Recreation has been defined both as activity undertaken during leisure and as activity without regard to leisure. It has been considered both cathartic activity and without regard to whether it provided catharsis. Such differences indicate that recreation is sometimes viewed as a means to an end and other times as an end in itself. Whether or not recreation is limited to "moral" activity is subject to question, and the concomitant problem of "moral according to whom?" is usually left unanswered. Finally there is disagreement as to whether recreation is primarily determined by the nature of the activity, the attitude of the respondent toward the activity, or the respondent's psychological state during the activity.

LEISURE IN PREVIOUS CENTURIES

PRE-INDUSTRIAL SOCIETIES

In most pre-industrial societies the majority of people worked, and still work, so hard to sustain themselves and their families that their lives are almost devoid of leisure in the modern sense. The life of the peasant, and it should be remembered that most people in our world are still peasants, was and continues to be a continuous round of labor. To conclude from this, however, that people in pre-industrial societies have nothing equivalent to our concept of recreation and leisure would be unwarranted. But it is true that there is no *deliberate* leisure, nothing that is the result of the exercise of individual choice. In such societies all time is utilized, if not in work, then in other "structured activities." Such festivities as weddings, christenings, birthdays and fiestas are common, but they all have an obligatory character in addition to serving as leisure or recreation.

In simpler societies the line between labor and leisure is not so sharply drawn. Primitive people tend to approach a great many of their daily activities as if they were play. The orientation of their lives is toward long periods of work interspersed with occasional rest or periods involving intense expenditures of energy. In these societies, there are no clearly defined periods of leisure as such, but economic activities such as hunting or market selling have their recreational aspects in that songs are sung and stories are told at work. Although such societies do have activities that would be considered recreation, the idea of having a special time set aside for this purpose is generally unfamiliar. One of the biggest differences in the role of leisure in such societies is that leisure is structured by the rhythm of necessary daily tasks and of the seasons. It is integrated into the people's daily life rather than existing as a separate part of it.

ANCIENT GREECE

Many of our ideas concerning leisure were first formulated by the ancient Greeks. As noted in the definitions, leisure was not just contrasted to work. There was also a contrast to action. Aristotle spoke of the life of leisure *vs.* the life of action. But he went on to insist that no occupation could be regarded as leisure, nor could leisure be anything related to an occupation. His view was that the goal of being occupied should be only to obtain leisure, or, as it may be more popularly translated, we are unleisurely in order to have leisure. The Greek conception of leisure was really part, and the very central part, of a wider conception of the nature of a free man. The Greeks saw the capacity to use leisure wisely as the basis of the free man's whole life. The actual range of activities that qualified as leisure was, however, severely restricted. Aristotle decided only two were worthy of the name leisure: music and contemplation.

There are, of course, many objections that can be raised against this whole concept of leisure. Prominent among these is the fact that Greek society was based on slave labor; the style of life and leisure regarded as appropriate to free men was in fact that of a privileged elite. It may be that technological and social advances will make it possible in the society of the future for the majority of people to be free from the necessity of work, and hence free to fill their lives with music and contemplation. But to rule out the whole range of creative activities beyond these two, which people in past Greek societies have chosen when free from economic necessity, would be to narrow unnecessarily the experience of leisure.

It is relevant to point out that what we have been discussing is the Greek leisure *ideal,* which is not necessarily consistent with the Greek *practice* of leisure. Games, for instance, were a major part of the education of the privileged leisure class. Military needs led to a heavy emphasis on physical feats of daring accuracy and endurance. The early Olympic games included foot races, wrestling, boxing, chariot racing and oratory. The large stadiums and gymnasiums held athletic events, while open-air amphitheaters afforded areas for music, dance and dramatic festivals. Public baths offered a setting for diversion and relaxation. So perhaps it is fair to say that there is not much difference between the range of leisure opportunities for some of the people then and that of most people today. It should also be noted that the leisure ideal was limited in ancient Greece to the minority, and this situation probably remains so to a different minority today.

THE MIDDLE AGES THROUGH THE INDUSTRIAL REVOLUTION

In many earlier societies the amount of leisure enjoyed by the ordinary citizen or non-slave worker was much greater than that available to the average worker during the Industrial Revolution. The Roman passion for free time reached its climax in the fourth century, when holidays numbered 175. Whatever the work schedules of slaves and women, leisure for the ruling class, for administrative and professional men, would never again be so abundant. By contrast, in France and England from the late Middle Ages to about 1800, the trend in manual occupations was toward longer working hours. The working week for factory workers in these countries and in America had by the mid-nineteenth century reached 70 hours or more. Farm workers were exceptions to this trend; they worked very long hours during the whole period, with some reduction only in the twentieth century.

The decline of leisure from the end of the Middle Ages to the height of the Industrial Revolution is not, however, to be measured only by the increase in working hours. In pre-industrial society, work was incorporated into everyday life and leisure time was not a separate section of the day. Work carried on in the fields or within the home itself was accompanied by friendly conversations concerning the business of village life. It was only when work came to be done in a special place, at a special, separate time and under special conditions, that leisure came to be demanded as a right.

It can, however, be argued that leisure never really existed for the mass of people until it was won as a separate part of life from their excessively long working hours. Leisure could therefore be regarded as a product of industrial society, and indeed it does seem that the reduction in working hours was accomplished by the introduction of forms of leisure typical of the social structure and circumstances of the time. In contrast to leisure in medieval times, which had to be justified by some kind of enforced public ritual or ceremony, the new leisure time of the industrial working classes was largely filled by various amusement industries. Industrial society developed into a mass production and consumer society, and this became evident in both the conditions and contents of leisure. More densely populated areas began to spring up as people left the land and moved closer to the factory or shop where they were employed. When they did this, they began to form cities, but whereas in the countryside and small villages they were used to having land on which to play, in the cities, no provision was made for setting aside recreation areas and facilities. The organized recreation movement came about in response to this situation.

LEISURE IN THE 20TH CENTURY

It was during the twentieth century that leisure became a separate social institution in industrialized nations. That is, provisions were made so that, during specified periods of time and under certain conditions, people could pursue desired experiences which they found pleasurable. While members of former societies all pursued pleasurable activities within the context of their daily life and social roles, our modern industrial societies differ in the extent to which (a) leisure and work have been split into *separate* areas of life, and (b) leisure activity is chosen on an *individual* basis, with a minimum of prescribed roles. In addition, material standards of living achieved by contemporary industrial societies have opened up undreamed of possibilities for leisure experience. Whereas pre-industrial cultures often prescribed the role of the individual in all life experiences, and individuals were restricted in the material resources necessary for many leisure experiences, our modern society permits more individual freedom in the selection of leisure experience and provides a better economic base for millions to seek leisure in whatever form they choose. In short, industrial societies have created what might be termed an increased "leisure potential." That is, if a person wants leisure rather than economically compelled activity, and will accept the consequences of choosing it, there are significant portions of his life that can be devoted to more than the endless round of labor that most people in the world have traditionally experienced and still do. This is not to say that all people will choose to do this, but merely that the potential exists. Such a situation has been variously viewed as a problem, a challenge or a utopian post-industrial society in which the end of scarcity has brought about "mass leisure."

While many factors have contributed to this leisure potential, the following have been most important during the last hundred years:

1. *The increased production of material goods through the application of technology.* This increased productivity, often 2 to 3 percent per year during the last half-century, has meant that the worker has the potential for more leisure if the material standard of living is kept the same.

2. *The creation of labor-saving devices for household maintenance and other essential duties.* Labor-saving devices for maintaining households and other living spaces have meant that if the level of maintenance required stays the same and it takes less time to achieve that level, more time is available for leisure. Sometimes, however, the result of this has been an increase in the desired level of maintenance.

3. *The decline of the influence of social institutions such as the church and the family in establishing predetermined roles for individuals in all aspects of life.* This has, in effect, produced more individual discretion in the selection of activities. Changes in religious beliefs concerning man's relationship to the macrocosm and the decline of the influence of secular religion in the twentieth century have made man exercise his will to a greater extent than before, since fewer usable guidelines for behavior exist which are based upon religious doctrine.

4. *Differences in attitudes toward pleasure.* It appears that contemporary society has become a pleasure-seeking one. The Puritans' distrust of pleasure and the Christian belief in original sin have both declined in popularity,

thus diminishing many individuals' need to justify their lives. As de Grazia mentions, the "leisure kind," who have existed in small numbers in every society, have not felt the need to justify their lives, and have, therefore, devoted most of their energies to pursuing what *they* wanted to do rather than what someone else wanted them to do.[2] It is evident that this attitude is far more prevalent today than it was in the past.

5. *Substantial increase in the education level of individuals.* Valuing certain leisure activities is usually a product of exposure. For instance, an individual may not value reading novels until he has been exposed to several and been taught about them. The increased education of the average citizen has caused an expansion of interest in various activities which, coupled with the rise in disposable income, has brought about greater interest in obtaining leisure and a greater diversity of interests during leisure.

6. *Lack of physical fatigue associated with many forms of employment.* In most pre-industrial societies, which were primarily agrarian or hunter-gatherer societies, work was physically exhausting. Because of this, recreation or leisure was synonymous with resting or relaxing, but little else. The exhausting demands of work prevented life away from work from realizing its potential. Today many forms of work involve a minimum of physical energy and therefore leave the individual in a position to enjoy a variety of leisure activities that require intensive energy.

7. *An increase in discretionary income.* While some leisure activities cost the participant nothing in terms of money, most today have some cost associated with them. Because of this, the rise in personal disposable income during the last three decades has resulted in a generally proportionate rise in leisure spending and thus in the potential to participate in many activities.

Unfortunately, these same societal conditions that have created the increased *potential* for recreation and leisure have also created a number of other factors that have either negated this potential or altered the meaning of leisure in our society. Among such factors are the following:

1. *Limitless materialism.* Many people in our society today have an inability to satiate their material desires. The acceleration of consumption has found no limits, even though we have no societal justification for it. The acquisition, maintenance and use of the vast number of material goods which we increasingly want takes time and increases the amount of work we are compelled to undertake in order to sustain our life style.

2. *Increased societal complexity and change.* Coping with the increased complexity and accelerated rate of change within our society has blunted our leisure potential in a number of ways. Decisions have become more complicated and time-consuming in a society where planning and regulation by government are increasingly necessary and where citizens expect a greater role in that process. The average individual is being forced to absorb more and more information, often of a complex technical nature, at an increasingly accelerated rate. Some scientists believe that much of the pathological behavior evidenced in most industrialized societies is due to "brain overloading"—a condition brought about by the constant mental strain resulting from the increased tempo of everyday life and the political, technical and moral changes to which man must adapt.

3. *The increasing demands of labor.* While the amount of time spent at work has doubtlessly decreased since the turn of the century, evidence is con-

tradictory concerning whether there has been any further decrease in the amount of work activities since World War II. Many statistics argue against any decrease. There has been a 70 percent increase in the number of people employed in service occupations during the last decade, while the percentage of those producing goods has decreased. Services are devourers of time because live performance and personal contact are involved, service workers are less efficient and capital cannot be substituted for labor. The amount of overtime done by wage earners has also been increasing, and the amount of dual job holding has increased. In addition, the percentage of adult women employed in the labor force has now increased to almost 50 percent. Almost 20 percent of full-time workers in our society work 48 hours a week or more.

4. *The carryover of "work values" into leisure.* Many of the goals, methods and styles of our work institutions are increasingly spilling over into our leisure institutions. In much of our "leisure" activity, no less than in our "work" activity, we place a high value on advanced planning and goal setting, competition, incremental improvement through the mastery of special knowledge and technique, the efficient utilization of time and winning. What has emerged is a situation in which one worries about doing the activity sufficiently well regardless of whether it is work or leisure. This seriousness of approach has led to the decline of many forms of pleasure.

In summary, while our potential for leisure has increased, we are nowhere near the society of leisure about which so much has been written. One explanation for what has happened during the last 50 years has sometimes been called "time deepening."

"TIME DEEPENING"

A study of people's use of time in 12 nations sponsored by UNESCO determined the following:

> **Our pretests suggest that the more a person is part of an industrial society with a very high density of communication, and the more educated a person, the more likely he is to do a number of activities simultaneously. While it is generally true that everyone—regardless of status or nationality—has the same 24 hours at his disposal, there is actually something like "time deepening" (to coin a term in analogy to capital deepening): if a person develops the ability to do several things simultaneously, he can crowd a greater number of activities into the same 24 hours.**[40]

Meyersohn and others have referred to this concept as "the more, the more."[41] This reference is to a dynamic concept of energy, suggesting that under pressure of expanding interest and motivation, the more a person does, the more he wants to do, and vice versa. Such a concept does not view energy as a fixed commodity which can be spent on either activity A or activity B. Instead, it assumes that some individuals have a higher rate of "doing" than others. Such a theory, if true, would negate the importance of the amount of leisure time as a predictor of leisure behavior. That is, attendance rates and participation rates in recreation and leisure activities could go up even though the amount of non-work time did not increase. This may be a plausible explanation for what has happened during the last two decades.

If this is the case, certainly "time deepening" has not been accomplished without tremendous psychological stress. Stress, indeed, is the great killer of our society. Each year 4 to 8 million Americans need psychiatric assistance, 125,000 are hospitalized for depression, 200,000 undergo treatment in outpatient clinics, and 50,000 commit suicide. This phenomenon on a smaller scale is also true in other post-industrial societies. It may be argued that such stress will disappear as man in industrial societies evolves into a creature capable of higher and higher levels of activity. Perhaps the desire to experience all things, so prevalent in our society, can be realized in a few more generations, after adaption to a new, faster life style takes place. Such a development, however, might become only one more form of the mindless consumerism that plagues our society with the belief that more is better. To choose everything is, in some sense, not to choose at all. Choosing involves sacrifice and doing and being one thing at the cost of not doing and being other things. The Greeks, long ago, believed that leisure was a quality of life and that in many senses, a life of leisure was a difficult one. It involved finding out who you are. To do this requires an environment of simplicity, tranquility and timelessness. If leisure in this sense is to grow in our society, we may actually begin to see declines in participation rates in leisure activities. Time deepening, in short, may be reversed.

RECREATION, PARK AND LEISURE SERVICE ORGANIZATIONS

The leisure activities of modern man are increasingly influenced by formal organizations. Much has been written about man's increasing interdependence in a highly technological society. This interdependence extends to many forms of leisure behavior. The Industrial Revolution created a partitioning of work and leisure in which work activity became specialized, removed from the home, and scheduled to suit those who owned the means of production. As people moved from the countryside into increasingly larger urban areas to be near the factories, many of the traditional forms of leisure activity were no longer possible. Additionally, urbanization brought about new modes of leisure activity in response to new life styles. Both these situations led to the growth of leisure service organizations—formal organizations whose primary function is the provision of leisure services to the general population or some specific subset of that population. The rise of such organizations on a large scale is a twentieth-century phenomenon. While it continues to be true that the majority of people's leisure time is spent in or around their household, the combination of increasing mobility, additional discretionary income, and more available time has increased both the scope and the importance of leisure service organizations.

Another reason for the increased importance of leisure service organizations is the change in the function of leisure. Today, leisure activities serve not only as rest, relaxation, diversion or catharsis, as they formerly did, but also as self-expression which is sometimes central to one's understanding of the world and one's place in it. Additionally, leisure activities may serve as a medium for making new friends or simply being with old ones. The economic self-sufficiency which a fraction of the world's population has enjoyed during the past few decades has raised the central question of purpose for millions: What should we do with our time, and why? Recreation, park and leisure service organizations hold out various visions of the answer to this central question. While leisure activities are "freely" chosen, leisure service organizations, public, private and commercial, exert tremendous influence on individuals by shaping the choices of leisure activities to which they have access, the environment in which they take place, and the qualitative aspects of such activity. While leisure service agencies may shape individual values as directly as organizations with other purposes, this transmission of values is often not recognized. Many leisure service agencies give the impression of being value-free, that is, in effect merely supplying people with what they already desire. If, however, as Bertrand Russell has observed, the ability to use leisure wisely is the final test of civilization, then leisure service organizations play an important role in shaping the values of individuals who will take that test.

THE MISSIONS OF RECREATION, PARK AND LEISURE SERVICE ORGANIZATIONS

Because organizations that provide leisure services are quite diverse, they use different methods to determine their missions. Some organizations, such as the Boy Scouts, have an historic mission which is much more highly specified than, for instance, a municipal recreation and park department. All leisure service organizations, however, are faced with common questions dealing with (1) goals, (2) the translation of these goals into specific actions, (3) the clientele to be served, (4) the specific leisure activities with which the agency should be concerned, (5) the areas, facilities and equipment the organization needs to provide their leisure activities, (6) the role of the user, client or citizen in determining the organization's actions and (7) the method of determining the organization's success. In this and succeeding chapters, we will examine the methods used by leisure service organizations to find answers to these questions.

Perhaps the first question to be asked in determining a mission for a leisure service agency is whether the process of choice should attempt to be a rational, scientific one or whether it should rely more heavily upon intuition, the beliefs of citizens and administrators, or other societal goals that may be furthered through the use of recreation. Currently many leisure service organizations are attempting to become more "scientific" in their operations, using systematically collected and analyzed data as a basis for operation. As we will see throughout this book, however, the "scientific" planning and administration of leisure service organizations does not mean that such organizations can operate in an "objective" or "value-free" manner. To some extent, in fact, the opposite is true. The more that leisure service organizations collect information and analyze it concerning their operations, the more they are pressured to specifically state their values. Information in itself does not provide decisions. It only provides a better base from which to make decisions. Such decisions are still reflections of values. Merely gathering information that shows that one park is more heavily used than another, for instance, does not lead to a decision as to whether users in that area should have more parkland until the organization plugs in its values concerning the relationship of user rates to provision of parkland. The leisure service organization may feel that each resident should have the same consideration in the provision of parkland, whether he or she uses such parks frequently or not. This is not to imply that leisure service organizations should not attempt to improve the information base from which they operate, but only to note that information alone will not remove the decision-making process from the realm of human belief, nor should it.

Roles of Leisure Service Agencies

Most leisure service agencies fulfill one or more of the following roles:

Promoter of Specific Leisure Activities and Facilities. Many leisure service organizations seek to interest people in participating in specific recreation and leisure activities with which they are not presently involved. In some cases, this is done in the belief that the leisure activity being promoted is "superior" to other choices of activity which the individual might make during his or her free time. Many outdoor recreation organizations act on the assumption that the activities that they promote are more worthwhile than other activities.

Bowling centers, for instance, sponsor advertisements concerning the joy of bowling. Some state or provincial leisure service agencies promote various sports and athletic activities for those who currently do not participate, in the hope that if people become involved in such sports they will become more physically fit, both for their own betterment and for that of society. In some mental hospitals, therapeutic recreation workers encourage emotionally disturbed patients to grow plants, whether or not the patient had such an interest previously, in the belief that it is a valuable step in learning to accept responsibility. In all of these cases, the agency wants the person to modify his or her behavior to include certain forms of leisure activity. The leisure service organization serves as a stimulus to awaken this interest in the individual. Since a given leisure activity is valued only after some form of exposure to it, the organization justifies its approach by saying that the individual may not appreciate the happiness found in, for instance, sailing, because he or she has never been exposed to it. A child playing basketball all summer in a ghetto area may not desire to go camping until exposed to a camping program, and may need to be introduced to such a program one step at a time or on a number of occasions before he or she can make a judgment about whether it is worth doing.

Culturally Neutral Provider. When acting as a neutral agent, the leisure service organization seeks to provide or sponsor whatever leisure activities, facilities or services its clients express interest in. In this role, it is assumed that the agency has no right to impose its own values upon its clients and should cater to existing leisure interests rather than attempting to create new ones. The chief task of the agency is to accurately identify what leisure experiences people wish to participate in and to supply them. The determination of leisure desires may involve community surveys, citizens boards or councils, public hearings or the collection of information concerning participation in a variety of leisure activities. As was stated earlier, it is impossible for the agency to avoid having its own values enter into the decision-making process. The agency may, however, consciously seek to minimize the role its own values play in the operation of its program, and in this role it seeks to do that.

Social Change Agent. Some leisure service agencies seek to bring about change in people's behavior or in societal conditions through the use of leisure activity. Such change goes beyond creating interest in a given activity. In such "social engineering" the leisure activity serves as a means to an end; a technique or tool to change and hopefully improve society. Some commercial leisure service organizations use golf or tennis as a means of interesting people in purchasing condominiums. Boys' Clubs sponsor afterschool programs for teenage boys in the hope of averting delinquent behavior. Nature programs in county park systems may be initiated to change the attitudes of young children toward the outdoors and to foster an attitude of "stewardship" toward the land. Employee-based recreation programs are often sponsored to help attract potential employees and to improve the morale of those already employed in order to improve company productivity. For a leisure service organization to effectively act as a change agent, there must be an ideal situation articulated for the agency to work toward. Sometimes the goals articulated are criticized as being incomplete or even unworthy. Thus, the goal of giving elder citizens "something to do" may be criticized for seeming to assume that the elderly would have nothing to do unless some activity were "given" to them. Another criticism is that the question of purpose of activity is often left unanswered, as is the question of its importance.

The recent interest in "leisure counselling" reflects the belief that people can be helped to use their leisure in more satisfying ways. However, leisure service agencies that sponsor such programs often find that counselling leads to the agency's making judgments about which activities are potentially more worthwhile, which may not always be desirable.

Coordinator of Leisure Opportunities. As a coordinator of leisure opportunities within a community, the leisure service organization seeks to maximize the citizen's opportunities to participate in a wide variety of leisure activities. The organization, in this role, takes the initiative in bringing together representatives of commercial, private and public leisure service agencies in order to share information, avoid duplicating each other's efforts, and plan ways that will allow joint cooperative use of each agency's programs and facilities. As a coordinator of leisure opportunities, the leisure service agency tries to make the citizen familiar with the total range of leisure opportunities within his or her community. Often particular attention is given to informing new residents of the community about such opportunities. The coordinator role assumes that it is desirable for the agency to take a "systems" approach to leisure opportunity rather than acting independently or in conflict with other agencies. In many cases the citizen is primarily interested in a given leisure activity rather than in who the sponsor of the activity is. A swimmer, for instance, will be interested in having the opportunity to swim in a clean, well-maintained pool at a nominal cost regardless of what organization maintains the pool. It is conceivable that many different leisure service organizations could successfully provide this service: commercial neighborhood pools, YMCAs, municipal recreation and park departments, public schools and so on. Because of this, it would appear desirable for all the agencies who could potentially provide this service to consult with each other to avoid duplicating services. This belief, however, is by no means unchallenged. Grodzins, for instance, has argued that an overlapping of functions by leisure-service agencies is actually desirable.

Provider for the Recreationally Dependent. This role starts with the assumption that the leisure service agency should direct its major effort toward providing services to those who are highly dependent upon the agency for meaningful leisure experience or who have a minimum of alternatives to using these services. Some people, it is assumed, are fortunate enough to have a wide variety of leisure opportunities to choose from because of their relatively good health, income, mobility, education and so forth. While these people may depend upon leisure service agencies for some of their leisure experiences, they are not dependent *to the same extent* as those who are in poor physical or mental health or who have less income, less mobility or less education. The leisure service organization tries to compensate for this inequity of opportunity in regard to play, recreation, open space and related areas. There are, of course, no absolute guidelines as to what characteristics constitute a high degree of recreation dependency. Many would argue, for instance, that it is possible to be poor and still enjoy a rewarding variety of leisure experiences. When dealing with an issue as basic as where children can play, however, it quickly becomes apparent that in urban poverty areas where apartments are small and overcrowded child's play opportunities are very limited unless some organized effort is made to provide parks, playgrounds and programs of leisure activities. The physically handicapped may likewise enjoy a variety of leisure activities with the support of interested organizations in their community, but such help is not always forthcoming. The rationale for a public leisure service agency to provide services for the recreationally dependent is that it should be a "provider of last resort," responsible for helping meet the leisure needs and desires of those for whom no one else can or will provide. Much the same argument is made concerning the responsibility of government to provide employment for those who cannot find work during a recession or depression.

Enhancement of the Physical Environment. Many leisure service agencies have, as a primary role, the protection and improvement of the environment. Many types of leisure activities are dependent upon certain environmental features or conditions which most people cannot supply individually in urban or suburban areas. In addition, the *quality* of the leisure experience may be highly dependent upon environmental conditions. Boating in a polluted lake is a markedly different experience from boating in a clear, clean one. A number of these leisure activities are often referred to as "land-based" and include boating, camping, backpacking, hunting and mountaineering. To accommodate such activities, leisure service agencies maintain a variety of areas and facilities.

Some leisure service agencies also perform services that contribute to the "quality of life" of a community, such as planting shade trees, acquiring stream valley parks, preserving historical sites and unique natural areas, and protecting wildlife.

The Question of Needs and Desires. All leisure service organizations, regardless of the role they fulfill, are obligated to make certain assumptions about the leisure needs and desires of those they serve. These assumptions, to the extent that the organization controls its own actions, provide the basis of the agency's operation. It is impossible for an agency to operate without making certain implicit or explicit assumptions about recreation or leisure needs, and all methods of determining needs ultimately require the expression of values. As Mercer points out, the term "recreation need" is often used without an attempt to define what is meant by "need."[42] The bases of recreation need are pluralistic; that is, there is more than one valid conceptualization of need. Following are the five major ways of determining recreation needs and desires.

1. Determining the attitudes and opinions of people toward a range of alternative leisure experiences which the agency could conceivably provide. This may be done primarily in one of two ways: (a) through survey research, and (b) through involvement of citizens on councils, boards, public hearings and other means of participation.

2. Applying standards, guidelines and other expert judgments concerning the desirable services, level of services, quality of services and distribution of services to be performed. This is usually done (a) by applying existing standards and guidelines, or (b) through the use of consultants for planning and evaluation.

3. Making inventories of present participation patterns and leisure-related areas and facilities, and planning future recreation or leisure services as an extension of what already exists.

4. Comparing potential participants in terms of recreation or leisure service needs and evaluating their comparative needs with regard to the supply of leisure services available. Such a comparison is usually made within different geographic areas of a city or county.

5. Assuming that leisure needs and desires are primarily a function of "created interest" and therefore seeking to publicize (advertise) and stimulate interest in certain leisure activities regardless of whether potential participants presently value the activity. Sometimes this approach is said to act upon "latent" recreation needs or desires, since it is assumed that people will come to value the activity after they have been exposed to it.

In the following chapters, the foundations and operation of a number of types of recreation, park and leisure services will be examined. As we will see, their conceptualizations of recreation often vary.

REFERENCES

1. Rolf B. Meyersohn, "Americans Off Duty," in Wilma Donahue et al., eds., *Free Time—Challenge to Later Maturity* (Ann Arbor: University of Michigan Press, 1958), p. 46.
2. Sebastian de Grazia, *Of Time, Work, and Leisure* (New York: The Twentieth Century Fund, 1961), pp. 19, 87, 65, 405, 19, 246.
3. Thorstein Veblen, *The Theory of the Leisure Class* (New York: B. W. Heubsch, 1899), p. 40.
4. Aline Ripert, "The Sociology of Leisure in the United States," *International Social Science Journal,* Vol. IX, Winter, 1960, p. 597.
5. Ankit Vitomar, "The Social Planning of Leisure," *International Social Science Journal,* Vol. IX, Winter, 1960, p. 576.
6. Herbert L. May and Dorothy Petgen, *Leisure and Its Uses* (New York: A. S. Barnes and Co., 1928), p. 3.
7. Henry Pratt Fairchild, ed., *Dictionary of Sociology* (New York: Philosophical Library, 1944), p. 175.
8. Eric Larrabee and Rolf Meyersohn, eds., *Mass Leisure* (Glencoe: The Free Press, 1958), pp. 2, 252.
9. Zulie Nakhooda, *Leisure and Recreation in Society* (Allahabad, India: Kitab Mahal, 1961), pp. 7, 14.
10. Wilbert, E. Moore, *Man, Time, and Society* (New York: John Wiley and Sons, 1963), p. 35.
11. Paul Weiss, "A Philosophical Definition of Leisure," *Quest,* Vol. V, December, 1965, p. 1.
12. George Soule, "The Economics of Leisure," *Annals of the American Academy of Political and Social Science,* Vol. 313, September, 1957, p. 16.
13. Joffre Dumazedier, "Current Problems of the Sociology of Leisure," *International Social Science Journal,* Vol. XII, Winter, 1960, p. 526.

14. Martin H. Neumeyer and Ester S. Neumeyer, *Leisure and Recreation,* 3rd ed. (New York: Ronald Press, 1958), pp. 14, 15.
15. August Heckscher, "The Gift of Time," *NEA Journal,* Vol. 46, May, 1957, p. 328.
16. Lawrence Suhm, Mary Ann Jorgensen and Ray O. Jondahl, *Leisure, Recreation and the Good Life in Wisconsin* (Madison: The Republican Party of Wisconsin, 1966), p. 16.
17. Max Kaplan, "Toward a Theory of Leisure for Social Gerontology," in Robert W. Kleemeier, ed., *Aging and Leisure* (New York: Oxford University Press, 1961). pp. 392., 22.
18. Bennett M. Berger, "The Sociology of Leisure: Some Suggestions," *Industrial Relations,* February, 1962, p. 38.
19. Max Kaplan, *Leisure in America* (New York: John Wiley and Sons, 1960), pp. 21, 22, 47.
20. Charles K. Brightbill, "Leisure . . . Its Meanings and Implications," *Recreation,* Vol. LVII, January, 1964, p. 10.
21. Gerald B. Fitzgerald, *Community Organization for Recreation* (New York: A. S. Barnes and Company, 1948), p. 34.
22. Paul Goodman, "Leisure: Purposeful or Purposeless," in Pauline Madow, ed., *Recreation in America* (New York: H. W. Wilson Co., 1965), p. 31.
23. Joffre Dumazedier and Nicole Latrouche, "Work and Leisure in Sociology," *Industrial Relations,* Vol. I, February, 1962, pp. 20–21.
24. John E. Anderson, "Psychological Aspects of the Use of Free Time," in Wilma Donahue et al., eds., *Free Time—Challenge to Later Maturity* (Ann Arbor: University of Michigan Press, 1958), p. 45.
25. Erwin O. Smigel, "The Problem of Leisure Time in an Industrial Society," in *Computer Technology* (New York: Industrial Counselors, Inc., 1975), p. 105.
26. David Riesman, *The Lonely Crowd* (New Haven: Yale University Press, 1950), p. 17.
27. David Dempsey, "Myth of the New Leisure Class," *New York Times Magazine,* January 26, 1958, p. 24.
28. Nels Anderson, *Work and Leisure* (New York: Glencoe Press, 1961), p. 255.
29. Joseph Pieper, *Leisure the Basis of Culture* (New York: New American Library, 1952), p. 40.
30. C. E. Rainwater, *Journal of Applied Sociology,* Vol. VII, May–June, 1923, p. 259.
31. Herbert L. May and Dorothy Petgen, *Leisure and Its Uses* (New York: A. S. Barnes and Co., 1928), p. 3.
32. Margaret Mead, "The Pattern of Leisure in Contemporary American Culture," in Eric Larrabee and Rolf Meyersohn, eds., *Mass Leisure* (Glencoe, Illinois: The Free Press, 1958, pp. 11–12.
33. C. Gilbert Wrenn and D. L. Harley, *Time On Their Hands* (Washington, D.C.: American Council on Education. 1941), p. xv.
34. Henry Fairchild, ed., *Dictionary of Sociology* (New York: Philosophical Library, 1944), pp. 251–252.
35. John L. Hutchinson, *Principles of Recreation* (New York: A. S. Barnes and Co., 1949), p. 17.
36. Charles E. Doell and Gerald B. Fitzgerald, *A Brief History of Parks and Recreation in the United States* (Chicago: The Athletic Institute, 1954), p. 127.
37. G. Ott Romney, *Off the Job Living* (New York: A. S. Barnes and Company, 1945), p. 14.
38. Elliott Avedon, *Therapeutic Recreation Service* (Englewood Cliffs, New Jersey: Prentice-Hall, 1974).
39. David E. Gray and Seymour Greben, "Future Perspectives," *Parks and Recreation,* July, 1974, p. 49.
40. Erwin Scheuch, "The Time Budget Interview," in Alexander Szalai, ed., *The Use of Time—Daily Activities of Urban and Suburban Populations* (The Hague, Netherlands: Mouton, 1972), p. 77.
41. Rolf Meyersohn, "Television and the Rest of Leisure," *Public Opinion Quarterly,* 1:111–112, 1968.
42. David Mercer, "The Concept of Recreation Need," *Journal of Leisure Research,* Winter, 1973.

QUESTIONS

1. What does "leisure" mean as the ancient Greeks conceptualized it?
2. What disagreements are found among the various definitions of the word "recreation"?
3. Can leisure be said to be a new phenomenon of the twentieth century?
4. What are some primary roles assumed by recreation, park and leisure service organizations?
5. What do we mean when we say that the bases of recreation needs are "pluralistic"?

The world's population will double in the next 30 years. Cities will increasingly be where most people "pursue happiness."
(U.S. Bureau of Outdoor Recreation)

ABOUT THE AUTHOR

Diana R. Dunn received her B.S. degree in Secondary Education in 1959 and her M.S. degree in Education Administration in 1963, both from the University of Dayton. She joined the staff of the city of Dayton, Bureau of Recreation in 1956, became a Recreation Center Director in 1957, then Supervisor of City-wide Performing Arts in 1960. In 1963, Dr. Dunn became Supervisor of Recreation for the Anaheim, California, Department of Parks and Recreation. In 1966, she began doctoral work in recreation and parks and sociology at The Pennsylvania State University, under the sponsorship of the U.S. Department of Health, Education and Welfare, Office of Education, Bureau of Research. She received her Ph.D. in 1970.

Dr. Dunn became Director of Research for the National Recreation and Park Association in 1969. Her duties included stimulating research on problems and issues in recreation and leisure and also conducting studies for the association. She served as Managing Editor of the scholarly quarterly *Journal of Leisure Research,* organized and participated in many national and international research symposia, and prepared congressional testimony relating to recreation. She was director of a study of 25 United States cities which dealt with urban recreation opportunities in America's intercities. In 1972, Dr. Dunn joined the faculty at Temple University in Philadelphia as Associate Professor of Recreation and Leisure Studies. In 1975, she served as director of research for the World Leisure and Recreation Association for HABITAT (the United Nations Conference on Human Settlements), helping to develop a state-of-the-world report on leisure and recreation for the June 1976 U.N. conference in Vancouver, British Columbia. In 1977, Dr. Dunn became professor and coordinator of the recreation program at the University of Arizona at Tucson. She served as president of the 7,000-member American Association for Leisure and Recreation during the 1977–1978 term. She has authored and edited scholarly and professional books, articles, monographs, and reviews. Her writing has appeared in *The Congressional Record, U.S. News and World Report, The Washington Post,* and many other places.

Her avocations include photography, backpacking and collecting kaleidoscopes.

chapter 2

URBAN RECREATION

GLOBAL URBAN PERSPECTIVES

The world is urbanizing. From an almost entirely rural planet at the beginning of this century, the Earth will be largely urban by the end of it (Fig. 2–1). In 1900, only a handful of cities in the world had a population of over 1 million; a "great city" was defined as one having 100,000 or more inhabitants. In 1960, there were 109 cities with over 1 million inhabitants; in 1975, there were 191. Three megalopoles are approaching the 50 million mark (Tokaido, Boswash and northern Europe). Predictions indicate that many "megaregions" of over 100 million persons will exist throughout the world by the year 2000.

These figures do not reflect simply a spectacular migration of people from rural areas to cities; they indicate enormous absolute population increases as well (Fig. 2–2).

What does it mean that the population of the world will double in the next 30 years, adding 3,500 million people to the human family? First, nearly

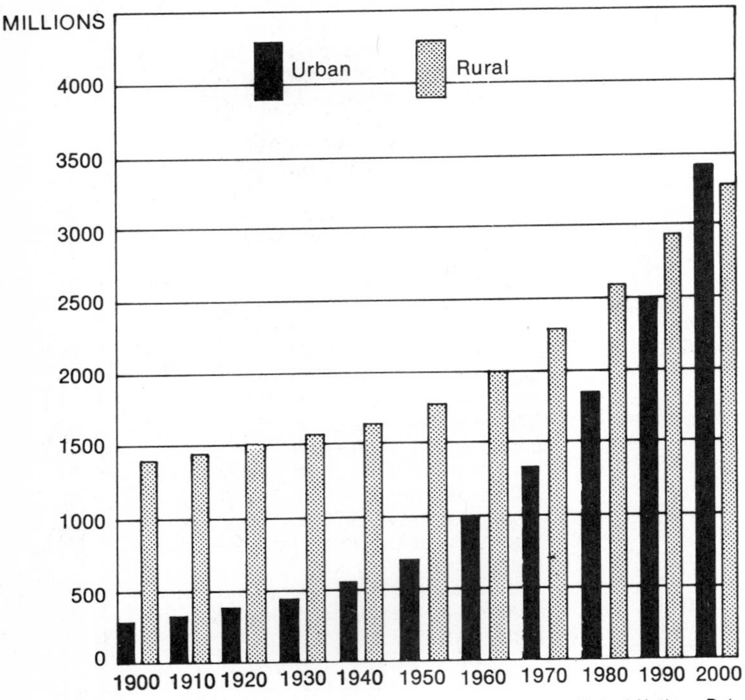

FIGURE 2–1 Comparison of the world's urban and rural populations. (From Barbara Ward and René Dubos, *Only One Earth: The Care and Maintenance of a Small Planet.* New York: W. W. Norton and Co., 1972, p. 9.)

all these new millions are going to live in towns and cities. That means building the equivalent of 3,500 cities of one million inhabitants each. Second, even with an average family of six, 3,500 million people will need nearly 600 million housing units—more than exist in the entire world today. Finally, at current birth-death ratios, the number of children who will be born and survive through childhood in this 30-year span will exceed 5,000 million. Considering the needs of these young people alone, enormous numbers of doctors, teachers, schoolrooms and playgrounds will be required.

Towns and cities throughout the world are already in a state of crisis, failing to provide basic facilities and services. Problems of unemployment, pollution, congestion, slums and squatter settlements, inadequate transportation, social alienation and crime are mounting everywhere. Despite all of the technological and industrial progress of the past century, United Nations official Enrique Penalosa declared, "The lot in the life of the majority of mankind is worse than ever."[3] British economist Barbara Ward agreed: "On balance, human settlements are simply not felt to be fulfilling (their) promise. In many ways, they grossly contradict it. They represent a spectrum of failure."[4]

What constitutes a benevolent urban environment, a "successful city"? Toward what condition should the human race aspire and strive? There is no authoritatively established definition or measure. Barbara Ward stated flatly

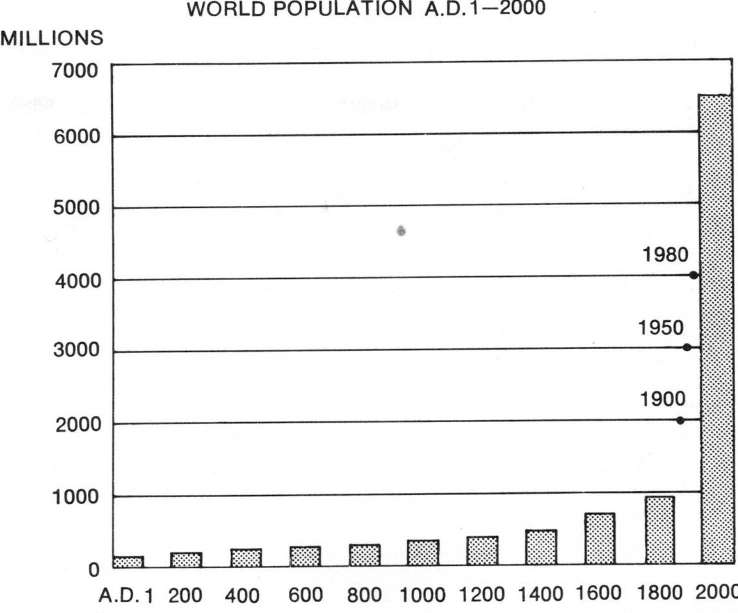

FIGURE 2–2 World population growth from A.D. 1–2000. (From Barbara Ward and René Dubos, *Only One Earth: The Care and Maintenance of a Small Planet.* New York: W. W. Norton and Co., 1972, p. 6.)

that ". . .a first priority is to stimulate the preparation of minimum agreed upon standards for the biological success of human beings in their settlements."[5] The goal of mankind would then be to achieve these minimum standards everywhere, and to achieve higher standards wherever possible. "Once the biological minimum is secured," Ward prophesied, "the range of man's cultural, intellectual and spiritual needs is as wide as the globe itself."[6]

Just as there are no minimum standards or universal goals for such basic human needs as food, water, shelter and health, so there are no authoritatively established measures for such secondary human needs as recreation. Goals, standards, objectives or other measures or statements that might be used to define minimum recreation needs of people living in cities do not exist on the global level.

URBAN GROWTH AND DECLINE IN THE UNITED STATES

URBANIZATION

The forces that precipitated the leisure and recreation movement in the United States did not exist when the country was largely rural; they developed while the nation was urbanizing and industrializing. Being an urban phenomenon, the leisure and recreation movement has had only a very brief history in this country.

In the first U.S. census, in 1790, a bare 5 percent of the country's 4

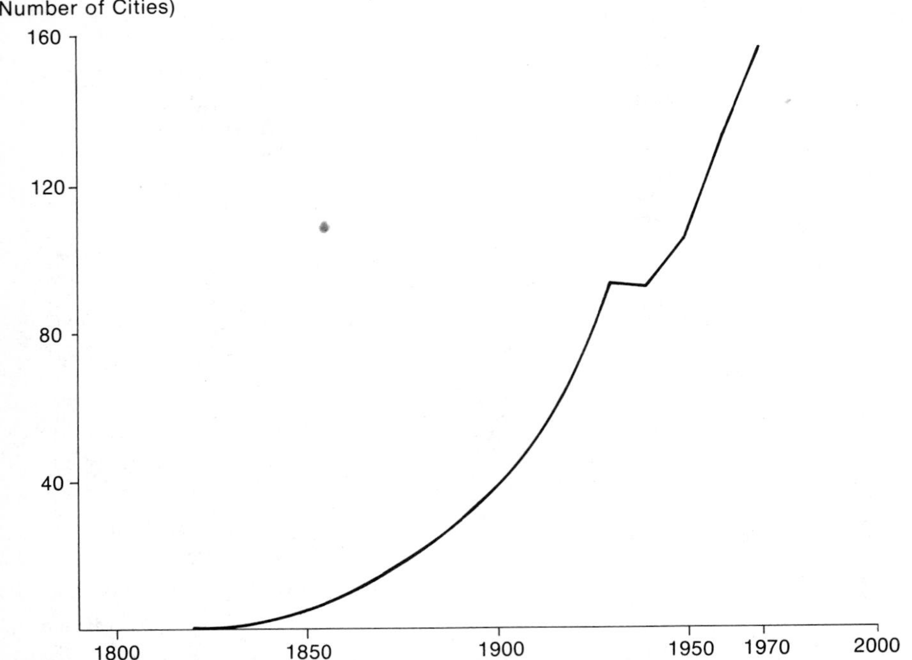

FIGURE 2–3 Graph showing increase in the number of U.S. cities with populations of over 100,000, during the period from 1820 to 1970.

million people resided in places with populations over 2,500—the definition of an "urban area." No cities had more than 50,000 people (Figs. 2–3 and 2–4). Indeed, 185 years ago, only four cities had more than 10,000 people: New York (49,000); Philadelphia (28,500); Boston (18,000); and Baltimore (13,500).

Just 60 years later, in 1850, much had changed. Fifteen per cent of the 23 million Americans lived in urban areas. Six cities had over 100,000 people (Cincinnati, 115,500; New Orleans, 116,000; Boston, 137,000; Baltimore, 169,000;

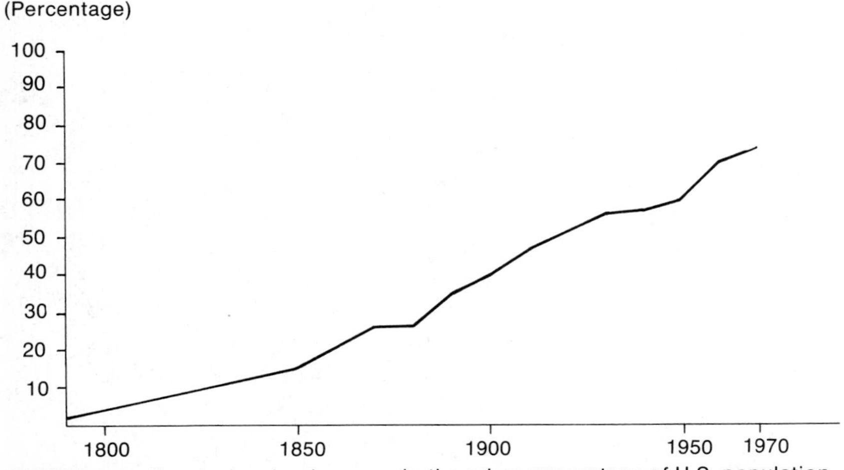

FIGURE 2–4 Graph showing increase in the urban percentage of U.S. population from 1790 to 1970.

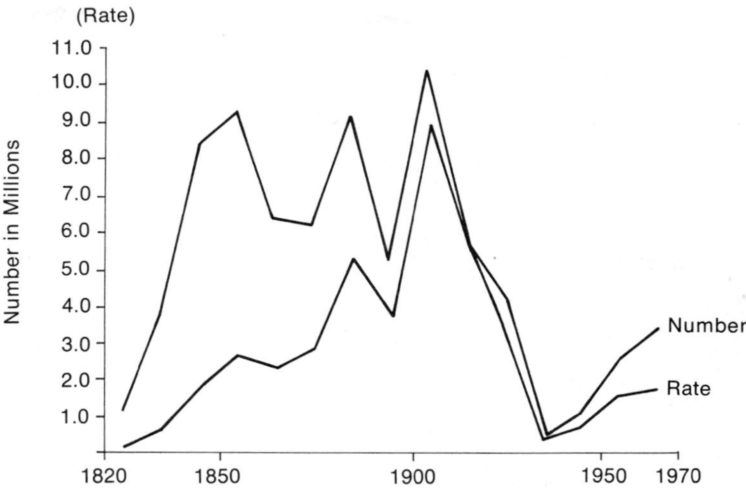

Figure 2–5 Graph showing the number of immigrants and the rate of immigration into the United States from 1820 to 1970.

Philadelphia, 121,000; and New York, 696,000). The future giant city of Chicago had but 30,000 inhabitants, while Houston had only 2,396.

By 1900, 40 percent of the nation's 76 million people lived in urban aggregations. The country had three cities with populations of over 1 million (New York, Philadelphia and Chicago); 12 with populations of between ¼ and 1 million; and 32 with between 100,000 and 1 million inhabitants.

Such tremendous growth of population in American cities did not result from simple absolute population increases alone. A great migration from rural areas to metropolitan areas also contributed, as Americans sought both better jobs and better lives. Immigration also contributed importantly to the rapid growth of U.S. cities (Fig. 2–5). In the first decade of this century, the highest immigration rate ever was recorded—10.4. Nearly 9 million immigrants came to this country during the decade, which the nation began with a population of 76 million and ended with a population of 92 million. Between 1905 and 1907, over a million mostly unskilled, poor "huddled masses yearning to breathe free" arrived at the so-called golden doors of ill-prepared U.S. cities annually.

By the middle of the twentieth century, after two world wars and a great depression, 60 percent of the U.S. population were urban dwellers. Detroit and Los Angeles raised the number of million-plus cities to five, and the country had 36 cities with populations of between ¼ and 1 million and more than 100 cities with populations of over 100,000.

The last national census, conducted in 1970, concluded that 74 percent of the more than 200 million Americans lived in urban areas. It identified six cities with more than 1 million inhabitants (Houston was added); 50 more with between ¼ and 1 million people; and 153 cities with over 100,000.

The meaning of the word "city" had become complex, and more precise designations developed. Terms such as central city (usually the political city), suburbs, small or independent cities, and countryside provided a more accurate description of the population (see Fig. 2–6).

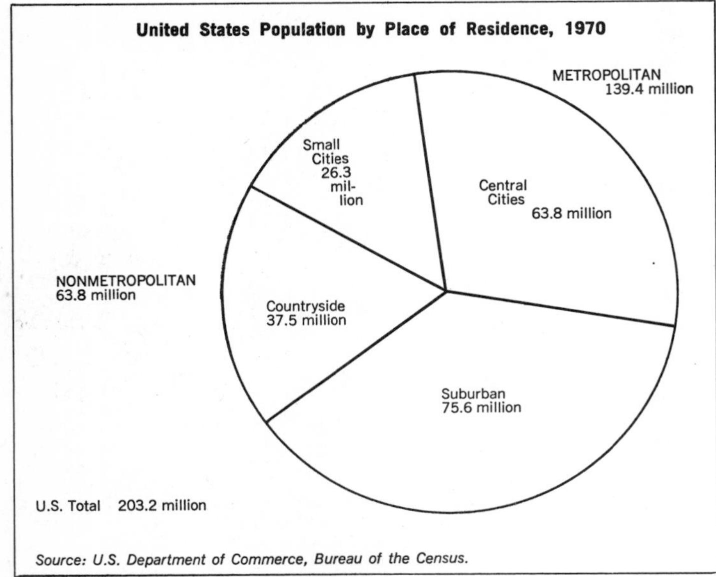

FIGURE 2–6

SUBURBANIZATION

Urbanization in the United States had a reciprocal—deconcentration—a phenomenon manifested in the United States by the growth of suburbs. In general, the older and larger cities began to deconcentrate earlier, and the pattern spread to newer and smaller places with the passage of time. This trend began in the middle of the last century; the peak density of New York City, for example, was recorded in the 1850's. New York began to exhibit relative deconcentration about that time, and was joined by nine other large cities by 1900.

On the whole, the largest cities of the United States were growing more rapidly than their outlying areas until the 1920's. The great tide of suburbanization, however, began in earnest after World War I, when, coincidentally, automobile registrations began their dramatic rise in this country (Fig. 2–7). Passenger car registrations grew dramatically from 8,000 in 1900 to

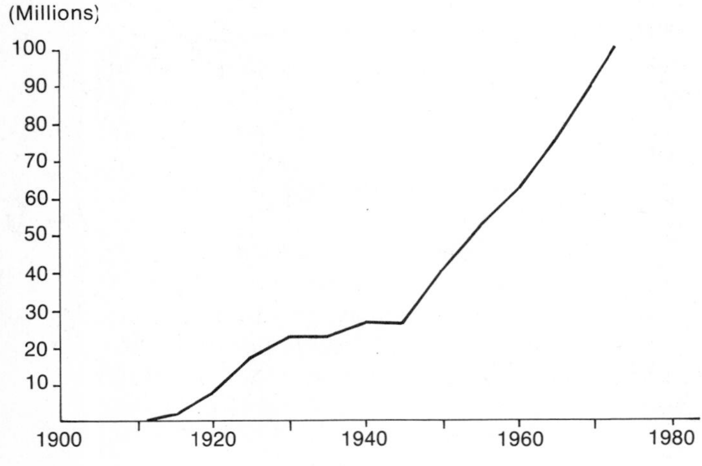

FIGURE 2–7 Graph showing increase in the number of passenger cars registered in the United States between 1900 and 1973.

nearly 90 million by 1970. After the automobile revolution, the growth of areas lying beyond the city's political boundaries tended to be more rapid. In the 1930's, these outlying areas began to capture greater proportions of the overall growth of the nation than did the central cities. Metropolitan central cities, although increasing in number, have contained smaller and smaller proportions of the total metropolitan population since approximately World War I, and this trend still continues today.

"RE-RURALIZATION"

A greater percentage of Americans lived in cities over 100,000 and in cities over 250,000 in 1950 than lived in such cities by 1970. Since 1970, even more important shifts have been documented. The United States has entered a new migratory phase: back to the country. Some 30 million Americans had been added to the nation's metropolitan areas since World War II, but 1976 statistics revealed that city dwellers were returning to rurality in growing numbers. The U.S. Bureau of the Census reported that between March 1970 and March 1975, ". . .persons moving from metropolitan areas exceeded movers to metropolitan areas by 1.6 million."[7]

General patterns indicate that Americans are heading for the sun-belt—the South and the Southwest. They are seeking a simpler life, and are hoping to avoid the high cost of urban living, crime and other urban ills.

Metropolitan area desertion is creating new problems for cities—less tax revenue, abandoned housing, empty schools and a larger percentage of the less mobile poor. Smaller communities face new problems too, such as how to handle more people, build more service delivery systems and obtain more revenue.

RECREATION IN THE CITIES

HISTORY

Urbanization, industrialization, immigration, improved mobility, new technology and an increasingly affluent middle class were among the phenomena that changed urban recreation patterns greatly in the early twentieth century. The recreation movement was born in an era of reformers and child-savers who believed in close supervision of an adolescent's leisure time activities. In the East and Midwest, settlement houses were supported by philanthropists. The settlement house was the first bulwark against the evils lurking for youth in the slums of a rapidly urbanizing and industrializing nation. In addition, several youth-serving organizations such as the Boy Scouts, Girl Scouts and Camp Fire Girls came into being. Providing healthy recreation was equated with the amelioration of social pathologies, especially for the underprivileged and particularly underprivileged youth. The common root during this period was the belief in the ability of recreation to solve social problems; this social welfare orientation perceived recreation to be a means to an end.

Initially, recreation opportunities were supported by philanthropic interests or private groups. Early in the present century, however, recreation also became a municipal government function, as a result of citizen demands for parks and then for organized recreation services. Soon the idea that recreation is a fundamental and universal human need and that all people need recreation became the commitment and rallying cry of the newly established public service profession. Meeting the needs and interests of all people became the motto: "The program should provide equal opportunity for all, regardless of race, creed, social status, economic need, sex, age, interest, or mental or physical capacity."[8] More succinctly, "The comprehensive program of recreation should be based upon the needs, interests and abilities of all the people."

During World War I, however, a schism developed between urban public recreation and the private and voluntary sector. In the following decades, public recreation joined with parks, and assumed a much less evangelical stance; recreation became an end in itself. Professionals in recreation were resource managers and activity leaders—period. The private and voluntary recreation organizations proceeded in the social welfare mold, viewing recreation as an important weapon in their arsenal aimed at improving lives and communities. Over the years, narrowing lines of professionalism within the ranks of both groups resulted in a lack of communication and coordination between them.

In the 1960's, the influences of the War on Poverty, federal categorical funding, public opinion, the civil rights movement and urban unrest all had tremendous impact on public and voluntary recreation services in the metropolitan areas of the United States. The public park and recreation profession responded somewhat to its original concern for the disadvantaged in urban America. The modification in commitment reflected a renewed emphasis, stressing that while all people need recreation, "people are unequal in their needs for community-supported recreation services."[9] Indeed, it was no longer heresy to observe that a great many people had no need at all for public or voluntary recreation services.

URBAN RECREATION PROVIDERS

All nations possess unique "mixes" of urban recreation providers, and the United States is no exception. The heterogeneity of governmental units, private and voluntary agencies, and commercial enterprises that own and operate recreation resources complicates efforts to determine the dimensions of the total national leisure resource base or even the total leisure resource

TABLE 2–1 Main Providers of Recreation Opportunity for People in Cities in the U.S. and in Selected Countries[10]

Provider	Estimates (%)	
	United States	*Other Countries*
Local government	20	20
National government	5	13
Commercial	20	14
Schools	5	11
Home/Individual/Clubs	20	14
Private and voluntary organizations	15	10
Labor	5	5
Industry	5	4
Religious institutions	5	3
	100	100

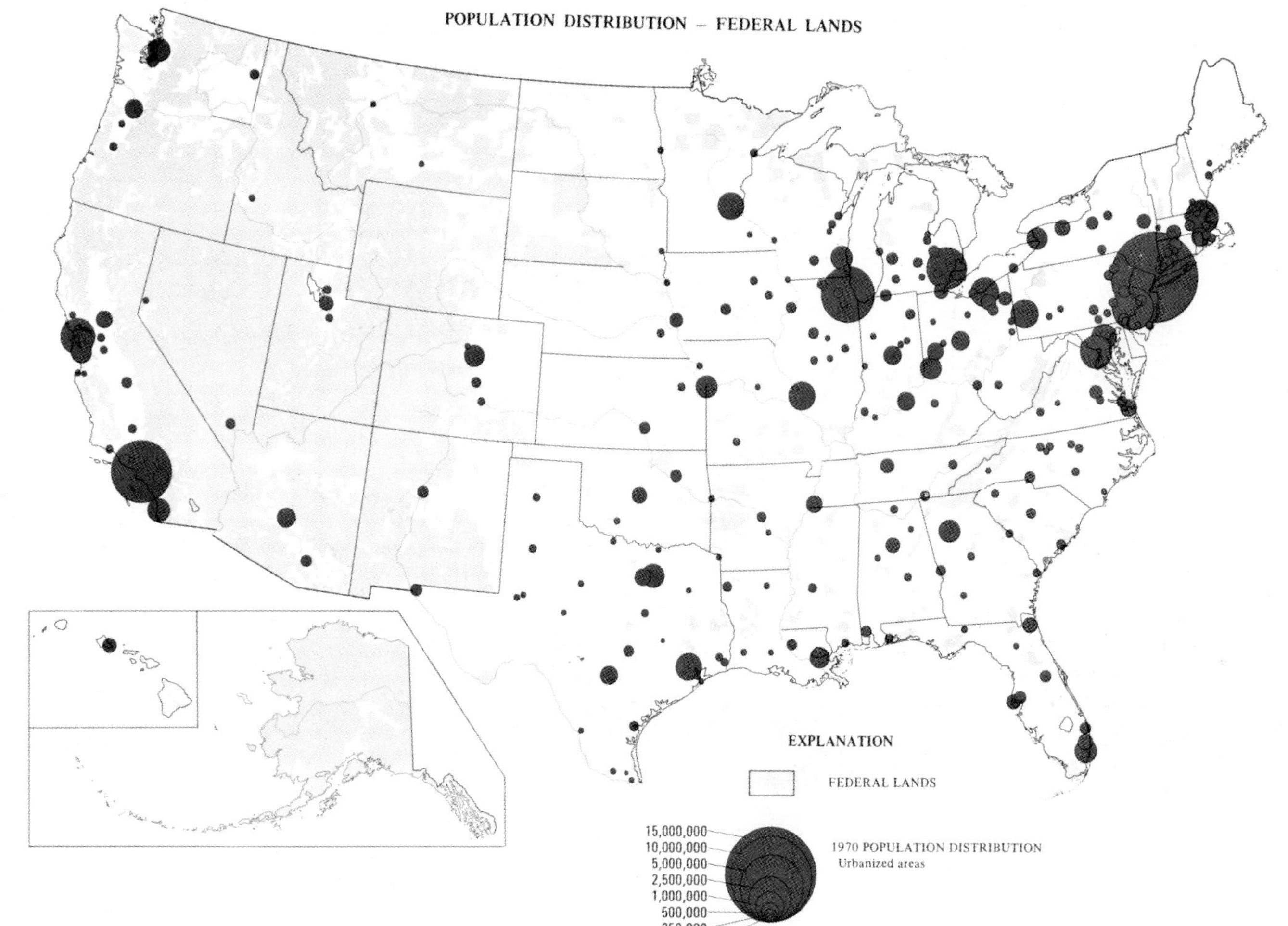

FIGURE 2–8 Comparison of population distribution with federal land holdings in the United States as of 1970. (From *Outdoor Recreation: A Legacy for America*, U.S. Department of the Interior, Bureau of Outdoor Recreation, Washington, D.C., U.S. Government Printing Office, 1973, p. 14.)

base for a particular city. The scope of resources is broad, ranging from the backyard swimming pool to bowling alleys, sports stadiums, amusement parks, cultural centers, campgrounds and resorts, to name but a few.

A 1975 study sought to determine how the main providers of recreation opportunity for people in cities were distributed percentagewise in the United States *vs.* selected other countries. Table 2–1 shows the results.

The complexity of such estimates becomes more apparent when one reflects, for example, that although municipal park and recreation departments now spend about $2 billion annually to serve urban citizens, recreation spending in America has been estimated to exceed 150 billion dollars per year. Both philosophically and operationally, however, it is safe to submit that the urban recreation delivery system in the United States is unique in the world.

While the federal interest in cities and their inner-city areas intensified considerably during the 1960's and early 1970's, less than 1 percent of the recreation areas in inner-city areas were federally operated in 1970. (Less than 3 percent were operated by state and county governments.) Figure 2–8

TABLE 2–2 Comparison and Contrast Study of Public, Private

	Philosophy of Recreation
Public	Enrichment of the life of the total community by providing opportunities for the worthy use of leisure. Nonprofit in nature.
Private	Enrichment of the life of participating members by offering opportunities for worthy use of leisure, frequently with emphasis on the group and the individual. Nonprofit in nature.
Commercial	Attempt to satisfy public demands in an effort to produce profit. Dollars from, as well as for, recreation.
	Objectives of Recreation
Public	To provide leisure opportunities that contribute to the social, physical, educational, cultural, and general well-being of the community and its people.
Private	Similar to public, but limited by membership, race, religion, age, and the like. To provide opportunities for close group association with emphasis on citizenship, behavior, and life philosophy values. To provide activities that appeal to members.
Commercial	To provide activities or programs which will appeal to customers. To meet competition. To net profit. To serve the public.
	Administrative Organization
Public	Governmental agencies (federal, state, county, and local).
Private	Boy Scouts, settlements, Girl Scouts, Camp Fire Girls, "Y" organizations, and others.
Commercial	Corporations, syndicates, partnerships, private ownerships. Examples: motion picture, television, and radio companies, resorts, bowling centers, skating rinks.
	Finance
Public	Primarily by taxes. Also by gifts, grants, trust funds, small charges, and fees to defray cost.
Private	By gifts, grants, endowments, donations, drives, and membership fees.
Commercial	By the owner or promoters. By the users: admission and charges.

illustrates vividly the maldistribution of federal land holdings with respect to the population of the United States. Clearly federal lands, including those used for recreation purposes, are not located where the people are.

Non-federal providers of recreation opportunities for urban populations cannot be overlooked, for their contributions are substantial. Sessoms has provided a succinct comparison and contrast of the three main types of agencies serving the recreation needs of urban populations in the United States (Table 2–2). The public, private and commercial sectors encompass all of the recreation resources, programs and services commonly found in U.S. cities.

A 1974 study determined that "the quasi-public, private and voluntary agencies provided a substantial and important dimension of the recreation opportunity for low-income inner-city residents."[13] (It was noted that had commercial and family recreation been a part of the study, public resource commitment would have constituted a very minor contribution to urban recreation opportunity.)

A summary of the open space areas, facilities, personnel and volunteers according to sector is presented in Figure 2–9. While public agencies

(Voluntary Agencies), and Commercial Recreation[12]

	Program
Public	Designed to provide a wide variety of activities, year-round, for all groups, regardless of age, sex, race, creed, social or economic status.
Private	Designed to provide programs of a specialized nature for groups and in keeping with the aims and objectives of the agency.
Commercial	Program designed to tap spending power in compliance with state and local laws.
	Membership
Public	Unlimited—open to all.
Private	Limited by organizational restrictions, such as age, sex, religion, and the like.
Commercial	Limited by: Law (local, state, and federal). Social conception regarding status and strata in some places. Economics—limited to those who have the price to pay.
	Facilities
Public	Community buildings, parks (national, state, local), athletic fields, playgrounds, playfields, stadiums, camps, beaches, museums, zoos, golf courses, school facilities, etc.
Private	Settlement houses, youth centers, churches, play areas, clubs, camps, and others.
Commercial	Theaters, clubs, taverns, night clubs, lounges, racetracks, bowling lanes, stadiums, and others.
	Leadership
Public	Professionally prepared to provide extensive recreation programs for large numbers of people. Frequently subject to Civil Service regulations. Volunteers as well as professionals. College training facilities growing.
Private	Professionally prepared to provide programs on a social group-work basis. Employed at discretion of managing agency. Volunteers as well as professionals.
Commercial	Frequently trained by employing agency. Employed to secure greatest financial returns. Employed and retained at the discretion of the employer. *No* volunteers.

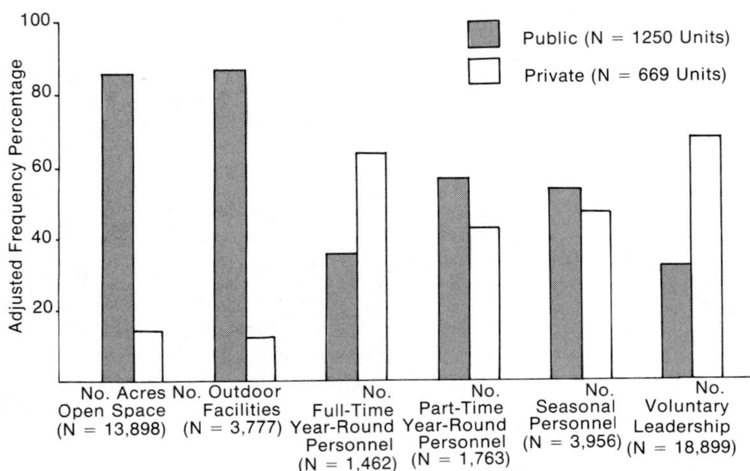

FIGURE 2–9 Sector classification analysis of space, facilities, personnel and volunteers in 1,919 study units. (From *Open Space and Recreation Opportunity in America's Inner Cities*, prepared for the U.S. Department of Housing and Urban Development by the National Recreation and Park Association, 1974, p. 63.)

operated far more acres of open space and outdoor recreation facilities than did those in the private sector, the private agencies had more full-time year-round personnel involved in recreation and related functions. The private sector was also much more involved in the utilization of voluntary leadership. While the public agencies had a slightly greater number of part-time year-round personnel, the private agencies had a far greater number of full-time year-round personnel assigned to inner-city recreation areas. In addition, buildings in the inner-city areas were most likely to be operated by private agencies.

PUBLIC RECREATION IN U.S. CITIES

Data and information about recreation and parks supported by local public agencies are available from two principal sources: (1) the National Recreation and Park Association and its predecessor organizations, and (2) special studies undertaken by other organizations, professionals and educators. This section highlights findings on selected subjects from several recent studies.

Every five years, the National Recreation and Park Association surveys the local public recreation and park agencies in a continuing effort to document the status and direction of the field. The most recent data are available from a survey of 2,301 cities with populations of more than 10,000, conducted by the International City Management Association (ICMA) in cooperation with the National Recreation and Park Association (NRPA) in 1975.[15]

Of 1,123 cities submitting reports, 88 percent had full-time year-round recreation and/or recreation and park agencies (Table 2–3). Two thirds of the cities had combined recreation and park functions, revealing the end of the 1960's trend of consolidating separate departments (Table 2–4). Cities with populations between 250,000 and 500,000 more often had joint park and recreation departments than those having more than 500,000 or less than

TABLE 2–3 Cities that Provide Full-Time, Year-Round Recreation and/or Park Programs and Services[16]

Classification	No. of Cities Reporting (A)	Yes		No	
		No.	% of (A)	No.	% of (A)
Total, all cities	1,123	986	88	137	12
Population group					
Over 500,000	14	14	100	0	0
250,000–500,000	19	19	100	0	0
100,000–249,999	54	51	94	3	6
50,000– 99,999	140	132	94	8	6
25,000– 49,999	276	247	89	29	11
10,000– 24,999	620	523	84	97	16
Geographic region					
Northeast	297	265	89	32	11
North Central	319	251	79	68	21
South	254	237	93	17	7
West	253	233	92	20	8
Metro/city type					
Central	192	181	94	11	6
Suburban	639	545	85	94	15
Independent	292	260	89	32	11
Form of government					
Mayor-council	377	316	84	61	16
Council manager	656	589	90	67	10
Commission	41	35	85	6	15
Town meeting	35	32	91	3	9
Rep. town meeting	14	14	100	0	0

TABLE 2–4 Departments or Agencies Responsible for Providing Recreation and/or Park Programs in 1975[17]

	Number	Percentage*
Department of Parks and Recreation	652	66
Department of Recreation	177	18
Department of Parks	27	3
Department of Public Works	12	1
Department of Parks and Recreation and Public Works	15	2
Departments of Parks and Recreation and Human Resources	3	–
Departments of Parks and Recreation and Conservation	1	–
Department of Parks and Recreation and Other	4	–
Departments of Parks and Public Works	4	–
Departments of Parks and Other	1	–
Departments of Human Resources and Conservation	1	–
Departments of Parks and Recreation, Public Works, and Conservation	1	–

*Percentages when totaled do not add to 100 percent because some respondents only answered the first part of the question on which the percentage is based.

250,000 inhabitants. The northeastern cities had fewer combined departments than did cities in other regions.

Differences in both city size and geographic region seemed to affect the kind of administrative organization of the recreation and park department. In addition, central cities were more likely to have had a combined park and recreation department than were suburban cities or independent cities. A larger percentage of cities with a commission form of government had joint park and recreation departments than did cities with mayor-council or council-manager governments.

The main reason for the trend toward merging previously separate departments was economic. Despite the attractiveness of savings, however, many have been reluctant and skeptical of such consolidations, feeling that the humanistic strength of recreation had to give way to the pragmatic force of resource- and facility-oriented leadership. This will be an important indicator to observe in coming years; it may be a bellwether of the philosophic direction of the field.

Although no comparable figures are available for subsequent years, in 1970 most local park and recreation agencies had citizen boards or commissions. Policy-making bodies were the most prevalent type (45 percent), followed by advisory (39 percent). Seventy percent of the members of these bodies were appointed, while 18 percent were elected.[18]

GOALS AND OBJECTIVES

Judson O. Allen, keynote speaker at a national forum on *Modernizing Urban Park and Recreation Systems,* convened by the National Recreation and Park Association in 1971, observed: "The only way to assure that park and recreation services will achieve and retain an effective role in the complex business of delivering services to the community is to work within a systematic, interrelated, goal-oriented framework."[19]

The development of goals and objectives usually makes up a substantial section of any recreation textbook; however, as noted earlier, real goals and objectives in real cities are usually vague or even nonexistent. One researcher, after studying six large U.S. cities during the summer of 1970, reported:

> **Most of the face-to-face leaders could not verbally tell me what their specific objectives were in a given program. In other words, they didn't know what they were striving for. Most agencies could not offer me in print their underlying philosophy of parks and recreation and a listing of their program objectives.[20]**

Researchers who studied the recreation programs of 25 large U.S. cities could not find any statements of explicit goals that could help city officials with limited resources establish real priorities. This lack of specific objectives increases the difficulty of decision-making when there are competing claims by advocate groups for direct and indirect components of the total inner-city recreation system. Nowhere, according to the study, were goals or objectives sufficiently defined to enable managers to make wise decisions regarding the distribution of funds among mass transit, art museums, library systems, adult education programs, playground leadership, park maintenance, pollution abatement or public safety.

CITIZEN PARTICIPATION

Citizens participate in decisions affecting recreation opportunities in their cities in many ways. Most cities have boards or commissions designated to make policies concerning parks and recreation. Many also have advisory council systems that represent geographic areas of the city or are linked to recreation centers or playgrounds. Thousands of citizens serve as volunteers in urban recreation and park departments, frequently influencing greatly the course of events and the quantity and quality of services.

Several investigators have reported problems with respect to citizen participation in the cities of the nation, however. For example, after many months of study in Philadelphia during 1971, Godbey concluded that "Poverty area recreation advisory councils are unlikely to successfully function or compete with middle-class councils in a comparatively centralized recreation allocation system."[21]

A 1974 study determined that ". . .if by citizen participation we mean the involvement of large numbers of low-income inner-city residents in processes which affect the quantity, quality and nature of their recreation opportunity, it is largely a myth." However, data and field observations revealed that the presence or absence of even modest citizen involvement had an important bearing on such factors as the amount of open space, number of park and recreation personnel, number of outdoor facilities, programs, unit maintenance and other critical functions.[22]

There is general support at the local, state and federal levels for the involvement of citizens in recreation and park matters. However, maximization of this participation has not been realized in many situations.

COOPERATION

Over the years, urban public park and recreation agencies have been criticized because they have not cooperated with other agencies at the local level. In 1972, for example, Richard Kraus, in his fine study for the Community Council of Greater New York, stated, "One of the most serious problems affecting urban park and recreation departments today is the lack of coordination among all municipal departments and organizations offering recreation services."[23]

Isolated examples had been heralded, however, which indicated that many innovative departments have extended their services by working closely with citizen groups, other public and private agencies, and various businesses and industries. This type of united effort was dubbed "synergetic programming," or the process of combining the unique resources of more than one agency to produce leisure services which could not be carried out successfully by one agency acting alone. A study to determine the extent of this type of effort was conducted in 1974, with responses coming from 103 cities having populations of over 100,000.[24] More than half the respondents indicated that their cities had more than 10 synergetic programs in 1973. Cities along the Great Lakes generally had more synergetic programs than cities in other regions; cities in the southeast had fewer such programs. Sports activities were the main focus of synergetic programming, although cultural and festival events and activities were also quite popular. Voluntary groups, educational institutions and service clubs were most frequently mentioned as groups and agencies with which departments cooperated.

Administrative commitment is the first requirement for implementing synergetic programming. A typical statement was received from the superintendent of the Flint (Michigan) Recreation and Park Board, James A. Bruce:

> **I believe sincerely that . . . cooperation between agencies cannot be legislated. Rather, it is an attitude of the administrators themselves. I submit to you that it is the responsibility of the municipal recreation departments to extend the arm of their total community program through cooperative planning and working with other agencies within the community. If you do not want to cooperate with other agencies, hundreds of excuses can be found to enhance this attitude and the total program in your community will thus be limited to the financial and physical resources of the municipal department. However, if an attitude of community cooperation is adopted, tremendous good can be accomplished. . . . No longer are you limited to the assets of the municipal department, but the sky is the limit and the total resources of the community can go to work for a total community recreation program. We know this is true because it has happened for us in Flint.[25]**

In addition to the necessity for commitment, a synergetic programming process was identified. Figure 2–10 highlights the steps in this process, starting from the idea and proceeding through implementation to possible repetition.

Municipal recreation agencies have had a long history of interaction with the public schools in the United States. The most obvious reason has been the recognition that school buildings, facilities, equipment and open spaces can be used during non school time by the community, thus saving tax dollars. In 1975, 96 percent of the recreation departments reported they cooperated with their local school systems. Such cooperation is often informal, however, and only 58 percent indicated the cooperative arrangements were based on a formal written agreement (Table 2–5). Large cities and Western cities had greater formal cooperation. The extent of school-recreation cooperation varies, but the most common cooperation involved the use of school buildings and grounds by recreation agencies during non school time.

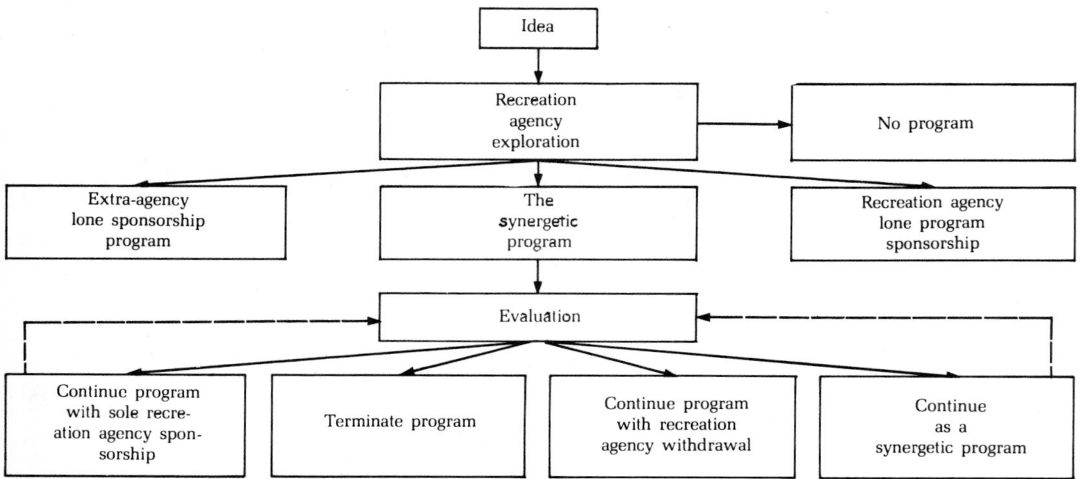

FIGURE 2–10 The Synergetic Programming Process. (From Diana R. Dunn and Lamarr A. Phillips, "Synergetic Programming, or 2 + 2 = 5," *Parks & Recreation*, Vol. 10, No. 3, March, 1975, p. 36.)

TABLE 2–5 Basis and Extensiveness of Cooperation Between Agency and Schools in the Utilization of School Facilities for Recreation Purposes[27]

Classification	No. of Cities Cooperating with Schools	Cooperation Based on a Formal, Written Contract or Agreement				Extensiveness of Cooperation[1]											
		Yes		No		Use of School Grounds[2]		Use of School Building Facilities[2]		Receipt of Monies for Recreation Purposes		Use of School Buses for Recreation Purposes		Developing/ Planning Joint Facilities		Other	
	(A)	*No.*	*% of (A)*	*No.*	*% of (A)*	*No.*	*% of (A)*	*No.*	*% of (A)*	*No.*	*% of (A)*	*No.*	*% of (A)*	*No.*	*% of (A)*	*No.*	*% of (A)*
Total, all cities	935	546	58	351	38	777	83	826	88	116	12	223	24	432	46	82	9
Population group																	
Over 500,000	14	9	64	3	21	12	86	13	93	1	7	1	7	9	64	3	21
250,000–500,000	18	13	72	3	17	13	72	18	100	2	11	2	11	14	78	3	17
100,000–249,999	50	32	64	15	30	40	80	43	86	8	16	4	8	27	54	7	14
50,000– 99,999	127	80	63	42	33	111	87	120	94	23	18	33	26	71	56	12	9
25,000– 49,999	239	144	60	82	34	208	87	211	88	27	11	67	28	116	49	24	10
10,000– 24,999	487	268	55	206	42	393	81	421	86	55	11	116	24	195	40	33	7
Geographic region																	
Northeast	255	119	47	126	49	212	83	238	93	22	9	66	26	87	34	16	6
North Central	232	130	56	96	41	191	82	203	88	26	11	45	19	106	46	22	9
South	218	117	54	90	41	166	76	170	78	6	3	38	17	96	44	28	13
West	230	180	78	39	17	208	90	215	93	62	27	74	32	143	62	16	7

[1]Percentages, when totaled, exceeded 100% owing to multiple responses allowed.
[2]Use of this facility after school hours, on weekends, and holidays.

However, all is not rosy. A field researcher reported in 1974:

> **. . . school facilities were empty 99 percent of the time . . . maintenance in many school playgrounds was minimal due to paved asphalt play areas. The play environment was dull and uninviting because one can see nothing but black surfaces and in some instances, broken glass crowning the hard surface areas.[28]**

The study reported further:

> **Ironically, it was the educational system which seemed to have "given up." Due to vandalism and other antisocial acts, and to the vagaries of the bureaucratic system, large numbers of inner-city school playgrounds were padlocked after school hours, and were therefore not a viable part of community leisure resources. (Some were even padlocked during the school day to prevent use by truant students from nearby schools.)[29]**

The nation's outdoor recreation plan also recognized the following dilemma:

> **Schools are fairly evenly distributed, represent a sizable portion of publicly owned lands, and may be the public areas most accessible to urban residents. School facilities, however, represent one of the least utilized public resources. They are used for their primary purpose during only a portion of daylight hours and for only one-half to three-quarters of the year. Many are vacant when recreation pressures are greatest—on weekends and during winter and summer vacations. However, many administrators are reluctant to make the school facilities available because of fear of damage, inability to control use, and liability in case of injury.[30]**

FINANCE

Historically, the property tax has been the main source of revenue for urban recreation services, as it has been for other municipal services. In competition for scarce local monies, the field of recreation and parks has traditionally been "low on the totem pole" when compared to most other claimants, such as policy and fire. Although the figures may not be precisely comparable, recent urban fiscal crises may account for the decline of revenue by municipal recreation agencies from $1,137,000 in 1970 to $931,687 in 1975. Sources of revenue for 1975 appear in Table 2–6. Western cities reported the highest mean revenue, while northeastern cities reported the lowest. Central

TABLE 2–6 Mean and Median Amounts of Revenue Obtained from Various Sources in Last Complete Fiscal Year[31]

Sources of Revenue	No. of Cities Reporting	Mean ($)	Median ($)
Local public appropriations	681	747,419	193,833
Fees and charges	601	144,558	33,000
Private funds	140	22,579	3,000
State funds and/or grants	191	106,921	40,000
Federal funds and/or grants	319	233,519	75,000
Other sources	130	189,679	36,600
Total revenue	806	931,687	218,041

TABLE 2–7 Mean and Median Departmental Budget for Last Complete Fiscal Year[32]

Classification	Operating Budget			Capital Budget			Total Departmental Budget (Operating and Capital)		
	No. of Cities Reporting	*Mean ($)*	*Median ($)*	*No. of Cities Reporting*	*Mean ($)*	*Median ($)*	*No. of Cities Reporting*	*Mean ($)*	*Median ($)*
Total, all cities	829	848,300	202,000	730	349,400	45,000	854	1,130,800	264,300
Population group									
Over 500,000	14	22,144,100	12,903,600	14	7,474,600	6,589,200	14	29,618,800	21,332,600
250,000–500,000	14	4,718,300	4,454,500	13	1,978,400	656,000	14	6,015,300	5,409,700
100,000–249,999	46	1,831,300	1,648,100	40	694,400	474,400	47	2,406,200	2,233,000
50,000– 99,999	107	966,800	800,000	104	374,100	174,000	110	1,318,600	1,127,100
25,000– 49,999	202	367,900	317,500	180	153,100	44,800	207	496,900	393,000
10,000– 24,999	446	146,100	111,600	379	80,300	25,400	462	229,000	140,600
Geographic region									
Northeast	212	878,600	111,000	160	337,800	23,500	218	1,104,800	129,300
North Central	209	550,600	160,900	186	144,000	42,700	217	693,500	228,600
South	199	824,200	216,000	184	385,700	47,000	205	1,158,100	293,100
West	209	1,138,100	358,300	200	516,100	100,500	214	1,574,400	567,200
Metro/city type									
Central	150	3,366,200	958,600	139	1,283,500	226,500	155	4,378,200	1,214,200
Suburban	454	343,800	164,600	383	156,900	35,000	467	473,100	211,200
Independent	225	187,600	139,600	208	79,400	36,400	232	285,000	180,600
Form of government									
Mayor-council	251	1,475,400	146,700	209	475,100	41,600	257	1,852,100	202,000
Council-manager	512	604,100	233,400	465	314,500	50,000	530	861,100	320,200
Commission	31	540,600	336,700	28	303,700	61,100	30	840,700	453,100
Town meeting	24	110,000	94,000	21	27,500	20,000	25	128,100	112,000
Rep. town meeting	11	382,800	124,400	7	59,900	13,500	12	403,000	164,600

TABLE 2–8 Various Mean and Median Expenditures (total operating and capital budget) in the Last Complete Fiscal Year[37]

Expenditures	No. of Cities Reporting	Mean ($)	Median ($)
Salaries and wages	732	656,154	138,865
Operation and maintenance	727	234,127	60,000
Capital (construction and improvement)	628	289,089	39,745
Land acquisition	129	290,054	54,000
Other	119	100,745	25,058

cities reported substantially higher revenue from all sources than did suburban or independent cities. Mayor-council cities had higher average revenues than did other forms of government.

It is likely that matching funds from the Land and Water Conservation Fund (see Chapter 4) account for the fact that many cities reported very large revenues from federal sources. Such monies would have been used for land acquisition and development.

In 1975, cities reportedly spent an average of $1.1 million for operating and capital expenditures for recreation and parks. Operations were 75 percent of this total, up from about 70 percent in 1970 (Table 2–7).

Not surprisingly, larger cities spent larger sums for recreation than did smaller ones. Western cities and central cities also spent on the average more money for recreation than did either cities in the other geographic regions or suburban or independent cities.

Following a long tradition, the largest municipal outlay was for salaries and wages (Table 2–8). The highest average expenditure for this function occured in the West.

Between 1967 and 1970, local agencies reported a decline in the number of bond issues passed and in the amount of capital outlay. Although more recent statistics are unavailable, it appears that, given the fiscal crises with which cities are currently faced, these measures have probably not shown any marked improvement.

A 1974 study concluded that public park and recreation systems in America's largest cities were in critical financial condition. Field researchers found crumbling facilities, staff cutbacks and slashed services in many cities.[34]

The 1974 study noted that large cities spent considerably more money for public parks and recreation than did the medium and small cities, even though there were fewer large cities in that study. Figure 2–11 shows the 1970 per capita operating expenditures for the 25 large study cities. The 25-city average was $9.93 per capita. The study staff, after tours through the study cities, determined that that amount was inadequate. It was inadequate in some areas to maintain even minimum safety levels of maintenance. The study recommended that per capita local park and recreation operating expenditures be at least $20 on the average instead of the then-current figure of $10.

PERSONNEL

Nearly 40,000 full-time (up from 34,133 reported in 1970) and 111,684 part-time recreation employees (up from 76,222 in 1970) were reported by cities in 1975 (Table 2–9). Larger cities had more employees and the West

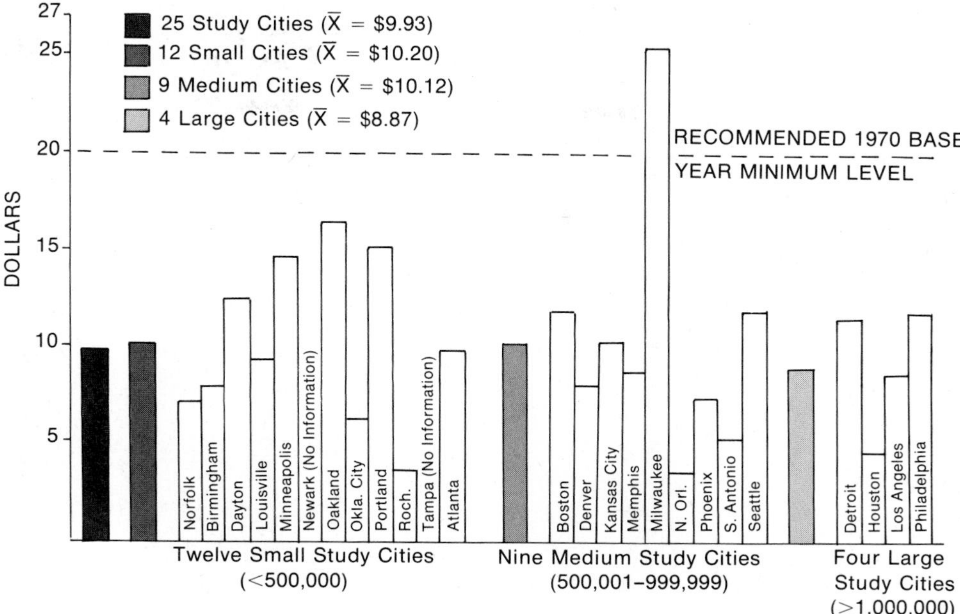

FIGURE 2–11 Per capita park and recreation operating expenditures in 25 study cities (1970). (From *Open Space and Recreation Opportunity in America's Inner Cities,* prepared for the U.S. Department of Housing and Urban Development by the National Recreation and Park Association, 1974, p. 71.)

TABLE 2–9 Average Number of Employees[36]

Classification	Full-time Employees			Part-time Employees		
	No. of Cities Reporting	*Mean*	*Median*	*No. of Cities Reporting*	*Mean*	*Median*
Total, all cities	909	44	11	908	123	61
Population group						
Over 500,000	14	1,045	841	14	1,465	923
250,000–500,000	18	304	304	17	543	543
100,000–249,000	42	105	104	49	277	214
50,000– 99,999	128	47	41	123	172	138
25,000– 49,999	236	19	15	230	95	75
10,000– 24,999	464	8	7	475	53	39
Geographic region						
Northeast	230	28	5	242	123	66
North Central	232	28	9	233	115	68
South	223	58	18	216	116	39
West	224	62	18	217	137	73
Metro/city type						
Central	173	165	54	169	323	150
Suburban	492	17	9	500	87	60
Independent	244	12	9	239	57	40
Form of government						
Mayor-council	280	68	9	286	166	63
Council-manager	558	34	14	546	103	62
Commission	32	35	17	31	121	80
Town meeting	27	3	3	31	54	41
Rep. town meeting	12	19	9	14	163	161

TABLE 2–10 Average Number of Employees by Occupational Category[37]

Occupational Category	Full-time Employees			Part-time Employees		
	No. of Cities Reporting	*Mean*[1]	*% of Cities Employing*	*No. of Cities Reporting*	*Mean*[1]	*% of Cities Employing*[2]
Total, all cities	909	...	100	908	...	100
Executive	744	1	82	26	1	...
Assistant director of parks and recreation	243	1	27	40	1	...
Division heads	228	2	25	41	2	...
Superintendent of parks	346	1	38	8	1	...
Superintendent of recreation	287	1	32	33	1	...
Administrative support staff	206	3	23	70	2	1
Clerical occupations	627	3	69	307	2	34
Related park professionals	87	5	10	26	2	...
District supervisors of parks	70	3	8	6	2	...
Park managers	119	3	13	20	5	...
Park rangers and police	77	5	8	62	7	1
Foremen	546	3	60	34	4	...
Skilled park personnel	469	12	52	95	10	10
Semiskilled and nonskilled personnel	528	31	58	465	33	51
District supervisors of recreation	75	3	8	28	3	...
Recreation supervisors	370	3	41	346	12	38
Recreation center directors	229	6	25	140	6	15
Recreation facility managers	128	4	14	229	6	25
Activity specialists	138	8	15	548	29	60
Recreation program leaders	119	12	13	642	51	71
Attendants and aides	79	14	9	593	53	65

[1]Leaders (...) indicate data not applicable.
[2]Leaders (...) indicate less than 0.5%.

and South had more than the Northeast and North Central. Central cities had substantially more than suburban and independent cities, and mayor-council cities had more recreation employees than other government types.

Table 2–10 reveals that in 1975, 82 percent of the reporting cities employed a full-time executive. Recreation leadership positions were primarily part-time positions; only 15 percent of the cities reportedly employed full-time activity specialists and only 13 percent employed full-time recreation program leaders. Clerical workers, foremen, and semi-skilled and non-skilled personnel made up the major group of full-time employees.

In 1970, about 25 percent of local parks and recreation departments had formally organized and recognized unions or employee bargaining units. No subsequent information is available.

Interestingly, women were a majority early in the history of the urban recreation (play) movement. By 1910, fully 65 percent of all the recreation workers in U.S. cities were women. This percentage has constantly diminished, and by 1970 was reduced to only 36 percent. This same general trend can be documented with respect to the number of full-time year-round recreation workers in U.S. cities. The percentage of women declined from 49 percent in 1928 (the first year that this statistic was recorded) to 38 percent in the depths of the depression; rose to 53 percent during World War II; and has declined steadily since to about 23 percent in 1970 (Figs. 2–12 and 2–13).

A more recent study by Henkel and Godbey[38a] estimated that 84,000 people were employed in local, county or state recreation and park agencies. Among such agencies, however, 40 percent currently had a hiring freeze in effect, reflecting the crisis in local government financing.

SPACE

Most cities grew before the concepts of comprehensive land use planning or open space planning were developed. Particularly in older cities, open space near large residential areas may be inadequate. Acquisition of open space has throughout this century been an important dimension of urban

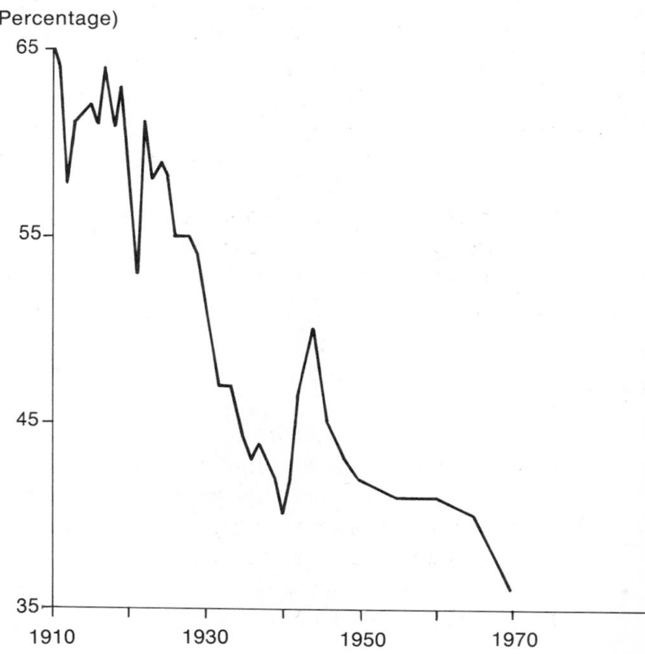

FIGURE 2–12 Percentage of female recreation workers reported by U.S. cities, 1910–1970.

FIGURE 2–13 Percentage of full-time year-round female recreation workers reported by U.S. cities, 1928–1970.

recreation departments. Federal programs such as Model Cities, the Land and Water Conservation Fund and the "Legacy of Parks" Surplus Property Program aided in this quest but, largely because of various matching fund restrictions, were not utilized to their fullest potential in many cities.

In 1975, cities reported acreage in three categories: reserved open space, undeveloped land and developed land (Table 2–11). Open space was generally related to city population size. Western cities usually had larger amounts of reserved land, whereas southern cities had more undeveloped land. Central cities consistently had more open space of all three types than did suburban or independent cities.

Although encroachment of urban park and recreation open space has been a highly volatile issue, a 1974 study reported that 23 large U.S. cities lost an average of less than 20 acres between 1965 and 1970. In most cases, this encroachment was due to street and highway construction, while school construction ranked second. Despite the encroachment, however, the cities had an average gain of 215 acres during the five year period. Since population decreased in over half the cities, the net gain was considered substantial. Figures do not reflect, of course, the historic and unique qualities of some of the acreage lost.[39]

FACILITIES

Facilities are important components of the urban recreation system. In 1975 common facilities included tennis courts, ball diamonds, athletic fields, basketball courts and recreation centers. Facilities infrequently reported were indoor/outdoor swimming pools, outdoor recreation centers, indoor ice skating rinks and resident camps.

Regional differences existed: southern cities reported more baseball diamonds, basketball courts, athletic fields and outdoor tennis courts and day

TABLE 2–11 Acres of Land for Parks and Recreation[38]

Classification	Reserved Open Space[1]					Undeveloped Land[2]				
	No. of Cities Reporting	*Mean*	*Median*	*Low*	*High*	*No. of Cities Reporting*	*Mean*	*Median*	*Low*	*High*
Total, all cities	327	588.8	70.0	1.0	20,911.0	628	215.6	60.0	1.0	7,495.0
Over 500,000	4	9,717.2	8,971.5	14.8	20,911.0	8	1,449.3	1,184.0	147.9	3,532.0
250,000–500,000	13	2,086.0	1,020.1	14.0	14,800.0	14	1,545.9	696.6	92.0	7,495.0
100,000–249,999	20	2,098.3	250.0	4.0	13,265.0	36	435.9	177.0	6.1	3,654.0
50,000– 99,999	46	548.0	110.0	3.0	8,400.0	87	292.6	105.2	2.0	5,000.0
25,000– 49,999	87	203.8	65.0	1.0	3,000.0	157	221.5	71.3	1.0	5,380.0
10,000– 24,999	157	202.7	40.0	1.0	3,522.0	326	80.5	39.8	1.0	1,500.0

Classification	Developed Land					Total				
	No. of Cities Reporting	*Mean*	*Median*	*Low*	*High*	*No. of Cities Reporting*	*Mean*	*Median*	*Low*	*High*
Total, all cities	770	345.3	100.0	1.0	12,315.0	826	759.4	197.9	2.0	24,449.0
Over 500,000	9	6,867.9	5,680.9	1,916.0	12,315.0	11	12,979.2	9,200.0	5,716.6	24,440.0
250,000–500,000	16	1,920.7	1;900.0	46.0	6,000.0	18	4,888.3	3,371.8	400.0	23,504.0
100,000–249,999	40	917.2	813.5	22.0	4,517.0	42	2,297.3	1,175.0	22.0	21,171.0
50,000– 99,999	104	474.9	288.0	10.0	10,000.0	112	928.3	403.0	15.0	17,000.0
25,000– 49,999	196	228.7	152.0	1.0	1,786.0	212	447.3	272.8	2.0	6,155.9
10,000– 24,999	405	101.8	60.0	1.0	1,800.0	431	234.9	114.0	2.0	4,657.0

[1]Reserved open space refers to acquired land that will never be developed.
[2]Undeveloped land is land not yet developed, but which will be in the future.

TABLE 2–12 Recreation Facilities Owned or Controlled by the City[40]

Facility	Lighted					Unlighted					Total				
	No. of Cities Reporting	*Mean*	*Median*	*Low*	*High*	*No. of Cities Reporting*	*Mean*	*Median*	*Low*	*High*	*No. of Cities Reporting*	*Mean*	*Median*	*Low*	*High*
Athletic fields	369	3	2	1	111	487	6	3	1	107	616	7	4	1	213
Baseball diamonds	557	3	2	1	69	624	5	3	1	96	822	6	4	1	74
Softball diamonds	62	3	2	1	93	604	6	4	1	89	812	7	5	1	95
Basketball courts	522	5	2	1	277	601	7	3	1	97	801	9	4	1	321
Nine hole golf course	12	1	1	1	2	117	1	1	1	7	137	1	1	1	7
Eighteen hole golf course	19	1	1	1	2	176	1	1	1	31	205	1	1	1	13
Stadiums	166	1	1	1	8	33	1	1	1	2	195	1	1	1	10
Indoor pools	...	...	...	...	...	...	...	...	...	...	121	1	1	1	11
Outdoor pools	459	2	1	1	70	170	2	1	1	37	602	2	2	1	72
Combined indoor-outdoor pools	15	1	1	1	3	3	1	...[1]	1	2	26	1	1	1	3
Portable pools	13	3	2	1	14	32	4	2	1	86	50	4	2	1	86
Bathing beaches	32	2	1	1	27	174	2	1	1	25	215	2	1	1	52
Marinas	49	1	1	1	8	42	1	1	1	8	94	1	1	1	8
Boat launching facilities	90	1	1	1	5	194	1	1	1	12	284	1	1	1	12
Bicycle paths restricted to cyclists (miles)	...	...	...	...	...	...	...	...	...	...	179	9.2	4.5	0.1	66.0
Indoor ice skating rinks	...	...	...	...	...	...	...	...	...	...	64	1	1	1	15
Outdoor ice-skating rinks	211	3	2	1	53	139	3	2	1	34	305	4	3	1	53
Artificial ice-skating rinks	55	1	1	1	11	14	2	2	1	8	72	2	1	1	11
Outdoor recreation centers	28	1	1	1	4	74	1	1	1	13	111	1	1	1	20
Recreation centers	...	...	...	...	...	...	...	...	...	...	672	5	2	1	150
Indoor tennis courts	...	...	...	...	...	...	...	...	...	...	32	4	2	1	36
Outdoor tennis courts	618	9	6	1	175	533	10	5	1	174	854	14	9	1	522
Day camps	53	1	1	1	9	178	2	1	1	74	294	2	1	1	74
Resident camps	32	1	1	1	6	23	1	1	1	1	73	1	1	1	8
Outdoor theatres	88	1	1	1	6	62	1	1	1	8	162	1	1	1	8
Zoos	41	1	1	1	1	43	1	1	1	1	100	1	1	1	2
Museums	68	1	1	1	5	18	1	1	1	3	107	1	1	1	6
Nature centers	37	1	1	1	6	83	1	1	1	6	141	1	1	1	6

Leaders (...) indicate data not applicable.
[1]Median statistics are meaningless when there are under four respondents.

camps than did cities in other regions. North-central cities had more outdoor ice skating rinks; northeastern cities more portable pools and indoor tennis courts; western cities more miles of bicycle trails and bathing beaches (Table 2–12).

OPERATIONS

The continuation of a traditional irony was again documented in 1975; although the purpose of public recreation agencies is to provide people with facilities, programs and services to meet their needs, very few agencies were found to be open after 10 P.M. Even fewer agencies provided services on weekends and holidays. Not one city with a population of over 500,000 reported provision of services between midnight and 8 A.M. on any day. Most services appeared to be scheduled for people who have free time between 8 A.M. and 6 P.M. on weekdays—certainly a minority.

Outreach programs designed to service those unable to participate in the more traditional programs showed great promise. Mobile equipment and facilities, roving leader efforts and toy loans were among those reported. Table 2–13 presents the types of outreach programs and facilities reported in 1975.

Despite the passage of public accommodations and equal housing legislation, current housing patterns in the cities continue to cause racial segregation at most urban recreation areas. A 1974 study found that most inner-city areas were consistently used by one social or ethnic group. Social philosophers who once saw urban open space and recreational activities as providing opportunity for ethnic and racial interaction would be hard pressed to document their theses in inner cities today. Homogeneous groups, largely reflecting homogeneous housing patterns, prevent this ideal from being reached. The study found that in some cities, youth and adult athletic league boundaries were carefully drawn to insure that interracial games would not occur during regular season play. Tournaments were carefully scheduled in "neutral territory."[42]

TABLE 2–13 Outreach Programs and Facilities (N = 624)

Program/Facility	Number	Percentage*
Roving Leader Personnel	284	46
Mobile and Portable Recreation Equipment and Facilities	242	39
Closing of Streets at Certain Times for Use as Recreation Areas	139	22
Use of Fire Stations	46	7
Services and/or Equipment to Persons in Correctional Institutions	56	9
Services and/or Equipment to Persons in Orphanages, Nursing Homes and Hospitals	139	22
Services and/or Equipment to Shut-ins	65	10
Toy Loan Center	28	4
Recreational Use of Fire Hydrants	52	8
Show Wagons	145	23
Shopping Center Programs	92	15
Storefront Recreation Center Programs	43	7
Use of Libraries	293	47

*Percentages exceed 100 percent since many respondents indicate more than one type of outreach program or facility.

UNDERUTILIZATION

In its most basic sense, underutilization means a park, playground, center or other recreation resource with no one there. With the exception of forced activity situations such as school recesses or prison exercise periods, people are not compelled to avail themselves of public recreation opportunities. Thus, if very few or no people choose to go to a particular park or other resource, then that resource becomes underutilized. Several writers and speakers have diagnosed this problem in many U.S. cities over the past few years. Combined evidence supports the contention of the 1971–1972 *Annual Report to the President and to the Council on Environmental Quality* of the Citizens' Advisory Committee on Environmental Quality: "Most of the time, most playgrounds are far too little used, and a good number are almost vacant most of the time."[43]

After studying the problem, Seymour M. Gold questioned:

> **Do urban populations really need public neighborhood parks if they cannot be located, designed, and managed to attract potential users and accommodate their recreational needs, or can the recreational needs of urban populations be accommodated better in private, regional, and national parks or other forms of leisure and recreational activities that generally take place outside of neighborhood parks?**

Gold stated further that "The record now indicates we may have, through neglect or indifference to user objectives, overlooked or avoided the phenomenon of nonuse." He predicted the possible demise of urban recreation systems if this professional challenge is not squarely faced.[44]

SPECIAL POPULATIONS

Increasing numbers of the old and the disadvantaged live in America's cities, and municipal recreation agencies are responding to their special needs. In 1975, cities reported that senior citizens were provided with the greatest number of recreation services, with pre-school children, the mentally retarded, the disadvantaged and the physically handicapped receiving somewhat fewer services (Table 2–14). Large cities were more likely to provide such services than smaller ones. Local public appropriations were most often used to support services to special populations (Table 2–15).

Accessibility is often a problem for special populations; if they cannot get to and from recreation centers and programs, the services offered will be of little use to them. In 1975, over two thirds of the cities with more than 50,000 inhabitants had a policy of making facilities usable and accessible to the physically handicapped. Over half the cities with populations of over 100,000 reported providing special transportation to recreation programs for persons unable to get to them by other means.[47]

In 1975, about 3,800 salaried personnel provided services for over 1¼ million disadvantaged individuals; there were 1,368 personnel for almost 1 million senior citizens; 1,850 personnel for ¼ million pre-school children; 714 personnel for 57,000 physically handicapped; and 1,244 personnel for 97,020 mentally retarded.[48]

PLANNING AND RESEARCH

A report based on a survey taken by the International City Management Association, the National Recreation and Park Association and The Urban Institute in 1971 shed considerable light on the planning capability and

TABLE 2–14 Cities Providing Special Recreation and/or Park Programs to Various Special Groups[45]

Classification	No. of Cities Reporting (A)	Mentally Retarded		Physically Handicapped		Senior Citizens		Preschool Children		Disadvantaged[1]	
		No.	% of (A)	No.	% of (A)	No.	% of (A)	No.	% of (A)	No.	% of (A)
Total, all cities	952	514	54	468	49	792	83	620	65	482	51
Population group											
Over 500,000	14	13	93	13	93	14	100	13	93	12	86
250,000–500,000	18	18	100	17	94	18	100	14	78	16	89
100,000–249,999	51	37	73	39	76	46	90	36	71	38	75
50,000– 99,999	131	95	73	84	64	117	89	92	70	75	57
25,000– 49,999	238	139	58	128	54	208	87	156	66	108	45
10,000– 24,999	500	212	42	187	37	389	78	309	62	233	47
Geographic region											
Northeast	252	148	59	126	50	198	79	136	54	103	41
North Central	238	123	52	107	45	198	83	149	63	116	49
South	231	130	56	113	49	182	79	143	62	133	58
West	231	113	49	122	53	214	93	192	83	130	56
Metro/city type											
Central	180	129	72	123	68	159	88	117	65	124	69
Suburban	523	253	48	225	43	437	84	368	70	215	41
Independent	249	132	53	120	48	196	79	135	54	143	57
Form of government											
Mayor-council	305	166	54	141	46	238	78	169	55	138	45
Council-manager	569	303	53	287	50	493	87	406	71	310	54
Commission	35	17	49	18	51	30	86	18	51	23	66
Town meeting	30	16	53	15	50	22	73	21	70	8	27
Rep. town meeting	13	12	92	7	54	9	69	6	46	3	23

[1]The disadvantaged, for purposes of this survey, are defined as those persons who have been denied social, economic, educational, cultural, or emotional opportunities because of race, ethnic background, religion, or socioeconomic condition.

TABLE 2–15 Funding Sources for Recreation Services for Special Groups[46]

Special Group	No. of Cities Reporting (A)	Funding Sources[1]: Local Public Appro-priations		Fees and Charges		Private		Federal		State	
		No.	*% of (A)*	*No.*	*% of (A)*	*No.*	*% of (A)*	*No.*	*% of (A)*	*No.*	*% of (A)*
Mentally retarded	514	368	72	70	14	64	12	31	6	75	15
Physically handicapped	468	322	69	59	13	46	10	22	5	48	10
Senior citizens	792	602	76	166	21	48	6	80	10	61	8
Preschool children	620	390	63	246	40	17	3	14	2	18	3
Disadvantaged	482	299	62	28	6	15	3	86	18	32	7

[1]Percentages, when totaled, exceed 100%, since some respondents noted more than one source.

activity of large city park and recreation departments.[49] Surveys were sent to all U.S. cities having more than 100,000 inhabitants, and to a sample of smaller cities. Of the 119 reporting cities, 41 percent had full-time facility-open space planners, and 29 percent had full-time recreation program planning analysts. Table 2–16 shows that the larger cities had more planning capability than did the smaller jurisdictions, insofar as full-time recreation planning staffs were concerned.

Mayor-council governments tended to have more planning capability than did council-manager cities. Public recreation agencies were most frequently responsible for recreation planning in all the cities; however, the larger the city, the more diffuse was the program planning function. Some 84 percent of the cities reported comprehensive park and recreation plans. About one half of these included only facilities, one third had both facilities and programs, and 4 percent had just programs alone. City size did not seem to influence whether or not cities had comprehensive plans.

Special studies and analyses were sometimes conducted by the cities. Table 2–17 shows the subjects of these investigations, and indicates that a substantial number were concerned with the wants and needs of people as members of special groups. About 55 percent of the cities had conducted citizen surveys of recreation interests or participation within the 3 years previous to the study.

Some 72 percent of the cities reported satisfaction with facility-space planning information; about 64 percent were happy with their recreation program analysis information.

Needed most to strengthen recreation facility space and program planning were, according to respondents, more funds (25 percent), more and better information concerning user needs and preferences (21 percent), greater public involvement (18 percent) and more and better governmental cooperation (11 percent).

The report concluded:

> **The majority of park and recreation agencies claim that they are satisfied with their planning, analysis, and evaluation information. However, a sizeable minority of these agencies—about one-third—state they are dissatisfied, especially with the program planning information. A recurring theme, particularly in the cities, is a desire for more and better information on user needs and preferences.**[52]

TABLE 2–16 Cities with Full-Time Recreation Planning Staffs[50]

Classification	No. of Jurisdictions Reporting *(A)*	Jurisdictions with Full-Time Recreation Planning Staffs			Facility-Space Planners		Program Analysts	
		No.	*% of (A)*	*Median Staff Size*	*No.*	*% of (A)*	*No.*	*% of (A)*
Total, all cities	119	54	45	4	49	41	34	29
Population group								
Over 500,000	17	14	82	5	12	71	9	53
250,000–500,000	18	15	83	4	13	72	11	61
100,000–250,000	58	19	33	3	19	33	11	19
50,000–100,000	16	6	38	3	5	31	3	19
Less than 50,000	10	0	0	0	0	0	0	0

TABLE 2–17 Subjects of Special Studies and Analyses Conducted by the Cities[51]

Subject	Cities: Total Responding, 85 (A)	
	No. Reporting	*% of (A)*
Facilities and open space	19	22
Needs of specific population group, such as teen-agers and elderly	18	21
General management, including organization, fees, and maintenance	17	20
Program evaluation or analysis	15	18
Recreation "needs"	8	9
Activity preference	5	6
Identification of users	2	2
Tourism	0	0
Other	1	1

The 1975 Congress for Recreation and Parks, held in Dallas, Texas, included a 1½ day Institute which focused on the process of researcher–urban practitioner dialogue.[53] The objectives were to identify information needs, share findings from recent studies, seek new and better ways to implement new information and develop mechanisms for continuing a productive conversation between urban recreation practitioners, researchers and educators. An overview of urban recreation technology and research emphasized that, despite the fact that the population has shifted from being a largely rural to a largely urban one in this century, the commitment to research in recreation has remained in the hinterlands. There is no critical mass of recreation researchers focused on urban recreation as there now is focused on outdoor recreation research in the United States. Urban recreation studies have been noncumulative in nature, owing to the wide range of their sponsors, staff, substantive topics, and geographic location and level. Urban recreation research in this country has in fact diminished at the same time that there has been an increasing concern for such information at the international level. (Unprecedented emphasis was placed on leisure and recreation by the planners of HABITAT—the United Nations Conference on Human Settlements, held in June 1976.)

Top U.S. urban recreation administrators and supervisors provided stimulation for researchers at the 1975 Dallas Institute by talking frankly about "what I need to know." Many "researchable problems" were presented, ranging from, "If my department went out of business tomorrow, would my city be better or worse?" to "How can we continue to function efficiently with the addition of an average of one new layer of bureaucracy annually at the *local* level?"

Urban researcher Richard Kraus provided closing observations at the final session of the Institute. He noted the lack of research in the field of urban recreation and the declining commitment to it. He underscored the gap between what the practitioners attending the Institute said that they needed to know and the kinds of research being done and reported at the Institute. This, he emphasized, pointed up the relevance of the Institute and the need for continuing dialogue between urban recreation and park administrators and the people doing and funding research.

Unfortunately, no research reported or mentioned at the Institute had been initiated or commissioned by an urban recreation and park agency or by any consortium of such agencies. Nevertheless, the expectation prevailed among urban recreation and park practitioners that policy-relevant research and management-oriented information should be available to them. The dilemma of "from where or from whom" this research was going to come remained for future resolution.

THE FUTURE

" 'Save Cities' Loses Its Power as Campaign Slogan" screamed a headline well in advance of the 1976 presidential elections. Many writers reported similar sentiments during the long campaign; cities were not big issues as they had been in the late sixties and early seventies. Other problems loomed larger for the majority of Americans. What does this portend for urban recreation?

Crystal-ball gazing is hazardous, but it seems likely that, as the cities go, so will go urban recreation in America. Most concur that central cities are in trouble and that their problems are getting worse. There is much evidence that urban recreation is similarly plagued and will continue to be so for the forseeable future. Even with its longer history and experience in supplying urban recreation, the United States cannot yet provide impressive urban recreation models for the rest of the world to imitate.[54]

In the recent past, the population has been migrating from the central cities to the suburbs and beyond. So too have recreation and park professionals. A singular exception seems to be the dynamic area of therapeutic recreation (see Chapter 6), which is now benefiting from federal intervention in its behalf. Monies currently not available in other urban settings *are* being made available to those serving special populations. To be sure, professionals in therapeutic recreation will probably continue to declare that funds are insufficient, but in many communities they are important bases for programmatic efforts.

As for the mainstream of American life, there seems no doubt that urban recreation will not survive as we know it today, but will continue to change to accommodate our changing needs. Certainly the coming years will be challenging ones for those who choose to commit their careers to recreation in the cities.

It is appropriate, even urgent, to search seriously for reasonable and realistic alternatives to shortsighted "what-we-will-need-in-the-future-is-more-of-what-we-have-now" attitudes. There is no reason why we cannot retain what works and is desirable and to replace what will be obsolete.

Needed today are active efforts to devise and determine the most beneficial and feasible forms of recreation for individuals and society at large, to inform the public of alternatives and their relative costs and benefits, and to solicit aggressively citizen support for needed resources. Some may be reluctant to assume such leadership roles; the question of who should must be resolved.

Who is best qualified to assess the present resources and probable future resource limitations facing every popular leisure activity? Who should scientifically document the relative merits of various activities for citizens of every age? Who should devise and popularize new high-density participant sport and recreation forums? Who should endeavor to maximize potential use of present and future resources and facilities around the clock and around the calendar? Who should minimize the environmental impacts of recreation activities and their attendant facilities, equipment and transportation requirements? Who should insist that the rhetoric of lifetime sports conform realistically to probable future resources as well as beneficial activity forms? Who should be certain that skills, values and interests fostered through formal and informal recreation programs will not be frustrated by lack of accessible resources and facilities? Who will decide whether limited assets will be committed to acquiring increasingly precious open space, developing playgrounds for children, building bicycle trails, supporting the performing arts, providing senior citizens' centers, transporting handicapped persons to special programs, underwriting subventions for adult education, keeping libraries open on weekends, expanding recreation opportunities for inmates of correctional institutions, or constructing new sports complexes?

The alternative to dynamic and aggressive professional leadership to resolve these tasks is intervention and control of the leisure destiny of the nation's cities by anyone who *will* assume leadership and responsibility.

In the meantime, perhaps we can dream of a "successful city." It would be, of course, a place where people are living in equilibrium with their environment and in harmony with each other. There would be no pollution, racism or sexism, and open space and clean air, water and streets would be the rule rather than the exception. The ideal city would be a place where everyone enjoyed good health; where safety, food and education were sufficient for all; where transportation and shelter were adequate; where life, liberty and the pursuit of happiness were realistically attainable; and where the Golden Rule was not subverted—in neighborhoods or throughout the city.

REFERENCES

1. Barbara Ward and René Dubos, *Only One Earth: The Care and Maintenance of a Small Planet* (New York: W. W. Norton and Co., 1972), p. 9.
2. Ibid., p. 6.
3. "We Cannot Go On As We Are Today," *Habitat World: United Nations Habitat Secretariat News*, June, 1974, No. 2, pp. 1–2.
4. Barbara Ward, *Human Settlements: Crisis and Opportunity* (Ottawa: Information Canada, 1974), p. 13.
5. Ibid., p. 11.
6. Ibid., p. 12.
7. Gay Pauley, "American Families Reverse Trend and Move Farther Out," *The Sunday Bulletin* (Philadelphia), March 28, 1976, p. 7.
8. Reynold E. Carlson, Theodore R. Deppe and Janet R. Maclean, *Recreation in American Life* (Belmont, California: Wadsworth Publishing Co., 1963), p. 14.
9. David E. Gray, "The Case for Compensatory Recreation," *Parks & Recreation*, April, 1969, p. 23.
10. *Beyond Survival: Leisure and Recreation in Human Settlements, A Global Survey*, prepared and submitted to HABITAT: UN Conference on Human Settlements by the World Leisure and Recreation Association, 1975, p. 33.
11. *Outdoor Recreation: A Legacy for America*, U.S. Department of the Interior, Bureau of Outdoor Recreation, U.S. Government Printing Office, Washington, D.C., 1973, p. 14.
12. H. Douglas Sessoms, Harold D. Meyer and Charles K. Brightbill, *Leisure Services: The Organized Recreation and Park System* (Englewood Cliffs, New Jersey: Prentice-Hall, 1975), pp. 13–15.
13. *Open Space and Recreation Opportunity in America's Inner Cities*, prepared for the U.S. Department of Housing and Urban Development by the National Recreation and Park Association, 1974, p. 62.
14. Ibid., p. 63.
15. *Municipal Recreation and Park Services and Programs: 1975*, International City Management Association Urban Data Service Report 10/75, 14 pp.
16. Ibid., p. 2.
17. Ibid., p. 3.

18. "Local Parks and Recreation," *Parks & Recreation,* Vol. 6, No. 8, August, 1971, p. 19.
19. Judson O. Allen, "An Approach to Recreation Planning," in *Modernizing Urban Park and Recreation Systems* (Arlington, Virginia: National Recreation and Park Association, 1972), p. 20.
20. *Open Space and Recreation Opportunity in America's Inner Cities,* op. cit., p. 66.
21. Geoffrey Godbey, "Recreation Advisory Councils and the Poor—A Second Look," *Parks & Recreation,* Vol. 7, No. 11, November, 1972, pp. 28–31, 41–43.
22. *Open Space and Recreation Opportunity in America's Inner Cities,* op. cit., pp. 44–45.
23. *Urban Parks and Recreation: Challenge of the 1970's,* prepared by the Community Council of Greater New York, February, 1972, p. 57.
24. Diana R. Dunn and Lamarr A. Phillips, "Synergetic Programming, or 2+2=5," *Parks & Recreation,* Vol. 10, No. 3, March, 1975, pp. 24–26, 36.
25. Ibid., p. 26.
26. Ibid., p. 36.
27. *Municipal Recreation and Park Services and Programs: 1975,* op. cit., p. 6.
28. *Open Space and Recreation Opportunity in America's Inner Cities,* op. cit., p. 43.
29. Ibid., p. 44.
30. *Outdoor Recreation: A Legacy for America,* op. cit., p. 16.
31. *Municipal Recreation and Park Services and Programs: 1975,* op. cit., p. 4.
32. Ibid.
33. Ibid.
34. *Open Space and Recreation Opportunity in America's Inner Cities,* op. cit., p. 70.
35. Ibid., p. 71.
36. *Municipal Recreation and Park Services and Programs: 1975,* op. cit., p. 5.
37. Ibid.
38. Ibid., p. 13.
38a. Donald Henkel and Geoffrey Godbey, *Parks, Recreation and Leisure Services—Employment In the Public Sector: Status and Trends* (Arlington, Virginia, National Recreation and Park Association, 1977).
39. *Open Space and Recreation Opportunity in America's Inner Cities,* op. cit., p. 32.
40. *Municipal Recreation and Park Services and Programs: 1975,* op. cit., p. 12.
41. Ibid., p. 11.
42. *Open Space and Recreation Opportunity in America's Inner Cities,* op. cit., pp. 44–45.
43. Ibid., p. 42.
44. Seymour Gold, "Nonuse of Neighborhood Parks," *American Institute of Planners Journal,* November, 1972, pp. 369–378.
45. *Municipal Recreation and Park Services and Programs: 1975,* op. cit., p. 7.
46. Ibid., p. 8.
47. Ibid., pp. 8–9.
48. Ibid., p. 9.
49. Robert Brown and Donald Fisk, *Recreation Planning and Analysis in Local Government* (Washington, D.C.: The Urban Institute, 1973), 70 pp.
50. Ibid., p. 55.
51. Ibid., p. 59.
52. Ibid., pp. 56–57.
53. Diana R. Dunn, "Reflections on the 1975 National Urban Recreation Technology Applications Institute," *Journal of Leisure Research,* Vol. 8, No. 1, 1976, pp. 66–68.
54. Diana R. Dunn, "Urban Recreation: No Models to Mimic," *Society and Leisure,* No. 4, 1975, in pp. 7–26.

QUESTIONS

1. What do the concepts "suburbanization" and "re-ruralization" mean in terms of (a) recreation and leisure services for Americans, and (b) your professional goals?

2. Based on your own experience, contrast the relative importance of urban public, private and commercial recreation services and facilities to you personally.

3. Examine your personal participation (or that of your friends or relatives) in decision-making processes influencing the leisure life of people in your home town or neighborhood.

4. What phenomena do you believe will most affect the recreation opportunities of U.S. urban residents during the next decade? Quarter century?

5. Describe recreation as you believe it should exist in a "successful city."

A family contemplates waterfalls in Yosemite National Park.
(U.S. Bureau of Outdoor Recreation)

chapter 3

THE ROLE OF THE FEDERAL GOVERNMENT IN RECREATION, PARK AND LEISURE SERVICES

While the role of the federal government in providing recreation, park and leisure services is vast, generally it has evolved as a by-product of other interests and functions, such as conserving natural resources or improving the quality of life in urban areas. Currently, nine major federal agencies operate under legislation or executive mandate permitting them to sponsor and fund public leisure services. Over 80 agencies, commissions, committees and councils are engaged in over 300 separate programs for outdoor recreation alone. Generally the federal government has operated under the philosophy that alternatives to federal provision of recreation opportunities should be allowed to develop to their maximum capability.

However, in spite of this, federal government involvement in recreation, park and leisure services continues. A number of social critics have questioned the involvement of government in such services, particularly at the federal level. A primary criticism of such involvement has been that government will use the sponsorship of leisure services as a means of social control. In effect, it is argued that government will seek to modify the beliefs and behavior of citizens in ways that meet the needs of the state. Since leisure or recreation is often thought of as freely chosen behavior, attempts to control such behavior are sometimes viewed with alarm. Certainly we have seen many governments use sport as a method of gaining political support, as entertainment and celebrations to draw the public's attention away from pressing social problems and so on. Perhaps it can be argued that government must advance *some* values in the leisure services they sponsor, but the *degree* of control should be questioned. Additionally, the individual should be free to not use such services if he or she so chooses, and to play a role in shaping them.

It has also been argued that government, particularly at the federal level, has no effective way of determining what people *want* to do during their leisure time. While this is true to some degree, particularly in a pluralistic society such as our own, other national organizations concerned with recreation face a similar problem. Local government is sometimes thought to be the only appropriate level for government involvement in recreation, since it is closest to the people and thought to be able to determine the leisure needs and interests of its residents most easily. While this is generally true, in some cases, such as preserving a large natural area for recreational use, local government may need help from the state and federal governments.

A common charge against the government is that it sometimes brings about results that are the opposite of what it wishes to accomplish. The desire of the federal government to promote a "return to nature" ethic, for instance, has led to the provision of outdoor recreation areas which often become overrun with visitors and increasingly resemble built-up urban areas. A development of parks as part of a problem to combat juvenile delinquency may sometimes increase delinquency by providing an attractive place for the commission of crime.

Government is also thought to be reactionary in its provision of recreation—sponsoring activities only after they are acceptable to the majority, and failing to experiment. Although such charges are often true, it must be said in fairness that government is also criticized when it is experimental. It may be argued that government is not the appropriate agency to be in the forefront of innovation in regard to leisure behavior, since organizations with a limited constituency may more easily gain support for innovation.

Although the U.S. federal government in particular is criticized for its involvement in recreation, park and leisure services, the provision of such opportunities appears to be a vital part of its concern for the social welfare of its citizens, particularly in a country that is dedicated to "the pursuit of happiness." Pursuing happiness in a highly interdependent society often makes government involvement necessary, even federal involvement. Such involvement may include serving as a "provider of last resort," undertaking large-scale funding of resources that aren't commercially feasible, establishing health and safety regulations, promoting art forms that cannot survive without economic assistance, and so on. Perhaps in the last analysis the question should be asked: "What will be missing if government involvement in recreation, park and leisure services is absent?"

FUNCTIONS

The primary functions of the federal government in regard to recreation, park and leisure services may be classified as follows:

Advisement. Assisting various public and private agencies in promoting, encouraging, fostering, stimulating and improving recreation, park and leisure services.

Coordination. Coordinating federal and state plans, policies and programs in a number of areas, especially in regard to outdoor recreation.

Credit Provision. Providing credit to states, other levels of government, private associations and individuals.

Grants. Administrating grants-in-aid, cost-sharing and other financial assistance programs for public agencies, private organizations and individuals.

Land and Water Resource Management. Acquiring land and water areas and administrating construction, maintenance and management of these areas.

Leadership, Supervision and Instruction of Recreation Programs. In certain circumstances, providing recreation leadership and supervision, such as in the parks of our nation's capital, and instruction, such as the environmental interpretation program led by rangers of the National Park Service.

Planning. Developing plans for recreation, park and leisure services at the national, regional, state, county and municipal levels, and in other local areas.

Regulatory. Regulating, controlling or adjusting public activities of a recreational nature. Regulating and controlling the uses of natural resources, by establishing recreational boating and flying safety measures, water quality standards, and so on. Regulating recreation personnel requirements in veterans' hospitals, homes for the aged using Medicare funds, and so on.

Research. Conducting research activities through analyses and investigations to solve problems and to increase knowledge pertaining to man's use of leisure.

Technical Assistance. Providing technical assistance and counsel to federal agencies, states and their political subdivisions, private organizations and individuals.

INVOLVEMENT

A large number of federal agencies are involved in recreation, park and leisure services. These agencies fall into three general groups: (1) those in which recreation is a primary function; (2) those which emphasize recreation but administer it as one of several other basic purposes; and (3) those which administer recreation as a relatively minor function. We may further divide such agencies into those that are involved in land management and those that are not. Table 3–1 shows the number of programs in outdoor recreation at the federal level and the types of functions performed.

Let us examine the role of some of these agencies.

DEPARTMENT OF HEALTH, EDUCATION AND WELFARE

Perhaps foremost among these agencies is the Department of Health, Education and Welfare, which heads federal efforts to meet the need for public leisure services and facilities. HEW also helps meet the leisure-service needs of special populations, such as the ill and the handicapped. The *Children's Bureau* deals with improving community-based services for children and youth, including opportunities for play. In this capacity, the Children's Bureau works with a number of state and/or national agencies and organizations. The *Administration on Aging,* which has responsibility for most federal-level programs dealing with older adults, provides grants to train professional staff. The *Rehabilitation Services Administration* is involved with vocational rehabilitation programs designed to help those who are mentally or physically disabled, and administers laws pertaining to this purpose. College and university programs providing specialized training in therapeutic recreation receive grants for curriculum development and scholarships from the *Vocational Services Administration.*

DEPARTMENT OF HOUSING AND URBAN DEVELOPMENT

The Department of Housing and Urban Development, which is involved in the development of public housing, slum clearance, provision of open space and community facilities, and mass transit, contributes to the recreation effort by providing large-scale assistance in planning parks, multi-purpose community centers, recreation centers and playgrounds, and urban

TABLE 3–1 Number of Federal Programs in Outdoor Recreation by Department, Agency and Function, 1973*

Departments—Agencies	Advisory	Coordination	Credit	Grants	Information	Miscellaneous	Regulatory	Research	Resource Management	Technical Assistance	Training
Department of Agriculture											
Agricultural Research Service								1			
Agricultural Stabilization and Conservation Service				6							
Cooperative State Research Service				1							
Economic Research Service								2			
Extension Service	1	1			1			1		2	1
Farmer Cooperative Service					1			1		1	
Farmers Home Administration			3								
Forest Service				3	3			3	3	2	
Rural Electrification Administration			1								
Soil Conservation Service		2		1	1	2				2	
Department of Commerce											
Bureau of the Census								1		1	
Bureau of Domestic Commerce					1			1			
Economic Development Administration			3	3				1		1	
Environmental Data Service					1						
National Marine Fisheries Service	1				1	1	1	2	3	1	
National Weather Service					1						
Office of Coastal Environment	1							1		1	
Office of Marine Recreation		1									
Office of Regional Economic Coordination										1	
Office of Sea Grant	1		1								
United States Travel Service					2			1			
Department of Defense											
Army Corps of Engineers (Civil Functions)					2	3	1	1	3		
Departments of Army, Navy, and Air Force									1		
Office of the Director of Civilian Marksmanship				1							2
Office of Economic Adjustment						1					
Department of Health, Education and Welfare											
Administration on Aging				2							
Children's Bureau					1					1	
Health Services and Mental Health Administration					1			3		2	1
National Institute of Mental Health				2				1			
Office of Education				4				1			
Rehabilitation Services Administration				3				1			
Department of Housing and Urban Development											
Community Planning and Management				1							
Housing Management			1								
Office of the Assistant Secretary for Housing Production and Mortgage Credit and Federal Housing		1	2								
Office of Research and Technology								1			
Public Housing Recreation Facilities				1							
Department of the Interior											
Bureau of Indian Affairs			1	1					1	1	
Bureau of Land Management				1	1	1	1	1	1		
Bureau of Mines				1							
Bureau of Outdoor Recreation		2		1	1	1		4		1	
Bureau of Reclamation				1	2				1		
Bureau of Sport Fisheries and Wildlife		1		4	2		1	3	4	4	1
Geological Survey						1		1			
National Park Service		1		1	3	1		3	3	1	2
Office of Water Resources Research								3			
Department of Labor											
Bureau of Labor Statistics								1			
Manpower Administration				6						1	4

TABLE 3–1 Number of Federal Programs in Outdoor Recreation by Department, Agency and Function, 1973* *(Continued)*

Departments—Agencies	Advisory	Coordination	Credit	Grants	Information	Miscellaneous	Regulatory	Research	Resource Management	Technical Assistance	Training
Department of Transportation											
Federal Aviation Administration				1			1			1	
Federal Highway Administration				3				3	1	1	
United States Coast Guard				1	1	4	5	1			2
Independent Agencies, Boards, Commissions, Committees, and Councils											
Advisory Board on National Parks, Historic Sites, Buildings and Monuments	1										
Advisory Commission on Intergovernmental Relations	1							1			
Advisory Committee on State and Private Forestry	1										
Advisory Council on Historic Preservation	1	1									
Appalachian Regional Commission				3							
Atomic Energy Commission						1			1		
Citizens Advisory Board on Environmental Quality	1										
Council on Environmental Quality	1	1			1						
Delaware River Basin Commission							1	1			
Environmental Protection Agency				6	1		2	2		2	
Farm Credit Administration			1								
Federal Farm Credit Board	1										
Federal Power Commission	1				1		1				
Federal Reserve System								1			
General Services Administration											
Property Management						1					
Public Buildings Service						1					
Marine Safety Council							1				
Migratory Bird Conservation Commission						1					
National Board for the Promotion of Rifle Practice											1
National Forest Reserve Commission						1					
National Marine Fisheries Service				1				1			
National Park Foundation						1					
President's Committee on Mental Retardation	1				1						
President's Council on Physical Fitness and Sports					1			1		1	
President's Air Quality and Water Pollution Control Advisory Board	1										
Public Advisory Committee on Soil and Water Conservation	1										
Regional River Basin Commissions (7)		7									
Roosevelt Campobello International Park Commission									1		
Small Business Administration			4		1			1		3	3
Smithsonian Institution						1					
Tennessee Valley Authority				1	3	1		3	2	1	
Veterans Administration			1			2					
Water Resources Council		1		1	1						
Total Programs	15	19	18	61	37	26	15	54	25	32	17
Total Agencies	15	17	10	28	27	19	10	34	13	22	9

*From *Outdoor Recreation—A Legacy for America.* Washington, D.C., U.S. Department of the Interior, 1973.

beautification projects. The Demonstration Cities and Metropolitan Development Act of 1966 provided funding of up to 80 per cent for historical preservation, acquisition and development of parkland, community centers, playgrounds and so on. The Model Cities Program of 1976 provided extensive planning grants to further urban renewal efforts, with recreation and parks an important planning consideration.

DEPARTMENT OF AGRICULTURE

Within the Department of Agriculture, the *Federal Extension Service* provides financial and consultant services to groups seeking to develop community leisure services. The *Forest Service,* which manages over 180 million acres of grassland and forest, became more directly involved in the provision of recreation opportunities after the passing of the Multiple Use Act of 1960. Although the Forest Service was created in 1905 primarily to manage forest lands reserved by presidential proclamation, Forest Service employees soon found themselves attempting to manage recreation in order to lessen the risk of forest fires. From this initial involvement, the Forest Service has greatly increased its involvement in recreation under the Multiple Use Act of 1960, which established the policy that our national forests were to be managed for outdoor recreation, range, timber, and wildlife and fish purposes. No longer were such resources to be administered only in order to maximize financial profit. Today, areas administered by the U.S. Forest Service receive almost as many visits for recreation purposes as there are people in the United States. As Douglass points out, in Pennsylvania, there are more armed men (800,000) in the forests on the opening day of deer season than were in the field on both sides of the Vietnam War.[1]

DEPARTMENT OF THE INTERIOR

Many of the agencies that manage land for recreation and other purposes are located within the Department of the Interior. As the map in Figure 3–1 shows, nearly one third of the land in the United States is owned by the federal government. The *Bureau of Land Management* maintains vast land holdings, including 42 percent of the 162 million acres in 11 western states, which are managed for multiple purposes, including recreation. The *Fish and Wildlife Service,* concerned with fish and game management, provides a variety of recreational opportunities on approximately one third of the land under its administration. Hunters and fishermen are assisted by the *Bureau of Sport Fisheries and Wildlife* and the *Bureau of Commercial Fisheries,* both of which operate within the Fish and Wildlife Service. Through the provision of wildlife refuge areas on public lands, fish hatcheries, areas for the production of water fowl, and opportunities to camp and study nature at wildlife refuge areas, the interests of a number of outdoor recreationists are met. The *Bureau of Reclamation* has responsibility for recreation on 242 recreation areas at land reclamation areas in 17 western states. It is primarily responsible for water resource development for irrigation and for power.

An important new bureau in the Department of Interior is the *Bureau of Outdoor Recreation.* Let us examine its origins in detail.

Federal interest and involvement in recreation became more direct with

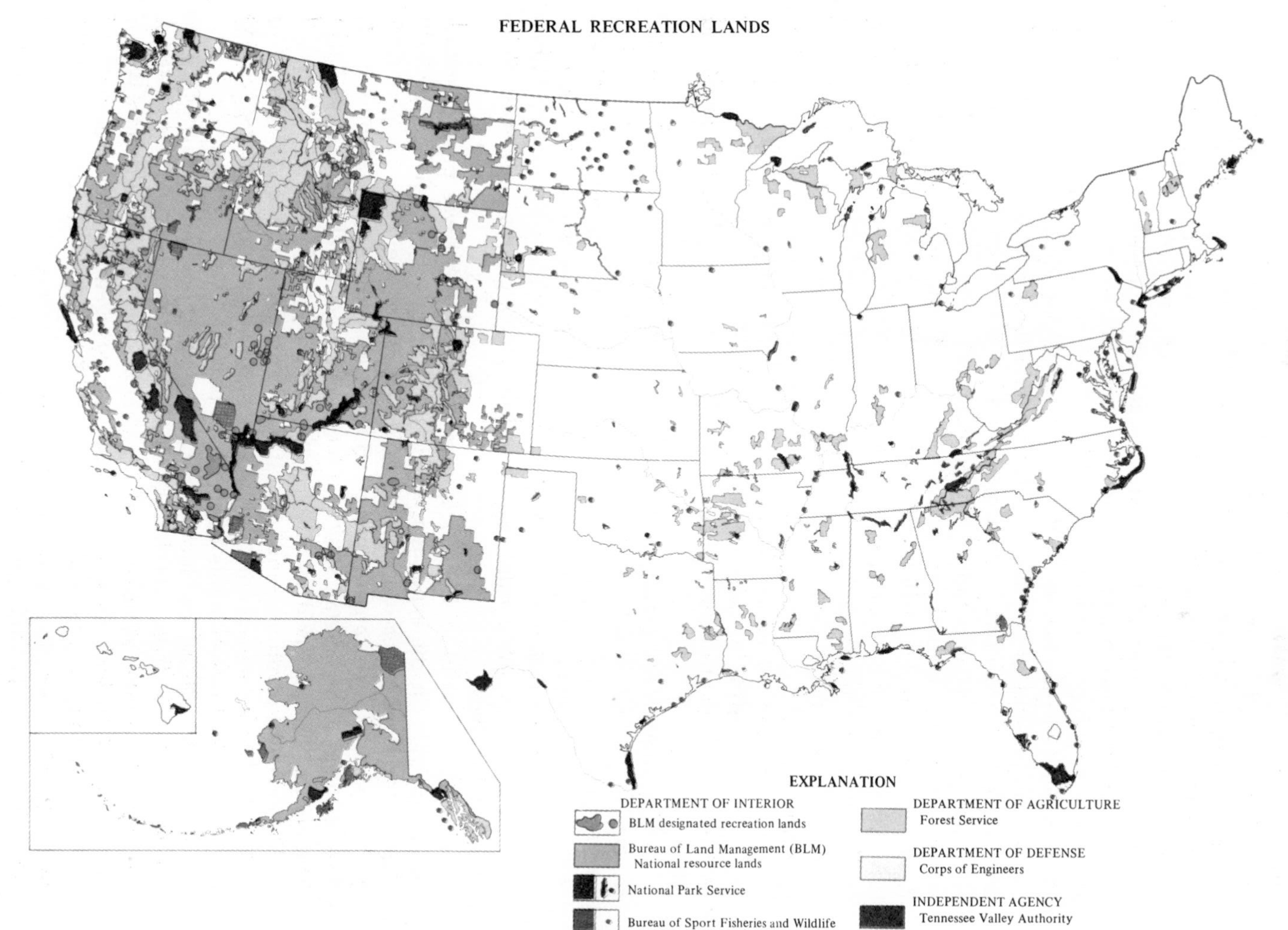

FIGURE 3–1 Federal recreation lands. (From *Outdoor Recreation – A Legacy.*)

the creation of the *Outdoor Recreation Resources Review Commission (ORRRC)* in 1958. This commission, which was created by bipartisan congressional action, undertook studies in order to recommend ways of meeting increased public demand for outdoor recreation. After three years of study, the commission submitted recommendations calling for (1) a national outdoor recreation policy; (2) guidelines for the management of outdoor recreation resources; (3) expansion, modification and intensification of present programs to meet increasing demand; (4) establishment of a Bureau of Outdoor Recreation in the federal government; and (5) a federal grants-in-aid program to the states.

The federal government's reaction to these recommendations was generally quite positive. A presidential message to Congress on conservation in 1962 announced the creation of the *Bureau of Outdoor Recreation (BOR)* within the Department of the Interior, responsible for coordinating federal outdoor recreation programs, state assistance and research, and for encouraging state and regional cooperation, undertaking recreation surveys and formulating a nationwide outdoor recreation plan. At the same time, President Kennedy followed suggestions of the ORRRC by establishing the federal-level *Recreation Advisory Council.* The Bureau of Outdoor Recreation provided staff support for the Recreation Advisory Council, which then issued several policy circulars pertaining to outdoor recreation, public health aspects of outdoor recreation, plans for a national program of scenic roads and parkways, guides for federal outdoor recreation investment, federal policy governing the reporting of recreational use of federal recreation areas, and nonfederal management of the recreation facilities on federally owned lands and waters.

These statements significantly influenced national policy on outdoor recreation. In 1966, the Recreation Advisory Council became the *President's Council on Recreation and Natural Beauty,* with broader authority concerning environmental protection. A similar citizen's committee was also appointed. The major accomplishment of the new council and the citizens' committee was a report on the natural environment. Both groups, however, were terminated in 1969.

In 1965, the Land and Water Conservation Fund Act was passed, which provided funds for the expanded acquisition of lands by the federal government for outdoor recreation, as well as for grants to the states for planning, acquisition and development of recreation areas. To date, over $1 billion has been spent in joint federal, state and local investments. The Legacy of Parks Program in 1971 increased by 50 percent the money available under the Land and Water Conservation Fund Act. It also provided for the conversion of surplus federal properties into public parks and recreation areas at discounts to state and local governments of up to 100 percent.

In 1970, a national outdoor recreation plan through the year 2000 was completed by the BOR and the Department of the Interior. This report, submitted to former President Nixon by his Secretary of the Interior, Walter Hickel, estimated that it would cost $42 billion to begin to meet the nation's future recreational needs. The study tried to balance the needs of the poor, the handicapped and the aged with those of the average citizen. It identified the following geographic areas as having the greatest recreational need: Pittsburgh, New York–Newark, Chicago, Philadelphia–Camden, Washington–Baltimore, Boston–Providence, Cleveland, Milwaukee, Cincinnati, Denver, Minneapolis—St. Paul, New Orleans and Buffalo. Finally, it recommended that the Pentagon release many forts, fields and other facilities for use as public play areas.

This report, which cost over $7 million to produce, was never made public by the Nixon administration, who felt it was inflationary. Instead, the BOR completed preparation of a revised nationwide outdoor recreation plan, after holding extensive forums to obtain public and private views on the plan. This plan was released by the Nixon administration, but was much less ambitious. Although the plan indicated continued administrative support for granting appropriations to the Land and Water Conservation Fund and enlarging the range of projects available for funding to state and local governments, many other features of the plan have been condemned by recreation and conservation organizations. As an editorial in *Parks and Recreation* magazine states:

> **Astonishingly, the plan contains no inkling of priorities. It does not even assert that defining priorities is a relevant issue. It relegates the problem of recreation for the ill and handicapped to two paragraphs on architectural barriers.**
>
> **It almost completely ignores research needs, especially in their human and behavioral implications.**
>
> **The plan gives no thought to the need for well-educated and trained professional manpower in parks and recreation.**
>
> **The plan focuses on land and facilities but largely ignores operations, interpretation, and programs. It asserts an urban focus but suggests little to meet urban needs.**[2]

To many, the plan signaled at least a temporary reversal in federal leadership in outdoor recreation. After former President Nixon resigned owing to his role in the Watergate scandal, President Ford continued to de-emphasize federal involvement in outdoor recreation.

In spite of this situation, the Bureau has continued to work toward the development of a National Outdoor Plan for 1978. The Carter administration has appeared to be supportive of outdoor recreation in its initial actions, although full appropriation of Land and Water Conservation Fund monies has not been assured.

The *National Park Service,* which administers areas of national significance because of their natural, historic, recreation or cultural resources, will not be dealt with here, since it is treated in detail in Chapter 4.

A number of other federal government agencies are involved in recreation, park and leisure services, as discussed in the following paragraphs.

NATIONAL ENDOWMENT FOR THE ARTS

The creation by Congress of the National Endowment for the Arts in 1965 helped to encourage the spread of high-quality art across the country. It also marked a turning point in governmental support of culture. By 1973 the federal government's expenditure per year on the fine arts was an estimated $42.5 million. Part of these funds is used to support ballet, opera and orchestras, which must either be subsidized or else charge such high prices for performances that all but the wealthy are excluded. Other funding has included appreciation and educational projects for school children and direct grants to artists. Since private contributions to the fine arts are estimated at $85 million per year, the government's role as a patron must be considered a substantial one.

ARMY CORPS OF ENGINEERS

The Army Corps of Engineers maintains and improves rivers and other waterways to enhance navigation and control floods. In performing this function, the agency makes improvements on existing beaches and also constructs new beaches, harbors and waterways. The Corps also operates 350 reservoirs. A great deal of recreation activity takes place on these facilities.

TENNESSEE VALLEY AUTHORITY

The Tennessee Valley Authority, originally created in 1933 to develop the Tennessee River for navigation, flood control and electrical power, created a series of multi-purpose dams which had tremendous outdoor recreation potential. Although recreation was not a specified purpose in establishing these dams, it was soon obvious that huge recreation opportunities had been created. Boating, camping, hiking and backpacking have grown tremendously in these areas.

ARMED FORCES

Each of our Armed Forces maintains a Special Services division which provides organized recreation programs for members of the Armed Forces and their dependents. Over 10,000 people were employed by the Army Special Services alone in 1970. Additionally, recreation leadership and facilities are supplied to those in Veterans' Hospitals.

PRESIDENT'S COUNCIL ON PHYSICAL FITNESS AND SPORTS

The President's Council on Physical Fitness and Sports was organized in 1956 after a number of alarming reports about the lack of fitness of the nation's youth were made public. It developed a suggested physical fitness program that was widely accepted by the nation's schools and has recently developed fitness programs for adults as well as launching a media campaign to stress the importance of physical fitness to everyone.

FEDERAL INVOLVEMENT IN CANADA

In Canada, according to Balmer, the federal government has been involved in recreation in the following areas:

1. The preservation of scenic areas, natural environments, primitive areas and historic sites of national significance
2. Management of federal lands, both urban and ex-urban, for the broadest possible recreation benefit consistent with other essential uses
3. The promotion of national health and welfare in cooperation with the provinces, often through support of recreation programs
4. The support of cultural programs, often having a leisure orientation
5. Development of regional assistance programs designed to offset major disparities of an economic and social nature across the country
6. Support and promotion of the tourist industry, with emphasis on export tourism and inter-provincial travel[3]

Nineteen federal departments or agencies are involved in park and recreation programs or funding, or both. The *Ministry of State for Urban*

Affairs, for instance, is responsible for coordinating federal programs in urban areas, including open space and recreation programs. The *Department of the Environment* is responsible for recreation opportunities as they relate to lands, forests, wildlife, fisheries, water management and atmosphere environment. The *Department of Indian Affairs and Northern Development* owns and manages national parks and historic sites and areas. From 1973 to 1974 it had a total operating and capital budget of over $90 million. The *Central Mortgage and Housing Corporation* currently has the greatest potential in terms of urban open space acquisition, because of the mechanisms for park development contained in the National Housing Act. Balmer concluded, however, that the Canadian federal government's role in the provision of leisure services had evolved without any specific policy designed to coordinate the efforts of the individual departments.

A SUMMARY OF FEDERAL ASSISTANCE LEGISLATION

While a huge number of laws indirectly affect recreation, park and leisure services, the following public laws have affected such services quite directly.

10.904 WATERSHED PROTECTION AND FLOOD PREVENTION

Federal Agency: Soil Conservation Service, Department of Agriculture.

Objectives: To provide technical and financial assistance in planning and carrying out works of improvement to protect, develop and utilize the land and water resources in small watersheds.

Use and Restrictions: Assistance is provided in planning, designing and installing watershed works of improvement; to include public recreation. SCS will provide up to 50 percent of the total costs.

3.522 ENVIRONMENTAL EDUCATION

Federal Agency: Office of Education, Department of Health, Education and Welfare.

Objectives: To educate citizens on the problems of environmental quality and ecological balance.

Uses and Restrictions: (1) Community education projects; (2) environmental education centers and inservice training for non-educational personnel; and (3) curriculum supplementary materials development. HEW will provide up to 80 percent the first year, 60 percent the second year and 40 percent the third year of the total costs.

14.203 COMPREHENSIVE PLANNING ASSISTANCE (701)

Federal Agency: Community Planning and Management, Department of Housing and Urban Development.

Objectives: To strengthen planning and decision-making capabilities of chief executives of state, area-wide and local agencies.

Uses and Restrictions: A broad range of planning and management activities may be supported by these grants. Grants are normally for two thirds of the costs.

14.302 NEIGHBORHOOD FACILITIES GRANTS

Federal Agency: Community Development, Department of Housing and Urban Development.

Objectives: To provide funds for community service centers, offer a wide range of facilities and activities.

Uses and Restrictions: Funds may be used only for the construction of centers, or for the acquisition, expansion or rehabilitation of neighborhood centers. HUD will provide up to two thirds of the total development costs.

14.303 OPEN SPACE LAND PROGRAMS

Federal Agency: Community Development, Department of Housing and Urban Development.

Objectives: To help communities meet the rapidly growing recreation needs of urban areas by assisting these communities in acquiring and developing parkland.

Uses and Restrictions: Acquisition and development of open space land. HUD will provide no more than 50 percent of the costs of acquisition and development.

14.304 PUBLIC FACILITIES LOANS (PFL)

Federal Agency: Community Development, Department of Housing and Urban Development.

Objectives: To provide loans for the development of essential public works when credit is not otherwise available at reasonable terms.

Uses and Restrictions: Loans are made to finance construction of a variety of public works, including recreation facilities. HUD loans may be made up to cover 100 percent of the project development costs.

15.202 PUBLIC LAND FOR RECREATION, PUBLIC PURPOSES AND HISTORIC MONUMENTS

Federal Agency: Bureau of Land Management, Department of the Interior.

Objectives: To permit qualified applicants to lease or acquire available public land for historical monuments, recreation and public purposes.

Uses and Restrictions: Available public lands may be used for health, education, public recreation, historical monuments, and other recreational and public purposes. BLM will sell lands at $2.50 per acre with a minimum payment of $10 per lease.

15.400 OUTDOOR RECREATION—ACQUISITION AND DEVELOPMENT

Federal Agency: Bureau of Outdoor Recreation, Department of the Interior.

Objectives: To provide financial assistance to the states and their political subdivisions for the acquisition and development of outdoor recreation areas and facilities for the general public, to meet current and future needs.

Uses and Restrictions: Acquisition and development grants may be used for a wide range of outdoor recreation projects. Facilities must be open to the general public. Fund monies are not available for the operation or maintenance of facilities. Not more than 50 percent of the project may be federally financed.

15.402 OUTDOOR RECREATION TECHNICAL ASSISTANCE

Federal Agency: Bureau of Outdoor Recreation, Department of the Interior.

Objectives: To assist other federal agencies, private interests, states, and local governments in the development and operation of effective programs to meet public needs for outdoor recreation and related environmental quality.

Uses and Restrictions: Advisory and technical assistance.

15.906 PARK AND RECREATION TECHNICAL ASSISTANCE

Federal Agency: National Park Service, Department of the Interior.

Objectives: To provide technical assistance to state and local agencies for planning, developing and managing their park and recreation areas.

Uses and Restrictions: Technical and advisory service.

15.907 PARK PRACTICE PROGRAM

Federal Agency: National Park Service, Department of the Interior.

Objectives: To serve as a means of disseminating information to park and recreation officials about tried and proven (a) designs for park, structures and facilities, and (b) improved methods of administration and operation.

Uses and Restrictions: Park practice publications are used as guides by park and recreation officials in planning, designing and administering their facilities.

17.222 NEIGHBORHOOD YOUTH CORPS (NYC)

Federal Agency: Manpower Administration, Department of Labor.

Objectives: To provide opportunities to students of low-income families to earn sufficient funds to remain in school while receiving useful work experience, and to provide work experience, training and support services for youths from low-income families who have dropped out of school, to enable them to return to school or to acquire skills that will improve their employability.

Uses and Restrictions: The NYC has 3 major components: (1) an in-school program to provide part-time work for students of high school age from low-income families; (2) a summer program that provides these students with job opportunities during the summer months; and (3) an out-of-school program to provide economically deprived school dropouts with practical work experience. The federal government will finance up to 90 percent of the cost of these programs.

39.002 DISPOSAL OF FEDERAL SURPLUS REAL PROPERTY

Federal Agency: General Services Administration.

Objectives: To dispose of surplus real property.

Uses and Restrictions: Surplus real property may be conveyed for park or recreation use and public health or educational purposes at discounts up to 100 percent. Surplus real property conveyed for public park or recreation use must be used for purposes so conveyed in perpetuity.

45.001 PROMOTION OF THE ARTS—ARCHITECTURE AND ENVIRONMENTAL ARTS

Federal Agency: National Endowment for the Arts, National Foundation on the Arts and Humanities.

Objectives: To provide grants for various projects, including research in architecture, landscape architecture and environmental design.

Uses and Restrictions: Grants may be used for projects fostering professional education and development, environmental education and public awareness, and research and design projects. The federal government usually provides up to 50 percent of the funding.

54.010 PROMOTION OF THE ARTS—EXPANSION ARTS

Federal Agency: National Endowment for the Arts, National Foundations for the Arts and Humanities.

Objectives: To provide grants to professionally directed, community-based arts organizations involved with urban, suburban, and rural communities.

Uses and Restrictions: The grants may be used for instruction and training in the arts at all levels. Federal monies to be matched dollar for dollar.

THE FUTURE

It is difficult to speculate on the future of federal involvement in recreation, park and leisure services. The federal government seems to be coming closer to recognizing recreation, park and leisure services as a legitimate concern, particularly with regard to outdoor recreation. The urban crises of the 1960's stimulated crash programs of aid to the major urban areas, and a high priority was given to recreation and parks, but such sources of aid have largely dried up. The concept of revenue sharing, in which block grants are passed from the federal government to state governments, has often meant that *decisions* about such expenditures for recreation, park and leisure services are passed along to state or even local governments. While it does not seem likely that recreation will become a *top* priority of the federal government, certainly the strong Congressional support for the Land and Water Conservation Fund and the heightened visibility of the issue of public recreation and parks in the 1976 presidential campaign indicates some renewed support. Also, amendments to the Land and Water Conservation Act, passed in 1976, will result in increased spending for outdoor recreation, which will reach nearly $1 billion a year by 1980. Perhaps it is safe only to predict that recreation, park and leisure services will continue to be quite sensitive to changes in political trends at the federal level.

REFERENCES

1. Robert W. Douglas, *Forest Recreation,* 2nd ed. (New York: Pergamon Press, 1975).
2. "Half A Plan," *Parks and Recreation,* January, 1974, p. 25.
3. Kenneth Balmer, "Recreation and Parks In Canada: Federal Involvements," *Recreation Canada,* March 31, 1973, pp. 7–8.

QUESTIONS

1. What are some criticisms of government involvement in recreation?
2. What functions does the federal government undertake in regard to recreation?
3. What is the National Endowment for the Arts?
4. What are the duties of the Bureau of Outdoor Recreation?
5. Is the involvement of the federal government in recreation justified? Why or why not?

Bicycling along the C & O Canal in a National Historical Park. (U.S. Department of the Interior, National Park Service Photo)

ABOUT THE AUTHOR

William R. Failor has 21 years of service with the U.S. Department of the Interior—18 with the National Park Service and 3 with the Bureau of Outdoor Recreation. Before assuming his present position with the C & O Canal National Historical Park, he was Superintendent of National Capital Parks - Central in Washington, D.C. He has held positions in the Office of Resource Planning, the Northeast Regional Office and the Office of Design and Construction with the Park Service. Upon establishment of the Bureau of Outdoor Recreation in 1963, he organized their 17-state Northeast Regional Office in Philadelphia. Bill is a registered landscape architect in the states of New York, Pennsylvania and Maryland.

After graduating from Penn State University in 1950, Bill spent four years with Clifton E. Rodgers and Associates in Harrisburg, Pennsylvania, before moving to Ohio and assuming the position of Assistant Director/Secretary for the Toledo Metropolitan Park System. Bill attended Muhlenberg College and Geneva College, and did graduate work in public administration at American University. He likes sports and is an avid music fan and landscape horticulturist.

Bill and his family are active in the United Church of Christ. He is a member of the American Society of Landscape Architects, the National Recreation and Parks Association, the Maryland Recreation and Parks Association, the Nature Conservancy and the National Trust for Historic Preservation.

chapter 4

THE NATIONAL PARK SERVICE

In April 1972, as a part of the 100th Anniversary of the National Parks, a symposium was held in Yosemite National Park to discuss what a national park system should be, where it is now, and where it should be going.

The National Park Service as a leisure-serving organization and the National Parks as places for leisure pursuits were put in proper perspective by the discussion group on National Parks and Young America at the Yosemite Symposium:

> **We do not, most of us, live in parks. We live, rather, in a nation, the United States, and it is within that unit that the search for diversity is most meaningful. In contrast to an increasingly urbanized, mechanized, noisy and crowded society, the parks stand out as quiet, natural, open and wild places. As such, they represent a chance for different kinds of experiences—for diversity. To the extent to which parks are maintained as places which contrast sharply with the rest of our society, diversity will be maximized. If, however, they become more like every place else (even though that would represent a gain in diversity within the parks), diversity will be lost over-all, and our lives would be poorer.**[1]

The parks managed by the National Park Service are not places for the pursuit of leisure activities per se, but rather places of natural, scientific and historic significance, which people may visit to enjoy and obtain an understanding of the values for which these national treasures were created and are being preserved.

The National Parks as places to visit are well known. Visitation to the 293 National Park Service areas exceeded 265 million in 1976. In spite of the popularity of many parks with the American public, few understand the purpose and relationships of the areas that make up the National Park System, or the responsibilities of the National Park Service to preserve and manage these parks.

The purpose of this chapter is to make a few observations about the National Park Service, the system of parks it manages and its challenges; and to encourage investigation, study and research into the many areas that make up the National Park System.

ORIGIN AND TRENDS

National Park Service management follows the principles in the statement of the National Park purpose contained in the Act of Congress of August 25, 1916, commonly referred to as the "Organic Act" which created the National Park Service:

> **. . . the Service thus established shall promote and regulate the use of the Federal areas known as national parks, monuments and reservations . . . by such means and measures as to conform to the fundamental purpose of the said parks, monuments and reservations, which purpose is to conserve the scenery and the natural and historic objects and the wildlife therein and to provide for the enjoyment of the same in such manner and by such means as will leave them unimpaired for the enjoyment of future generations . . .**[2]

The system of national parks began with the preservation by the Congress of large natural areas of the West, such as Yellowstone National Park. It has grown from this park's origin in 1872 into a vast and complex system of some 293 parks of immense variety, preserved not only for natural purposes but also for scientific, historical, recreational and cultural purposes of significance to the Nation as a whole.

The diversity of the National Park System can be illustrated by citing Mount McKinley National Park, an area of more than 2 million acres that preserves the highest mountain in North America and vast glaciers of the Alaska Range, as contrasted with Ford's Theater National Historic Site, a one-quarter acre area on 10th Street in Washington, D.C., which consists only of the small theater where President Lincoln was assassinated on April 14, 1865, and the house where he died the following day.

In the beginning the system included only large natural wonderlands of the West, such as Yellowstone, Yosemite and Glacier National Parks. Historic areas became a large segment of the system in 1933, when President Franklin D. Roosevelt transferred 50 historic sites to the National Park Service in a gigantic reorganization of the federal government. Later, under authority of the Park, Parkway and Recreation Area Study Act of 1936, national parkways, such as the Blue Ridge and the Natchez Trace, were added to the system. National Recreation Areas became popular after World War II, when many coastal and lakeshore areas were added.

As an outgrowth of the Outdoor Recreation Resources Review Commission study report, "Outdoor Recreation for America," in 1962, an increased awareness of the need for national recreation areas near large metropolitan areas became apparent. To meet the growing needs of the urban sectors of the nation, several large recreation areas were established during the early 1970's, such as Golden Gate in California, Gateway in New York, and Cuyahoga Valley in Ohio. Another development of the late 1960's was the Summer in the Parks and Parks for All Seasons programs, which originated in the National Capital Parks around Washington, D.C. These programs aimed to "bring parks to the people" by developing activities that emphasized the interrelationships of people in the urban regions. Park settings were used for a variety of cultural activities—living history programs, drama, music and art forms—to convey the inherent meaning of the parks. Summer in the Parks had a profound influence on the traditional interpretive programs and management of the National Parks.

EARLY HISTORY

In the early exploration and discoveries of the land that now makes up the United States, the primary objective seemed to be "to take possession" for economic advancement and the accumulation of materials and wealth. Little consideration was given to protecting the environment or conserving natural resources.

Later, however, as settlements began to spread across North America, some people began to think in terms of preserving large areas of natural beauty and setting them aside to keep and protect "for all time." The impetus for preserving unique areas of natural beauty came primarily from the military people of the eighteenth century, who during their tours of duty took special note of and kept diaries on many unusual places in the West.

Public thinking was also influenced by many poets and writers of the early eighteenth century. One of the earliest was George Catlin (1796–1872), an American painter and student of Indian life from Philadelphia. He traveled widely throughout America, studying Indian tribes and writing about his experiences with American Indian cultures and their environments.

FIRST NATIONAL PARK

Many people believe that the National Park System really began with the preservation of Yosemite Valley in 1864, when the Congress gave the area to the state of California for use as a "public park and recreation area." John Muir (1838–1914), a worldwide explorer and naturalist and the founder of the Sierra Club, aroused much interest in the area through his enthusiastic writings about the valley's magnificent beauty.

Congress established "the first" National Park with the passage of the Yellowstone National Park Act on March 1, 1872. This set aside 2 million acres "as a public park or pleasuring ground for the benefit and enjoyment of the people." The protection of Yellowstone resulted from the famous Washburn-Langford-Doane expedition of 1870 into the Montana Territory. Heading the party was General Henry D. Washburn, Surveyor-General of the territory and a former congressman. Nathaniel P. Langford was a writer and lecturer, and Lieutenant Gustavus C. Doane led a small group of cavalrymen responsible for protecting the civilian party. At the end of their expedition they saw and named the most famous geyser in the park "Old Faithful." This group, and other explorers that followed, wrote numerous articles and made many speeches on the value of the area to the nation, and of the need to set it aside for preservation in perpetuity.

COMMERCIAL INTERESTS

As exploration and settlement of the West grew, so did commercial interests—in prospecting, timbering and collecting artifacts, primarily from the ancient Southwest Indian cliff dwellers, which brought tremendous prices in eastern markets. William C. Everhart, Assistant Director of the National Park Service, in his book on the National Park Service (1972), describes the attitude of early settlers to preservation:

> **For the pioneer settlers who followed Lewis and Clark into the American West, wilderness was the cruel and dangerous enemy that had to be conquered, and there was no higher aspiration than to make the trackless wasteland blossom like a flower. In the course of his visit to the United States in 1831, Alexis de Tocqueville, the French statesman and political philosopher, fulfilled a lifelong urge by traveling to Michigan to see "primitive country". Men he encountered could comprehend neither his craving for wilderness nor his indifference to such traditional frontier pursuits as land speculation, timber-stealing from the public domain, and destruction of the American Indian in the name of progress and religion. Americans had a different set of values, their vision "fixed upon another sight . . . the march across these wilds, draining swamps, turning the course of rivers, peopling solitudes, and subduing nature."**

Meanwhile, similar activities were happening in the east. In 1828, a commercial venture was started in Georgetown in the District of Columbia. The Chesapeake and Ohio Canal Company wanted to build a cheap mode of water transportation through western Maryland to the Ohio Valley through a natural wilderness in the flood plain of the Potomac River. The project was doomed to failure by nature's floods and the introduction of a faster mode of transportation—the railroads. Interestingly, the canal is now a National Historical Park, as a result of its purchase by the department of the Interior in 1938 and the support of concerned citizens such as former Supreme Court Justice William O. Douglas, who wanted to preserve, in his words, "a ribbon of green alongside the Potomac as a slender refuge of nature and tranquility."

ANTIQUITIES ACT

The first significant piece of legislation passed by the Congress toward the formation of a national system of parks was the "Antiquities Act" of June 8, 1906. It culminated the efforts to stop the looting, speculation and desecration of many of the prehistoric Indian sites and villages that had been going on in the southwestern part of the United States and introduced natural resource protection as a national concern. The Antiquities Act authorized the President to establish National Monuments by proclamation; these would include such things as historic landmarks, prehistoric structures, and objects of scientific interest situated upon lands controlled by the federal government. Although this Act is used sparingly today, it was exercised extensively in the early part of the twentieth century.

Theodore Roosevelt was the first President to make conservation a national goal. He convened the first conference on conservation in 1908. In his opening remarks at the conference he declared, ". . . It seems to me time for the country to take account of its natural resources, and to inquire how long they are likely to last." Before his term expired, President Roosevelt proclaimed 18 acres as National Monuments, one of the most significant being the pre-Columbian cliff dwellings area of Mesa Verde, now a national park.

TURN OF THE CENTURY

During the early 1900's much momentum was being generated toward the creation of a system of national parks through nationwide publicity and by many individuals of great influence and integrity. One of these individuals was Stephen T. Mather, a man of boundless energy, influence and wealth. He is frequently referred to as "the father of the National Park Service." Mr. Mather used much of his personal wealth, as many individuals have done throughout the history of the Park Service, to promote and sell the preservation of areas for inclusion in the National Park system.

Stephen Mather came to Washington in 1915 in response to a letter from the then Secretary of the Interior Franklin K. Lane, who was his friend. Mr. Mather had written to complain about the conditions in the national parks of that day. Secretary Lane wrote in reply: "Dear Steve—If you don't like the way the national parks are being run, come on down to Washington and run them yourself." Mather became Assistant to the Secretary of the Interior in January 1915 and, along with another Californian, Horace Albright, set out to establish an organization to administer the national parks which over the years has become a model for the world.

The immediate job that faced Mather was getting legislation passed to establish a new parks bureau for the 31 national parks and monuments which existed in 1915. Through Mather's genius in public relations and organization and through his persistence, Congress in 1916 passed the Act that established the National Park Service.

The Act is the most significant piece of legislation to National Park Service management. It provides a broad framework of policy for the administration of park areas of the system. Students planning to enter the National Park Service should study the "legislative history" of this act and other acts authorizing national park areas, in order to understand the concepts and trends in the development of National Park legislation. Knowledge of the legislative *history* of a bill, or "legislative intent" as it is sometimes called, is frequently more important to the interpretation of policy and management directions than the acts themselves. A thorough study and analysis of the legislative histories of park legislation is basic to the understanding of the "public will" as bills proceed through the hearings and deliberations of the Congress.

TYPES OF AREAS ADMINISTERED BY THE NATIONAL PARK SERVICE

All parks administered by the National Park Service are a part of the National Park System because they are of *national significance;* that is, they represent part of the nation's historic and cultural heritage, natural wonders of the country or national recreation needs. Management of each park is directed to one or more of these purposes.

In reviewing the legislation that has shaped the National Park Service, it can be seen that the Congress has included within the system three different categories of areas—*natural, historic* and *recreational.* Specific management criteria and policy have been formulated to support each category or combination thereof.

It is true, of course, that some parks in the system are more spectacular than others. But each park is an expression of something special—some manifestation of natural forces, scenic beauty or historic significance.

For those who love to explore the wilderness on foot or horseback there are parks with vast areas that have been untouched. Wildflower lovers and bird lovers know which parks present the best opportunities. Park visitors are filled with admiration and awe at the natural beauty they find, and are impressed by the ways in which the history of the nation is portrayed in hundreds of park areas. To sum up, the National Park System provides adventure and diversity for everyone.

Natural Areas. In the "natural areas" category are the parks and monuments which are primarily of scenic and scientific interest. They preserve the superlative examples of our nation's scenic beauty, its wilderness, plants and wildlife. This category contains some of the oldest parks in the system, such as Yellowstone and Yosemite National Parks, Acadia National Park, and the White Sands and Joshua Tree National Monuments.

Historical Areas. The "historical areas" group contains all national historic sites and some monuments, and comprises the largest number of areas within the system. It also includes parks established for prehistoric values. The nomenclature of areas in this category is fixed by the Congress and is sometimes confusing. It includes: national historical parks, national monuments (not to be confused with those areas in the natural category), national military parks, national memorials and monuments, national military parks and battlefields, and national historic sites. A few examples of areas in this category are Colonial and Independence National Historical Parks, Bandelier National Monument, Federal Hall National Memorial, the Washington Monument, Golden Spike and Robert Frost National Historic Sites, and Gettysburg National Military Park.

Recreational Areas. The "recreational areas" group is relatively new and includes National Seashores and Lakeshores, National Parkways and Riverways, and National Recreation areas. These areas either preserve a particular physical resource or serve a fundamental purpose, usually recreation. Examples in this category are Cape Cod and Cape Hatteras National Seashores, the Blue Ridge Parkway, Delaware Water Gap National Recreation Area, Pictured Rocks National Lakeshore, Buffalo River National Riverway, and Golden Gate and Gateway National Recreation Areas, the latter two being primarily urban recreation resource areas.

Cultural Areas. A fourth and the newest category is the "cultural group," sometimes included with the historical category. It consists of only two areas at the moment—Wolf Trap Farm Park for the Performing Arts and The John F. Kennedy Center for the Performing Arts. Ford's Theatre in Washington, D.C. is also a significant cultural resource. Cultural events are important to other areas of the system, particularly folk art and nature crafts.

Cultural activities require "resource space," but are usually not designated as a part of the basic park resource area.

THE NATIONAL PARK SYSTEM PLAN

The formulation of a well-rounded system of parks requires a good representation of the best examples in the above categories, and existing and potential park areas which qualify for inclusion in the national park system make up what is called a "National Park System Plan."

Planning for a system of national parks has been an ongoing endeavor since the first national areas were established. A more systematic approach to nationwide planning for parks at the national level began with the passage of the Park, Parkway and Recreational Area Study Act of 1936. This Act enabled the Park Service to study and expand its system of parks by authorizing broad studies of potential park areas and providing assistance to states and local communities for expansion and development of their park systems.

Many park areas, particularly in the recreation category, have been added to the system through comprehensive resource studies, such as the Atlantic Coastline survey and Great Lakes studies of the 1950's, and the more recent Gulf and Pacific coastline studies.

The creation of the Bureau of Outdoor Recreation in 1963, an outgrowth of the Outdoor Recreation Resources Review Commission Study of 1962, caused a shift in emphasis of agency responsibility and brought nationwide parks and outdoor recreation planning to that agency. The National Park Service, however, continues to exercise a strong role in the study and planning of potential National Park System areas, through its participation in interagency task groups and by acting as the lead agency in nationwide planning efforts.

Other federal land managing agencies share responsibilities in outdoor Recreation and Parks planning. Among these are the U.S. Forest Service, the Army Corps of Engineers, the Bureau of Reclamation, the Bureau of Land Management and the U.S. Fish and Wildlife Service. The National Park Service frequently enters into agreements with these agencies for cooperative management of land and water resources having national recreation significance. Cooperative management arrangements are also formulated through congressional action.

Much attention has been given by the Park Service in recent years to regional planning requirements for areas currently within the system and proposed additions to the system.

THEMES

In classifying the areas which are part of the National Park System—natural, historic and recreational—the National Park Service has established historic and natural history themes with the objective of defining a National Park System that has balance and is representative of the nation's natural phenomena and historical heritage.

Natural History and Regional Themes. Natural history themes and natural regions are based largely on Fenneman's physiographic divisions of the nation (1928). This classification gives primary consideration to the geologic histories, structures and landforms of the various regions, and their influence on climates, soils, vegetation and animal life associated with them.

The natural history themes, in their broadest definitions, are a series of categories encompassing essentially all of the natural phenomena of the country. For example, Yellowstone and Grand Teton National Parks portray nearly all of the natural phenomena existing in the Middle Rocky Mountains region of Fenneman's classification, while the Appalachian Plateaus, although not a part of the National Park System, *are* represented in National Forests and scattered State Parks. The National Park System's best examples of natural regions in Fenneman's classification are located in the West, while the best representations of natural regions in the East are located in the Appalachian Ranges region, represented by the Shenandoah and Great Smoky Mountains National Parks and the Blue Ridge Parkway; and in the state of Florida, represented by the Everglades National Park and the new Big Cypress National Preserve. In sum, natural region and natural history theme representations in the National Park System are complex issues, requiring continuing study and analysis.

American History Themes. American history is also organized into themes and subthemes to provide an orderly framework for preservation of areas on a national basis. Many themes that are not represented in the National Park System *are* preserved by other levels of government or private organizations. The National Historic Landmark Preservation program also promotes the preservation of historic sites according to the historic theme classification.

There are nine general historic theme groupings which demonstrate the development of the nation: (1) The Original Inhabitants; (2) European Exploration and Settlement; (3) Development of the English Colonies; (4) Major American Wars; (5) Political and Military Affairs; (6) Westward Expansion; (7) America at Work; (8) The Contemplative Society; and (9) Society and Social Conscience. Forty-three subthemes have been identified which are basic study units for consideration of historic areas of national significance.

It must be remembered that there are few areas within the National Park System which fall entirely within a single classification, be it natural, scientific, historic or recreational. Many natural areas contain important historic resources that should be preserved to demonstrate various ways of life in American history. For example, old farmsteads and mountain villages are preserved in the Great Smoky Mountains National Park to demonstrate early settlements and life in that region of the country. There are also historic areas that contain representations of natural history themes, an example being the C. & O. Canal National Historical Park, which was created not only to preserve an example of America At Work (Transportation) but also to protect the scenic beauty and natural environment of the shoreline of the Potomac River in the State of Maryland.

MANAGEMENT

Following the Act of August 25, 1916, the then Secretary of the Interior Franklin K. Lane outlined to Stephen T. Mather, Director of the Service, management principles that were to guide the Service in its management of the areas then included within the system. This set of principles is sometimes called the Magna Carta of the National Parks and remains to this day a significant guide for National Parks management. The principles state, in part:

> **. . . for the information of the public an outline of the administrative policy in which the new Service will adhere may now be announced. This policy is based on three broad principles: *first*, that the national parks must be maintained in absolutely unimpaired form for the use of future generations as well as those of our own time; *second*, that they are set apart for the use, observations, health, and pleasure of the people; and *third*, that the national interest must dictate all decisions affecting public or private enterprise in the parks.**

Even though all of the parks managed by the National Park Service are operated under the mandate of the 1916 Act, the purpose and intent of each park is not the same. Indeed, each park has been set aside because of its uniqueness and individuality as a place of national significance worthy of preservation.

Many social and economic changes have taken place since the park system was first established that greatly affect the approach to the management of the parks. In the early years of the Park Service there was a need to promote visitation. Today, however, because of the increased mobility of our expanding population, the emphasis is on the dispersal of park visitors to the less crowded areas within the more popular parks, and to lesser known areas of the system.

Once identified mainly with the West, more than half of the units currently within the National Park System are now located east of the Mississippi River. Whereas the parks in earlier times were primarily natural areas, today two thirds of the system consists of historical and recreational areas near and within urban regions, such as Golden Gate Park in San Francisco. Management must recognize the diversity of the areas within the system and treat each one individually; the Mall in Washington, D.C., cannot be managed in the same manner as Yellowstone National Park. Such diversity requires a great deal of flexibility on the part of the people who operate the parks.

As stated previously, the Park Service has recognized three primary categories—natural, historic and recreational—for management of the different park areas. These categories are valid for some of the parks in each category, but many parks have characteristics of two or all three categories. The Service is currently placing greater emphasis on *land* classifications within each park, so that the resources of each area can be properly identified and managed in terms of their inherent values and provision of appropriate visitor facilities.

Management of the National Park Service begins with the main mission of the organization, which is to conserve the scenery, the natural and historic objects, and the wildlife of each park, and to provide for the enjoyment of each park in a manner that will leave it unimpaired for future generations. Simply stated, this means to care for the parks, help people enjoy the parks, and to do both in a way that insures the integrity of the parks for continued use for all time.

Management Objectives

The National Park Service management objectives are arranged in five broad areas of emphasis that give flexibility and latitude for management and program innovation. The five areas are Resource Management, Visitor Services, Interpretation, Maintenance, and Planning and Development. Administration could be considered as a sixth function.

Resource Management

Resource Management in National Park Service terms means management of the land, water and wildlife resources within a park. It includes the study and management of the ecology of a park and its surroundings. As defined by Freeman Tilden, a noted naturalist, *ecology* is the understanding of animal and plant life in their home environment and their relationship with other forms of life, including man. Resource management goes beyond the park boundaries, in considering the broader aspects of the environment within which the park is located.

Resource management also includes establishing classification systems for the park in terms of its environmental setting by defining natural, historic and recreational zones and establishing programs for their protection and care. Research and continuing evaluation of these values are essential to effective park resource management.

Visitor Services

Visitor Services is a term somewhat unique to the National Park Service. It includes the services needed by park visitors to insure their comfort and protection while visiting the park. Visitor Services may be considered synonymous with "public service," insuring that visitors are made to feel welcome in the park and that information services will be designed to help them enjoy their stay and provide for their safety. Respect for individual preferences and expectations consistent with the preservation of the park resources, the rights of others, and safety are important considerations in Visitor Services programs.

While every employee in the park is involved with visitor services in one way or another, the function is the full time concern of specific groups within the park, particularly the Park Rangers, concessions personnel and those specifically involved in visitor protection and safety. Interpretation may sometimes be considered a part of Visitor Services, but usually is considered as a function of its own, particularly in the larger parks.

CONCESSIONS. Concessions include food services, overnight accommodations, gas station operations and a variety of recreation services and equipment rentals. They are a big business in some parks, whereas many of the smaller parks have few or no concessions. Concession facilities and services are provided only when they are necessary for the visitor's enjoyment of the area, or when the services do not exist or cannot be developed outside of the park boundary. The policies and management of many park concessions have come under close review and scrutiny by the Congress in recent years. A balance must be achieved between concession services needed within the park as opposed to those services that can be more conveniently provided or relocated outside park boundaries or in nearby communities, thus lessening the impact on park resources.

Concession management is an expertise important in many parks within the National Park system. Total revenues of concession activities throughout the Park Service are currently about $170 million annually.

Interpretation

Interpretation in park operations is a term that frequently confuses many people. Webster defines the word *interpret* as ". . . to explain or tell the meaning of." In simple terms, interpretation is the art of communicating the "park story" to the visitors, or, as a former Park Service director defined it ". . . the art of making the park experience meaningful."

One of the major contributions of the National Park Service over the years has been the development of interpretation into a professional expertise. Some people, in particular those who have devoted their career to this pioneering activity, believe that interpretation is *the* most important function of the National Park Service.

Interpretation takes many forms—talks, guided tours, living history demonstrations, exhibits, film presentations, publications and museums. The test of the Park Service's interpretative activities is their capacity to enhance the enjoyment and understanding of the parks for the visitor. Interpretation must give the visitor a perception of and an appreciation for the park resources and the intangible values they represent. It must foster an environmental awareness of the natural and man-made environment, and instill in the visitor a recognition and acceptance of conditions imposed upon him so that the parks may be preserved for the future.

In recent years interpretation has involved the sociological aspects of park programs in "bringing the parks to the people." This has been achieved through outreach programs such as "Summer in the Park," "Parks For All Seasons," and environmental education and living history programs. These programs attempt to put more emphasis on the cultural heritage of the various national and ethnic groups that make up the United States and their contributions to American life. Some negative questions have been raised about the involvement of the Park Service in these programs and its future role in these activities. Be that as it may, they have brought many innovative ideas into the interpretative spectrum of the parks, and have significantly contributed to making interpretation more meaningful and interesting to the park visitor.

The subtleties of interpretative needs and skills are often overlooked or not fully recognized in organizational staffing. In tight budget situations, the interpretive function frequently loses out in the competition with other park functions for funds. Interpretation is too often looked upon as a "frill" in the budget process, particularly when cuts have to be made. In spite of these limitations however, the National Park Service maintains a strong leadership role in the field of interpretation.

Maintenance and Development

Maintenance is the largest function of park operations in terms of manpower and funds allocations. It has been estimated that 60 percent of the total Park Service budget goes toward the maintenance of physical resources. This is understandable, considering the extent of the maintenance requirements of the road and trail systems of the parks, visitor and information centers, historic buildings and features, administrative structures and housing, campgrounds and picnic areas, the parkgrounds themselves, utility systems, and the elaborate array of "park furnishings" consisting of signs and markers, wayside exhibits, tables, seats and the like.

Maintenance is divided, for budget and programming purposes, into "Buildings and Utilities" and "Roads and Trails." Grounds maintenance, a significant part of the operation in some parks, can be considered a third subdivision, but is usually included with buildings and utilities. Grounds maintenance is primarily concerned with landscape horticulture displays and agronomy practices.

Maintenance is a growing field in the National Park Service. Once considered a static function staffed largely by local residents, it is emerging as an attractive ladder toward a career in management. It was once thought of as heresy if a park maintenance chief ever became a superintendent, but this picture is now changing.

There are two reasons for the emergence of maintenance as a profession in park operations. The first is the increasing emphasis on preserving the environment that has been brought to bear on maintenance activities and the second is great technical expertise now required in restoring and maintaining historic structures and grounds. The knowledge and skills required in both of these areas has been given increased attention as a basic requirement in maintenance management.

As with interpretation, it is often difficult to obtain adequate funding for a sustained preventive maintenance program. In the public sector, it always seems easier to obtain funds to "rebuild or construct" rather than "maintain and prevent."

ADMINISTRATIVE SERVICES

The function that holds the entire park system together is the *administrative operations*—the business side of parks management. This function keeps the organization moving through the bureaucracy of government. Important elements of administration are program planning and budgeting; financial management; property management; procurement and contracting; clerical support; personnel management; and employee development.

Efficient administrative procedures are the basic ingredients for effective administrative practices in the public bureaucracy. They make all functions of park operation work smoothly because they relieve the staff of the burden of many time-consuming business details. Support and assistance are the two basic functions of parks administration.

Three areas of administration deserve mention: record keeping, program planning and budgeting, and personnel management.

Record Keeping

Record keeping is a very important aspect of public administration, where the accountability of actions and the expenditure of public funds is a basic trust. Government operations are often criticized for their excessive paper processes and red tape. Forms management, record keeping, data processing and the retrieval of information are areas that require constant attention.

Program Planning and Budgeting

Program planning and budgeting are processes closely integrated with the system of "management by objectives." *Program* in park management refers to a group of related activities with a target or an objective for accomplishment. Some examples of programs within the framework of park operations are fire control, wildlife management, environmental education, employee training, construction and safety. *Program planning* means defining all of the needs of a park, arranging them into categories of activities and formulating strategies for their accomplishment. Budgeting converts programs into the dollars needed for the people and resources required to accomplish the tasks. This is not solely an administrative task, but rather a total effort of the park staff, sometimes with public input.

Administration's role is to see that the programs and budget requests are in the proper form and are understandable for their circuitous route through the budget process. The emphasis is not so much on doing things by rote, but rather on determining the quality of each project according to its needs and justifications, and on the suggested strategies for program accomplishment.

Personnel Management

Personnel management is often characterized as involving too much paper work and skills training, and not enough of actually working with employees on effective performance and job satisfaction. The abilities, expectations and performance of employees of the Park Service should be dealt with more carefully in terms of on-the-job requirements and performance standards. Park work cannot be characterized as an assembly line operation in which a person does just one or two things. Park work, by its very nature, is more generalized, with one person performing many tasks. There is a need for civil service job standards to reflect more flexibility and diversity in their application to parks operations.

Administrative personnel must keep the mission of the National Park Service constantly in mind, and be sensitive to the fact that park employees are there for the purpose of conserving and protecting the parks' resources and providing for the enjoyment of the visiting public.

ORGANIZATION

The basic unit of National Park Service organization is the park. Organizational structure of a park is based on the various functions needed to carry out the mission and work of each area. Variations occur from park to park, depending upon the scope of the park's programs, the nature and size of the park, the number of visitors to be served, and the complexion of the land and water resources. The following chart shows the basic arrangement of park management functions discussed above.

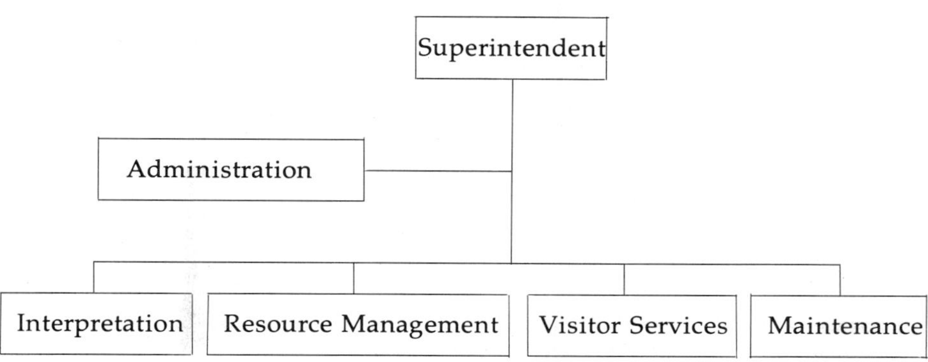

THE PARK SUPERINTENDENT

People who are unfamiliar with the Park Service organization frequently ask, when introduced to a superintendent, "What do you do?" Surprised somewhat by this question, he describes his role in the simplest terms possible.

The superintendent is the general manager of the park, responsible for all operations, employees and public relations. In former times the superintendent often was a resource management person trained in forestry, wildlife management, natural resources or related fields. In recent years superintendents have been people selected on the basis of their overview and skill in public administration and management. Frequently they are ambassadors for the National Park Service and the Department of the Interior in the state and regions in which the park is located. The day-to-day operations of the park are usually handled by an operations officer or assistant superintendent.

The position of Superintendent is the focus of career ladders in management within the National Park Service. With few exceptions, experience as a superintendent is a prerequisite for positions of higher responsibility both in the regions and in the Washington headquarters offices of the Service.

PEOPLE OF THE NATIONAL PARKS

Working and living in or near a National Park area under the special conditions existing in each park is one of the most distinctive features of a career in the National Park Service, even in the newer urban parks. To most employees of the Park Service, their position is not just a job, it's a "way of life." Working and living together, particularly in remote areas and often under inconvenient conditions, inspires them to improvise and help each other, and lifelong and endearing friendships result.

Because of occasional hardship and inconvenient circumstances, hospitality is a common trait that has permeated the entire Park Service organization and the visitors they serve. Notwithstanding the occasional gripe letter from an irate visitor who did not find things to his liking, the Park Service is lauded for its friendly and helpful approach. It gives the visitor a feeling of caring, assurance and security.

The diverse viewpoints of Park Service people about preservation and use of the parks constitute a strong ingredient in the organization's character—the old conflict of natural resource orientation versus people orientation. The requirement to learn about the nature, character and opportunities of each park as the employee moves about the system produces a fundamental understanding of man's relationship with his environment.

These characteristics have sometimes been referred to as a mystique of the Park Service organization—esprit de corps, dedication and unselfishness among the people of the National Parks.

Many disciplines and backgrounds are represented by the people of the National Park Service. In the early days of the system, most park specialists were persons with a natural resource orientation. In recent years, however, park specialists are obtaining a better "people orientation," and are being selected for this quality, particularly in management. People in the social and political sciences and in the recreation and parks specialties are finding greater opportunity in the Park Service.

People who make up the park staff may be grouped into five general categories—the Park Ranger, the Administrative Specialist, the Maintenance Specialist, the Cultural Specialist and the Scientific Specialist. Of these, the Park Ranger has the most contact with the public, and thus we will discuss that category in detail here.

The Park Ranger

To the park visitor, all uniformed employees are rangers, the persons one approaches for information and assistance. The traditional National Park Service uniform transcends many personnel types, and regardless of their official duties, most visitors consider everyone on the park staff a ranger.

The title "Ranger" has a long tradition in the Park Service. Basically it means a person in a role of assistance and protection—assistance to the people who visit the parks and protection of the park resources and the visitors who use them. In a truer sense, a park ranger is both a generalist and a specialist. He is a generalist in maintaining continuing contact with the public and helping them to enjoy and use the park resources. He is the general overseer of resource management by virtue of being constantly in touch with the park's resources. The ranger applies policies and regulations in ways that protect the resources as well as the visitor. Rangers are specialists in having skills in land and water search and rescue operations, and in the ability to handle themselves in the out-of-doors.

With the ever-rising numbers of visitors to the parks, there is little doubt that the ranger will find he has more and more responsibility for management of people as he performs his dual role of preserving the parks and assuring that visitors have an enjoyable yet safe experience.

Other specialists may have a ranger title, such as Ranger-Historian, Ranger-Naturalist, or Ranger-Interpreter, but as the title notes, these people represent and operate in a more specialized sphere of park operations. The 025 "Ranger Series" of the personnel classification system of the U.S. Civil Service Commission is the management classification for the Park Service.

Besides the ranger, many specialty types are represented in park operations to carry out plans and programs. The fields of horticulture and historic preservation maintenance are very prominent in the National Capital Park and in historic areas where urban park landscapes and historic restorations are important elements of park development. Engineers, architects, landscape architects and environmental specialists have important roles, as do many maintenance specialists.

THE WASHINGTON OFFICE

A study of the organization of the Washington Office quickly conveys the involvement and influence of the Park Service within the federal government and throughout the nation and the world in "park affairs." (See Fig. 4–1.)

Organization of the nine regional offices of the Service is in many respects a copy of the Washington Office, without the functions necessary to operate within the federal establishment in Washington and with the Congress.

The Park Service has a special role in the field of historic preservation and assistance to the states. It also has the responsibility to cooperate with

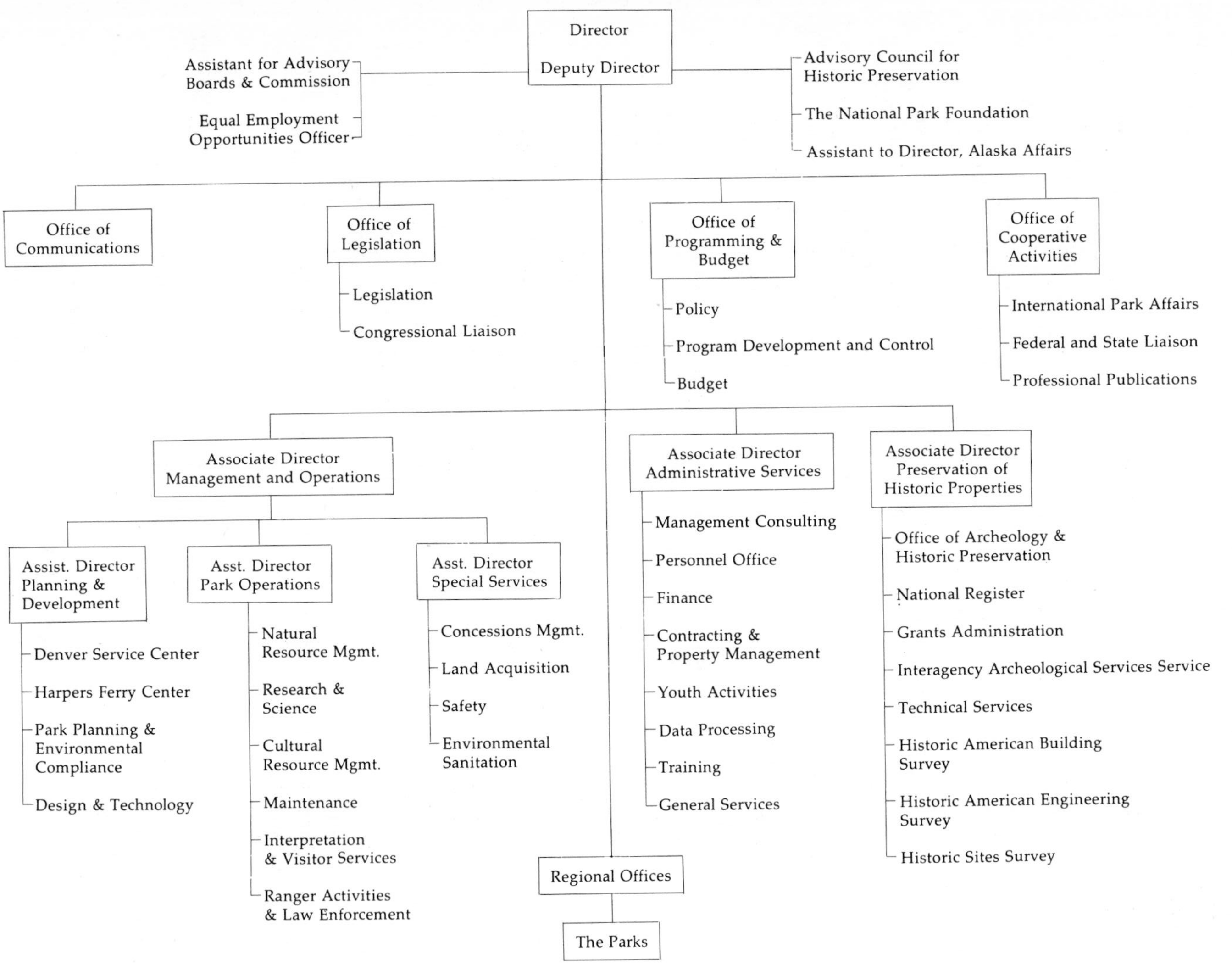

FIGURE 4–2 National Park Service Organization

any agency of government, with the private sector, and with foreign governments whenever Park Service expertise and views can contribute to programs of park planning, management and environmental preservation.

The Director

Much of the Director's attention is devoted to the work within the executive branch and in congressional activities. Much of his time is spent preparing for and appearing at hearings of the Interior Department, the Office of Management and Budget, and congressional committees, explaining and justifying Park Service programs for which funds are being requested and authorizations sought. Maintaining these and other relations with a broad constituency of public and private groups throughout the nation is an awesome task. A call from a congressional committee, congressman or citizens' group frequently precipitates a review or study on a problem involving the total organization.

The primary function of the director's office is policy formulation and direction, but by no means does the director work in a vacuum removed from the regions and the parks. Frequent interchanges take place in task group problem solving or park and regional matters. The Washington Office is very sensitive to input "from the field" in the formulation of policy and guidelines on a host of operational problems.

There are two reasons for this approach; first, most of the people in the Washington office have served in many of the parks and regional offices during their careers and are intimately familiar and genuinely concerned about many conditions and problems of the parks; and, second, the smallness of the Park Service organization makes it imperative to draw upon the expertise of employees throughout the Service in helping to resolve and develop approaches and policies for the organization. It is not uncommon for a park superintendent or regional director to head a task group under Washington Office direction for a considerable period of time.

The Denver Service Center in Denver, Colorado, and the Harpers Ferry Center in Harpers Ferry, West Virginia, are large units of several hundred people that serve the parks in providing design, construction and master planning services. The Harpers Ferry Center is concerned primarily with interpretive planning and design of exhibits, museums and audiovisual services.

Historic Preservation

The Historic Sites Act of 1935 gave extensive responsibilities to the Secretary of Interior through the National Park Service to effect a national policy of historic preservation, and authorized a survey of historic sites of national importance.

The National Historic Preservation Act of 1966 broadly expanded federal support to states and local governments in the preservation of all historic properties, including a grant program. These responsibilities, managed from the Office of Archeology and Historic Preservation, not only define and determine appropriate treatment of historic properties within the National Park Service, but also offer an extensive program of assistance to the states. A system of review has been established whereby proposals affecting historic properties and environments, particularly areas on the National Register of Historic Places, are reviewed by the historic preservation officer of the respective states and the Advisory Council for Historic Preservation for concurrence and compliance. The relationship of these functions is shown in Figure 4–2.

International Affairs

The National Park Service, through its division of International Park Affairs, has brought its philosophy and expertise in the administration of national parks to many countries of the world. For example, in 1967 a team was sent to Turkey to assist that government in planning a system of 11 national parks. Countries of the Middle East, Africa and South America have also been aided in establishing national parks. More recently emphasis has been placed on information and exchange programs with Canada, Japan, Spain, Mexico and other nations of the world, with the view that the National Park Service gains as much benefit from these associations as it gives.

Legislation

As Stephen Mather found out in 1915, the best plans of men go astray if they can't be sold to the national administration and to the Congress. While every administration and Congress has given support to the National Parks, albeit in varying degrees, "a majority" must agree in order to enact the legislation necessary to obtain budget approval to support a system of National Parks. The Congress has been in a favorable frame of mind over the last 20 years in establishing more than 80 new National Park areas. In the competition for the "federal dollar," a more formidable task has been to obtain the funds and manpower needed to staff and operate these new parks, and at the same time to sustain the financing necessary to operate the old areas.

There are six congressional committees primarily involved with National Park Service affairs: the House of Representatives Committee on Interior and Insular Affairs and its subcommittee on National Parks and Insular Affairs; the Senate Committee on Energy and Natural Resources and its subcommittee on Parks and Recreation; and the Interior Appropriations Committees of the House and Senate.

GROWTH PERIODS

In the history of the National Park Service there have been four periods which have brought a flurry of growth to the system in terms of expansion of areas and facilities.

1906 to 1930

The first of these occurred at the beginning of this century, when a substantial number of park areas were established subsequent to the Antiquities Act of 1906. Before his terms expired, President Theodore Roosevelt proclaimed the first 18 national monuments, the administration of which was left to whichever federal agency had jurisdiction over the land. This was, of course, before the establishment of the National Park Service.

After the establishment of the Service in 1916, the early 1920's found the National Park System containing 54 units—21 National Parks and 33 National Monuments.

1930 to 1940

During the Great Depression years of the 1930's, the Park Service experienced a period of fantastic growth. President Franklin Roosevelt's reorganization of the executive branch in 1933 transferred dozens of areas from other agencies, such as battlefield parks and historic sites from the jurisdiction of the War Department to that of the Park Service. The Historic Sites Act of 1935 and the Park, Parkway and Recreation Area Study Act of 1936 established a national policy of preserving historic places and marked the beginning of planning for outdoor recreation on a national scale.

The 1930's also saw new areas added to the system, such as the Blue Ridge Parkway and Lake Mead National Recreation Area. In the seven years of the Civilian Conservation Corps (CCC) from 1933 to 1940, program expansions included the establishment of 650 campsites and the employment of over 7000 persons engaged in facility design and construction throughout the National Park System.

1940 to 1960

During World War II park resources and facilities deteriorated badly. However, thanks to public support and much editorializing in magazines and newspapers throughout the country, a 10-year development program called "Mission 66" was created in 1956. This brought the 180 parks in the system at that time up to standard by 1966, the 50th anniversary of the establishment of the National Park Service.

As a result of enthusiastic endorsement by President Dwight D. Eisenhower and the Congress, "Mission 66" brought rejuvenation to the parks' worn-out facilities and many new developments to meet the demands of ever-increasing numbers of visitors. Substantial increases in staff provided badly needed protection activities and resumption of lapsed interpretive and visitor service programs that had lapsed during the War years and early fifties. Two training centers were established at Grand Canyon National Park and at Harpers Ferry, West Virginia, forming the nucleus of one of the most comprehensive training programs in the federal government.

The 1960's

The 1960's saw sea and lakeshore areas and new historical parks added to the system. The Atlantic Coastline Survey, the Great Lakes Survey ("Our Fourth Shore"), the Gulf Coast Survey and the activities of the Outdoor Recreation Resources Review Commission created an increased awareness and effort in establishing additions to the National Park System before the opportunities were lost to development and other land uses.

The creation of the Bureau of Outdoor Recreation in 1963 and the establishment of the Land and Water Conservation Fund in 1964 brought new impetus to state and federal agencies to meet outdoor recreation demands and needs. The Conservation Fund has greatly aided the National Park Service by providing a continuing flow of capital for the acquisition of new park areas and many inholding areas within existing parks.

Supplementing the role of the Bureau of Outdoor Recreation in nationwide outdoor recreation planning and national resources studies, the National Park Service today enjoys a strong position in identifying and evaluating land and water resources for potential "national significance."

PRESENT OPPORTUNITIES

Over the years the National Park System has grown from a small group of large natural areas, including a number of national monuments basically located in natural settings, to a diverse and complex number of some 293 natural, historic, recreational and cultural resource areas, with additional units being added regularly by congressional action. New park proposals in the state of Alaska would create nine new areas with unique features not presently represented in the system, along with expansion of two existing park areas (Mount McKinley and Katmai). In combined size these areas amount to 15 Yellowstone Parks, or 32 million acres, and their addition would represent a doubling of the amount of land now within the nation's park system bringing it to 62 million acres.

COMPLEXITY AND CONFLICTS

The increased complexity of the National Park System often raises questions as to how it should be organized to best meet the changing needs of society and the demands to preserve its unique resources. Some fear that the increased involvement in recreational and cultural areas in recent years is diluting the Service's capacity to manage the outstanding natural and historic treasures of the nation.

Recreation vs. Parks

In this connection, it is interesting to note the direction in which the country as a whole has been moving during the last 20 years, particularly at the local level, toward combining parks and recreation departments. This unified approach is intended to meet both citizens' needs for outdoor recreation pursuits and the requirements for preservation of the park environments within which recreation activities take place.

The term "recreation and parks" has caused much confusion among those responsible for managing outdoor recreation and park areas. Historically, the word "parks" has meant land and water resources, while "recreation" has referred to the programs and activities that people engage in on the land and waters of park areas.

This raises an interesting question of natural area versus recreational area management in the National Park Service. Are there valid reasons why Cape Hatteras and Point Reyes National Seashores (commonly referred to as recreation areas) should be managed as recreation areas while the 400,000-

acre Sequoia National Park, one of the original national parks, is managed as a natural area?

Certainly the preservation of representative examples of the natural coastlines of the country and their ecological processes, as represented by Cape Hatteras and Point Reyes, are every bit as important to preserve and as difficult to manage as the oldest and largest living trees represented in the giant sequoia groves of Sequoia National Park. Just because the visitor may have more actual "recreation" at Cape Hatteras or Point Reyes, by fishing, swimming, surfing or boating, doesn't make these places any less important from a natural point of view.

"Recreation" in our society, has a definite connotation of some sort of action taking place, whereas our idea of "parks" seems to have a strong relationship to more passive activities. One might argue the latter by pointing out that the physical stamina required in exploring the wilderness areas of the national parks does not exactly fit the description of "passive."

People in the recreation field seem to avoid using the term "parks" and tend to categorize everything as some type of recreation; by the same token, parks people shy away from the term recreation, probably because of the historic connotation recreation has developed in our society and the risks of diluting the preservation requirements related to parks.

Perhaps the concept of *re-creation* offers a better approach to peoples' use of park resources. At any rate, the attitudes and forces that have developed over the years as a result of the "parks *vs.* recreation," "resource approach *vs.* people approach," "active *vs.* passive approach" and other conflicts have to be reckoned with not only in the National Park Service, but in the Parks and Recreation field in general. Resolutions to these conflicts are needed in order to clarify the missions and purposes of the areas that fall under the general labels of parks and recreation. The two must somehow be brought together in a manner that supports both the inherent natural values of the land and water resources that make up our parks and the programs and activities that constitute what we call "recreation," without one group feeling threatened by the other.

The approach to management of the diverse areas of the National Park System is well stated in the introduction to the current management policies of the National Park Service:

> **Our management guidance must recognize the diversity of areas in the System, a diversity which is increasing with the addition of major urban recreation areas such as Golden Gate in San Francisco, Gateway in New York and New Jersey, and the Cuyahoga Valley between Cleveland and Akron in Ohio.**
>
> **Even though all of the parks come under the mandate of the Act of August 25, 1916, establishing the National Park Service, it is clear that the purpose and intent of each is not the same as the others. Clearly, we cannot manage the Mall in Washington, D.C., as we do Yellowstone National Park; nor can we manage Independence National Historical Park in Philadelphia as we do the Lake Mead National Recreation Area. In 1964 we recognized three management categories—natural, historic, and recreational—to encompass this diversity. These are valid for some parks in each category, but others have characteristics of two, or all three categories. Accordingly, we are laying greater stress on land classification within the parks so that resources may be appropriately identified and managed in terms of their inherent values and appropriate uses.**

A clear challenge for the future is to effectively carry out the scientific research needed to clarify and support land classifications within the parks and the "carrying capacities" appropriate to support appropriate uses.

Preservation vs. Use

Since the beginning of the National Park Service, the conflict between two factors, preservation and use, has been involved in every discussion affecting the parks. The issue is never clear-cut and will always be an integral part of decision making and management of park resources.

Reconciling the need for preservation with those who believe that the "parks are for people" will always be a major challenge to Park Service management, especially in the political climate in which public parks must be managed today. People certainly approach the parks from many angles. One observer of the conflicting demands of preservation and use believed that it will simply always be a problem, for the perfect solution is never truly attainable and it is impossible to please everyone.

> **We may agree that it is a counsel of perfection, for even the discreet use of a wilderness area cannot help being in some degree of impairment. But why split hairs about it? The intent of Congress was high and good, and the very difficulty of fulfilling the injunction has been one of the fruitful challenges that has reached down through the personnel of the National Park Service to the loneliest laborer in the most remote spot.**[6]

The Historic Preservation Act of 1966 and the Environment Policy Act of 1969 placed a broader obligation on the Service and on all public agencies to review plans and developments in terms of how they will affect the parks and the environments within which they are situated. To effectively deal with the trivia which is too often employed to obscure and interfere with the evaluation of larger environmental issues is a continuing challenge in public park management.

Titles of Park Units

Another challenge is the confusion that currently exists in the titles of park units of the National Park System. Many names do not conform to the category they represent and within which they are managed, e.g., natural, historic or recreational. A typical problem is the use of the term "monument," which comes from the Antiquities Act of 1906, which authorizes the President to set aside areas by proclamation as national monuments. The term *monument* or *memorial* in general usage refers to structures in memory or in honor of a person, such as the Washington Monument, the Cabrillo National Monument, the Lincoln Memorial and the De Soto National Memorial. However, there are many areas titled as monuments and memorials which have little relationship to the type of area they represent. Two classic examples are Dinosaur National Monument, a 200,000-acre area of spectacular canyons in Colorado that contains fossil remains of dinosaurs and other ancient animals, and Death Valley National Monument, a 2-million-acre area containing the best representation of desert landscape in the country. Both of these are basically managed as natural areas and should correctly be designated as national parks. Another striking example of faulty classification is the monument nomenclature of Federal Hall National Memorial and Katmai National Monument, the former being the building on Wall Street in downtown Manhattan where President George Washington was inaugurated as the first President of the United States, and the latter (Katmai) being a vast volcanic area consisting of nearly 3 million acres in Alaska.

Just as much confusion exists within the historic category. Arkansas Post, site of the first permanent French settlement in the Lower Mississippi Valley, is called a monument rather than an historical park. The birthplace and home of Booker T. Washington in Virginia is designated a national monument but is in fact an historic site. Castillio de San Marcos, the oldest fort in the continental United States, is also called a monument rather than an historic site.

It would seem reasonable to rename all areas that commemorate the historic heritage of the nation as national (historic) parks regardless of their size, and to reclassify all monument areas that basically preserve outstanding natural features as national parks. The terms monument and memorial would be reserved for those features that were created to honor or memorialize individuals. Certainly a thorough reclassification of national park system area titles would make a worthy contribution to better public understanding of the country's national parks and their administration.

CURRENT CHALLENGES

The National Park Service has been hard pressed over the past 15 years to keep pace with the growth of its system in terms of the money and personnel needed to manage and operate it. Since 1960, over 100 new areas have been added. Visitation has grown from 127 million in 1960 to 256 million in 1976, an increase of 100 percent. In addition, operational workload has increased as a result of new and more stringent environmental quality, safety and public health legislation.

Operating funds and employment levels for some areas have continually fallen behind to keep up with the demand to staff and operate new areas. Visitor services in older areas have been reduced, maintenance deferred, personnel positions transferred and rehabilitation and construction projects delayed. The result has been a general dilution of services and an alarming deterioration of physical facilities throughout the system.

The Park Service has attempted to encourage visitation to lesser known areas, but many of these parks are too small and inconveniently located to attract an appreciable number of visitors away from the more popular parks. Unfortunately, even when people do visit lesser known areas, they tend to stop as well at old traditional parks that may be located nearby, thus causing as much congestion as ever.

Moreover, since each park in the system has been established for the unique values it possesses, it does not necessarily follow that visitors will go to an area in lieu of Grand Canyon, for example, when "the Canyon" is the only one of its kind in the nation. Overcrowding will have to be resolved at the park itself, by such means as dispersing crowds and limiting and controlling visitation and use.

Vandalism and impairment of natural and historic resources is also on the increase because of heavier visitation, the proximity of more and more parks to large population centers, and the lack of personnel to protect park resources. The absence of uniformed personnel is frequently an invitation to those who are out to vandalize and do mischievous acts.

Parks cannot manage themselves. Indeed, most new areas, and many old ones, require much more intensive management *after* they become a park, in order to properly convert existing land uses to park purposes and to reclaim areas to their true natural state and ecological balance. These processes are years in the making. Adequate staff must be on hand to interpret park values and to educate the public on their proper protection and enjoyment.

It is virtually impossible to keep new areas closed or to curtail visitor services and facilities to the point where the lack of them will keep visitors away. It won't happen. Since public parks are created for human enjoyment, the public pressure to open new areas is so great that management will do its best to accommodate visitation, no matter how meager the budget or inadequate the staff. The results can be disastrous.

Therefore, adequate staffing and development of new areas is essential if park resources and values are to be preserved and be worthy of the natural and historic heritage for which they were created. They should not be left to disintegrate. The Park Service will continue to face a real challenge for many years in developing strategies to obtain adequate funding and manpower resources for the preservation and protection of its park system.

THE FUTURE

The National Park System as a "national resource" that preserves the best of our natural environment, historical heritage and recreational resources is well established. The desire of people to keep and preserve these priceless areas as "outdoor museums" seems inherent, comparable to their desire to preserve their creativity through inventions, art, music and literature. The basic difference is that parks are *living* museums and are ever-changing.

Parks are a combination of people's creative desire for aesthetics and the "order of things" as presented in the natural world; their preservation allows successive generations of people to see how they relate to the living environment.

These priceless areas increase in value throughout history, in both a tangible and an intangible sense. As unique environmental resources become scarce or diminish, people's interest and desire to preserve them increases.

People's desire for the "finer things of life" has been increasing rapidly in modern times, as less and less time is spent in providing for the basic needs of food, clothing and shelter. Thus parks, and the opportunities they provide to increase the quality of life, will continue to attract people's attention and concern.

The future for a broader system of national parks seems assured by the increased desire of people and their representatives in the national government to preserve more areas of the nation's unique natural, historic and recreational resources.

REFERENCES

1. *National Parks for the Future,* An appraisal of the National Parks as they begin their second century in a changing America (Washington, D.C.: The Conservation Foundation, 1972), p. 7.
2. Act of August 25, 1916 (39 Stat. 535).
3. William C. Everhart, *The National Park Service* (New York: Praeger, 1972), p. 6.
4. Administrative Policies for Natural Areas of the National Park Service, U.S. Department of the Interior, National Park Service, Appendix A, February, 1967, p. 55.
5. Management Policies, U.S. Department of the Interior, National Park Service, 1975.
6. Everhart, *The National Park Service,* p. 83.

QUESTIONS

1. What is your concept of the National Park System? How does it differ from the National Park Service?

2. What forces and interest led to the establishment of the National Park Service? Explain.

3. Why are the functions of the Director's office essential to the management of the National Park Service and what relationships do they have with the parks?

4. What is meant by the "resource approach" and the "people approach" in park management?

5. Explain the primary categories of National Park area management. How do they differ? How would you categorize them?

Many state park systems are the result of public work programs of the federal government during the 1930's, which created "recreation demonstration areas."
(U.S. Bureau of Outdoor Recreation)

ABOUT THE AUTHOR

Jerry Wettstone is a native of central Pennsylvania and attended the Pennsylvania State University, receiving a B.S. degree in Physical Education in 1962 and an M.Ed. in Recreation and Parks in 1963. His master's thesis was entitled: "State Park User Fees and Charges—Problems of Administration."

Mr. Wettstone held the position of State Parks Supervisor with the Indiana Department of Natural Resources between 1964 and 1966, before returning to work with the Commonwealth of Pennsylvania. His initial positon was with the Project 70 Open Space Program Office, and subsequent to its inclusion in the new Department of Community Affairs in 1966, he was promoted to the position of Director of the Recreation and Conservation Bureau.

Under his direction, the Bureau has grown to become one of the outstanding local advisory agencies of any state in the nation. The Bureau administers the local funds from the Federal Land and Water Conservation Fund, and concurrently provides a range of technical advisory services to local governments.

chapter 5

STATE RECREATION ROLE—NATURAL RESOURCE FIELD

INTRODUCTION

Although the states are the basic units of government in this country, their activities in the park and recreation field have been less extensive in the past than those of the city and federal governments.

The initial role assumed by the states was restricted to the area of natural resources. The state park movement actually preceded that of the federal government, when in 1864 the state of California on its own established what was later to become Yosemite National Park. State fish and game activities were also among the early state initiatives in the field. It wasn't until the 1900's however, that parks were officially acquired or forest tracts preserved by the state governments. Much of the initial impetus came from the eastern states, which had no public lands but were experiencing urbanization, or which had inherited tax delinquent lands that had been lumbered over and abandoned.

A major boost for park and recreation efforts at all three governmental levels came during the Great Depression of the 1930's. Public employment and public works programs of the federal government pioneered the development of "recreation demonstration areas," which are now largely part of state park systems.

The financing of recreation and park programs at the state level was initially derived chiefly from state general funds. The post-war period and particularly the 1960's have seen a major increase in bond programs for capital investments. Additionally, several states derive significant operating revenues from user fees, such as those charged for admissions or for special facilities such as lodges or campgrounds.

In dealing with recreation issues, state governments are located in the pivotal middle position in our three-layer governmental system. They work with a variety of federal agencies and establish enabling powers and are responsible for assisting their local political subdivisions. States have increasingly come to be recognized by the federal government as the proper agencies for administering fiscal programs directed to local governments or individuals, because they are more familiar with local needs and possess a regional perspective.

The sophistication of state government park and recreation enterprises differs considerably from state to state, somewhat in relation to the degree of urbanization of the state and the level of federal activity. As with other functional areas, some states have particularly advanced services in some sections of the field, such as New York's youth recreation activities, while their services in other areas may be average or less than average. Generally, however, it can be expected that most of the states have at least a minimal level of coverage of the four functional areas of park and recreational service. These areas are:

1. Natural resource–based park and recreation services
2. Park and recreation services in a human service context
3. Assistance to local governments
4. Assistance to private sector agencies

The states have developed their natural resources and recreation services in many ways, and they administer them under a variety of organizational structures. Some agencies are responsible for broad functional areas such as natural resources, while in other states there is more subdivision, leading to the establishment of separate agencies for fish, game, historic sites, and so on.

STATE RECREATION ROLE–NATURAL RESOURCE FIELD

The initial role of the states in the parks and recreation field was to conserve unique land areas and care and see to the propagation of fish and game. As noted earlier, the state park movement got under way in 1864, when the state of California took the initiative to preserve what is now Yosemite National Park.

The agency responsible for park and recreation functions bears different names in different states, the trend of the 1970's being to consolidate agencies dealing with these functions and those dealing with environmental regulation into single departments of natural resources or environmental protection. However, in some states, historic or fish and game interests have been so strong that the agencies controlling them have continued to exist as independent commissions.

Until the 1950's, the principal criterion for state park selection was that the area possess unique scenic, historic or geologic features. However, recent philosophy has recognized that this practice often resulted in parks located too far from where the majority of people lived, and current site selection policies place greater emphasis on accessibility to population centers and the degree to which the resource can accommodate a greater variety of recreational facilities and ever-increasing numbers of visitors. An important implication of these new policies is that natural amenities must often be created through such means as reforestation programs, in order to take advantage of land areas that are close to population centers but do not have the natural resources required of a state park.

The increasing sensitivity of state park planners to serving people's needs as well as preserving unique areas has led to a number of other innovations and adaptations. One change, prompted by the increasing demand for swimming and the decline in stream water quality in urban areas has been the inclusion of swimming pools in state parks. In order to provide a more natural-looking setting for swimming, Pennsylvania has been building many free-form style pools in its new state parks, and in many parks the state has also built lakes for fishing and boating.

During the 1960's, a number of states began to develop elaborate overnight lodges that offered lodging and dining facilities comparable to modern commercial motels. Tennessee, Ohio, Kentucky, Oklahoma and West Virginia were among the first to establish such accommodations. Indiana modernized its system of lodges, which dated back to the 1930's. One of the major objectives behind these initiatives was that it was in the economic interest of the state to provide such accommodations in order to attract tourists to the parks and provide a facility that would encourage them to stay for several days. (This trend of the 1960's, however, has not been carried forward into the 1970's, although it is too early to draw conclusions on whether or not it will reoccur.)

Because of the budgetary challenge faced by the state governments to pay off the revenue bonds that financed the construction of the lodges, it became vital that they maximize their use. A concurrent development, therefore, was that of "programming" lodge areas for visitors. Golf courses and tennis courts were constructed and instructional programs in these sports were established. South Carolina has even seen fit to develop an arts and crafts program for its state park visitors.

Overnight facilities in state parks have also undergone dramatic changes. The increasing use of elaborate trailers has meant that the primitive tent site is no longer accepted by the average camper. More and more camp sites are being provided with electric and sanitary connections, and served by buildings containing flush toilets and hot showers.

Another trend that has developed is the provision of formalized outdoor education interpretive programs in state parks, going beyond the traditional evening campground programs. Most state park systems, working in conjunction with local school districts, have established special interpretive centers or laboratories throughout the state for use by local school districts.

Another concession that park officials have had to make to today's American outdoorsman has been in services to motorized recreation equipment. Motor boat sales skyrocketed quickly in the 1950's and 1960's, followed by snowmobiles, trail bikes, and other motorized all-terrain vehicles. Because of the potential damage such machines may cause to the environment, the issue of providing services to them is still very controversial; the trend appears to be that governmental agencies will restrict motorized equipment to appropriate areas where its use can be controlled.

Some states, particularly Vermont and New Hampshire, have a history of state involvement in ski areas. However, even though this sport has experienced tremendous growth, state park and natural resource agencies have not assured major responsibility for the development of such areas. They have been largely supported by private enterprise, with some states providing land areas for development on a long-term lease basis.

While many of the trends in state park planning and use have been toward more intensive use of state parks, there have been several trends counter to this as well. One of these has been the identification of certain natural areas within state parks, which, because of their delicate nature, have had special limitations placed on their use and development. Examples of such areas would be geologically unstable or fragile areas such as cliffs, rock ledges, waterfalls and bogs.

A second extensive recreation movement among state natural resource and park agencies has been to identify and plan for the preservation of wild and scenic rivers. This comes from a recognition that, even though these areas are not owned or managed outright by state governments as an entity of the state park system, the last free-flowing scenic rivers are still a special recreation resource area of great significance because of their unspoiled character. Some states, in cooperation with local government officials, are attempting to develop planning and zoning controls on the shorelines of these areas, where they cannot be acquired for protection.

State natural resource agencies and various state historic agencies have also developed extensive programs and sites for the preservation of historic sites and industries. The focal point of such efforts is usually the state's museum, although this single facility is quite often complimented by a series of historic sites and structures across the state, which interpret significant historic events or present exhibits on the lives of citizens who shaped the direction of the state and the nation.

STATE RECREATION ROLE—HUMAN SERVICES

Perhaps one of the most difficult areas of state service to analyze is that of recreation programming for citizens, particularly the disadvantaged citizen. The analysis is difficult because the programs are often fractionalized among a number of departments and special commissions, are often quite minimal and are frequently not even categorized under the term "recreation."

Some of the state's special programs for citizens pre-date the open space thrust of the 1960's, while others are quite recent, having developed as outgrowths of state and national recognition of the needs of such special populations as the aged, the young (see box), racial minorities and the physically and mentally handicapped.

NEW YORK'S YOUTH COMMISSION

New York's Youth Commission represents one of the outstanding special missions of a state government in a human service area of the parks and recreation field. Begun at the end of World War II, at a time when the problems of leisure time and the concern for juvenile delinquency were attracting major attention, the agency had a primary thrust to aid local communities in developing and improving youth recreation programs.

The Youth Commission has, since 1945, provided financial assistance for recreation programs and leadership for programs. Field representatives of the agency have provided technical assistance on the establishment and conduct of such programs as well.

With the advent of special state financial programs for outdoor recreation in the 1960's, New York's program of grants for recreation program expenses became even more unique, because almost every state grant program is limited to grants for capital projects, and cannot be used for financing operation of recreation programs.

In 1960, the Commission was renamed the Division for Youth, and a second priority area was mandated toward innovating with rehabilitation treatment facilities. In 1970, drug treatment centers became a third mission area.

One of the largest recreation roles exercised by state governments is one that is relatively unknown to the general public; namely, the provision of recreation services to those special populations residing in state institutions. Therapeutic recreation programs for the residents of state hospitals and correctional facilities have improved considerably over the past decade, and the operation budgets and staff employed quite often are comparable to those of the state park operations.

A growing mental health treatment philosophy, coupled with state financial problems, led to a movement in the 1970's toward deinstitutionalization. This means that those patients who are not gaining any additional medical benefits from staying in large institutional settings, and who can support themselves in an individual or small group living environment, are being discharged into community settings. As a result, the states have been challenged to train staff in private nursing homes, or in local governments, to deal with the special problems of these individuals. A new trend is emerging of state employment of Therapeutic Recreation Advisors who work not in institutions, but out of regional service centers in communities. The State of Georgia employed five such individuals in 1976.

Because of the limited social service responsibilities of local and state governments in areas outside of institutional settings, special state programs such as New York's Youth Commission are rare indeed. Programs that do relate to recreation are frequently run by the state cabinet agency that administers the federal health and welfare programs. The state's role is often limited to merely the administration of funds, such as those under the Social Security Act or the Older Americans Act, with contracts for social services provided to non-profit groups such as Y's or the Salvation Army. While the programs are labeled as social enrichment programs, they are largely recreational in nature. Federal Medicare and Medicaid regulations now require private nursing homes to provide some therapeutic recreation services. State departments responsible for inspecting these facilities have in turn employed advisors in this area for developing programs to meet this requirement.

Perhaps no social institution in American life today has such a large influence as does education. In this field, the role of the states has grown significantly, particularly in providing an increasingly greater portion of the capital and operating budgets of elementary and secondary schools.

While recreation is not the primary function of school districts, it has generally enjoyed support by school officials as an important adjunct of education. State education officials concerned with demonstrating multiple use of state-subsidized school physical plants, and mindful of the broader human development mission of schools, have increasingly come to recognize the recreation and leisure service role of schools, and are advocating progressive local programs.

The terms "community education" and "community schools" are currently in vogue, and as part of their advisory activities, state education departments are encouraging social service programs within the school which encourage recreation efforts at the local level.

THE STATE RESPONSIBILITY TO LOCAL GOVERNMENTS

State governments were at one time as much regulatory agents as service agencies. Today, enforcement and regulation are no longer the main functions of state governments. They are now primarily service agencies, engaged in promoting the public welfare. It is the role of state governments, as in welfare, education, and law enforcement, to assist the local governments, at their request, in doing their job.

One of the first efforts at pinpointing the emergence of and need for a state role in assisting its political subdivisions in developing community recreation programs and services was made by Harold D. Meyer and Charles K. Brightbill in their book *State Recreation.* Their list of the functions of a state recreation authority is still applicable today:

> 1. Prepare surveys, studies and appraisals of state-wide and specific community recreation needs and conditions.
> 2. Assist in organizing for community recreation and in helping establish and improve local recreation systems.
> 3. Assist in methods of financing and budgeting for local recreation.
> 4. Provide assistance in securing and improving local and state legislation and related legal recreation problems.
> 5. Help develop and enrich total recreation opportunities and programs to meet the varied interests of entire communities.
> 6. Serve as a clearinghouse for the exchange and dissemination of information regarding recreation, including that related to programs, plans and services.
> 7. Assist in the preparation of long-range local plans for recreation and in the layout and design of recreation areas and facilities.
> 8. Promote and promulgate standards of recreation leadership, finance, areas and facilities and program.
> 9. Assist in recruiting, planning and training professional and volunteer recreational personnel.
> 10. Secure wider use of existing local and state recreation areas and facilities.
> 11. Influence the development of commercial recreation.
> 12. Promote institutes, conferences and meetings in the best interests of recreation.

13. Coordinate federal, state and local recreation efforts for systematic application within the state.

14. Investigate and help meet recreation needs in special settings such as rural areas, in industry, in institutions, in religious groups and the like.

15. Formulate, in cooperation with other state agencies, interested organizations and citizens, a comprehensive recreation policy for the state.

16. Provide and administer supplementary financial assistance to the political subdivisions as the need arises and as funds are made available for the purpose.[1]

The needs of local government cover a wide range of issues and problems in the park, recreation and conservation field. Local officials require publications, on-site advice and financial assistance. Their concerns range from how to organize a recreation program to how to preserve a piece of open space. Communities need help in interpreting legal statutes and in designing park and recreation areas. They seek assistance in negotiating school-municipal agreements to gain access to other public facilities, and they want to know what other communities are doing. These and a host of other needs require a strong state advisory capability.

The fact that our citizens receive the majority of their recreation services at the local level is a fact that can easily be overlooked when one looks at the statistics on the park and recreation acreage owned by the state or federal government *vs.* that owned by the local governments. Typically, local lands make up less than 5 per cent of those owned by the state and federal government, yet the majority of recreation activity days are controlled at the local level. This clearly indicates that the local portion of the total park and recreation system of a state carries a heavy burden, and thus state services to this sector are altogether proper.

The local governments, which are political subdivisions of the state, have always been in the front line when it comes to providing services to the people. While state governments have for some time had special departments of education that have been responsible for assisting local school districts, the provision of coordinated services to the local municipal governments through departments of community or local affairs is as recent as the late 1960's. These departments represent agencies with excellent potential for the provision of local recreation assistance. To date, however, only Pennsylvania, New Jersey, Virginia, Minnesota, and Oklahoma have seen fit to locate recreation missions within them.

CASE STUDY: LOCAL ASSISTANCE PROGRAM: PENNSYLVANIA DEPARTMENT OF COMMUNITY AFFAIRS

Pennsylvania had a recreation consultant working for its State Planning Board as far back as 1948. The Recreation Consultant provided advisory services to local governments on the organization and conduct of community recreation programs. The state also has had, since 1943, a progressive program of grants to school districts for assisting with the creation and operation of extensive recreation programs.

In 1964, the state voters approved a special $70 million open space acquisition program entitled "Project 70." It permitted the state to launch a large-scale six-year program for the purchase of disappearing lands for new state parks, fishing access to waterways, public hunting lands and community parks and open space. The sum of $40 million was allocated for the purchase of the regional parks. Twenty million dollars was provided for grants to local municipalities, and $10 million went for the acquisition of hunting lands and waterways.

The 1965 session of the Pennsylvania General Assembly created a new cabinet-level agency—the Department of Community Affairs—the first such state department in the country. The Recreation Consultant and the staff employed to administer the local government portion of the Project 70 program were absorbed into the new department and reorganized as the Bureau of Recreation and Conservation. The Bureau's mission was to combine its responsibilities of administering the local open space bond program with the broader mission of the Department, which was to provide advisory assistance to local governments. The latter role was similar to that previously exercised by the single recreation consultant of the State Planning Board.

The fact that the Department also provides technical and financial assistance to local governments in related functional service areas such as comprehensive community planning, redevelopment and housing, human resources, police and fire, public works, and municipal administration and finance, provides for an environment of coordinated local service. The Department is somewhat unique in that it is organized for a consolidated approach to a single clientele—local governments—rather than being organized to handle a single governmental function such as recreation or natural resources.

One of the key operating features of the Department, which has facilitated its on-site assistance programs, is that it has been able to deploy its technical advisors in five regional offices at key geographic locations throughout the state. The Recreation and Parks Advisors in each regional office are within two hours of almost every municipality in the state. The Advisor can utilize the experience and expertise of his co-workers in the office. Their specialized knowledge may include planning, housing, human resources and municipal administration. This pooling of knowledge allows the regional office to take advantage of programs and referrals stimulated in the other areas. For example, urban renewal efforts in dense cities previously lacking sufficient open space can recreate open space. Comprehensive planning programs undertaken by newly urbanizing communities lead to the dedication of parkland by developers.

The general goal of the Bureau is to improve the living environment of the state's communities, particularly for the children of those communities. In reaching toward this goal, the Bureau is advocating the creation of year-round park and recreation programs in all communities or groups of communities having at least 15,000 inhabitants. In order to achieve this, intergovernmental cooperation among municipalities and between school districts and municipalities is advocated.

In keeping with one of the general missions of the Department—that of providing for the training of municipal officials—the Recreation and Conservation Bureau annually conducts regional recreation workshops for elected, appointed and salaried municipal officials. Topics include the roles of park and recreation boards, park maintenance, recreation planning standards and school-municipal cooperation in recreation. Other special training involves working with counties to conduct playground leaders workshops for employees of county municipalities.

Planning and research has become an important activity of the Department of Community Affairs. It not only provides and supports the technical assistance mission of the field advisors, but projects needs and demands as part of the local government participation in the Federal Land and Water Conservation Fund Program. Two examples of short-term research projects are financial and administrative analyses of municipal swimming pool and tennis operations. A survey of local park users has provided more insight into the socioeconomic relationships of participation patterns.

In the conservation and environmental field, publications have been prepared to help local officials in planning, park and environmental commissions understand technical subjects such as mandatory land dedication ordinances, easements and the preparation of inventories of environmentally sensitive areas. In cooperation with the Department of Environmental Resources, the Bureau provides consultation on the organization of Environmental Advisory Councils at the local level, and helps them to organize programs for addressing priority concerns.

One of the primary roles of the Bureau continues to be that of administering the financial assistance program for local governments that is supported by the Federal Land and Water Conservation Fund. Bureau staff do more than just inform local governments about application procedures. They become involved with the community in identifying capital development priorities, and in analyzing site alternatives. A strong advocacy is provided for quality in design, starting from the preparation of a site master plan and proceeding down to the functioning of material specifications. Technical advice is given on land acquisition projects as well, to yield the best result at a resonable price.

STATE RECREATION ROLE—PRIVATE ASSISTANCE

Recreation, like other vital social services, does not belong to government alone. As a governmental entity with responsibility for directly operating programs and facilities, state governments are not noted for exercising strong assistance initiatives to the private sector, be it individuals or corporations. As state recreation planning programs have improved however, more state recreation policy setters have come to recognize that the private sector plays a more significant role than does government in meeting people's recreation needs. Having realized this, the states are doing an increasingly better job of coordinating with and assisting their fellow providers in the private sector.

One of the state-related agencies, the Cooperative Extension Service of the state agricultural college, is typically the principal agent in providing advisory assistance to the private sector. Historically, the Extension Service primarily worked with individual farmers, or farming-related groups such as a farm grange or county 4-H club, in planning social recreation programs.

In recent years, the clientele served by the Extension Service, through groups of Recreation Specialists, has included small businessmen in rural areas who organize such recreation enterprises as vacation farms, fee fishing lakes and campgrounds. The advice given to these individuals includes research data and economic information that will assist the client to determine whether his proposed project has an income potential. Planning advice is also given on site suitability, facility design and potential operation and maintenance problems.

Usually the only other state agency that has any relationship to the private sector is a tourist development agency in the State Commerce or Economic Development Department. The economic significance of recreational travel (commonly referred to as tourism) was given increased recognition in the 1960's, and many states now provide special information and promotional programs on public and private sites and resorts that can attract in- and out-of-state visitors.

Perhaps the area in which state recreation roles will see their next new initiative will be in increased technical and financial assistance to the private profit and non-profit sector. In the future, states may expand beyond tourist information services and provide market analysis and planning assistance to private businessmen. Such services could enable the private sector to provide those recreation services which public agencies are unable to meet with their finances, or which the public agencies feel are more appropriately assigned to the private sector. Low-interest loans for recreation development may be routinely offered by states in the future.

INTER-AGENCY RECREATION COMMITTEES

As the parks and recreation movement grew during and after World War II, those in the field advocated the creation of state government agencies that would be assigned broader coordinative and advocatory roles in parks and recreation. State inter-agency councils or boards were recommended by many and by 1950 at least four states had created such agencies.

While approximately four states did follow through with executive orders or legislation to create new recreation agencies, most of them were semi-autonomous committees, commissions or boards. The only states to create cabinet-level departments have been California and Idaho, while New York, because of state constitutional limitations on the number of departments created an Office of Parks and Recreation under the Governor's Office.

The purpose of state recreation committees is to foster coordination and cooperative planning of recreation efforts among a number of state agencies. The establishment of such committees can stimulate greater understanding of responsibilities, and, through economies of scale, can often lead to the employment of full-time staff to advance recreation efforts where the same staff level could not previously be justified within individual agencies.

Potential shortcomings of such agencies exist as well. Possibly most serious is the problem of gaining a strong commitment of the member agencies to the decisions of the main agency. Without a defined mission and staff capability to carry it out, the committee can easily become nothing more than a discussion forum that meets less and less frequently to a point at which it exists in name only.

In the past decade, the centralization-decentralization pendulum of political philosophy has swung more in the direction of centralization where recreation is concerned. Many of the functions of the new semi-autonomous recreation councils of the post–World War II period have either been abolished or absorbed by state constitutional reform, which has consolidated independent agencies into departments of the state governments. One of the first state agencies created, the North Carolina Recreation Council, was abolished in 1969 as a result of reorganization of the state government. The Georgia Recreation Commission experienced a similar demise several years later.

With the passage of the Federal Land and Water Conservation Fund program, together with various state bond issues, Arizona, Missouri, North Dakota, Virginia, Wyoming and Washington, among other states, chose to create Outdoor Recreation Commissions. Since most states spread the annual appropriations from the fund among several state departments and local governments, they needed staff capability to participate in the program. Additionally, the states were required to prepare a statewide comprehensive outdoor recreation plan to participate in the program. The establishment of an inter-agency committee, which would provide a staff pool for program administration and a forum for providing input from diverse groups in order to prepare the state plan, was a proper choice for these states.

CASE STUDY: WASHINGTON INTER-AGENCY COMMITTEE FOR OUTDOOR RECREATION

The Committee was established in 1964 along with special state legislation to create a special Outdoor Recreation Account financed from a special state bond issue and marine fuel takes. The Committee was directed to assist state and local agencies in the acquisition and development of outdoor recreation resources. In 1967, legislation was passed to add the statewide comprehensive outdoor recreation planning responsibility to the Committee.

The Committee consists of 12 members, including five citizen members appointed by the governor, and the directors of the seven state agencies most directly concerned with outdoor recreation. These agencies are the Departments of Commerce and Economic Development, Ecology, Fisheries, Game, Highways, Natural Resources, and the State Parks and Recreation Commission.

Structurally, the Committee staff is deployed in three sections—planning, project administration and administration. The Planning Section maintains the state outdoor recreation plan and involves itself with special task force projects on rivers, trails, wilderness and power plant citing. It also prepares the outdoor recreation capital budget for the state. The Project Administration Section does the staff work for the review and presentation of issues for Committee decision, and handles the various state agency and local government requests for financial assistance for land acquisition and development. The Administration Section handles all fiscal, personnel and clerical functions.

STATE OUTDOOR RECREATION THRUST OF THE 1960's

One of the most significant influences upon park and recreation actions at all levels of government was the report entitled *Outdoor Recreation for America.*[2] Released in 1962 to the President and Congress, this pioneering report represented the first comprehensive national analysis of the outdoor recreation activities and demands of Americans.

The Report's revelations of the magnitude of outdoor recreation pursuits and future needs captured the attention of policy setters at all levels, and triggered a series of actions that heavily influenced state government actions in the field during the 1960's and are still affecting state actions today.

STATES IN THE PIVOTAL ROLE

Outdoor Recreation for America spotlighted the fact that state governments should play the pivotal role in the national effort to improve outdoor recreation opportunities. The report observed that the states occupy the key middle position in our complex system of government, having both program experience and the legal authority to work effectively with the federal and local governments. Accordingly, Congress identified the states as the major recipients of the Land and Water Conservation Funds.

PRIORITY ATTENTION TO THE OUT-OF-DOORS

The state governments in the pre- and post-war period had primarily focused on the natural resources of parks, concentrating on preserving unique forest and water tracts for public parks or preserves and stimulating an abundant fish and wildlife supply for public fishing and hunting. The depression years and the war years did serve to increase attention to the purely "recreational" side of the field somewhat, although state activities in recreation were still not of the magnitude of agencies at the local level. After World War II, two or three states undertook initiatives to establish state recreation councils to improve state and local recreation programs.

One impact of the report *Outdoor Recreation for America* was to stimulate an even stronger state focus on the out-of-doors and on the land and facility side of park and recreation activities. The report emphasized the economic and social significance of parks and open space in American life and dramatized the shortcomings of the then-existing public parks in meeting the projected needs for the years 1976 through 2000.

DYNAMIC NEW FINANCING FOR OUTDOOR RECREATION

Outdoor Recreation for America carried with it several significant recommendations which were subsequently implemented by Congress. One of these was the passage of a federal grants-in-aid program to provide matching funds to the states to stimulate recreation planning and assist in acquiring lands and developing facilities for public outdoor recreation. The Federal Land and Water Conservation Fund Act was passed in 1965, with a 25-year life span. The Act provided a significant level of funding, much of which was to come from specially earmarked revenues, much the same as the highway trust fund.

The fact that the money appropriated to the states was also authorized for aid to local governments introduced to many states a new role. With the exception of the few urban states that had already passed state-financed programs authorizing grants to localities, most states had never perceived their role to be beyond that of setting aside unique state park, fishing, hunting and historic areas. The challenge of involvement in projects at the municipal level was a new one for the state park officials who were designated responsible for this new program.

The involvement of state governments in administrating financial assistance programs to local governments marked a new era in state roles in parks and recreation. In some states it has generated a special local government assistance function to local governments which has moved beyond merely processing grant requests. These states are also providing advice and technical assistance services as well, covering the organization, financing and conduct of recreation programs. States are now serving as clearinghouses for local agencies and are providing research, training and other resource and educational materials.

A second Federal grants-in-aid program was also authorized in 1965 under the administrative auspices of the Department of Housing and Urban Development. It was entitled the "Open Space Land Program." Its distinctive differences, from the state government perspective, were that it was for *urban* land acquisition rather than statewide projects, and that it was administered exclusively by the federal government.

The states had previously had to finance their acquisition and development projects, modest as they were, primarily from annual appropriations of their legislatures. Triggered by dramatic findings of the *Outdoor Recreation for American* report, a number of states having major urban areas passed major open space bond programs of their own, to supplement the federal assistance program and to help meet the matching fund requirements. New York, even took action in advance of the report, when the state's voters approved a $100 million bond issue in 1960 and again in 1962. New Jersey, Wisconsin, Pennsylvania, Michigan and California passed programs during the period from 1961 to 1965. By 1970, at least 27 states had some type of park and recreation program for providing aid and advice to local governments.[3]

STATE COMPREHENSIVE PLANNING INITIATIVES

Another impact of the report and passage of the Land and Water Conservation Fund Act was the initiation of statewide comprehensive outdoor recreation planning. The Land and Water Conservation Fund Act specified that, in order to participate in the program, each state be required to prepare a plan that would include an evaluation of the supply and demand of outdoor recreation in the state; a program for the implementation of the plan; and other necessary information determined by the Secretary of the Interior. Prior to this requirement, the only state to have undertaken any comprehensive planning in the field was California, which started its plan in 1957 and released it in 1960.

These plans, which must be updated every five years, have had a significant influence upon the maturation rate of state government roles in the outdoor recreation field. While these influences are not always apparent because some states have done only the minimum necessary to maintain eligibility for the grants program, the second and third generation planning programs are causing many states to look deeper into such issues as urban needs and the role of private enterprise, which will continue to influence state actions in future years.

The states, like the federal and local governments, have the constant problem of coordinating their several recreation-related activities. Although it has long been recommended, there has not been any significant action to consolidate all recreation-related functions into a single department. Without such consolidation, the need for inter-agency statewide comprehensive planning is vital, if past precedents and data are not to continue to dictate future courses.

Recognition of the need to combine the various agencies that presently deal with recreation has fostered planning that would undoubtedly not have otherwise occurred. It has required that the states make a critical evaluation of their multi-faceted activities and determine their proper direction. This comprehensive planning requirement will probably be recognized in years to come as having had as positive an influence on shaping the future of state recreation services as any other factor.

In the first 10 years of the program, about $25 million were invested into the plans of the 50 states and the District of Columbia. A new state recreation professional, the Recreation Planner, can now be found in each state, addressing the outdoor recreation needs and demands of his citizens.

Most states have chosen to vest the responsibility for the state plan with the department that serves as the liaison agency with the Federal Bureau of Outdoor Recreation in administering the Land and Water Conservation Fund program. This agency almost always is the conservation or natural resource department of the state government. A few states have utilized their existing state planning agencies for preparing the document.

One of the disadvantages associated with vesting the responsibility for the state outdoor recreation plan with the state natural resources agency is that the range of priorities and recommendations may be limited by the built-in orientation of the agency. While the use of a more independent state planning office is not without some disadvantages of its own, such agencies do have the potential for taking a more independent and perhaps tough look at state and local recreation priorities.

Perhaps the single most limiting factor in the recreation planning programs of the states to date is the fact that the planning is artificially constrained by the word "outdoor." While the states traditionally have been involved primarily with outdoor activities, the recreation and leisure needs of an urban American public include many indoor pursuits as well. Notwithstanding the limitations of the Federal Land and Water Conservation Fund, the more progressive states in the future will recognize the artificiality of partial planning, and will correct this shortcoming themselves.

THE STATES AND URBAN AMERICA

Of the many social disparities and problems that exist, perhaps the most perplexing is the condition of the urban areas of our nation. The central cities are the principal place of residence of the poor, the minorities and the handicapped. These individuals are the most deprived of all of our citizens of the opportunities to improve the quality of their lives.

The state government's role in addressing the particular recreation needs of these citizens is minimal at best. Within the three-tiered government system, local governments traditionally are responsible for providing direct programs and services to their citizens. Tragically, however, as inner cities become the primary place of residence of the disadvantaged and the more mobile and affluent individuals and corporations move to the suburban fringe areas, the city governments of our country become less capable of meeting the needs that history has conferred upon them to handle.

Because of its' emergence as a national issue, and because the state planning guidelines of the Federal Bureau of Outdoor Recreation require it, all states typically include a section on "urban recreation" in their statewide outdoor recreation plans. These sections in the plans produced to date are remarkable for their brevity and uniformity among the states and for the degree to which responsibility is assigned to local governments. The state outdoor recreation role in meeting urban needs is usually defined as working to locate state park areas closer to urban areas, although there is no trend toward actually locating state parks *within* core cities.

While the states to date have collectively maintained a policy of allocating the responsibility for providing parks and programs in cities to local governments, they do have the prerogative of providing financial or technical assistance to local governments. The Federal Land and Water Conservation Fund makes annual appropriations to the states, which can in turn grant them to local governments.

Unfortunately, the record of state investments under urban recreation programs reflects little apparent desire to help the cities meet their needs. In a report entitled *Recreation in the Cities: Who Gains from Federal Aid?*,[4] John M. Burdick found that in the first 10 years of the programs, cities had been almost uniformly squeezed out of full participation.

While one of the major facility needs of urban areas in meeting the recreation needs of citizens on a year-round basis is for the development of indoor, multi-purpose centers, no state has as yet undertaken a program to provide assistance in this regard. The states are, however, providing heavy capital and operating subsidies for local school facilities, and these facilities have great potential for meeting broad leisure service needs. Most state school funding formulas are flexible enough to cover problems of density and income deficiency.

REFERENCES

1. Harold D. Meyer and Charles K. Brightbill, *State Recreation: Organization and Administration* (New York: A. S. Barnes and Co., 1950), pp. 88–89.
2. Outdoor Recreation Resources Review Commission, *Outdoor Recreation for America,* (Washington, D.C.: Government Printing Office, 1962).
3. Joseph E. Hoffman, Jr., "State Grants-in-Aid Program for Outdoor Recreation—Acquisition, Planning and Development," October, 1971.
4. John M. Burdick, *Recreation in the Cities: Who Gains from Federal Aid?* (Washington, D.C.: Center for Growth Alternatives, 1975).

QUESTIONS

1. What are the four broad areas of state government activity in the parks and recreation field?
2. Describe some of the trends in state recreation services to local governments.
3. What features are special about the role of the states in the three-level governmental system?
4. What influences has the report of the Outdoor Recreation Resources Review Commission had on state activities?

Making recreation facilities available to everyone who wants to use them is a major challenge that has only recently begun to receive attention.
(U.S. Bureau of Outdoor Recreation)

ABOUT THE AUTHOR

Fred Humphrey received a B.A. degree from Tarkio, Missouri, College, an M.A. from the University of Iowa, and a Ph.D. from Pennsylvania State University. He is registered with the National Therapeutic Recreation Society as a Master Therapeutic Recreation Specialist and has had 14 years of clinical experience as Director of Therapeutic Recreation and Director of Activity Therapies in various rehabilitation settings. Dr. Humphrey developed the Therapeutic Recreation option at both the undergraduate and graduate levels at the University of Iowa, and at Penn State and Temple Universities. His textbook on *Conceptual Issues in Therapeutic Recreation* is currently in preparation.

Dr. Humphrey's professional participation includes the following: member, Board of Trustees, NRPA; President, NTRS; Chairman, Hospital Section, American Recreation Society; currently Editor, *Therapeutic Recreation Journal;* member, Professional Registration Boards, NRPA and NTRS; and participant on numerous federal advisory committees and review panels. He is a recipient of the Distinguished Service Award from the NTRS, and is the author of numerous federal grant proposals funded by the Bureau of Education for the Handicapped, the Rehabilitation Services Administration, and the National Institute of Mental Health.

His leisure interests include family, golf, music, conversation and professional sports.

chapter 6

THERAPEUTIC RECREATION—SERVICE AND PROCESS

Therapeutic recreation, the newest area of specialization within the broader field of recreation, park and leisure services, concerns the utilization of recreation experiences as a facet of the rehabilitation process, in both institutional and community settings. In order to gain a basic understanding of the many aspects of therapeutic recreation, both as a service and as a process, the following topics and issues merit exploration: (1) historic perspectives; (2) definition of the field of service; (3) scope and objectives; (4) delivery systems for therapeutic recreation service; (5) cooperative relationships; (6) professionalism; and (7) current societal status and trends.

HISTORIC PERSPECTIVES ON RECREATION AND REHABILITATION

PRE- AND POST-CHRISTIAN SOCIETIES

As O'Morrow states, "disease and disability are as old as life itself," and the histories of both the rehabilitation process and the use and development of recreation experiences as an essential part of this process have not been chronicled in definitive form.[1] However, the inclusion of recreational activities, such as music, dance, games and athletics, in the life style of people can be traced to prehistoric artifacts, and these same activities have been related to people's treatment of various illnesses and disabilities, according to the earliest historic documents.

Historic artifacts show that the earliest civilizations (Babylon, Jericho, Egypt) participated in music and dancing; they engaged in sports and festivals; they had table games and children's toys and many other activities and items of equipment we today classify as recreational. Evidence indicates that many of these early cultures attributed illness and disability to demons, evil spirits and transgressions against the gods. Although there are no records that clearly note the use of recreation to prevent or treat illness and disability in these cultures, there is documented support for the fact that many ritualistic activities (which we today call recreational) were engaged in to appease the gods. One of the most specific early references to the use of a recreational activity for therapeutic purposes is the biblical story of David playing his harp to relieve Saul from the ill effects of evil spirits.[2]

The Cultures of Greece and Rome

Although the Greeks originally attributed most illnesses to the gods, they probably led the way among ancient cultures in the transformation of medicine to a non-religious art. Temples and shrines built to Asclepius, and to his daughters Hygieia and Panacea, were the principal early medical centers in Greece. As early as the fifth century B.C., some of these temples had assumed many of the characteristics of modern health spas. They provided the seekers of the Greek health ideal of a balanced state of well-being in soul, mind and body with not only places of worship but also lodging, hospitals, gymnasiums, libraries, and large stadiums and theaters with capacities as high as 16,000.[3, 4]

Huizinga states that Plato, in the fourth century B.C., unreservedly recognized the link between ritual and play as a given fact.[5] As pointed out by Frye and Peters, ". . . concern for the human body, the temporal dwelling of the soul, has always been a vital tie between health and religion."[6] With a relationship to both health and religion, recreation served as a connecting pathway between the two.

It was during the age of Pericles that the transformation of medicine from a ritualistic to a scientific base occurred; and with the rise of the Roman Empire, Greek medical advances were instituted in Rome and further developed. The significant contributions of the Romans included an expanded system of public health services to prevent social dysfunction and to provide enlightened treatment programs for the emotionally ill. At the heart of many of the new approaches to psychiatric rehabilitation was increased attention to recreational activities such as music, dance, poetry and games.

The Middle Ages

There is evidence that countries in Asia and the Middle East were at least as advanced as their European counterparts during the early Middle Ages. Sketchy records indicate that recreation was used in treatment programs in China and India as early as 190 A.D., according to Avedon. Charaka, an Indian physician of this period, advocated that it was the hospital's responsibility to supply toys and games for patients—an enlightened position that is far from being effectively accepted in institutional programs even today. It is Avedon's interpretation that Jewish and Moslem physicians of the early Middle Ages were more advanced than their European counterparts, not only in their approaches to medicine but also in their comprehensive social rehabilitation programs. It was not until the thirteenth century that Arab physicians introduced their advanced methods to Europe.[7]

From approximately 200 to 1500 A.D., religious emphasis was on the spiritual rather than the physical aspects of life, and those denying man's need for recreation appeared to have the upper hand. The period from 1500 to 1700 can be classified as a period of transition in the health field, for although there was much new scientific knowledge, it was largely unapplied in medical practice. Particularly tragic was the treatment of the emotionally ill, who were tortured and burned in the witch-hunting frenzy created by religious zealots.[8]

The 18th and 19th Centuries

The late 1700's and early 1800's saw a renewal of interest in the therapeutic value of recreation and work activities in the rehabilitation process, especially in the psychiatric setting. The efforts and writings of Dr. Phillippe Pinel, an eighteenth century French physician, had a significant influence on the conscious use of recreation activities for therapeutic purposes as his humane treatment regime spread through the British Isles and to the Western Hemisphere. Dr. Benjamin Rush, the first superintendent of the Pennsylvania Hospital of Philadelphia (1812), Dr. Thomas Eddy, New York Hospital (1815), and Dr. Wyman, McLean Hospital, Waverly, Massachusetts (1822) were the earliest recorded supporters of recreation activities in institutional settings in the United States. Between 1843 and 1848, there were reports describing the extensive recreation programs at Hanwell Asylum in London, the value of music in treating emotional illness and the fact that the asylum was providing pianos, flutes, clarinets and violins for patients' use. Florence Nightingale, more commonly known for her work in nursing, was the last great pioneer of the nineteenth century in behalf of recreation programs in institutional settings. At the midpoint of this century, she introduced innovations that have since become established parts of military life and military hospitals. The provision of classrooms and instruction, reading rooms, barracks social rooms and recreation huts came about through her efforts. Her book, *Notes on Nursing* (1873), gave attention to such items as color variety, visits by babies, the value of pets, and the use of music in therapy, and discussed a range of recreation-oriented issues.[9]

The United States in the 20th Century

The formal recreation movement began its development in the United States during the latter part of the nineteenth century, but it was almost exclusively oriented toward community recreation and restricted to large urban areas, particularly those areas with extensive economic and social problems. Although therapeutic recreation (hospital recreation) did not enter the mainstream of the recreation movement until after World War II, recreation programs in psychiatric settings had grown to the point where, in 1913, one hospital in the United States reported the chartering of a train to take 500 patients on a picnic.[10] Between 1893 and 1914, recreation programs for the visually impaired were developed in New York City by the Industrial Home for the Blind, the New York Association for the Blind (Lighthouse) and the Jewish Guild for the Blind. The Vineland, New Jersey, Training School in 1915 reported on a variety of recreation approaches used in "treating" or "training" retardates.

World War I stimulated an expansion of recreation services in military hospitals serving general medical, surgical and psychiatric patients. Shortly after the entry of the United States into the war, the American Red Cross began to provide some recreation services in military hospitals, and by the end of the war, recreation programs were being offered in wards and convalescent homes. The Red Cross has continued to employ and assign recreation workers to military hospitals to this day, while the responsibility for programs in veterans' hospitals was transferred to the United States Veterans' Bureau (Veterans' Administration) in 1931.

The growth of therapeutic recreation in non-military settings between World Wars I and II was relatively slow. There are individual examples of great progress such as the one previously mentioned of a psychiatric hospital chartering a train for a picnic, but the overall status of program development was essentially static. One outstanding exception was the program at the Lincoln (Illinois) State School and Colony. Under the direction of Bertha Schlotter and Margaret Svendsen, a conceptually sound and well-structured program designed to teach social and functional skills to the retarded was instituted. This pioneering program was highly successful, and the evaluation report of the three-year project, originally published in 1932, has been reissued in 1951, 1956 and 1959. The report considers a number of concepts and issues that were innovative for their time, such as the recorded observations and analyses of the responses of mentally retarded children to various play activities, suggestions concerning play equipment, and classification of play activities according to mental age, degree of motor activity and degree of social organization. One chapter presents a socio-psychological analysis of the play activities used in the experimental program.[11]

The United States Since World War II

The greatest single period of growth in recognition of the value of therapeutic recreation and a resultant development of programs in institutional settings occurred during World War II and in the decade that followed. The efforts of the American National Red Cross in expanding programs in military hospitals, both in the United States and overseas, brought attention to the value of therapeutic recreation to both the morale and treatment of hospitalized servicemen. Red Cross recreation programs became permanently established after World War II and have continued to the present time as a valuable facet of the peacetime as well as emergency services to the armed forces.

Immediately following World War II (1945), another landmark in the growth of therapeutic recreation occurred in the form of the establishment of the Recreation Service of the Hospital Services Division within Veterans' Administration hospitals nationwide. In 1960, recreation services were structured within the Recreation Section of the Physical Medicine and Rehabilitation Service of the V.A. hospitals. The programs and professional staffing patterns that were developed in V.A. hospitals were outstanding, and this national showcase for therapeutic recreation had much to do with the subsequent development of recreation programs in state psychiatric hospitals, state schools for the retarded, physical rehabilitation centers and other types of treatment centers throughout the country. The V.A. efforts in therapeutic recreation peaked in the mid-1960's, at which time a program of Central Office (Washington) consultants in each activity area (occupational therapy, therapeutic recreation, and so on) was dropped. While excellent therapeutic recreation programs currently exist in nearly all V.A. hospitals, the support for such programs must exist within each hospital, and such support, unfortunately, has been far from universal.

State hospitals and state schools have been roughly 10 years behind V.A. Hospitals in mounting concentrated efforts to develop comprehensive therapeutic recreation programs. While examples have been given of programs in the early 1900's, it was not until the mid-1950's that these were more than isolated examples. It could be said that the 1950's represented the decade of emphasis on mental health programs and the 1960's the decade of emphasis on programs for the mentally retarded. Therapeutic recreation program development in state-funded settings has followed the same pattern.

While deinstitutionalization, community placement, development of community resources and transitional experiences were not uncommon in the late 1950's, the decade from 1965 to 1975 is especially noted for its emphasis on a community orientation for all types of institutional programs. Therapeutic recreation is presently suffering from separation anxieties as it attempts to cut the umbilical cord of institutional isolation and become a full partner of public, private and commercial recreation programs in the broader community. Today, in addition to the programs of such agencies as community mental health and mental retardation centers, physical rehabilitation centers, and the like, programs developed by public recreation agencies to serve ill, handicapped, racially isolated and other excluded individuals living independently in the community have made a significant contribution to fulfilling the longstanding public recreation motto of "recreation for all."

DEFINITION OF FIELD OF SERVICE

EVOLUTION OF TERMINOLOGY

An examination of how the terminology that has been applied to therapeutic recreation has evolved provides an excellent basis for understanding this field of service. In its earliest organized form, this area of recreation was given the site-specific descriptor of *hospital recreation*. The historical background of therapeutic recreation shows that its greatest initial acceptance was in psychiatric hospitals, followed by its use in institutions for the retarded, physical rehabilitation centers, institutions serving the aged, penal and correctional settings and, most recently, the community.

Within the medical community it has been said, in reference to the treatment and rehabilitation process, that anyone of any importance is doing therapy. It was therefore inevitable that, essentially because of status pressures, recreation in the rehabilitation process would be characterized as "therapy" and its definition limited to the medical model, with its emphasis on illness and treatment. During this period of its conceptual evaluation, recreation in the rehabilitation process was first designated *medical recreation* and then *recreation therapy*—a term that finally encompassed many of the concepts and practices of therapeutic recreation at the present time.

THERAPEUTIC RECREATION AS BOTH A SERVICE AND PROCESS

The term therapeutic recreation, which originated in the 1950's and began to appear in the literature as early as 1957,[12] must be understood as being both a *service* and a *process.* Therapeutic recreation *service* refers to the understandings, approaches and skills that an individual must have to effectively involve an ill or otherwise excluded person in a recreation-oriented experience. Working in therapeutic recreation requires a wide range of knowledge across a continuum that includes personality development dynamics, medical terminology, impairing conditions, anatomy and kinesiology, leadership approaches, activity analysis, activity skills, adaptation of activities, architectural barriers and many other areas. Within this context, it becomes readily apparent that the efforts in the field of therapeutic recreation to the present time have been highly oriented to the service side of the field.

Therapeutic recreation as a *process* refers to the dynamics of what may be described as the catalyst-facilitator role, the indirect service role or the enabler role. It appears that, for the foreseeable future, therapeutic recreators will neither be trained, nor hired if available, in sufficient numbers to provide direct service to the disabled population, which has been estimated by some investigators to be as high as 70 million, or 35 percent of the total population.[13] This estimate includes only those with some form of physical, emotional, social or intellectual problem and does not include offenders against the law. Therapeutic recreation as a process refers to the role of the therapeutic recreator in providing assistance to the recreation and parks profession, to related human services fields such as medicine, social work, psychology and education and to the families of disabled persons. The increasing reduction and elimination of architectural barriers to the disabled represents a classic example of how the therapeutic recreator, in the role of catalyst-facilitator combines his efforts with those of many others directed toward increasing the accessibility of recreation and park facilities to disabled persons. The net outcome of this is increased participation on the part of disabled persons in existing general programs that are not a part of a formalized therapeutic recreation service delivery system.

SCOPE AND OBJECTIVES OF THERAPEUTIC RECREATION

Within the context of the generic definition of therapeutic recreation as having both a service and process component, there are more specific delineations of how the service component functions. The transition in terminology from *recreation therapy* to *therapeutic recreation* provides an excellent framework within which to analyze the conceptual issues related to therapeutic recreation service.

The term "recreation therapy" uses therapy as the noun and recreation as the adjective, with the resultant strong implication that therapy—a specific technique or medication utilized with identifiable results—has taken place.

With reference to the prescription of specific recreation activities to be experienced for identifiable results, this use of the term is highly questionable. On the other hand, the term "therapeutic recreation" uses recreation as the noun and therapeutic as the modifier, the interpretation being that the recreation experience has the potential to be therapeutic for *all* people, whether disabled or normal. A host of issues must be given attention if the odds are to become favorable for the therapeutic potential of the recreation experience to become a reality for the participant(s): the appropriateness of the activity to the functional strengths of the participant(s); whether the activity is conducted in a group or on an individual basis; whether adaptations in the activity must be made to correspond to the functional level of the individual or group; whether attention must be given to architectural barriers; what leadership approaches are most appropriate; how the participant(s) will perceive the proposed experience; and the participant's level of readiness. These and many more factors must be considered.

"The Osmosis Halo of Activity Involvement" is suggested as an appropriate descriptor for the conceptual bind into which the activity professions (occupational therapy, physical education, music, dance, drama and recreation) have placed themselves. This conceptual bind is predicated on the unquestioned assumption that activity experience is inherently beneficial (therapeutic) for *all* those involved. In other words, participants gain something from the activity environment through an inevitable "soaking up" of its benefits, regardless of the conditions or content of the environment. Recreation has always been promoted as a basic human need, rather than analyzed in terms of its potential contribution to a number of human needs. This conceptual fallacy is at the root of the evolving premise that recreation can cure everything from schizophrenia to fallen arches.

The distinguishing characteristic about the therapeutic recreation approach is its utilization of the activity experience as a *tool* and its conceptual realization of the activity experience as being basically neutral. Implementation of the therapeutic recreation process involves four specific steps, as identified by O'Morrow: (1) an assessment of the individual's needs; (2) the development (planning) of goals for the therapeutic recreation effort, including analysis of the demands (cognitive, social and emotional, as well as physical) of proposed activities (individual or group) and environments (on the ward, in the community, in the home, etc.); (3) the actual involvement in a program experience; and (4) a continuing evaluation effort.[14]

DELIVERY SYSTEMS FOR THERAPEUTIC RECREATION

Despite a longstanding recognition that delivery systems for treatment and rehabilitation services to the ill and disabled should be integrated, they are in fact highly dichotomized into institutional and community segments. The extent of interaction, cooperative case planning, sharing of facilities and programs, and so on between institutions and community agencies falls far short of what would be highly desirable. Unfortunately, the organization of therapeutic recreation services follows essentially the same pattern. Therefore this section will summarize service delivery under the following headings: (1) Institutional program organization; (2) Community program organization; (3) Examples of transitional efforts.

INSTITUTIONAL PROGRAM ORGANIZATION

Therapeutic recreation programs are currently offered in institutional settings serving the emotionally ill, mentally retarded, physically impaired, aging, visually impaired, hearing impaired, those addicted to alcohol and/or drugs, and societal offenders ranging from those in short-term detention centers to those in maximum security prisons (both women and men). Treatment and rehabilitation programs also span the range of sponsorship from public and voluntary non-profit support to private settings. This wide range of disabilities and sponsorship leads to extensive variance in the quality of overall programs, staffing patterns, facilities and organizational structure in terms of the total program as well as therapeutic recreation.

The therapeutic recreation program or department is increasingly viewed as being a part of the treatment or rehabilitation services within the institutional environment, and hence has a structured relationship to the clinical director or head of medical services in the institution. However, the acceptance of therapeutic recreation, and the directness of its relationship to the clinical head, varies greatly and is almost always dependent on the quality of recreation services offered in each individual institution.

The larger the institution, the greater the tendency is for therapeutic recreation to be organized within a more specific structure, such as a Department of Activity Therapies, Rehabilitation Therapies, and so on. Included in such a department will be found some or all of the following activity-oriented disciplines, in addition to therapeutic recreation: occupational therapy, music therapy, dance therapy, drama therapy, vocational therapy or rehabilitation, volunteer services and library services. Since so many gray areas exist among these activity approaches, a coordinated and integrated activity therapies program should not only provide more effective activity experiences for those in institutions but also present the disciplines involved with the opportunity for a more forceful voice in the rehabilitation process.

Activity Areas in Therapeutic Recreation

The content potential for therapeutic recreation program development is as wide as human behavior. Examples of potential program areas include cooking, gardening, reading, creative writing, the writing and publication of an institutional newspaper or magazine, pantomine, drama, table games team sports, individual sports, field trips, community activities, travel (programs both throughout the United States and in foreign countries are becoming increasingly common for disabled individuals), and so on. Creativity is the key, as reflected in the example of a community mental health center that recently raised several hundred dollars to support a local wheelchair sports club through sponsorship of a "rockathon" (contestants kept a rocking chair going as long as possible) on the wards of the center.

By location, the five basic facets of an institutional therapeutic recreation program are (a) ward-centered programs; (b) off-ward programs during the day; (c) evening-weekend programs off the ward; (d) special events; and (e) programs utilizing community facilities while the individual is still institutionalized. Within these five general categories, participation occurs along a functional strengths–activity demands continuum that includes a variety of criteria such as individual-group, structured-unstructured, and so on, to help the therapeutic recreator determine the degree and kinds of activity that will most benefit the individual. A more detailed discussion of the five basic facets of an institutional therapeutic recreation program is presented in the following sections.

Ward-Centered Programs

As indicated, these are programs, either individual or group in orientation, conducted for the residents of a given ward within the constraints of the ward environment. In a continuum sense, the limitation in functional strengths of the participant(s) makes this approach the most appropriate one for patients confined to a hospital or other health institution. Creativity and effective leadership dynamics are at a premium in constructing a ward activity environment that has development potential as well as perceived motivational attractiveness for the participant.

Off-Ward Day Programs

As individuals grow in meeting the varying demands of the activity environment, they can be encouraged to eventually attend off-ward activity sessions. The key to an effective transition lies in limiting the environmental shock of the off-ward setting and initially maintaining the functional demands of the off-ward environment at a level no higher than that comfortably reached during on-ward experiences.

Evening-Weekend Programs

The ultimate goal of the therapeutic recreation experience is to assist the individual in developing a functional non-work segment of his life style in the community. For the great majority of people, the recreation experience occurs during the non-work segment of life—evenings, weekends, holidays, vacations, and so on. The evening-weekend program experience in an institutional setting is directed toward goal achievement in this area. The initial transition from day-program experiences, either on-ward or off-ward, requires a much greater degree of structure and leadership guidance than will be necessary later on. The ward program components should have been directed toward development of not only the functional strengths but also the activity skills that will lead to a realistic degree of success in the evening-weekend activities. Voluntary participation in recreation activities in the non-institutional community is a key to an effective non-work life style. Thus, the evening-weekend program has a significant built-in evaluative component in terms of this voluntary participation criterion.

Special Events

Programs in this category follow the same pattern as community-based programs, and are heavily oriented to holidays, historical dates and other special occasions. A key feature of the special events aspect of programming, one often overlooked in the emphasis on program development per se, is the great opportunity for community involvement in the institutional environment and the highly significant educational experiences that ensue. An example of a different kind of special event, which resulted in a high level of community involvement and education, was a "Family Recreation Day Program" developed by the author, at the Mental Health Institute, Clarinda, Iowa, in June 1959. The essence of the program was the opportunity for all residents of the hospital to invite as many family members and friends as desired to the hospital grounds for an old-fashioned picnic. Relatives and friends brought picnic lunches for themselves plus their hospitalized friend; the hospital furnished soft drinks and "the promise of a fun-filled day." The program format included morning religious services for all faiths, (with programs for children to attend while the adults were at services), a noon picnic, an afternoon of games and activities for children of all ages (ages 3 to 90 participated), a "leftovers" picnic in the evening for all who wished to attend, and an evening dance or movie (take your choice) for visitors and hospital residents. Many other features were added to the general format, such as awards to the Family Recreation Day Queen and King—the oldest lady and gentleman in attendance.

This activity, which attracted over a thousand visitors, has remained a special event to this day at the Iowa Mental Health Institute and was brought to another setting by the author when he assumed a position at the State Hospital in Jamestown, North Dakota, in 1961. It has since been adopted by many institutional settings in the United States and Canada. The key ingredients in the continued success of this program have been community involvement and interaction with hospital residents in a normal environment. As one resident remarked following the first Family Recreation Day, "You know, that was the first time in my life my parents ever played catch with me."

Programs Utilizing Community Facilities

Community involvement while the individual is still hospitalized represents not only the next step in developmental growth but also an important transitional stage in the patient's re-orientation to available community opportunities and resources. The range of program opportunities is limited only by the range available in the community, the financial resources of the therapeutic recreation department and/or program participants, and the attitude of the public recreation department, commercial recreation centers such as bowling alleys, and other community agencies. As previously mentioned, institutional and community-based programs serving the ill and disabled have not yet been effectively integrated; and involvement of the resident in the community, as a transitional phase of institutionalization, represents the vital link whereby this integration can occur.

COMMUNITY PROGRAM ORGANIZATION

It was stated earlier that development of a meaningful non-work segment of an individual's non-institutional life represents the ultimate goal of therapeutic recreation in the institutional setting. Add to this the fact that the great majority of ill and disabled individuals do not reside in institutions, and the focus is immediately on the community in terms of the greatest challenge facing therapeutic recreation. It has also been indicated that a dichotomy has existed too long between community recreators and therapeutic recreators in institutional settings. One reflection of this dichotomy has been the development of therapeutic recreation programs in the community which essentially serve the stabilized ill and disabled population—usually those of a higher functional level—and provide little opportunity for transitional involvement on the part of the increasingly sizable population of institutional dischargees. It has not been uncommon for institutions to find it necessary to develop transitional programs of their own until barriers to participation of their dischargees in community-based programs for the ill and disabled could be removed. Community agencies serving the ill and disabled are highly specialized in orientation and generally direct their services to only one impairing condition. This fact has led to organizational problems not only for public and community recreation agencies attempting to develop therapeutic recreation services but also for institutions attempting to develop integrated transitional programs for their residents. Kraus has identified six organizational sponsorship approaches to the provision of community therapeutic recreation services, and these will be discussed in the following section.[15]

PUBLIC RECREATION AGENCIES

While accurate and up-to-date survey data on a nationwide basis is not available, it can be estimated, based upon a limited number of statewide studies, that significantly fewer than one half of the public recreation departments in the United States have broad therapeutic recreation efforts. However, it must be quickly added that concrete efforts *are* being made to increase the number and scope of programs among public recreation departments across the country. Many of the initial efforts involve only summer or day or residential camping programs, but such efforts represent a legitimate first step toward assumption of full responsibility by public recreation departments for the disabled residents under their jurisdiction. An excellent example of statewide recognition of responsibility toward the disabled population is reflected in a resolution passed by the Oregon Parks and Recreation Society, February 1973, calling for increased state financial support to local jurisdictions for the provision of more comprehensive leisure services to disabled persons.[16] While it is impossible to identify accurately all the public recreation agencies that either have developed or are moving toward the development of effective and comprehensive community therapeutic recreation efforts, public recreation agencies in the following cities have been among the leaders in this effort: Kansas City, Missouri; Cincinnati, Ohio; Seattle, Washington; Philadelphia, Pennsylvania; Greensboro, North Carolina; Chicago, Illinois; Oak Park, Illinois; Washington, D.C., and Los Angeles, California.

The Northern Suburban Special Recreation Association (Chicago area) represents a unique cooperative effort in which seven suburban communities formed a special association to meet the recreation program needs of their disabled residents. Thanks to adequate financing and excellent staff and volunteer resources and facilities, an outstanding program effort has developed which far exceeds in both quality and quantity anything the individual communities could offer. A similar cooperative approach is developing today among nursing homes and extended care facilities that serve a predominately aging population. For example, five nursing homes located in the same area can each hire an aide-technician level person for a full-time assignment in the home and cooperatively employ a qualified therapeutic recreator to provide one day per week program guidance and evaluation efforts. Cooperative efforts can also include the joint purchase of major equipment items such as projectors and film rentals, sound systems, and so on.

A unique research-demonstration effort designed to develop a coordinated and integrated recreation service delivery model for disabled adults in a large urban area was instituted in 1974 by the Department of Recreation and Leisure Studies of Temple University, Philadelphia, under a grant from

Region III, Social and Rehabilitation Service, Department of Health, Education and Welfare. Special objectives or activities of this project include:

1. The decentralization of therapeutic recreation services through the development of regional-district program sites. The current therapeutic recreation effort of the Philadelphia Department of Recreation is essentially centralized in the Carousel House facility in Fairmount Park. Decentralization of the program to the many community centers throughout the city would greatly improve the delivery system.

2. The utilization of general therapeutic recreation services to decrease or eliminate the categorical delineation of services to a single condition of impairment, which so often occurs among voluntary agencies. Agencies with appropriate facilities are being encouraged, with Project financial assistance, to develop therapeutic recreation programs serving a target geographical area adjacent to their center rather than an exclusive target population chosen from a diagnostic standpoint.

3. A mini-grant process has been established whereby public, private and voluntary agencies can, on a city-wide basis, develop plans to offer integrated therapeutic recreation programs and receive Project financial support during the developmental phase.

4. The development of an effective referral process whereby available therapeutic recreation programs can most appropriately be used by those in need of and desiring the services. A key feature in this objective is an in-depth evaluation of each therapeutic recreation offering in terms of architectural barriers at the facility, leadership approaches, functional levels of participants, and so on. The weakness in many existing referral systems for community therapeutic recreation opportunities is that little is known about the program other than the title, time and place of meeting, and cost. As a graphic example, it is far better to make no referral at all than to refer a paraplegic in a wheelchair to a program conducted on the second floor of a building that has neither ramps to the first floor, an elevator to the second floor or doors wide enough to accommodate a wheelchair.

5. Development of an effective cooperative relationship with vocational rehabilitation personnel and facilities is a must if programs for adults are to be effective. This represents yet another facet that the Temple Project is attempting to incorporate into its model development.

ORGANIZATIONS SERVING SPECIFIC DISABILITIES

Increasingly, voluntary community organizations serving a specific disability are sponsoring recreation programs at the local level. Examples are the American Foundation for the Blind, national, state and local chapters of the Association for Retarded Citizens, the Arthritis and Rheumatism Foundation, the Muscular Dystrophy Association, the National Multiple Sclerosis Society, the National Easter Seal Society for Crippled Children and Adults and the United Cerebral Palsy Association. As in the case of public recreation agencies, program offerings vary from locale to locale and range from full-time, well-staffed efforts to infrequent special activities usually supported entirely through volunteer efforts.

SERVICE ORGANIZATIONS

Civic, service and fraternal organizations such as the Elks, Moose, Lions, Kiwanis and Jaycees (Junior Chambers of Commerce) have traditionally been involved in assisting with special programs, including recreation services, for the disabled. The Lions of North Carolina joined with the North Carolina Association for the Blind to develop Camp Dogwood, a camp and vacation center for the visually handicapped, and the Elks of North Dakota support the North Dakota Easter Seal Society in its annual operation of Camp Grassick, a summer-long program for physically handicapped children, adults and family units.

SPECIAL THERAPEUTIC RECREATION AGENCIES

One of the most outstanding examples of a special center is the Recreation Center for the Handicapped, Inc., in San Francisco, which has served the Bay Area since 1952. Founded and still directed by Janet Pomeroy, the Center has grown from serving a mere six children in one room to serving over 600 children, youths and adults. A recently completed additional building, primarily funded by a $667,424 construction grant under the Developmental Disabilities Act, makes it one of the most outstanding community facilities for the disabled to be found anywhere. However, as Pomeroy frequently emphasizes, successful programs can be developed regardless of surroundings, as evidenced by the fact that the Center's only facility for over 20 years was a two-level restaurant. Through the installation of ramps and rails, it was made functional for both wheelchairs as well as bedfast persons.[17]

COMMUNITY COUNCILS OR BOARDS

Community councils, although they are probably the least common and possibly most difficult method of organizing community therapeutic recreation programs, because of the need for interagency involvement and a wider base of community support, appear to hold great potential as service delivery mechanisms. The program that has received the greatest attention, because of its longevity and quality, is the Greater Kansas City Council on Recreation for the Handicapped.[18]

The Recreation Division of the Kansas City municipal government was a pioneer in developing special summer programs and day camp programs for orthopedically disabled, diabetic, cardiac, cerebral palsied and hearing-impaired children. Programs of this nature were offered in the early 1950's, and in 1955 a Supervisor of Special Recreation was appointed to develop a comprehensive year-round therapeutic recreation program.

Prior to the appointment of the Supervisor of Special Recreation, the Recreation Division approached a number of community agencies for advice and assistance. Agencies contacted included the National Foundation for Infantile Paralysis, the United Cerebral Palsy Association, the Jackson County Society for Crippled Children, the Kansas City Board of Education, the National Muscular Dystrophy Association, Goodwill Industries, the National Multiple Sclerosis Society and the Arthritis and Rheumatism Foundation. A unique aspect in the development of the Kansas City Council was the early participation of the Kansas City Veterans' Administration Hospital in the Council's efforts, for this represented one of the earliest major involvements of an institution in a cooperative community recreation effort for the disabled. Later participants in the Council effort included several agencies whose prime focus was not rehabilitation, including the YWCA, the Junior

League, Boys' Clubs, the American Red Cross, the Visiting Nurses' Association and others.

An initial survey to determine existing resources and unmet needs found that 11 different day and overnight camping, scouting, club and swimming programs were already being conducted for the disabled, but the following conditions represented critical unmet needs:

a. Existing programs were serving very few orthopedically handicapped children or adults.

b. Social deprivation was common among mobile adults who believed they were too disabled to participate in regular groups; lack of social contact was also a serious problem for unemployed teenagers who were no longer attending school.

c. The unmet needs of the homebound of all ages were acute.

d. The existing programs were so limited in both staff and budget that they were unable to respond effectively to the people they were attempting to serve.

Development of a formal structure called the Greater Kansas City Council of Recreation for the Handicapped grew out of the interests of the Recreation Division and the participating agencies and the issues that the survey brought into focus. Throughout its history, the evolving programs of the Council have been directed to one or more of the following elements:

a. A service delivery effort that has included programs for homebound children and adults, separate club programs for physically disabled adults and teenagers, a training program in home recreation activities for physically disabled children which is available to parents and interested volunteers, and participation-oriented television programs that are particularly oriented to the physically disabled.

b. A continuing survey and research effort.

c. A referral system.

d. The stimulation of public interest.

e. The development of further involvement on the part of community groups and the public at large.

f. The recruitment and training of professionals and volunteers to participate in the effort.

The activities of the Greater Kansas City Council on Recreation for the Handicapped have been covered in some detail, for it serves as an effective case history of community recreation efforts in behalf of the disabled. The approach, organizational format, scope of the program and basic objectives offer excellent guidelines for any community considering the implementation of a program in this area. The importance of interagency relationships, which will be treated briefly in the following section, is very effectively illustrated in the Kansas City effort.

COOPERATIVE RELATIONSHIPS

The theme of interdisciplinary and interagency cooperation has been emphasized throughout this chapter. Whether working within the institutional environment or in the community, an effective therapeutic recreator must not only plan toward but also participate in a continuum of cooperative efforts designed to create a more effective rehabilitation effort for those involved.

Within the institutional setting, the cooperative emphasis is on interdisciplinary relationships. Reference has been made to the Department of Activity Therapies, which is an organizational approach to making cooperation and interaction among the activity-oriented disciplines easier and more effective. In the broader institutional context, therapeutic recreators are increasingly functioning within a *team concept,* which expands the interactive challenges and opportunities to all rehabilitation disciplines—medicine, social work, psychology, nursing, special education, vocational rehabilitation and others. Probably no other facet of the treatment-rehabilitation approach permeates the total institutional environment to the extent that recreation does, and by the same token no other discipline finds itself interacting with as many other disciplines as does recreation. A therapeutic recreation program in an institutional environment cannot succeed without effective relationships with the dietary, engineering-maintenance and housekeeping departments, to name three examples. From these departments comes the food for refreshments, picnics and camping programs; the building, repair and alteration of facilities and equipment; and the "cleaning up of the mess" after that great party or special event. These ingredients are as important to a successful therapeutic recreation program as the psychiatrist's approval for his ward to participate in the event.

Human services agencies involved in the rehabilitation process in the community are generally organized around services to a specific disability category. Needs are identified and service responses to these needs are generally restricted to those who meet the categorical definition. This leads not only to fragmented efforts and many gaps in the service continuum but also frequently to a lower quality of services because resources become so diffused. The survey finding in Kansas City in 1955 that 11 agencies were providing recreation services to the disabled, with each limited in both quality and quantity, illustrates this point. An integrative mechanism, such as the Greater Kansas City Council on Recreation for the Handicapped, or the Health, Education and Welfare (SRS) Region III Project in Philadelphia, is a necessity if the interaction and cooperation necessary to eliminate the ineffectiveness of unilateral efforts is to be achieved.

PROFESSIONALISM

Parallel to the growth and development of therapeutic recreation as a recognized service specialization has been a growth in the professionalism exhibited by therapeutic recreators. The National Therapeutic Recreation Society (NTRS), a branch of the National Recreation and Parks Association (NRPA), has achieved both national and international recognition for its efforts in behalf of and contributions to the expansion of higher quality therapeutic recreation services in both institutional and community settings. Achievement of the current level of professional development represents a formalized effort of almost 30 years' duration.

The first professional group to be formed was the Hospital Recreation Section of the American Recreation Society in 1948. This group saw recreation in the rehabilitation process as a specialized facet of the larger recreation movement. In 1953, an autonomous group called the National Association of Recreation Therapists (NART) was formed. Individuals in this organization essentially represented state psychiatric hospitals and state schools for the retarded, and held a more exclusively clinical concept of the recreator's role in treatment centers. A third group, which originated in 1952, was the Recreation Therapy Section of the American Association for Health, Physical Education and Recreation (currently called the American Alliance of Health, Physical Education and Recreation), but this group never achieved an effective membership total or program effort. The NTRS came into being in 1966, following the merger of five national organizations to form the NRPA in 1965, and for the first time a united front of therapeutic recreation professionals existed.

While the professional development efforts of NTRS and its predecessors have included workshops, conferences, an institute at the annual NRPA Congress for Recreation and Parks, legislative activities, and so on, it is probably in the areas of publications and professional registration that the greatest impact has been made. The Hospital Section published a quarterly newsletter, the *Recreation in Treatment Centers Annual,* and a document entitled *Basic Concept of Hospital Recreation,* which received widespread attention. The NART published an excellent quarterly magazine, *Recreation for the Ill and Handicapped.* Since 1967, NTRS has combined these periodicals into the quarterly magazine, *Therapeutic Recreation Journal.*

The NTRS voluntary professional registration plan, and its antecedent, represent the first such plans developed in the entire recreation, park and leisure services movement. The Council for the Advancement of Hospital Recreation (CAHR), formed in 1953 to coordinate activities between the three professional organizations that developed between 1948 and 1953, established standards of qualification for hospital recreation workers in 1956. This program, called the National Voluntary Registration of Hospital Recreation Personnel, has operated with revisions to the present time, and is now the NTRS Voluntary Registration Plan.

CURRENT SOCIETAL STATUS AND TRENDS

Therapeutic recreation, while it has yet to realize much of its potential, probably has achieved as high a level of recognition and acceptance in as short a period of time as any discipline presently involved in the rehabilitation process. While it seems safe to predict that the role of therapeutic recreation in institutional settings will continue to grow for the remainder of this century, the frontier of therapeutic recreation for the next 25 years will be found in the development of an effective response to the leisure needs of the handicapped in the community. The following points are presented as the two major challenges to which therapeutic recreation must respond if the next 25 years are to produce growth and development that will exceed the progress of the past 25 and in the process develop an effective response to the community therapeutic recreation frontier:

a. Therapeutic recreation must cast aside the medical model, with its overriding emphasis on illness and impairment, and adopt a "wellness" model, which utilizes the individual's intact strengths, regardless of his station in life, as the contact point for effective activity involvement. Such a concept is not exclusive to community therapeutic recreation programs but is equally valid in the institutional environment.

b. Therapeutic recreation must conceptually and functionally accept the difference between the direct service approach and the process approach, and place increasing emphasis on the process approach. Only through a greater emphasis on the resource role of catalyst-facilitator by the therapeutic recreator can community recreators, rehabilitation agency staffs, volunteers, families of disabled individuals and the general public be enlightened to the leisure needs of the disabled and be able to effectively respond to these needs.

REFERENCES

1. G. S. O'Morrow, *Therapeutic Recreation: A Helping Profession* (Reston, Virginia: Reston Publishing Co., 1976), pp. 81–82.
2. E. M. Avedon, *Therapeutic Recreation Service: An Applied Behavioral Science Approach* (Englewood Cliffs, New Jersey: Prentice-Hall, 1974), pp. 2–5. Also, *The New English Bible,* I Samuel, *16*:14–23.
3. V. Frye and M. Peters, *Therapeutic Recreation: Its Theory, Philosophy, and Practice* (Harrisburg, Pennsylvania: Stackpole Co., 1972), p. 16.
4. Avedon, op. cit., pp. 5–6.
5. J. Huizinga, *Homo Ludens: A Study of the Play-Element in Culture* (Boston: Beacon Press, 1950), pp. 18–19.
6. Frye and Peters, op. cit., pp. 17–18.
7. Avedon, op. cit., pp. 6–9.
8. Frye and Peters, op. cit., p. 18.
9. Frye and Peters, op. cit., pp. 19–21.
10. *American Journal of Insanity,* Vol. 70, 1913, pp. 247–250.
11. B. E. Schlotter and M. Svendsen, *An Experiment in Recreation with the Mentally Retarded,* rev. ed. (Springfield, Illinois: Illinois Department of Public Welfare, 1959).
12. V. Rensvold, B. H. Hill, E. Boggs and M. W. Meyer, "Therapeutic Recreation," *Annals of the Academy of Political and Social Science,* Vol. 313, September, 1957, pp. 57–71.
13. O'Morrow, op. cit., p. 14.
14. O'Morrow, op. cit., pp. 178–201.
15. R. Kraus, *Therapeutic Recreation Service: Principles and Practices* (Philadelphia: W. B. Saunders Co., 1973), pp. 190–196.
16. J. Pomeroy, "The Handicapped Are Out of Hiding: Implications for Community Recreation," *Therapeutic Recreation Journal,* Vol. VIII, No. 3, 1974, pp. 121–122.
17. Ibid., pp. 120–128.
18. "Community Organization for Recreation for the Ill and Handicapped: The Kansas City Plan," *American Recreation Journal,* January–February, 1964, p. 19.

QUESTIONS

1. What guidelines to program development in therapeutic recreation can be elicited from its historical background?

2. Clearly distinguish the difference between therapeutic recreation as a service and as a process.

3. Identify and illustrate three issues which must be considered if the therapeutic potential of any activity experience is to be realized.

4. Compare and/or contrast the approaches to the delivery of therapeutic recreation services in an institutional environment, a community environment and a transitional environment.

5. Illustrate, with specific program examples or approaches, the "wellness" model and the catalyst-facilitator (process) role as these relate to the delivery of therapeutic recreation services.

Leisure activity is an increasingly important component of our economy.
(U.S. Bureau of Outdoor Recreation)

ABOUT THE AUTHOR

Karl F. Munson joined the Community Resource Development Staff of the Extension Service, U.S. Department of Agriculture in September 1970. Prior to joining the staff, he served as Project Leader, Recreation and Parks, at the University of Missouri, Columbia, for 1½ years.

His experience includes 6 years as Recreation and Community Activity Specialist with the Arkansas Extension Service, and 4 years with the University of Illinois as Extension Recreationist. In February of 1965 he joined the Federal Extension service as Program Leader, Outdoor Recreation, and served in this capacity until January, 1969.

Dr. Munson received his B.S. from the University of Illinois in 1950, his M.S. from Indiana University in 1954 and his Ph.D. from the University of Illinois in 1967.

He is an active member in the National Recreation and Park Association and is past chairman of the Personnel Advisory Committee and the American Camping Association. He also served as a board member of the Family Camping Federation and the Soil Conservation Society of America.

chapter 7

COMMERCIAL AND MEMBER-OWNED RECREATION FORMS

INTRODUCTION

In a nation where 60 percent of the labor force is engaged in service industries and a high proportion of service industries relate to recreation, the opportunities for business people with training in recreation are encouraging. There is going to be galloping demand for wide choices in ways of using leisure time. The recreation business person, trained to satisfy that demand, has a promising world of opportunity ahead.

> **A 1972 study by the Economic Unit of *U.S. News and World Report* estimated the leisure industry at $105 billion in 1972, up from $82.6 billion in 1969. The $105 billion was divided as follows: $50 billion for recreation-sports equipment and activities; $40 billion for vacations and recreation trips in the United States; $7.5 billion for travel abroad; $5.5 billion for vacation land and lots; and $2 billion for second homes. The article indicated that "a 'leisure boom' that has grown to phenomenal proportions will push $105 billion into the U.S. economy this year . . . And estimates are that the dollar volume of leisure-time expenditures will more than double during the decade of the '70s.[1]**

When one considers that most of this money is spent in the private sector of recreation (entrance, camping and other special recreation fees being the major consumer expense in the publicly owned recreation areas), it is little wonder that the Outdoor Recreation Resources Review Commission had the following to say in its 1963 report:

> **The most important single force in outdoor recreation is private endeavor-individual initiative, voluntary groups of many kinds, and commercial enterprise. Outdoor recreation starts on the front lawn or in the backyard. Day outings are often on private lands. People on weekend trips and vacations involving outdoor recreation usually patronize private accommodations, while some stay at privately owned cottages in seashore, lake or mountain settings. When they do use government-owned land, they are almost certain to patronize private business to prepare for a trip, to get to their destination, to make their stay more comfortable while there, to get home, and to enjoy the trip in retrospect.[2]**

Approximately two thirds of the nation's land and water areas and over 90 percent of the shorelines were in private ownership in 1965. Over 30 million acres of this land, water and shoreline area were utilized by the more than 130,000 recreation enterprises to provide outdoor recreation opportunities. More than 5.5 million of these acres were leased by recreation enterprises from the private sector (4.3 million) and government (1.2 million).[3]

DEFINITIONS

Outdoor recreation generally refers to those forms in which the participants are involved in some physical way. However, the term recreation also covers the entertainment field, in which the greater portion of the participants are spectators. One way of delineating the type of recreation to be discussed in this chapter is to say what it is *not.* It is not taxpayer-built or operated. It is built and operated on a self-liquidating and self-sustaining basis. It is intended to make a profit for its owner(s) or to pay for and at least sustain itself by the fees charged. In short, this is the "commercial sector" of recreation, with the understanding that it includes some not-for-profit forms.

The commercial sector covers a host of enterprises, including hotels, motels, and restaurants, sports tracks or arenas (including the professional athletes who perform in them), golf courses, tennis clubs, health clubs, theaters (including movies and dinner theaters), theme parks (such as Disneyland and Busch Gardens), swimming pools, private lakes for swimming, boating clubs and marinas, riding stables, fee fishing places, charter fishing boats, nature trails (even snake pits!), caves and caverns, sightseeing excursions, hunting guides, shooting preserves, pool halls, bowling centers, ski resorts, ice-skating arenas, vacation farms and dude ranches, vacation camps (youth camps), camping areas (for travel trailers or motor homes or tenting), adventure trips and picnicking areas.

Within each of these types can generally be found various subdivisions or variations. For example, riding stables may take the form of maintaining a string of riding horses for rent by the hour, with possibly instruction in riding for an additional charge. Another type of facility may also include, or may be solely devoted to, boarding and housing of horses owned by city dwellers. Some riding stables may be limited to ponies for the kiddies.

Commercial recreation also encompasses those individuals and companies that provide consulting, booking, managing and listing services, as well as those that manufacture, distribute and retail athletic equipment and supplies used by recreationists.

Some people like their recreation in a form that gives them a chance to actively participate physically. Some prefer to watch others actively participate while they simply relax and enjoy the entertainment. Thus we have recreation for participants and recreation for spectators.

Those who like their recreation to be of the active kind are further divided into those who like to travel away from home for it and those who want it near home. Nearly all active recreationists find themselves in both categories at different seasons of the year or at different stages in their lives. However, the need to divide the classes comes from the viewpoint of the entrepreneur, who must consider a different set of factors in planning for itinerant customers as distinguished from those who live nearby.

RECREATION FOR TRAVELERS

The ultimate in active recreation for travelers is to stay as close to nature as possible. Those who like to rough it are content to simply find a place among the trees to park their trailers or pitch their tents.

RECREATIONAL VEHICLES

Shortly after the end of World War II, people began to want to travel on vacations again. Many wanted to travel in their own automobiles rather than by public transportation. They didn't want to be burdened with unloading and loading their baggage every night and morning. They wanted, generally, to do their own homecooked meals (but not over campfires). They wanted to sleep away from the city's bright lights (but not on the ground). They wanted to be free to wander as they pleased across the country in a zig-zag course if they felt so inclined. So, to meet the needs of these tourists there developed a new industry—the builders of travel trailers. A report of the industry shows total retail sales of recreational vehicles in 1965 at $308,236,000 and in 1975 at $2,320,000,000 (with a dip in 1974 to $1,392,092,000 when the industry suffered from the petroleum shortage).

At first people with their travel trailers were able to find a place to park them in public parks along the way or in campgrounds built for tent campers or even on the grounds of some motels. This proved unsatisfactory, so enterprising businessmen and, in many cases, travel trailer owners, seeing the need, developed campgrounds designed specifically for travel trailers. As the builders of trailers added more and more conveniences to the interiors of the vehicles, the need grew for more sophisticated parking facilities, such as electrical outlets and sewage dumping stations to accommodate the self-contained trailers. There are an estimated 13,775 campgrounds in the U.S.[4]

People vacationing in travel trailers wanted to be able to make reservations ahead when they so desired. Businessmen, alert to their needs, developed campground directories and later associations of campgrounds through which they could communicate with each other to make such advanced reservations.

Travel trailer enthusiasts found that they enjoyed each other's company so much that they wanted to hold periodic get-togethers in which they toured as a group. This led to the formation of travel trailer clubs. This is the story of the wonderful world of travel trailers. It is a big industry. It had a real scare during the years of the gasoline shortages, but fears seem to have been allayed as of the present writing. An important outgrowth of the travel trailer that is getting an enthusiastic response is the motor home, which, as the name implies, is a travel trailer with its own motive power.

The business of listing trailer camps has in itself become one of the major enterprises, with catalogues being published yearly by at least half-a-dozen publishers. These catalogues provide information on nearly every question you might want to ask on the subject. Of course, in the American tradition, chains of travel trailer camps have developed, whereby you can travel from coast to coast using only one brand of camp. Most of these chains seem to be on a franchise basis, with local people actually owning and operating the facilities.

BIG GAME HUNTING

Big game hunting has long been the sport of, if not kings, then at least princes. In the twentieth century, getting to the places where big game is still to be found usually requires a considerable amount of traveling for most people in the United States. In addition, the outfitting of an expedition into big game country requires quite an expenditure of money. Teddy Roosevelt was a great exponent of the sport who gave it mass publicity. The sport has developed into one in which millions of hunters now participate every fall, not because costs have become lower but because greater numbers of Americans have become more affluent.

The increasing demand gave rise to the business of providing expeditions into the big game areas. There are more than 7,774,000 hunters who take to the woods every year in search of deer, elk or bear.[5] Today there are numerous outfitters and guides who specialize in this business.

Charges for an eight-day hunt are likely to run from $400 to $600 per person, with a minimum of three in the party. Horse, saddle, meals, packer, guide and camp equipment are furnished by the outfitter. The hunter generally furnishes only his gun and ammunition, hunting knife, sleeping bag and personal equipment, and meat sacks.

The season is short and beset with many financial as well as physical hazards, so the outfitters and guides must take in substantial receipts in a very short time if they are to remain in business.

BACKPACKING

True back-to-nature enthusiasts are those who take off on "shanks' mares" with only the barest essentials of man-made cooking utensils, bedding and extra clothing, and "backpack" from here to there. This is why certain areas of rivers and forests have been reserved for those who disdain modern conveniences in their recreation and don't want to spoil it by "civilized" contraptions. Wilderness areas and such trails as the Appalachian Trail are their natural habitat. They require some special clothing and equipment, but their purchases are modest in comparison with most forms of recreation.

WILDERNESS JOURNEYS

Wilderness journeys are now being taken by people who simply want to explore and mountain-climb, or take pictures, so there are outfitters and guides whose season has been extended into the non-hunting periods. There are also *wilderness schools* where the essentials of survival in the wilderness are taught, as well as mountain-climbing techniques.[6]

VACATION FARMS, DUDE RANCHES, AND ADVENTURE TRIPS

How pleasant it was for youngsters to spend their vacation days down on the farm was poignantly told by James Whitcomb Riley in his poem "Out To Old Aunt Mary's." Today there are not enough aunts and uncles or grandparents living on farms to provide thrilling farm experiences for all the city families that would like to have them. Instead, there are farm families that are making a business of hosting city people who long for the rustic life of the family farm for a few days or weeks. Despite the inflationary spiral, the cost of a week's bed and board with such a farm family is generally still within the $75–$100 range.

Dude ranches were started in the western states to satisfy the easterners' craving to live the romantic life of the cowboy. They specialize in such activities as riding the range and learning the cowboy vernacular, open air cookouts and impromptu rodeo performances by the resident cowboys. At the same time, most of the conveniences and amenities of the society set are retained. Modest prices generally are not a distinguishing feature of these places, although in recent years, some guest ranches have developed in the more modest price range, with less elaborate entertainment, of course.

Adventure trips include such experiences as mountaineering, cattle and horse drives, covered wagon trips, windjammer cruises, canoe and kayak trips, snowmobile excursions and ballooning.

All three of the classifications just discussed are promoted primarily by a New York lady with a zest for adventurous experiences. She started with the Farm Vacations Guide more than 25 years ago and has only recently come out with the Adventure Trip Guide.[7]

SKIING RESORTS

The skiing industry is one of the riskiest from a financial standpoint, since it depends to such a great extent on Mother Nature's willingness to provide snow at the proper time. The proper time, of course, is weekends, because that's when most skiers are able to indulge. Skiing is one of those sports that skyrocketed in popularity in a relatively short time. The development of mechanical ski lifts was the factor that made skiing possible on a massive scale. Snowmaking machines helped to make up for Mother Nature's frequent delinquency, but even they are limited in that the weather must stay cold enough for them to operate effectively, and at best they are not a completely satisfactory substitute for natural snow.

The tremendous size of the skiing industry is indicated by the 1974–75 economic report of the National Ski Areas Association. This report estimated that there were 34 million skier visits that year, with gross revenues of $405 million and payrolls of $91 million. Average days of operation for 1974–75 were 130, compared to 121 for the preceding season. This, together with an increase in revenue per skier visit from $6.76 to $7.10, caused average revenue to increase by 17.9 percent. The cost of a ski lift ticket for adults at all-day weekend rates was $7.94, an increase of 8.9 percent.[8]

The trend in the ski industry seems to be a holding pattern, with talk among the operators about the large "untapped skier market potential." However, "Ski area construction is at its lowest point since the ski boom started in the early 1950's," according to Cal Conniff, National Ski Area Association executive director, writing in the Fall 1975 issue of *Ski Area Management* magazine.[9]

TENNIS

Tennis is the "wonder sport" of the 1970's. The boom was undoubtedly the result of television, for the sport is not new at all. In fact, King Henry VIII was a devotee, and the tennis court was a landmark in the 1789 French revolution. For the most part, however, tennis remained a sport of the wealthy, who either belonged to exclusive clubs or were rich enough to have their own court on their estates. Public courts were made available to the American public early in the twentieth century. However, these were seldom kept in good shape, since they were for the most part clay-based and the clay was not too well attended. There were tennis teams in high schools and colleges, but very little attention was paid to the sport except once or twice a year when the newspapers devoted some space to the progress of the Davis Cup play, which determined the world championships. Then, in the late 1960's and early 1970's, television started showing professional tennis competition and the public discovered that it liked to watch the sport. Not only that, but people suddenly discovered that it was one of the most pleasant and cheapest ways to keep physically fit, and the tennis boom was on.

The December 1974 issue of *Tennis* magazine quotes a report by the A. C. Nielsen Co. polling firm on a 1970 survey that showed:

> **10.3 million persons playing tennis "from time to time" in the U.S. By 1973, the number had climbed to 20.2 million. This 1974 summer, when they ran another survey, it had soared to 33.9 million.**[10]

The same magazine reported that, according to a Harris Survey, spectator interest had increased so much that tennis had risen from being 12th among the major sports in 1972 to being 4th in 1974 (exceeded only by football, baseball and basketball).[11]

The zooming demand by the public has led to great proliferation in the number of courts available. This has resulted in a great increase in the number of construction firms specializing in tennis court construction. It now costs from $10,000 up to build an outside court, and in the neighborhood of $95,000 per court for an indoor court.

Tennis ranches are springing up all over the country, but mostly in the sun belt, where, to quote from the brochure of one famous establishment, you can stay for a weekly rate of $150 to $270 (food is extra), depending on the season of the year, and participate in a tennis clinic of 20 hours for $135. Most of the tennis ranches have at least part-time services of a well-known tennis professional. In fact, many of the ranches are owned by individual tennis stars. Hotels and motels are advertising the number of tennis courts available to their patrons. Condominiums are featuring tennis courts in their construction plans. How far it will go nobody knows, but of one thing you can be sure, there will be some fortunes made—and lost.

RESORTS

Andrew Hepburn, in his book *Great Resorts of North America,* states that:

> **From the days of Babylon, resorts were established and flourished in every region and in every age where a combination of four economic and social elements existed. The four elements were, and still are, wealth, leisure, suitable setting, and accessibility . . . perhaps suitably called the Sybaritic Law.[12]**
>
> **The court of the Pharaohs in ancient Egypt had resorts set in oases on the banks of the Nile, on islands in the Nile, and at Aswan and at Luxor . . .[13]**

The Romans introduced resorts with mineral baths wherever they colonized—from Aquae Solis in Britain to Ischia in the Bay of Naples.[14]

James Hilton's fictional Shangri-La was probably the epitome of the average person's fantasyland resort.

The first resorts in America were health springs in Bath County, Virginia—Warm Springs and White Sulphur Springs—established toward the end of the eighteenth century.[15]

The greatest growth in the number of luxury resorts in this country came with the spanning of the continent with railways. Many such resorts were built and owned by the railroads: "Sun Valley, in Idaho . . . was planned, built, and until quite recently was operated by the Union Pacific Railroad."[16]

Hepburn disclosed some of the more spectacular origins of some of the great resorts:

> **A barn with a spectacular view in the mountains of Vermont evolved into a small but distinguished resort called Mountain Top Inn. And a highway accident in New England started a hospitable farm owner on the way to developing the famous Mountain View House. The desperate needs of a Mexican woman attempting to homestead a patch of Arizona desert were responsible for the building of Paradise Inn, near Phoenix. A fishing camp that burned down on the shore of a Maine Lake triggered the development of one of the most luxurious resorts in the north woods, Severance Lodge. In New Hampshire a gruesome murder gave a big boost in patronage to the great seaside resort of Wentworth-by-the-Sea. And an automobile dealer's love of boating led to one of the most unusual boating resorts in the country, The Tides Inn, in the tidewater region of Virginia.[17]**

Many of these luxurious resort hotels, such as the Homestead in Virginia, the Greenbrier in West Virginia and the French Lick Springs Hotel in Indiana, have been kept up or refurbished and still provide luxurious surroundings. There are many more Americans now who are able to afford vacations at such resorts.

> **The rich still go, and so do the socially prominent, but they are lost in the new army of resort patrons. Resort life is different too. It is likely to be more luxurious; it is almost always more comfortable . . .**
>
> **Most students of the economy agree that there are probably several million American families that can afford the time and money regularly to visit the best resorts in the country, even though resort life is relatively expensive. There are additional millions that make occasional resort visits. And they take the children.[18]**

Because of this demand, there are some new large resorts just now going into use. Many of them combine vacation lodging and second home developments. Many of the new resorts initially plan for year-round use. Ski slopes are combined with golf courses, swimming pools, and tennis courts. Vail, Colorado, is one example, and Bryce Mountain, Virginia, is another.

Scattered throughout the country are thousands of more modest resorts. Some are heavily clustered in lake regions such as Lake George or the Finger Lakes in New York, Lake Champlain between New York and Vermont, The Great Lakes, the Lake of the Ozarks in Missouri and many, many others. The states of Minnesota and Wisconsin each have hundreds of lakes, a high percentage of which are sites of small fishing resorts, often just one resort per lake.

A Minnesota survey in 1970 covered 2,071 such resorts and 137 campgrounds.* The report showed the rates charged to be quite modest, running from $118.24 per week for a four-bedroom housekeeping cabin down to a low of $60.88 for a one-bedroom cabin.[20]

Another part of the report disclosed that the average resort size, statewide, is 7.4 units, and that more than one third of the resorts have facilities for campers. It also noted that "about 10 percent of Minnesota resorts now have some part of their facilities open for winter business (due to the advent of snowmobiling)."[21]

Wisconsin had 3300 businesses classified in 1966 as resorts, according to a report by R. A. Christiansen, S. D. Staniforth, and H. A. Johnson.[22]

Another study in 1965 of 47 resorts in Wisconsin scattered among ten lakes, all of them being European-type resorts, and the majority considered to be small operations, showed:

> **Twenty-four had less than five cabins. Only five had more than nine cabins. They averaged 17 acres of land with 505 feet of lake frontage. All were owner-operated with the period of ownership ranging from one to 34 years (average almost 12 years).**
>
> **At all resorts fishing was the major recreational activity and boats were provided for all cabins.**
>
> **The short recreation season was found to be a severe limitation. Rentals averaged about 10 weeks per cabin, early June through Labor Day.**
>
> **Income from the resort, in many instances, was a minor source of family income.[23]**

DEEP SEA FISHING

In most seaside resorts, fishing boats can be chartered to take parties out for a few hours or for a whole day of deep sea fishing. There is generally a minimum charge by the hour or by the day for a party of so many persons. The captain furnishes all the equipment, bait, coolers, ice, and so on.

CAVES

Certain areas, generally in mountainous country, have cave trips where sightseers are conducted on guided tours through spectacular formations

---

*It was estimated, however, that 506 resorts were not listed.[19]

made by dripping water over the centuries. Many of these are commercial establishments. Examples are the Luray Caverns in Virginia and the Cave of the Winds in Colorado.

RECREATION FOR LOCAL RESIDENTS

Year-round recreation is a part of the American scene, stimulated partly by the fact that we have more leisure time—owing to the shorter work day and week—and partly by the growing awareness of the need for regular exercise for health reasons. Hunting and fishing are probably the oldest forms of recreation for people who want to spend a few hours in recreational activity after work or on weekends, without much expense in money or time. As the demand grew and the natural supply shrank, both in small game and fish, alert businessmen stepped in to augment the supply. Now there are scattered throughout the nation fee fishing ponds where the fisherman can exercise his worms with more hope of getting some fish than in the overcrowded public lakes and streams, and shooting preserves where game birds are turned loose ahead of the hunter in a manner simulating natural conditions.

FEE FISHING PONDS AND LAKES

The development of these areas was greatly assisted by a program of the Department of Agriculture that paid farmers to build dams and impound water as conservation measures. The proliferation of watering ponds on farms and ranches helped distribute cattle and sheep-grazing more uniformly over pastures. It also conserved the water supply in low rainfall areas and reduced soil erosion. The planting of fish in these ponds added to the farmers' food supply and kept the pond from becoming swampy. This is how many fee fishing ponds got started. Now many farmers make it possible for a fisherman to loll on the bank with his line in the water for a charge of only a dollar or so per line, plus a charge of so much per pound for fish caught. There are an estimated 12,338 fee fishing ponds and fishing enterprises in the United States today.[24]

SHOOTING OR HUNTING PRESERVES

Hunting is a highly specialized business and thus is more costly to the customer. The business involves purchasing or hatching and raising the game birds—pheasants, quail, chukkers (partridge), and so on—keeping them penned under proper conditions until they can be released ahead of the hunters, providing bird dogs to assist the hunters if desired, and taking care of dressing and perhaps freezing the game. Shooting and hunting preserves in the United States total an estimated 1,412 as of 1975.[25]

GOLF

Golf has long been a sport that every sizeable community endeavored to make available to its residents. For years it remained a rather elite game, played mainly by those people who were able to afford membership in a country club, because that was where most golf courses were found. During the Depression and World War II, the number of golf facilities fell from 5,700 to 4,800.[26]

During the 1960's there was a strong move, encouraged by the U. S. Department of Agriculture, to increase the number of golf courses, especially in small rural communities, as a means of using to advantage the crop acres farmers were taking out of commission to reduce the agricultural surpluses. This caused an upsurge in the number of courses throughout the land and helped encourage industries to build in small communities where they had otherwise been reluctant to locate because of lack of recreational facilities for their workers.

Many of these golf courses were built under the auspices of local non-profit associations, with money borrowed from the Farmers' Home Administration. A move in the direction of removing the country club image was made by qualifying requirements for the government loans that there be no membership restrictions on account of race, religion or national origins. The number of golf courses in the U.S. reached an all-time high of 11,370 in 1975, with approximately half of these open to the public on a daily fee basis. There are now an estimated 16 million golfers in the United States.[27]

At the same time the Farmers' Home Administration also made loans to farmers to build income-producing golf courses on land not suitable for crops. This situation was satirized in the Lichty cartoon of a farmer leaning over the fence talking to a neighbor and saying, "You gotta diversify crops if you aim to keep up with progress, Lem! . . . This year I'm putting 20 acres to barley, 40 to corn and 95 to a public golf course." Many uninformed writers hooted at the idea of a farmer putting in an income-producing golf course. The farmers, who had the courage to ignore the jibes and had the business acumen to carry it off, found they could often make more net income per acre using their land for a golf course than they could producing crops and livestock that were already in surplus. They laughed all the way to the bank.

MARINAS

The Bureau of Reclamation, the Corps of Engineers and the Watershed program of the Soil Conservation Service, and the Farmers' Home Administration have done their work so thoroughly that there are few areas left in the United States that are more than a few hours drive from a body of water large enough to launch a motor boat. Where there are motor boats there must be marinas to serve them, even if only to provide a launching ramp and a gasoline pump. The number of motor boats sold in the United States is one of the most convincing bits of evidence of the growing affluence of the middle class American. Even in small towns in the dry western plains, one can always find at least a few high-powered motor boats parked on trailers in the driveway in back of the family automobile(s).

There are an estimated 9 million boat owners in the United States, with $15 billion invested in their boats and equipment.[28] The accoutrements that go with a boat range from fishing tackle to water skis, and the sale of these items provides a substantial portion of the income for the marina owner. In most cases, however, the most reliable source of income is from the rental of docking space for those patrons who prefer to leave their boats in the water during the season.

The 1976 report of the estimated consumer purchases of pleasure boats and equipment showed $2,539,600,000 total, which was exceeded only by the total spent for recreational vehicles.[29]

SWIMMING POOLS AND BEACHES

Public beaches on the oceans and lakes provide the basis for large numbers of concessionaires and suppliers of equipment, such as bathing suits, umbrellas, and locker and shower facilities. Other income-producing forms of swimming are private-for-profit and club-owned swimming pools. However, by far the biggest part of the swimming business is the building and servicing of family swimming pools in the backyards of 1,163,500 Americans.[30]

HEALTH CLUBS

This has a tendency to be a faddist type of business. People wishing to take off surplus weight are the foundation of the business, but there is also a large and growing number of businessmen who find exercise machines and saunas the most economical (timewise) way to keep their bodies in shape when their most strenuous activity otherwise is reaching for a cigarette. In 1976 Americans purchased $120.9 million worth of exercise equipment.[31]

BOWLING

"*Bowling* is the workingman's country club," someone has said. Anyone who has observed an evening of league play couldn't help but agree. The same camaraderie prevails there as will be found at a golf club. The bowling business surged forward after the development of automatic pinsetters, and it reached its peak in the 1960's with about 11,000 centers enclosing 260,000 lanes.[32] The two major bowling equipment manufacturers, AMF and Brunswick, struggled to outdo each other with the most generous financing terms.

Then the bubble burst. Many small businessmen lost their shirts and the big equipment manufacturers found themselves owners of more bowling centers than they knew what to do with. When the smoke cleared and the number of centers adjusted to fit the demand, there were, as of 1976, about 8,500 centers with 140,000 lanes.[33]

Bowling is able to weather recessions better than most recreation enterprises because it is one of the least costly of all sports. The experienced operators prefer to organize league play, which generally suffers very little from recession periods. In fact, one operator of a chain of bowling centers held his leagues together during a recession, when many team members were laid off, by deferring payments until the members went back to work.[34]

BILLIARDS

Once known as pool, with a looking-down-the-nose connotation to the term, the game of pocket billiards has climbed to a position of respectability in recent years, with many women now participating. However, it hasn't attained the mass participation of bowling, although the public spent an estimated $153.2 million on billiard equipment and supplies in 1976.[35]

OTHER ENTERPRISES

Opportunities abound for recreation entrepreneurs in such independently run recreation businesses as youth camps, riding stables, skating rinks (ice and roller), and picnicking and sports areas.

Youth Camps. Summer youth camps are a natural for farm families, especially if their farm is in lake or mountain country. Some have started out as vacation farms and then gradually came to specialize in youth until they became bonafide summer camps. There is an excellent nationwide accreditation and certification program carried on by the American Camping Association, with headquarters in Martinsville, Indiana. This is a model organization that other recreation categories would do well to follow. In addition to the summer camps, there are many day camps for children that are especially helpful to working mothers in looking after children during the summer vacation from public schools.

Riding Stables. Riding stables are another form of recreation that farmers can get into rather easily, because they have the land and are generally experienced in handling animals. All they have to learn is how to handle humans—which often turns out to be the big problem. Liability insurance is sometimes difficult to secure for a reasonable premium, but it can be done. A less hazardous type of horse recreation business is providing stables and boarding for horses owned by city people. In either case, location near a city or a resort area is a requisite of a successful business in this category.

Picnic and Sports Areas. Picnicking and sports areas thrive best when they are located fairly close to a population center. Here, competition with public parks is a major problem, the answer to which is providing food service with a convenience and appeal that will be the attraction to picnicking groups.

Skating Rinks. Ice skating rinks are expensive to build and keep up and cannot normally thrive without a large population center to draw upon. Roller skating rinks, on the other hand, seem to flourish in smaller communities but seem to have a faddist tendency; that is, enthusiasm wears out after a time and the operator must be prepared to move to another area.

RECREATION FOR SPECTATORS

It is certain that no sport started as a spectator sport, but simply as a form of competition between people with more energy than it took to secure the necessities of life. They devised games that afforded the opportunity to match strength and wits.

BASEBALL

Baseball started as just such a sport. It began in the days before the Civil War, in villages throughout New England and upper New York State. Connie Mack, longtime manager of the Philadelphia Athletics, tells about the early days of professional baseball, when he received "the then princely sum of ninety dollars a month for playing with the Meriden club."

> **Usually, a ball club was started by a lot of public-spirited businessmen in a town, who chipped into a common pot, out of which uniforms and equipment and a ball park were purchased . . . a team could be started and kept running on a capital investment of eight or ten thousand.**[36]

The National League was established in 1876, and in 1903 the first World Series was started.[37]

The National League now includes 12 teams (including one in Canada) and in 1975 had a total attendance of 16,600,630. The American League's 12 teams drew an attendance of 13,211,605 in 1975.[38] Pitching star "Catfish" Hunter set some sort of record in 1976 when he signed a contract with the New York Yankees that purportedly will yield him $3.5 million in the next five years.

The Commissioner of Baseball is headquartered at 75 Rockefeller Plaza, New York 10019. Headquarters of the National League is Mills Building, 220 Montgomery Street, San Francisco, California 94104. The American League Office is at 280 Park Avenue, New York 10017.[39]

BASKETBALL

Basketball was invented by James Naismith in December 1891, specifically for students of the School for Christian Workers in Springfield, Massachusetts.[40] Professional basketball teams are formed into two associations. The National Basketball Association has 18 teams, divided into 4 different groupings.[41] Their championship listings started in 1947.[42] The American Basketball Association, dating from 1968, is composed of 10 teams in two divisions.[43]

The NBA League Office is at 2 Pennsylvania Plaza, Suite 2010, New York 10001, and the ABA League Office is at 1700 Broadway, New York 20019.[44]

FOOTBALL

Football was started at Rugby school in England in 1823, and, according to the Encyclopedia Americana, was "Formalized by the Rugby Football Union in London in 1871." Professional football began in small towns of western Pennsylvania in the 1890's.[45] The National Football League now embraces all major professional football teams. It is made up of 26 teams and divided into the National Conference and the American Conference, each with 13 teams. Each conference is divided into three divisions.[46] Total attendance at the 182 games played in 1974 was 10,236,332.[47]

The NFL League Office is at 410 Park Avenue, New York 10022.[48]

The attempt to form a new World Football League lasted only one year, with 12 teams, and then collapsed.

All three sports seem to have reached some kind of culmination now in the New Orleans Superdome, which is big enough to accommodate any one of the three. It is as high as a 27-story building, covers 9 acres, can seat 95,000 people, cost $163 million to build, and lost $5 million in its first year of operation.[49]

It takes millions of dollars to own just one team of the big three professional sports. Even the food and drink business of catering to the spectators is a mammoth enterprise and not something that can be started by a "Mom and Pop" sized hot dog stand.

Bill Veeck, with Ed Linn, tells in the March 15, 1976, issue of *Sports Illustrated* how he arranged to buy the Chicago White Sox in 1975 from John Allyn, who couldn't meet the payroll for his players:

> **His proposition was that he would sell the club for $10 million, without the ball park and other real estate, or for $13.5 million with the park and the additional property.[50]**

Those are the kinds of operations financed by millionaire movie actors and business tycoons, and not the sort of thing the budding recreationist gets involved in. However, even the large spectator sports enterprises must have experts in the management of crowds and facilities in travel, feeding, and all the other arrangements that go to make up the final presentation of the entertainment for which the public is prepared to buy a ticket. These are the people that make it possible for the sports stars to be presented in a favorable and exciting light that will keep the spectators interested.

THEME PARKS

Theme parks are a form of entertainment that has only recently come into its own.

> **The most spectacular growth was recorded by the 40 major theme parks (the type which first appeared on the scene in 1955 when Walt Disney opened Disneyland in California). Last year the combined revenues of Disneyland and Disney World (Florida) set a new record of $68 million in revenue, a 19 percent increase over 1974.**
>
> **These theme parks outdraw professional sports by better than 40 percent. In 1974 the 68 teams in major league baseball, football, and basketball drew an audience of 46.9 million. In the same year 38 theme parks drew 76.5 million visitors.**
>
> **The Disney parks now account for almost one third of the theme park business, with Six Flags in second place, followed by Busch Gardens (5.1 million visitors in 1975).**[52]

Many of the theme parks contain wild animals in conditions simulating their natural habitats—even animals from such places as Africa. It is possible that these parks will take the place of circuses. These wildlife parks also represent a commercial counterpart to the modern public zoo.

Disney World, in Florida, is the ultimate in theme parks. On October 26, 1965, Governor Haydon Burns settled more than a year of guessing on the part of Floridians about what was going to happen in the Orlando area by announcing that Walt Disney was coming to Florida. By that time most of the land needed for Disney World had been bought or optioned. Florida would never be the same again.[53]

Professor Leonard E. Zehnder in his book *Florida's Disney World: Promises and Problems* says that Disney World is significant for many reasons:

> **One, the building of Walt Disney World was one of the most important economic events in the history of Florida. Two, it was the most widely publicized business venture in history . . . Three, Disney World is one of the major tourist destinations in the world. Four, it is the most extensive and expensive tourist attraction ever built. Five, Disney is Forida's major employer in the state's main industry: tourism. Six, the history of Walt Disney World provides an excellent case history of the development of a tourist area. It may be useful to planners in other areas contemplating similar developments.**[54]

A "news release circulated by Walt Disney World one year after it opened" makes some interesting points to show its mammoth proportions in the world of tourism:

> **On the basis of the first year total of 10,712,991 visitors from 'outside its borders,' the new Vacation Kingdom ranks No. 6 among the**

TABLE 7–1 Major Sources of Receipts and Paid Admissions – United States: 1972[51]
(Data are shown only for establishments with payroll)

Kind of Business	Establishments (number)	Receipts from Customers, Clients, and Patrons, by Source						Receipts from Other Sources ($1,000)	Paid Admissions ($1,000)
		Total ($1,000)	Admissions ($1,000)	Admission Taxes (State and Local) ($1,000)	Sales of Food, Refreshments, and Alcoholic Beverages ($1,000)	Share from Parimutuel Betting ($1,000)	Other ($1,000)		
Baseball clubs	152	120,207	81,910	2,966	4,720	–	30,611	19,811	29,544
Football clubs	46	144,440	99,518	4,371	907	–	39,644	22,364	18,010
Other professional sports (hockey, basketball, etc.) ...	173	151,193	94,758	3,321	2,098	–	51,016	9,918	30,993
Auto racetracks	593	102,989	81,675	1,163	8,348	–	11,803	1,983	(V)
Horse racetracks.....	247	684,232	82,550	13,512	9,076	528,003	51,091	20,405	58,332
Dog racetracks	43	106,020	5,840	967	2,329	91,883	5,001	584	12,979
Amusement parks ...	682	467,718	263,461	4,491	83,343	–	116,423	16,340	(NA)

> **'Nations' of the world; behind Spain, Italy, France, Canada and the U.S., but ahead of Austria, Germany, the United Kingdom and the rest.[55]**
>
> **The land which was purchased amounted to an impressive 27,400 acres, compared to the 230 total acres of Disneyland in California, where the actual theme park is on only 85 acres. The Florida purchase encompassed 43 square miles; twice the size of Manhattan Island, a little more than twice the size of the official city limits of Orlando, and about the same size as the city of San Francisco.[56]**

U.S. News and World Report for January 4, 1971, states that:

> **An unusual labor agreement is credited with having kept the peace for two years on a huge construction project (Disney World) . . . while strikes plagued the building industry elsewhere. . . . The Florida construction so far has employed some 3,500 workers in 18 unions, and more than 100 contractors.**
>
> **Despite the complexities, Disney World has escaped serious labor strife. In many other areas, prolonged shutdowns have occurred. President Nixon has stated that 1 out of 3 negotiations in construction has led to strikes.[57]**

Time magazine for October 18, 1971, states that:

> **The 6200 Disney World staffers, in general, are young: 3,300 are between 17 and 22, and every one of them is wholesome. . . . Boys must be short-haired, and girls are required to keep makeup at a minimum. . . . Once on the payroll, the kids were 'Disneyized' at Disney World University, where rose-colored glasses are part of the curriculum.[58]**

A *Sentinel* story by Dick Marlowe covered the topic of employment at Disney World. Here is part of the article:

> **Youth, neat appearance, enthusiasm, personality and that clean-cut look will win out over experience, says Tom Eastman, employment manager . . .**
>
> **Eastman says Walt Disney World would rather educate employes with the Disney philosophy than import experienced service personnel.**
>
> **The Disney 'philosphy' basically is simple—be nice to people.**
>
> **Newly hired hosts and hostesses will first go to school. Walt Disney World University will teach Disney history and philosophy.**
>
> **Eastman, 28, is an example of Disney's practice of promotion from within the ranks. Eastman went to work for Disney at the age of 18.**
>
> **Working his way through school as a Jungle Cruise ride operator, Eastman came up through the ranks.[59]**

An article quoted from *Forbes* magazine, May 1, 1971, gives the following information: The project was expected to cost $320,000,000 and by the time it was finished the company was expected to be "virtually debt free."[60] While the size and wealth of the Disney organization of today is almost beyond belief, among recreationists, its beginnings were almost unbelievable in the other direction.

A *Time* magazine article of January 3, 1972, tells how Walt Disney and his brother Roy started out in the business of entertaining people.

> **Walt was a young cartoonist and Roy had just left a tuberculosis sanatorium when they decided to start a Hollywood studio in 1923. For capital the two brothers pooled Walt's $40, Roy's $250 and $500 borrowed from an uncle.[61]**

Roy was the money manager of the team. Their climb to financial wealth covered a period of more than 30 years. Walt died before Disney World opened and Roy survived the opening glory by only 3 months.

Excerpts from a letter to the shareholders by Donn B. Tatum, Chairman of the Board, covering the 1972 annual report show how rapidly the money was rolling in by the end of the first year of Disney World:

> **At the same time, every other aspect of the Company's overall activities reached new levels of performance.**
>
> **In the process, our total assets increased by 22% to a total of $608,249,000, and our shareholders' equity grew to $460,619,000, an increase of 44% this year.**
>
> **Revenues were $328,830,000, an increase of 87.2% over the previous year; and a consolidated net income of the Company and its subsidiaries increased 51% to a total of $40,293,000, or $2.90 per share on a larger number of outstanding shares.[62]**

FESTIVALS, RODEOS AND SIMILAR SPECIAL EVENTS

There are apple festivals in the apple countries, snow festivals in the northern states, honey festivals, strawberry festivals, buckwheat festivals, and this is only a sampling of the list. Indian festivals are attracting more and more interest in recent years. Indian tribes are beginning to catch on to the white man's ways of attracting the tourist dollar.

The American Indian Calendar for 1976 lists 407 different Indian festivals in 27 states. These include well-known shows like the "Trail of Tears Drama" (June 19–Aug. 21) in Oklahoma and "Unto These Hills" (June 21–Aug. 30) in North Carolina. Celebrations total 59 in the New Mexico pueblos alone (10 at the Taos pueblo). In addition, the Eskimos of Alaska put on 37 different celebrations.[63]

Rodeos, a type of festival indigenous to America, are a part of almost every small town county fair in the west. Some have become quite prominent nationally, such as the Frontier Days in Cheyenne, Wyoming, and the Pendleton Roundup in Oregon. The Ski-Hi Stampede is the name of the annual rodeo in Colorado's San Luis Valley at 7,500 feet altitude. Most state fairs in the west feature rodeos, and indoor rodeos generally constitute the main entertainment at stock shows as well.

Professional rodeo companies contract with the big fairs and stock shows to put on the performances. They furnish the animals and the equipment and recruit the performers.

The Rodeo Cowboys Association keeps records of the points won by the different cowboys at performances all over the country, and at the end of the year announces the Rodeo Cowboy All Around Champion as well as the top money winner in each of 7 categories. Rodeo cowboys don't learn their trade from books. However, various colleges and universities in the west put on rodeo contests with rival institutions, so college students can no doubt start a career in rodeoing at the college level, just as baseball, basketball and football players do.

THEME RESTAURANTS

Theme restaurants have developed into a thriving business attracting many tourist dollars. The Knotts Berry Farm in California is perhaps one of the best known of this type. The Wall Drug Store in South Dakota is a variation of the same idea. The drug part of this establishment is minuscule compared to the sideshow and souvenir business. This is an excellent illustration of how a recreation business can be built up from the most unlikely beginning and with a particular type of advertising adapted to the conditions. Cleverly worded road signs begin advertising Wall Drug Store somewhere around 500 miles in each direction from the town of Wall. Bob Pennington reports that during World War II he saw a sign in Liège, Belgium, proclaiming "4,000 miles to Wall Drug Store."[64]

SECOND HOMES

The building of second homes away from the cities has become a booming business in recent years, and some developers have put together chains of such recreation second home clusters.

In some cases lakes have been built by the government or a local public body, and developers have been allowed to develop homesites around them. One such lake was built in Putnam County, Missouri, by a loan made to a group of citizens who had formed a non-profit association for the development of the county. Money to build the lake was loaned to the group by the Farmers' Home Administration. The lake and land surrounding it was then sold to a developer, who built second homes around it. Wherever there is suitable land in rolling, wooded country or near a lake or stream, it is not uncommon to find developers building second homes for sale to city dwellers.

In many cases such developments have taken place around artificial lakes built by the developers, simply because, as Harold LeJeune points out in a study made for the Upper Great Lakes Regional Commission,

> **With choice frontage on lakes and streams hard to find and expensive to purchase, real estate firms and individual developers have turned to constructing artificial lakes in order to increase the supply of water for recreation and of shoreland for home development.**[65]

He pointed out that questions have been raised about the undesirable effects on the environment brought about by some of these lake developments, however. Also, some taxpayers have questioned whether the increased tax base resulting from such developments will be adequate to pay for the increased costs of local government services.[66]

LeJeune's conclusions are favorable on both questions in the two projects his study covered. However, he raises a warning as to whether a community has given full consideration to the changes in life style that might occur from such developments and whether the local government should become more involved in controlling such developments in order to assure the retention of access by the native population to the area's resources.[67]

An article in *Investor* for October 1971 gives a report on "N. E. Isaacson —Developer of Lake Properties," who developed the projects studied by LeJeune. The import of this article is that while "Isaacson's sales figures place him in the middle of the nation's top ten land developers," his concern with the long-term environmental as well as financial impact on the local community sets him above "Most of the industry leaders (who) are west coast based promotion organizations characterized in the public eye as gamblers peddling postage stamp 'rural acreage' . . ."[68]

The "Big Picture for 1976" projects for 1977 for the east coast a slowdown in purchases of weekend homes and condominiums in resort areas.

> **Many resort developments of the past ten years were created on the premise that it was not the tourist but the sales of real estate that would keep the property viable and permit it to pay the high-interest loans obtained from the banks and other lenders. Today the lending institutions are finding themselves loaded with foreclosed properties located in resort areas from Maine to Florida.**[69]

PROVIDERS OF SUPPLIES AND SERVICES TO THE RECREATION BUSINESS

Supplying recreation businesses and recreationists is possibly a bigger source of profit than the actual fees for the sports and entertainment. For example, in the bowling supply business, AMF reported that revenues from bowling supplies were around $100 million in 1975, while Brunswick did roughly $50 million worth of business in supplies.[70]

Some golf clubs find they can make their payments on the mortgage out of the revenues brought in from renting golf cars to members and guests.

Parks and Recreation magazine's annual buyers' guide lists 424 categories of suppliers to the recreation industry, not including such well-known names as Spaulding.[71]

The following tabulation shows estimated consumer purchases of sporting goods by selected product categories.

Services allied to motion picture production numbered 855 establishments, with total receipts of $389,419,000 in 1972. Managers and promoters of baseball, football and other professional sports totaled 166 and grossed $97,064,000.[73]

The individual who invented the Frisbee has already made a fortune. Now he has started the idea of disc golf courses, which will increase his sale of Frisbees. The Frisbee is a plastic disc (about the same diameter as the traditional discus) which can be sailed through the air with the flick of the wrist.

Thus, while all of the forms of sports, entertainment, lodging and eating establishments discussed in this chapter are service industries that supply the public, there is a vast, almost unseen network of commercial establishments that supply and service those primary organizations. For example "producers, orchestras and entertainers" number 7,641 and took in $1,110,505,000 in 1972. Of these, the theatrical services numbered 1,249 and grossed $257,456,000.[74]

Another illustration is recreation planning consultants. There are adjuncts to the recreation industry that hold opportunities for great numbers of educated professionals who are trained in business management with a recreation orientation. The Annual Buyer's Guide in the January 1976 issue of

TABLE 7–2 Estimated Consumer Purchases of Sporting Goods by Selected Product Categories[72]

Category	$ Millions 1970	1976
Archery equipment	53.1	130.0
Baseball and softball equipment	66.9	173.6
Bicycles	318.3	957.9
Firearms and supplies	583.8	1,118.6
Fishing supplies	287.7	506.5
Golf equipment	348.8	587.4
Pleasure boats and equipment (including skiing, scuba-, and skin-diving equipment)	939.9	2,539.6
Snowmobiles	309.0	246.0
Tennis equipment	27.8	666.4
Camping equipment	86.5	386.4
Winter sports equipment	88.4	498.6
Athletic goods—team equipment		719.7
Football and basketball equipment		200.8
Billiard supplies and equipment		249.7
Exercise equipment		120.9
Recreational vehicles	1,149.9	2,700.0

Year	Total Estimated Consumer Purchases of Sporting Goods (Millions)
1965	$2,862
1970	4,795
1976	72

Parks and Recreation magazine lists 42 recreation consultant and planning firms.[75] The 1977 Directory of Products and Services in the *Ski Area Management* magazine for Winter 1977 lists 16 firms offering consultant and planning services in the ski business.[76]

Included in the category of suppliers and servicers of the recreation industry are the professional instructors, ranging all the way from football coaches to tennis and ski instructors. Abby Rand, in an article entitled "Take a Ski Instructor To Lunch" in the January 1977 *Signature* magazine, provides some insights on a ski instructor's lot. She reports that of the approximately "10,000 people in America who give ski lessons in exchange for money . . . only about 600 can work full-time during a complete December to mid-April season." Rand also reports that about 1 out of every 10 ski instructors is a woman, and

> **At Killington, the Vermont resort boasting one of America's most successful ski schools, about half the 123 instructors are women.**[77]
>
> **"Ski schools have become big business," says Rand, "and just as skiing itself has changed from an exotic sport to a high-stakes web of land developments, stock deals, mergers and spin-offs, so teaching techniques have become more intellectualized."**
>
> **American instructors tend to be college graduates, usually with degrees in education or physical education. Many have done graduate work.**

She quotes Werner Schuster, president of the Professional Ski Instructors of America, as saying, "You need successful educated people to talk to successful educated people."[78]

TYPICAL FORMS OF ORGANIZATION AND OPERATIONAL TECHNIQUES

INDIVIDUALLY OWNED ENTERPRISES

Individually owned enterprises are the most common form of recreational services. Restaurants, including theme restaurants and dinner theatres, motels, campgrounds, vacation farms and dude ranches, hunting and guide services, horseback riding stables, tennis ranches, golf courses, shooting preserves, marinas, health clubs, bowling centers, billiard parlors, moving picture and legitimate theatres, and travel agencies all tend to be individually owned. However, some in this group may be partnerships or local corporations. Restaurants, motels, bowling centers, movie theaters and, in recent years, campgrounds are sometimes parts of a nationwide chain or franchise.

LOCAL CORPORATIONS

Local corporations are likely to be the owners of such enterprises as arenas or stadia for professional football, basketball, hockey and horseracing, as well as owners of the individuals or teams that perform in those sports. This is also generally true of ski resorts, leisure- or rest-oriented resorts, festivals and amusement parks.

LARGE NATIONWIDE CORPORATIONS

Hotels, theme parks and second home developments at beaches and in the mountains (especially when they center around artificial lakes) are generally owned and operated by large nationwide corporations. There are many variations with corporation ownerships, too. Franchise operations are a common method of financing and managing some types of recreational enterprises. These have various forms, but generally ownership of the facility resides in some local individual or partnership or corporation. Often the franchise chain provides advertising aid and some management. This is often true when a popular name is the basis of the chain.

NON-PROFIT CLUBS, ASSOCIATIONS AND CORPORATIONS

These own and operate many recreation facilities, such as golf clubs, swimming pools, historic sites, homes or farms, festivals, nature trails, scenic gardens, theatres and second home developments at beaches, lakes or mountains. For many years most of the nation's golf clubs were owned and operated by non-profit country clubs. However, a recent report shows that daily fee golf courses now outnumber private courses.[79]

CONSUMER ORGANIZATIONS

Consumer organizations are another type of non-profit group. From snowmobiling to skiing and from camping to surfing, if there is an activity, then there are one or more organizations which promote that activity and inform their members of new products and places to go. Sometimes these groups stress conservation of the resources the activity uses, while other groups inform users of the latest techniques and equipment.

CONCESSION OPERATIONS

The concession-government business relationship has existed in various forms almost from the beginning of public recreation programs, and can be expected to continue at at least current levels in the future.

A Bureau of the Budget (now Office of Management and Budget) study report to the President revealed that, in fiscal year 1965, private investment by some 2,470 concessioners on federal recreation lands and waters was valued between $260 million and $290 million.[80] These investments included hotels, motels, trailer and other camping sites, restaurants, stores, service stations, marinas and skiing areas constructed and operated by private interests under contractual arrangements with the National Park Service, Forest Service, Army Corps of Engineers, Bureau of Sport Fisheries and Wildlife, Bureau of Reclamation and Tennessee Valley Authority.

Though some facilities have been built at federal expense, the majority of concessioners have had to finance the entire facility. This generally calls for a considerable percentage of capital to be invested in non-revenue-producing items, roads and parking areas, utilities, water supply and sewage disposal facilities, and other facilities.

In its 1966 report, the Bureau of the Budget estimated that by 1976, an additional investment of $350 million in new facilities would be needed on federal lands to meet rising demands. The Bureau stated: ". . . it is generally agreed that the use of concessioners offers the best means of providing the bulk of needed recreation facilities and services on federal lands."[81]

Thus, because of the large amounts of capital required by concessioners, this area tended to gravitate into the orbit of large corporations. The next step was for these large corporations to obtain concessions on a number of national parks, in an effort to obtain a monopoly.

This trend reached undesirable proportions when, in the words of an editorial in *National Parks and Conservation Magazine:*

> **. . . the concessioners tended to acquire substantial political influence and often influenced park management decisions heavily. Features of park management which might tend to draw crowds and bring profits to the concessioner, even though harmful to the basic purposes of the park, in terms of the protection of natural features, might be retained for long years after a widespread public understanding had emerged of their undesirability.**
>
> **Moreover, as time went on, and as the structure of American business tended toward chain systems, interlocking directorates, conglomerates and monopolies, combinations of corporations gained control of a number of concessions and achieved even greater influence in park policy determination. The influence was expressed at the offices of Park Superintendents and Regional Directors and also in Congress.**[82]

Thus, as so often happens, unchecked greed turned a good thing into an undesirable situation.

State and local governments utilize concessioners to provide needed services to a greater extent than does the federal government. Revenues to states from concessioners totaled $63 million and accounted for 9 percent of the total state recreation revenue in 1970.[83]

It is expected that the use of concessioners will increase as the public demands additional services and as competition for the financial resources of all levels of government becomes more acute.[84]

In addition to the enterprises directly involved in the provision of outdoor recreation opportunities, there is a large variety of related services, including bars, restaurants, sport shops, service stations, laundromats and bath houses.

MANUFACTURER-OPERATED ENTERPRISES—BOWLING

The bowling business underwent some atypical organizational and operational changes over the years. With the invention of automatic pinsetting machines and the nationwide televising of bowling matches, the bowling business took off like a rocket in the 1950's and 1960's. The demand for bowling equipment was so strong and profits in operation of the alleys were so great that the leading manufacturers of lanes and pinsetting machines were helping to set up alleys with what one writer called "ridiculously generous financing."[85] After a few years of this trend the inevitable result was that in many areas there were two bowling establishments where there was business enough for only one. The manufacturers found themselves repossessing more bowling alleys than they wanted. The major companies weathered the storm, however, and operated the centers, which they, in most cases inadvertently, acquired, and they are now making substantial profits from the sale of bowling supplies through these centers. An article in *Forbes* magazine for June 15, 1976, points out that "the average number of games bowled per lane per day—the key measure of success—is just about at its record level . . ."[86]

CURRENT TRENDS

In today's fast-moving world, most recreation activities are subject to rapid and far-reaching changes. Fortunes are likely to be made almost overnight by those who happen to be in the best position when some recreation form suddenly booms. This has happened in the recreation vehicle field, in bowling and in tennis over the last two decades. There may be sudden booms or busts in a number of fields, depending on certain underlying factors in our complex society. Some of the factors that bear on the trends are increasing leisure time, exercise as a promoter of physical and mental health, energy shortages, space constraints, availability of financing, increased participation of minorities, inflation, and television exposure.

LEISURE

Leisure is a continuing modifier of all we do in the recreation field. The tendency to delegate more and more manufacturing and servicing operations to machines leaves humans with an increasing amount of leisure time on their hands. The tendency of our society to use various forms of recreation to fill that leisure opens up a continually increasing field of opportunity to commercial recreation.

HEALTH

Ever since Teddy Roosevelt wrote his autobiography, promoting the vigorous outdoor life as a cure for most of the ills of the body and mind, Americans have gravitated more toward outdoor participant sports. Activities that do not require a big team of individuals are the ones that appeal to the greatest number of people. This is one reason why golf, tennis and bowling appeal to so many. They can be played in a meaningful and competitive way with only two people participating. The health factor can be depended on to continue accelerating the demand for such activity and hence increasing the need for supplies and services that fill the needs of such sports.

ENERGY SHORTAGE

There is no doubt that the amount of fossil fuels on which the modern world depends so heavily is limited, and we may be closer to the end of our lavish use of this energy source than many of us may want to face up to. Until substitute energy forms are discovered or developed, everything we do that uses energy is poised on the brink of sudden need for curtailment. We saw how the energy crisis of 1974 caused a sudden cutback in the recreation vehicle industry as well as the automobile industry in general. Most soundly-based industries in that field have now recovered as of this writing, but they are proceeding more cautiously.

Bicycling should have received a big boost from the energy crunch, especially since it is an individually-oriented sport. However, the energy shortage disappeared, temporarily at least, before many people had switched over to bicycling. Sailboating, however, was given a strong boost by the energy shortage and is rapidly overtaking power boating.

SPACE LIMITATIONS

As our population increases, the amount of land available to the average individual decreases. Hence there is mounting pressure to curtail sports that use large acreages. Golf was the primary sport to be affected by space constraints. This caused some modifications in the game; more par-3 courses were built and more golf cars were put into use to speed up play. ASTA's "The Big Picture—Travel '76" reveals that "Robert Trent Jones, the leading golf course architect, reports that he hasn't started a course in the U.S. in the past year." The same publication also reports that new courses are being built in the U.S. at the rate of 200 per year, but that old courses are disappearing at about the same rate.[87]

FINANCIAL LIMITATIONS

One of the problems of private recreation for profit is that of securing financing. Banks are slow to change and are not the least bit interested in financing untried ideas for making money out of furnishing recreational opportunities to the public. Government assistance in the field of private recreation has been very limited and sporadic. In 1962 the Congress authorized the Farmers' Home Administration to make loans to farmers and rural groups for the development and operation of recreational enterprises. During the most active years of this program, loans were made to farmers in 49 of the states for the development of income-producing recreational enterprises.

Most of the money was loaned at 5 percent interest, 40 years to repay on real estate and improvements. Money was also available through this source for purchase of equipment and for expenses of operating the enterprise; the repayment period for such uses varied from one to seven years. The recreational enterprises built with these loans included facilities for youth camps, golfing, marinas, hunting, camping, vacation farms, swimming, horseback riding, picnicking, sports and fishing. Some of these enterprises served vacationers from afar, but others received their principal patronage from the local communities. A survey of the repayment record on these loans showed them to be more profitable than loans made by the same agency for farming purposes.[88]

Recreation development loans were also made to rural groups to develop such facilities as golf courses, swimming pools, tennis courts and recreation complexes. While some of the loans were made to public bodies, the greater part were made to non-profit associations of local people, because of the difficulty of getting voter approval to incur indebtedness for recreation purposes. These types of loans were also made at 5 percent interest, with 40 years to repay. Loan repayment was made out of dues charged to the membership. For the most part, these clubs were a financial success and were able to keep up the payments on their loans.

Because the amount of loan funds available was always limited and also because FmHA was restricted by law to making such loans to communities of not over 5,000 inhabitants, this was a very limited program. It was understandable that the majority of voters in small towns did not relish the idea of incurring a bonded debt for building recreation facilities which most of them did not know how to use. It was much more appropriate to form a non-profit association of those who would make use of the recreational opportunities and would be responsible for repaying the debt.

This venture by the federal government into financing private, income-producing recreation was motivated by a number of factors. First, the report of the Outdoor Recreation Resources Review Commission pointed to a shortage of recreational facilities for America's exploding population. As one means of alleviating this shortage, the report recommended that financing be made available to private, commercial recreational facilities.[89]

Second, the Department of Agriculture had been struggling for several decades with the problem of what to do with the surplus acreage they were paying farmers to keep out of crop production. Orville Freeman, Secretary of Agriculture under the Kennedy Administration, conceived the idea that at least some of that land could be put to good use in providing recreational opportunities for city people and at the same time giving farmers who were willing to try something new a chance to make some money on the side by charging fees for the use of their land.

The third motivation for the recreation loan program was to try to make rural communities more attractive places to live. Since the 1920's farmers and rural residents had been leaving the hinterlands and flocking to the cities at an ever-accelerating rate. The vacuum they left in the countryside caused problems, and the overcrowding they caused in the cities created other problems. Industries were encouraged to locate in rural communities in an effort to reverse the trend. Yet industries had difficulty enticing workers away from the bright lights of the cities where they had more chances to take part in recreational activities. The answer was to stimulate recreation in the hinterlands, both to encourage immigration and to hold the current residents there. This worked as long as it went on, but the program was decelerated after 1969.

MINORITIES

Let's look at trends from another angle. Before 1954 black individuals were so submerged by the mores of our society that they had only a minor impact on the economy. Since 1954, however, they have played a role of increasing economic importance. As more and more of their essential needs (food, clothing and shelter) are met, they have more time and money for recreation. It would be reasonable to expect that blacks will have an increasing impact on the recreation market. The same principle applies to other minority groups, such as the Latins and the American Indians. Thus the social and economic emancipation of minority groups has gradually thrown open a whole new market for recreation. Minorities are participating more in such sports as golf, tennis and swimming. As they become more affluent and as social barriers continue to crumble, vacation resorts and beaches and many other recreation enterprises will find their business increasing. American Indian entrepreneurs are already becoming established in recreational enterprises. A folder put out by the American Indian Travel Commission lists

> **. . . over 100 campgrounds and trailer parks in the U.S. owned and/or operated by American Indians. They range from primitive facilities you can reach only by horseback to more deluxe accommodations. They are located from the Florida Everglades to the coast of Washington.[90]**

A similar folder lists 79 motels and resorts owned and/or operated by Indians and Alaskan natives throughout the United States.[91]

Inflation poses an ever-present threat to the recreation business. As people find that buying the necessities of life takes all their income, they must force themselves to cut down on recreation spending. This can take two forms—cutting down on the *amount* of recreation and looking for cheaper forms of recreation. The public can help check inflation by refusing to buy expensive goods and services. An article in *Changing Times* entitled "Good Vacation Lodgings—Cheap" tells about bed and board on college campuses during the summer months at substantially lower costs than current motel and hotel prices, and gives the name of a listing service of such accommodations. It tells about a Mountain club in upper New York State and New England with a network of campgrounds, hostels and lodges where rates are $15 daily per person with three meals.[92]

YOUTH HOSTELS

Despite the name, most youth hostels are open to people of any age.

> **There are now more than 150 hostels across the United States affiliated with American Youth Hostels (AYH). They are located in private homes, converted mansions, historic inns, colleges, converted motels and structures built expressly for the purpose. All are in close proximity to scenic, historic or recreational areas—the hostel in Washington, D.C. is eight blocks from the White House.[93]**

> **Generally, men and women lodge in separate dormitories, but some hostels provide family units. Rates range from about $1 to $3 per night, with a maximum stay of three nights at each hostel.[94]**

In many states state parks have lodgings where the charges are often lower than average. The *Changing Times* article also gives the addresses of places to write to for listings of state park lodging facilities.[95]

Many farmers provide lodging and meals for people who want to enjoy the peace and quiet away from the cities. There is a listing service for farm and ranch vacation places.[96]

TOURIST HOMES

You don't find much information readily available about the old-fashioned tourist home or guest house, but look closely and ask directions. They will turn up, low-priced and in key locations. One organization that does help in this area is Holiday Hosts in Washington, D.C., which "arranges accommodations for visitors in inspected and approved private homes and apartments."[97]

Public-interest groups have formed an organization to list accommodations such as youth hostels, YMCA's and YWCA's, college dormitories, church properties, institutional retreat centers and camping areas, according to the article.[98]

CROSS-COUNTRY SKIING

Cross-country skiing, or ski touring as it is sometimes called, has long been a favorite sport with some skiers, but it did not turn "commercial" until about five years ago, according to an article in *Ski Area Management* (Fall 1976 issue). The article goes on to say that:

> **Now, it is estimated that there are half a million langlaufers in the U.S., while the highest estimate placed on the number of downhill skiers is five million—and this after 40 years of lift-building and promoting.[99]**

There are differences of opinion as to whether cross-country skiing can be a profitable operation, but some operators are undoubtedly making money at it. The state of Minnesota assists the sport by paying "$2,000 a mile for the construction of either cross-country or skimobile trails . . ."[100]

Changing Times magazine for November 1974 gives the idea a boost by pointing out that:

> **Your investment in equipment is modest compared with downhill skiing. You don't need a lot of lessons to enjoy yourself, you don't have to join the crowds at the lifts and on the slopes at downhill facilities. Those are the reasons why cross-country—x-c as it is known to practitioners is such a fast growing winter sport in the United States.[101]**

The commercial possibilities are in charging by the head for use of the trails and from food and lodging income from the skiers.

INFLUENCE OF TELEVISION

No discussion of commerical recreation would be complete without mentioning the influence of TV on the industry. Numerous illustrations come to mind of how TV has popularized various sports greatly beyond what would otherwise have occurred. One has only to think of the booms in football, basketball, baseball, golf, bowling and tennis to realize the vast impact that television has had on recreation. TV holds within its hands the ability to make or break any sport from a financial standpoint.

So far, it seems, TV's influence has been for the best for all concerned. Its techniques have brought the TV viewer closer to the action—through the use of zoom lenses and instant playbacks—than even the referee or umpire is. Yet it has at the same time offered the overview—via the Goodyear blimp.

PROBLEMS AND SOLUTIONS

Recreation generally involves action. Action sometimes involves miscalculation, and that often means an injury. Injuries are the things lawsuits are made of.

LIABILITY

Liability of recreation establishments for injuries received on their premises is a leading problem of the business. There are insurance companies that insure recreation establishments against liability for injuries. However, such insurance is not uniformly available throughout the United States, and the rates are quite variable.

When a private entrepreneur invites the public onto his property to engage in recreational activities and accepts fees, he is responsible for their safety.

All persons who pay an entrance fee must be treated as invitees (persons who enter at the express or implied invitation of the owner, on the owner's business or for mutual advantage). The owner must exercise reasonable and ordinary care for the safety of invitees, warn them about all possible hazards, and protect them from other persons.

In general, an owner is not liable for injury unless negligence is proved. In turn, negligence is commonly defined as "failure to act as a reasonably prudent and careful person would under the circumstances."[102] The question of "reasonably prudent . . . under the circumstances"[103] is usually decided by jury trial.

The owner is responsible only for injury to trespassers (persons who enter without invitation for their own purposes and not for the owner's business) if their presence is discovered or reasonably expected. He must refrain from willfully injuring them, but has no duty to keep the premises safe or to warn unknowing trespassers of normal hazards. However, he must warn observed trespassers of imminent hazards or be liable for resultant injuries.

The owner's liability for injuries to licensees (persons entering not for the business of the owner, but where it is either expressed or implied that public use of land is permitted) is essentially the same as for trespassers, except that owners must use reasonable care to discover the presence of licensees and therefore warn them of imminent hazards.

Several states have enacted laws that intend to lighten the liability duty of the owners, with the objective of encouraging more rural landowners to open their properties for such recreational uses as fishing, hunting, and general hiking. The California statute is an example of at least one law in which the liability specifications have been changed to lighten the liability load of the landowner. However, the statute continues to hold the owner fully liable for all injuries if the visitor pays a fee for entering the property.[104]

FINANCING

Financing is a major problem with recreation entrepreneurs, to a greater extent than it is with other types of businesses that have a longer history. Banks are not accustomed to lending for recreation purposes, and many bankers are still infected with the work ethic to the extent that they do not encourage recreation for others.

The Outdoor Recreation Resource Review Commission in its Report to the President indicated that in the past, private enterprise has been limited largely to resort enterprises catering to high-income groups and to the development of private beaches, summer camps, riding stables, yacht clubs, ski areas, boating clubs, and shooting preserves. Since World War II, the scope of private activities has broadened somewhat in response to growing demands. However, the Commission concluded that despite the increasing demand, enterprises would not, for the most part, step forward to fill the gap in needed recreation facilities without a substantial increase in the availability of credit.[105]

The Commission indicated that there are opportunities for a number of types of recreation enterprises.[106] However, many enterprises, particularly smaller ones, report financing difficulties as an important limitation on expansion.

Specific financial-credit problems confronting private recreation entrepreneurs include:

1. Seasonality of business with resulting unstable loan repayment capability.
2. The high investment--low return aspect of some enterprises signifies a marginal investment alternative to both entrepreneur and lender.
3. The high cost of loan supervision. Lenders are unfamiliar with recreation enterprise features, and loan requests are frequently outside their normal "service" area.
4. The lack of collateral assets which typifies concessioner borrowers.

SEASONAL CHARACTERISTICS

The seasonal nature of most recreational businesses constitutes a distinct handicap. Summer enterprises in the northern states are the most severely affected. Some businesses are limited to a scant three months, and those in the mountains often operate even less than that. On the other hand, a cold season sport is one of the most seasonally vulnerable—skiing. Owners of ski resorts are wholly dependent on the vagaries of Mother Nature for snow, or at least cold enough weather to make artificial snow.

All outdoor sports are affected by wind, rain or intense heat, especially coming at times when the greatest crowds are expected.

Some recreation entrepreneurs have arranged to operate one recreation business in a northern state during the summer and then move to the south and operate another establishment during the winter months.

Others have found it possible to convert their northern-based recreation business to another type of income-producing enterprise in winter. For example, a summertime fee fishing lake can be used in winter for fee ice skating or fee fishing through the ice. A golf course in summer can be used for snowmobile trails in winter.

VANDALISM AND THEFT

Livestock and buildings shot by hunters and casual shooters, stolen gasoline and broken fences plague the farmer, while stolen or smashed equipment, fires, gas tanks with sand or sugar in them, broken tree tips and open gates are not uncommon experiences for the forest landholder. Broken tables, smashed toilet fixtures and lights, strewn rubbish and clogged toilets add to the cost of operating concessions and private campgrounds. It is not difficult to understand why private landholders are wary of opening their lands to the public.

Most vandalism is committed by youthful males in dark unpatrolled areas with few or no people around. Vandalism and theft can, however, occur in sunlit, crowded areas that are patrolled. Public apathy is the vandal's greatest ally.

Solutions

To solve some of the problems of vandalism and theft, the following measures are suggested:

1. **Build quality and stronger facilities to make it harder for vandals and thieves to have an impact. Studies indicate that recreation areas with better quality facilities experience less vandalism.**
2. **Strengthen the law enforcement and surveillance effort. Additional law enforcement personnel would help in those counties that are large in area but have small populations and understaffed law enforcement agencies. Private developments should be large enough to justify full-time supervisory staff presence.**
3. **Provide incentives or subsidies to landholders to offset vandalism and theft losses. This may persuade more landholders to open their lands to recreationists.**
4. **Increase dissemination of information on coping with vandalism. Much is already available.**

ENERGY SHORTAGE

Until this situation is solved, it will have a depressing effect on plans for expansion in some recreation fields. Businesses concerned with recreation vehicles are looking more conservatively at the future than they were a few years ago. Owners of motor boats face possible restrictions, because of the fuel they use and also because of the fuel it requires to get to the water.

The energy crisis could affect many types of recreation. While it may not mean going out of business, it could point to the need for reorienting the types of services offered, e.g., marina owners may have to direct their services away from motor boating and more in the direction of sailboating. People traveling to recreation spots may have to rely more on public transportation than they ever did before.

COMPETITION FROM PUBLIC FACILITIES

The economic success of private recreation enterprises is sometimes jeopardized by competition from low-priced public facilities and private operators with low monetary goals.

There is controversy between state and federal government and commercial recreation entrepreneurs as to the point at which public installations are competing with the private sector. Private campgrounds for modern recreation vehicles are the most controversial area, but restaurants, cottage and hotel rentals, and golf courses are other examples of public provision of recreation facilities that compete with commercial recreation business. There are a number of examples of installations representing substantial investment by the private sector that failed because they could not compete with later, less expensive developments by the state or federal government.

In competing for the public's business, public facilities have the following advantages over private enterprise offerings:

1. In a majority of cases public facilities are located nearer to the natural resource that initially attracted the visitor.
2. Interstate highway sign programs greatly favor public facilities.
3. Promotional and information programs for the public sector tend to overshadow the private sector's efforts.

However, a major disadvantage that should not be overlooked is that the location of tourist accommodations on public parklands can increase degradation of the very resources that were meant to be preserved.

Proposals That Would Help Solve the Problem

1. Public policy should aim toward increasing complementary and reducing competitive relationships between the private and public sectors.
2. Government should not provide services that can be more efficiently provided by the private sector, e.g., campgrounds, golf courses, ski facilities, vacation cabins and riding stables.
3. Government should provide business management advice (technical assistance) on how to conduct enterprise budget studies that will indicate the user charge that is needed to achieve the desired financial return on investment and management.
4. Government should conduct marketing studies to determine the price consumers are willing to pay for the various recreational services they seek.
5. Government should conduct marketing studies to determine the range of recreation charges by type of enterprise and important factors that influence the rate charged in various areas of the nation.
6. The federal government should assist state and local governmental agencies in compiling and disseminating information about the availability of private recreation facilities in their jurisdictions.

POOR BUSINESS MANAGEMENT

Many small recreation-oriented businesses suffer from lack of managerial abilities and skills. Owners and managers need assistance in financial management, investment analysis, pricing, personnel management, market analysis, advertising and promotion.

Often recreation enterprises are initiated by individuals or firms that are accustomed to producing or selling an impersonal product. Recreation, however, is a personal consumption item in which a wide variety of individuals with differing personalities are seeking satisfaction. Meeting this challenge requires special skills and aptitudes in working with people.

Some enterprise owners enter the recreation business to augment their main source of income. The very fact that their main income is low may indicate a lack of knowledge of basic business management practices.

Some enterprise owners (utility companies, for example) may enter the recreation business without adequate knowledge of the technical aspects of providing the necessary physical facilities for recreationists. For example, someone who knows little about the husbandry of horses may buy a riding stable; or the owner of a fee fishing enterprise may not know how to tend to the stocking and feeding of fish.

Suggested Solutions

1. The federal government could assist state agencies in providing a comprehensive public recreation advisory service.
2. Public agencies could provide technical assistance in business management, specifically on how to conduct budget studies that would indicate the user charge that is needed to achieve financial return on investment and management.
3. Government agencies could conduct marketing studies to determine the price consumers are willing to pay for the various recreation services they seek.
4. Professional and trade associations could encourage greater use of rosters of consultant firms offering planning and management assistance and provide more guidance on how to select and use consultants.
5. Public and private agencies could encourage the development of educational programs to provide management training.

UNIQUE OPPORTUNITIES

RAILROADS

Although in 1969 there were over 207,000 miles of railroad lines, between 1960 and 1969, the mileage in use decreased by over 10,000 miles. Additional abandonments of railroad lines are currently being proposed, owing to mergers and unprofitable operations.

In some instances, the railroad companies have retained ownership of their lands for other commercial purposes. In other cases, the land is being leased for recreational purposes.

Most of the nation's railroads have found it unprofitable to transport passengers. Some of their business has been taken over by the Amtrak Corporation, which might be induced to farm out segments of its passenger business to enterprising commercial recreationists. For example, a few years ago an alert young man saw an unfilled need of Florida vacationers who wanted to have their own automobiles to get around in but didn't want to drive the long journey from northern cities to Florida. He formed a corporation that leased transportation rights on existing railroads so that his trains could carry passengers and their automobiles.

There are numerous organizations of railroad buffs, some of whom have the courage to do what many of us would secretly like to do—operate a steam engine train. One such organization operates excursion trains that run from Washington, D.C., to various historic and scenic areas during the summer season. There may be hidden gold mines here for commercial-minded people who can bring together railroad property and railroad buffs and tourists who would like to have a vacation from fighting automobile traffic.

INDUSTRIAL PROPERTIES

Industrial organizations, including landholding forest, mining, and private utility concerns, often supply outdoor recreation opportunities for the general public. These are listed as non-profit, since the majority of these programs at best recapture only their operating costs.

Approximately 95 percent of the private forest industries are making about 65.6 million acres of land available for outdoor recreation.[107] Offered for public enjoyment are such diverse facilities as athletic fields, ice skating rinks, ski lifts, and picnic, camping and trailer park areas.

In addition to reservoirs and related land resources of public utility companies, thousands of miles of electrical and natural gas transmission lines right-of-ways provide opportunities for many outdoor recreation activities.

Thousands of acres of strip-mined land have been rehabilitated and converted into recreation sites. One such area has facilities for skiing and golf, and a number of once unattractive and hazardous quarries near populous areas have been filled with water to create attractive small lakes for public and commercial water-oriented recreation projects. The private utility companies, which also control vast amounts of land and water holdings, make many of their areas available for public recreation.

Private hydroelectric facilities have historically attracted large numbers of visitors, and most companies have either developed facilities or provided land and money to others for recreation facility development. Typical recreation facilities provided at hydroelectric plants include campgrounds, picnic areas, fishing and boating access, and swimming areas. At several areas, plant tours, excursion boat tours, museums, aerial tramways, and historical exhibits have been provided.

As of December 31, 1970, there were 428 private conventional hydroelectric facilities and 10 private pumped storage hydroelectric facilities under license by the Federal Power Commission.[108] Private utility and transportation right-of-ways may, in addition to being a recreation resource themselves, provide means of access to other recreation facilities. The possibilities of personal transport by means of these private right-of-ways have not yet been fully investigated, but it is likely that they will open new recreation opportunities to areas, either private or public, that were not previously available.

PRIVATE LAND IS WHERE THE PEOPLE ARE

About one third of the land in the United States is in federal ownership, and another 10 percent is owned by states, counties, and municipalities. However, approximately 60 percent of the nation's land and water area and over 90 percent of the shorelines are in private ownership.

Demands for recreation opportunities are mounting most rapidly in precisely those areas where public ownership of lands is least and private ownership greatest.

The settlement of our people in cities and the growth of densely settled metropolitan regions require conscious action to meet recreation needs that formerly could be met by individuals or by informal community arrangements. In rural communities, recreation was informally provided as part of reciprocal community relationships. For instance, tradesmen hunted or picnicked on the farmers' land in exchange for services to the farmers. In an urban and specialized society, however, people are dependent on institutional arrangements, on the market, and on public action to meet their recreation needs.

Land use customs and land patterns in the east, especially in those areas near population centers, limit the amount of open lands available for extensive outdoor recreational uses such as hiking and hunting. Some areas in the west have this problem to a smaller degree, but, because of the extensive federal land holdings in the west, a more prevalent problem is finding private land in suitable locations for private, intensively developed facilities to be used in conjunction with the federal lands.

Some of the overuse that is currently threatening the natural resources of many national parks could be alleviated by developing facilities *adjacent* to the national parks on private lands. In certain areas these facilities could be constructed on public lands and operated by concessionaires.

OPPORTUNITIES FOR COOPERATIVE SERVICE ORGANIZATION

There is no central information system concerned with private sector involvement and actions in outdoor recreation.

Private enterprises in recreation have been represented by literally dozens of trade associations and thousands of tourist promotion groups. This dispersement of leadership tends to prevent the industry from reaching its full potential.

Thus, in a nation that is so often over-organized, there is an overriding need to organize and/or strengthen cooperative services for the commercial sector of recreation for participants.

Advertising

Advertising is perhaps the most striking opportunity for small and medium sized recreational enterprises to organize to more effectively spread the word about what they have to offer. Why shouldn't fee fishing lakes, for example, work cooperatively to secure nationwide advertising?

All riding stables, to pick another example, have a message that should be brought to the public's attention. If the individual forms of recreation are not extensive enough to finance such advertising, surely the entire industry of outdoor recreation could muster the strength to advertise its wares. Such individually owned businesses as florists have developed cooperatives to advertise nationwide. The opportunity is waiting for some enterprising individual to organize an advertising campaign for commercial outdoor recreation.

Insurance

Liability insurance is not uniform in its rates for outdoor recreation. If recreation entrepreneurs organized, they could address the question of liability insurance with enough clout to induce insurance companies to listen, lest they start their own cooperative insurance company.

Standards

Uniform standards throughout the nation for all outdoor recreation enterprises would do much to improve their public image. This could be worked out if the entire industry would get together and establish guidelines and minimum requirements for recreation facilities. Some alert recreation-trained individual is going to grasp this opportunity to improve the business one day.

IDEAS FOR THE FUTURE

A partial answer to the biggest problem that faces most recreational enterprises—the shortness of the season—is showing promise in the installation of *slides on ski slopes for the summer season.* The Fall 1976 issue of *Ski Area Management* magazine describes two types of slides that are already in use. One is the Red Rumbler system, which:

> **. . . consists of a track made up of 7′6″ steel sections, coated with a polymeric urethane and having identical fittings. The rider goes down the slide on a polyethylene sled. The recommended top speed of 25 mph may be reached on the preferred grade of 12 percent.**
>
> **The Red Rumbler can be installed directly on a regular ski hill for summer use and removed for winter storage in the fall.**[109]

The same article describes another invention, the Alpine Slide:

> **. . . [it] is a permanent installation, and is made from asbestos cement. Sleds are controlled by the rider using a control stick. They can accelerate by moving the stick forward, which lifts the sled up from its runners onto wheels; or pull backward to apply the brakes to slow or stop the sled fully. For uphill transportation the sleds are hung on the chairlift.**[110]

Skateboard Bowls. The hazards of skateboarding on the streets and sidewalks, both to the young people on the skateboards and to less agile pedestrians, prompted the town of Ocean City in Maryland to build a skateboard bowl. The facility started with a ramp which dropped from 6.5 feet to 1 foot in approximately 35 feet, with a 5-foot curved wall at the end of the incline which could be ridden around as the wall tapered down to 6 inches in height.

According to "The Ocean Bowl Story," an article that appeared in the December 1976 issue of *Parks and Recreation* magazine, "An experienced skater could come off this wall at anytime to use the other slopes or the flat, open area to end his ride." Referring to the ramp, which is built of asphalt concrete, the article notes that "Skateboarders were on the ramp before the asphalt was completely cool, which helped to make the surface smooth and compact." Needless to say, this one bowl wasn't enough, and the one-half acre lot now contains two bowls.

The skateboarding bowl requires someone present at all times to supervise the facility and administer bandaids. There is also a problem of liability, which the city has anticipated by posting warning signs and requiring users to sign waivers.[111] Despite these drawbacks, skateboarding bowls could be a whole new industry for enterprising recreation entrepreneurs, as well as specialized contractors and manufacturers of specialized skateboards, knee pads, elbow pads, and protective headgear. It undoubtedly has more potential for the future than the hulahoop.

Shopping Center Amusement Parks are already with us, and according to an article in the December 1976 *Recreation and Parks* magazine:

> **. . . a cursory glance does indeed suggest that the factors of social safety, controlled environments, and available parking facilities favor shopping centers as a foci for future leisure and recreation activity development.**[112]

One such facility, 35 miles southwest of Chicago, opened in July 1975 as the world's first enclosed amusement park and shopping center. Another one, planned in New Jersey, would:

> **. . . offer an 18-hole golf course, ice and roller skating rinks, two indoor-outdoor Olympic-size swimming pools, eight indoor-outdoor tennis courts, a gymnasium, and a 32-lane bowling alley.**[113]

Automatic Computerized Scorekeeping Machines for Bowlers are already available at a cost of $3,600. Some people think that this is the comiñg thing, but others feel that the loss of the camaraderie that goes with the verbal jousting around the pencil-in-hand scorekeeper will detract too much from enjoyment of the game.[114]

Individual Submarines are a future possibility for nautically inclined recreationists, but they may not be available for a long time.[115]

Excursion Trips to the Moon have been demonstrated as technically feasible, but are as yet far from financially feasible.

RELATIONS BETWEEN PUBLIC AND COMMERCIAL RECREATION

Too little attention has been paid by the academic community to commercial recreation. Its importance in the number of people served and the monetary value of its services warrants much greater consideration.

Whenever recreation professionals gather for meetings and conferences, the commercial aspects of recreation are given only a cursory look; sometimes they are completely ignored.

There are several reasons for this. First, the commercial sector has not developed organizations to represent it widely on a general basis. There are organizations that represent different branches, such as the Recreation Vehicle Industry Association and the National Golf Foundation, but none that attempt to speak for all forms of commercial recreation.

Second, the National Recreation and Parks Association, which purports to represent the recreation industry nationally just as the American Medical Association represents the medical profession or the American Bar Association represents lawyers, has to date represented only those recreation professionals who serve the public sector.

Third, the commercial sector has not demanded representation in professional recreation councils, nor has it called upon the academic community to provide research or personnel for its industry.

Fourth, the graduates of recreation schools have gravitated toward the public sector because it offered more job security as well as the many benefits that all public employees enjoy.

What does all of this mean in terms of service to the public? Does it mean that there are less qualified people serving them on the commercial side than on the public side? This may be so. It is a matter worth examining by both sectors.

Janet Nelson, writing in *Ski Area Management* magazine, observes that "As the ski area business grows more sophisticated and more competitive, education counts in geometric proportions."[116] She concludes from the results of a survey made by *Ski Area Management* of colleges across the country, that "College ski management programs are going to be an increasingly important source for management personnel."[117]

The survey reports that colleges offering recreation programs with ski area management options included seven with four-year programs and two with two-year programs. Colleges offering ski management programs included one with a four-year program leading to an A.S. degree, three institutions offering two-year associate degrees, and one one-and-a-half–year program with a diploma. All either offered or required a period of training at a ski area.[118]

Nelson capsulizes her feeling with the statement that:

> **The ski school director with a college degree (in any subject) turns a better profit than the Austrian mountain boy with the dimpled smile and the charming accent. The mountain manager who understands hydraulics and surveying produces more and better snow than the off-season construction worker.**[119]

The above is an illustration of a very narrow and specialized kind of education including supervised practical experience.

All of the recreation curriculums should contain at least a minor in business and personnel management if the graduates are to consider the commercial setting as a career option. Probably those with a public recreation option would also benefit from more business management.

The career option in commercial recreation, therefore, has two more alternatives. One is to be a professional employee or manager for an established business, as discussed above. The second alternative is to use the knowledge gained from recreation education and field experience to develop a personal business in which the recreation professional would profit from returns to capital use as well as the normal returns to labor. This second alternative has not been a normal part of a recreation professional's career option as the community recreation career has. One reason is the historic dedication to public service in the recreation field. Another is the fear of risk in borrowing large amounts of capital. This is not the same as farming today, in which many new farmers are well-prepared college graduates.

Certainly there should not be any bitter rivalry between the two sectors of recreation. The mission of both should be to provide better service to the public. There should be friendly competition to see which can do this more effectively. If a particular need offers the opportunity for businessmen to serve the public on a profitable basis, then public administrators should encourage the private sector to take advantage of that opportunity. By the same token, if the commercial recreation entrepreneur finds himself unable to render the best service needed by the public, he should call upon the public sector for assistance. Under no circumstances should public administrators deliberately build facilities and services to try to take business away from commercial interests nearby that are already adequately providing those services at reasonable charges.

Is there adequate exchange of information and personnel between the academic community and recreation consultants? Or do they attempt to avoid each other?

Perhaps there should be a definition of general boundary lines. Shouldn't the public sector attempt to provide basic, no-frills recreation facilities and services free, or at minimum rates, and shouldn't it leave for the commercial sector the offering of more sophisticated facilities and services for those who can afford to pay more?

Some public officials have an emotional dedication concerning the responsibility of public agencies to supply quality recreation facility development. The public agencies *do* have a responsibility to provide quality recreation experiences for the public. However, it would take less money to encourage and regulate private direct recreation provision (both on and off public lands) than it would to directly provide all facilities and services with the public dollar. The rest of the tight public dollar could be used to provide non–income-producing recreation activities and to serve low-resource families that cannot afford the higher fee activities.

There are areas where only the commercial sector can adequately fill the needs, and yet those needs are not being adequately met. Why? Perhaps a nationwide conference should be called of representatives of the two sectors to draw up a statement of principles to guide *all* recreation professionals—public and private-commercial.

CRIME AND RECREATION

There is an obverse side to the commercial recreation coin. Its sole purpose is financial exploitation of the emotions. Most of it is outside the law.

In some cases it has been taken over by public agencies. This has been justified on the basis that if it can't be stopped, then by bringing it into the open, under public supervision, it can at least be controlled and the financial benefits retained by all of organized society instead of by a small group of organized criminals.

Drug abuse, gambling and prostitution constitute most of the "recreation" in this category. Any form of recreation can generally be corrupted by association with any of these three activities. Since participation in this side of the entertainment field is generally against the law, this book will make no attempt to analyze its financial potential.

Crime can penetrate any legitimate business or profession, and recreation is no exception.

REFERENCES

1. "Leisure Boom: Biggest Ever and Still Growing," *U.S. News and World Report,* April 12, 1972.
2. "Outdoor Recreation for America," A Report to the President and to the Congress by the Outdoor Recreation Resources Commission (the *ORRRC Report*), 1962, p. 157.
3. "Private Sector Study of Outdoor Recreation Enterprises," Chilton Research Service, 1965.
4. *Private Sector Inventory,* Estimates on the National Association of Conservation Districts Survey (NACD Survey).
5. *Nilo Farms* publication.
6. Paul Petzoldt, *The Wilderness Handbook* (New York: W. W. Norton and Co., 1974).
7. Pat Dickerman, *Farm, Ranch and Countryside Guide* and *Adventure Trip Guide,* 36 East 57 St., New York, New York 10022.
8. Cal Conniff, "Economic Study," *Ski Area Management,* Winter, 1976, p. 19.
9. "Growth or No Growth," *Ski Area Management,* Fall, 1975, p. 8.
10. *Tennis,* December, 1974. p. 16.
11. Ibid.
12. Andrew Hepburn, *Great Resorts of North America* (Garden City, New York: Doubleday, 1965), p. ix.
13. Ibid, p. x.
14. Ibid.
15. Ibid. p. xii.
16. Ibid., p. xiii.
17. Ibid., p. xv.
18. Ibid., p. xvi.
19. Dayton, M. Larson, and Laurence R. Simonson, *The Minnesota Resort and Campground Rate Structures, 1973, Special Report 50–1974,* Extension Service, University of Minnesota, p. 3.
20. Ibid., p. 4.
21. Ibid., p. 7.
22. R. A. Christiansen, S. D. Staniforth and H. A. Johnson, *Some Economic Aspects of American Plan Resorts in Wisconsin, 1967,* Research Report 72, University of Wisconsin and USDA.
23. Rollin Cooper, S. D. Staniforth, Aaron Johnson and R. A. Christiansen, *Cabin Resort Income In The Near North,* Research Report 35, 1965, p. 1.
24. *Private Sector Inventory* (NACD Survey).
25. *Nilo Farms* publication.
26. *National Golf Foundation* (707 Merchandise Mart, Chicago, Illinois 60654), Information Sheet ST 1, January 1, 1976.
27. Ibid.
28. "Showtime Showcase," *The Boating Industry,* Vol. 5, No. 1, Fall, 1976, p. 116.
29. Irwin Broh and Associates, 1001 East Touhy Ave., Des Plaines, Illinois 60018, from a report for the National Sporting Goods Association.
30. National Swimming Pool Institute, 2000 K St., N.W., Washington, D.C.
31. Broh, op. cit.
32. "Striking It Rich Again," *Forbes,* June 15, 1976, p. 68.
33. Ibid.
34. Ibid.
35. Broh, op. cit.
36. Connie Mack, "The Bad Old Days," *Saturday Evening Post,* May/June, 1976, p. 44.
37. Roger Kahn, "Baseball: State of the Game," *Esquire,* July, 1976, pp. 20–22.
38. *World Almanac & Book of Facts,* 1976, p. 839.
39. Ibid., p. 858.
40. Ibid., p. 839.
41. Ibid., p. 835.
42. Ibid., p. 836.
43. Ibid., p. 838.
44. Ibid., p. 858.
45. *Encyclopedia Americana,* 1976, Vol. 11, p. 531.
46. *World Almanac,* p. 860.

47. Ibid., p. 867.
48. Ibid., p. 859.
49. *Newsweek,* Jan. 26, 1976, p. 56.
50. Bill Veeck, with Ed Linn, "Back Where I Belong," *Sports Illustrated,* March 15, 1976, pp. 73–81.
51. *1972 Census of Selected Service Industries, Commercial Spectator Sports and Amusement Parks,* Table 24, Census Bureau, Suitland, Maryland.
52. "Commercial Travel Attractions—Theme Parks," *The Big Picture—Travel '76,* Annual Report World Travel Trends and Markets, Vol. 21, p. 33.
53. Leonard E. Zehnder, *Florida's Disney World: Promises and Problems* (Tallahassee, Florida: Peninsular Publishing Co., 1975), p. 5.
54. Ibid., p. 2.
55. Ibid., p. 3.
56. Ibid., p. 6.
57. Ibid., p. 178.
58. Ibid., p. 215.
59. Ibid., p. 185.
60. Ibid., p. 192.
61. Ibid., p. 236.
62. Ibid., p. 287.
63. "American Indian Calendar, 1976" Superintendent of Documents, Government Printing Office, Washington, D. C. 20402, pp. 1–37.
64. Interview with Robert M. Pennington, native of South Dakota.
65. Harold LeJeune, *Economic Impacts of Artificial Lake Development: Lakes Sherwood & Camelot—A Case History,* Inland Lakes Demonstration Project Report, Upper Great Lakes Regional Commission, May, 1972, p. 1.
66. Ibid., p. 2.
67. Ibid., pp. 41–45.
68. "N.E. Isaacson—Developer of Lake Properties," *Investor,* Vol. 2, No. 8, Unidex Publishing Co., Inc., 611 N. Broadway, Milwaukee, Wisconsin 53202, p. 33.
69. "Commercial Travel Attractions—Theme Parks," op. cit., p. 34.
70. "Striking It Rich Again."
71. *Parks & Recreation,* January, 1976, Official Publication of the National Recreation and Parks Association, 1601 N. Kent St., Arlington, Virginia 22209, pp. 70–102.
72. Broh, op. cit.
73. 1971 Census of Selected Service Industries SC72-A-52, Table 1, Census Bureau, Suitland, Maryland.
74. Ibid.
75. *Parks & Recreation,* op. cit., p. 79.
76. *Ski Area Management,* Winter, 1977, Vol. 16, No. 1, p. 57.
77. Abby Rand, "Take a Ski Instructor to Lunch," *Signature,* Media Services, Division of Diners Club, Inc., 260 Madison Ave., New York, New York 10016, p. 42.
78. Ibid., p. 44.
79. National Golf Foundation.
80. "Study of Concessions on Federal Lands Available for Public Recreation," Bureau of the Budget, October, 1966.
81. Ibid.
82. Editorial, *National Parks and Conservation Magazine,* December, 1974, p. 2.
83. *State Park Statistics, 1970,* National Conference on State Parks, National Recreation and Parks Association, August, 1971.
84. "Study of Concessions . . . ," *op. cit.*
85. "Striking It Rich Again."
86. Ibid.
87. "Commercial Travel Attractions—Theme Parks."
88. *For Your Information No. 59,* Publication Staff, Farmers' Home Administration, USDA, Washington, D.C. 20250, November 12, 1976.
89. *ORRRC Report,* p. 158.
90. *Campgrounds and Trailer Parks,* published by American Indian Travel Commission, Suite 550 Westland Bank Building, 10403 W. Colfax Ave., Lakewood, Colorado 80215.
91. "Motels & Resorts," published by American Indian Travel Commission, Suite 550 Westland Bank Building, 10403 W. Colfax Ave., Lakewood, Colorado 80215.
92. Changing Times, May, 1975, p. 18.
93. Ibid.
94. Ibid., p. 19.
95. Ibid., p. 20.
96. Ibid.
97. Ibid., p. 21.
98. Ibid.

99. *Ski Area Management,* Fall, 1976, Vol. 15, No. 4, p. 30.
100. Ibid.
101. "Like to Try Cross Country Skiing," *Changing Times,* November, 1974, p. 11.
102. *Liability and Insurance Protection,* Extension Bulletin 58, Cooperative Extension Service, Michigan State University, July, 1967, p. 4.
103. Ibid., p. 8.
104. Ibid., p. 5.
105. *ORRRC Report,* p. 158.
106. Ibid.
107. *American Forest Institute Report.*
108. *Recreation Opportunities At Hydroelectric Projects Licensed by the Federal Power Commission,* Federal Power Commission, October, 1970, Superintendent of Documents, U.S. Government Printing Office, Washington, D.C. 20402.
109. "Rumble and Slide to Summer Profits," *Ski Area Management,* Vol. 15, No. 4, Fall, 1976, p. 39.
110. Ibid.
111. "The Ocean Bowl Story," *Parks and Recreation,* December, 1976, p. 14.
112. "Leisure In The Modern Market Place," *Parks and Recreation,* December, 1976, p. 11.
113. Ibid., p. 10.
114. "Striking It Rich Again."
115. "Future Leisure Environments," USDA Forestry Research Paper NE-301, p. 7.
116. *Ski Area Management,* Vol. 14, No. 4, Fall, 1975, p. 30.
117. Ibid.
118. Ibid., p. 31.
119. Ibid., p. 30.

QUESTIONS

1. What distinguishing characteristic separates the recreation forms discussed in this chapter from other recreation forms?

2. This chapter divides commercial and member-owned recreation into four categories. Name them. Would you divide the subject differently? If so, how?

3. How would you describe a theme park? When was the first theme park built in the United States? What is its name and location?

4. What recreational activity do you think would be most severely affected by a sudden energy shortage? Why?

5. Do you think the recreation industry would be doomed if the United States was forced to cut its energy usage in half? Explain.

6. Name some commercial recreation forms in which you think a person with a degree in recreation could find employment. What types of jobs do you think would be offered?

7. What is a "vacation farm"?

8. What idea for the future could you propose that has not been mentioned in that section?

Employee recreation provides an opportunity for those who work together to become friends in a leisure setting. (U.S. Bureau of Outdoor Recreation)

ABOUT THE AUTHOR

Frank Guadagnolo, currently a faculty member at The Pennsylvania State University, completed his Bachelor's and Master's degree programs at California State University, Sacramento, and then received a Ph.D. degree from Oregon State University. Interlaced throughout his pursuit of advanced degrees was a ten-year span of full-time employment in the parks and recreation field. Upon receiving his undergraduate degree, Dr. Guadagnolo accepted a supervisory position with one of the nation's largest industrial recreation programs. During his tenure with the Aerojet General Corporation of Sacramento, California, the author was actively involved in all phases of employee recreation.

Upon completion of course work for the Master of Arts degree, Dr. Guadagnolo joined the West Coast community of El Cerrito, California, in the capacity of recreation supervisor. Early in 1969 he was appointed Director of the combined El Cerrito Parks and Recreation Department in El Cerrito. In the Fall of 1972 he returned to the academic setting, whereupon, after completing the doctoral program at Oregon State University, he joined The Pennsylvania State University faulty in the capacity of Assistant Professor. Currently his academic interests center on the psycho-social dimensions of leisure and the administration of parks and recreation field, particularly as related to collective bargaining and legal aspects.

chapter 8

EMPLOYEE RECREATION

The basic objective of industrial recreation is to recognize man's needs as a social entity.[3]

Robert W. Galvin
Chairman of the Board
Motorola Incorporated

LOOKING BACK

From its first provisions somewhat over 120 years ago, industrial recreation has developed into a multi-billion dollar leisure delivery system; some estimates suggest that a six billion dollar annual commitment will be reached by the end of the 1970's.[1] Although it is generally agreed that industrial recreation is a post--World War II movement, historically many of the current provisions had their beginnings during the 1800's and shortly after the turn of the nineteenth century.

It was well over a century ago that Frederick Engels suggested that employee excesses at the local pubs and brothels were results of impersonal and dehumanizing work conditions.[2] Although these observations were directed towards England's mill workers, similar conditions existed in the United States. At various times during the nineteenth century labor unions attempted to improve conditions; however, for the most part the brutalization of the American worker continued. Many of the early provisions of employee recreation could not be termed altruistic on the part of industry. Generally, management's decision to grant an employee benefit was predicated on the probable financial return. Equating the worker to a piece of machinery, management speculated that the provision of wholesome leisure alternatives might contribute to a much more efficient worker on Monday morning.

> **Employees, having failed to use their leisure time to get out of their rut, may return to the job feeling deeply mired.[3]**
>
> *Sanford McDonnell*
> *President and Chief Executive Officer*
> *McDonnell Douglas Corporation*

The development of a community library in 1854 by the Peacedale Manufacturing Company of Peacedale, Rhode Island, is generally recognized as the starting point in the industrial recreation movement. It was some 15 years later, however, before the first major effort in employee recreation came into existence. The Young Men's Christian Association promoted and sponsored a substantial number of recreation programs for thousands of workers employed along the Union Pacific Railroad. Commitments of full-time YMCA staff coupled with assistance from labor unions allowed the YMCA to begin offering employee recreation services in a variety of industries. To this day the YMCA has continued to play a major role in providing recreation services to business and industry.

As noted in Anderson's definitive historical examination of industrial recreation, several landmark developments occurred during the late 1800's, both in terms of facility development and services offered.[4] The Conant Thread Company (1870) is recognized as offering one of the first annual employee excursions; shortly thereafter, Allis Chalmers established the first annual company picnic. In 1878 the Ludlow Manufacturing Company established an employee game room; some 18 years later the firm formed what is considered the first employee recreation association.

Although a myriad of "firsts" could be cited, the most notable thrust during the 1880's and 1890's was the increasing sponsorship of competitive athletics. Leagues in baseball, riflery, rowing and a host of other team sports became the mainstay of industrial recreation. Interestingly, this emphasis on competitive athletics remained until only recently.

Even with the social movement prior to and during the turn of the nineteenth century, provisions for employee recreation were almost exclusively limited to the larger firms who were willing to financially underwrite such services. Surveys conducted during the 1920's identified just a few hundred companies who were offering any form of employee recreation.[5] During the 1920's recreation associations were formed which for the first time allowed smaller firms to collectively sponsor recreation activities. Frequently these associations sought co-sponsorship with municipalities, and thus were assured of needed facilities.

Until the Depression years industrial recreation encountered a slow but continuous growth. With the beginning of the Great Depression in 1929, however, significant reductions in funding for employee recreation became the rule. Management was hard pressed to defend expenditures on employee recreation while it was terminating substantial numbers of employees.

With the advent of World War II attention was once again directed toward the American worker. Employee unions and management alike began developing facilities which not only housed ongoing athletic programs but also served a broader range of leisure pursuits, including cultural, social and educational activities. Concurrent with the surge in industrial recreation was the creation of full-time professional positions. As with most movements, the industrial recreation directors were encountering growing pains. Therefore, under the guidance of Dr. Floyd Eastwood in 1941, the directors came together to share their common concerns. An outgrowth of this meeting was the formation of the Industrial Recreation Association, currently known as the National Industrial Recreation Association. The National Industrial Recreation Association will be explored in greater depth later in this chapter.

During the past quarter century industrial recreation has expanded both in the nature of services and in the total number of companies developing employee recreation programs. Gary McCormick, former President of NIRA, noted that some 50,000 privately owned American companies are now offering some form of employee recreation. He further noted that there are perhaps only 300 or so that have one or more full-time staff members, with the remaining firms staffing on a part-time basis or using volunteers and employee organizations for the development of programs.

Recreation dollars return dividends in the form of personal enrichment, improved health, higher morale, and greater productivity.[6]

Hon. A. Garnet Brown
Minister of Recreation
Province of Nova Scotia

REASON FOR BEING

With what has become a rather massive financial commitment by industry, one would assume that substantial evidence is available to convince management that dollars used for employee recreation are well spent, particularly as related to cost-benefit. In examining the research completed to date, however, the industrial recreation director would find little data in support of the often claimed values of employee recreation.[7,8]

Don Neer, former Executive Secretary of NIRA, itemized the benefits of industrial recreation, among them: improvement of physical health; reduction of tension and fatigue; employee recognition; leadership development; reduced absenteeism and job turnover; development of good community relations; breakdown of distinctions between race, creed and color, and between labor and management; development of friendships; protection of employees from adverse commercialized recreation areas; increase in employee involvement in company activities; and improvement of employee morale.[9]

While a few of these benefits may have a tinge of paternalism, for the most part, they can be characterized as positive. Obviously, some of them can be achieved by offering a series of leadership courses, instituting employee recognition programs, and so on. For many of the goals, however, the "jury is still out" as to whether such outcomes do in fact occur.

> **Recreation is a great equalizer, a good ice breaker, and often an incentive for employment, combatting absenteeism and turnover.[10]**
>
> *Samuel C. Johnson*
> *Chairman*
> *Johnson Wax*

Although reduction in the absenteeism rate is a goal of industrial recreation, in some instances employee recreation may increase the rate. For example, many firms must now cover their employees with workers' compensation whenever an employee is injured during company-sponsored recreation programs. For some firms, records indicate an annual outlay of several hundred thousand dollars for injuries sustained during company-sponsored employee recreation. Would the loss of man-hours/absenteeism rate have been as great if the company had had no provisions for employee recreation?

Paul Davis, Chairman of McLean Trucking Company, recently observed that "Employees have become polarized because of contract restrictions that tend to prohibit intermingling."[11] He contends that recreation serves to prevent such polarization. Again, little evidence is available to demonstrate that employee recreation serves as a "melting pot" between labor and management or union and non-union personnel. Some firms actually reinforce differences through the creation of separate facilities and programs based upon salary schedules, location on the organization chart, union membership, and so on.

Industry has cited all of Neer's goals in its justification of employee recreation; however, provisions for employee recreation have also been based on other factors. During periods of high employment, some firms have initiated comprehensive recreation programs as a basis for attracting top caliber employees. During the Sputnik era of the 1950's and early 1960's, many aerospace industries developed elaborate facilities and programs in an effort to secure an "edge" in attracting the nation's top scientists. Raymond Herzog, Chairman of Minnesota Mining and Manufacturing, acknowledges this point: "We feel that the 3M program exerts a strong positive influence on the quality of employees we attract and retain."[12]

Most recently, industry has begun to recognize that the company does not exist in a vacuum, thus suggesting an obligation to community. While many firms have been forced into new roles because of such concerns as environmental impact, others have taken the initiative. Former Chairman of the New York Stock Exchange James Needham concludes that "Recreation programs sponsored by the employer for the employee can contribute meaningfully to a personally rewarding spirit of community."[13] In a similar vein, Walter Fallon, President of Eastman Kodak, states, "We cannot isolate ourselves from the world around us, concentrating solely on what takes place in the office, the laboratory, or the plant."[14]

The difficulty in quantifying the expressed outcomes of recreation is not unique to the industrial setting; however, the exiguity of research examining the claimed benefits to employer and employee alike suggests the need for an orchestrated effort by all parties concerned. The most complete annotated bibliography on industrial recreation, developed by Schott and Crapo,[15] includes a chapter on the "Production-Recreation Relationship," yet few of the sources cited lend credence to the often verbalized values of industrial recreation. In the final analysis, management has been convinced of the value of employee recreation through personal observations and various forms of feedback. As Needham contends, "Though the rewards may not be calculable on a balance sheet, there is no doubt that they are there."[16]

SCOPE OF FACILITIES AND SERVICES

It is difficult to make any generalizations about industrial recreation facilities, since their development in any given company is primarily a function of management's attitude and the number of employees. Obviously there is a direct relationship between resources and company size; however, without management's blessing, the probability of large capital outlays is most unlikely. Even with the two major ingredients, many firms, owing to their decentralized structures, find it impractical to develop major recreational facilities; for instance, while airlines and insurance companies may engage thousands of employees, their small, geographically dispersed units make it difficult to develop large recreation complexes serving a goodly number of employees.

While smaller firms may be limited to a single unkept horseshoe pit behind the warehouse or dependent upon public and commercial facilities, there is a continually growing number of companies setting aside substantial acreage and hundreds of thousands of dollars for capital improvements. Tennis courts, Olympic-size swimming pools, bowling alleys, rifle ranges, softball diamonds, gymnasiums, and a host of other specialized facilities are common among dozens of the nation's larger industrial firms. In a few instances, under various financial arrangements, employer and employees have combined to develop recreation facilities valued well in excess of a million dollars.

Only a small percentage of this nation's more than 50,000 firms provide elaborate facilities, although an estimated 75 per cent of the companies having a thousand or more employees do provide some form of employee recreation. Two of the more unique features of industrial recreation are the diversity of programs and the special formats under which they are offered. Although industry frequently duplicates activities provided by local public recreation agencies and their private and commercial counterparts, the various programming emphases distinguish industry from other systems. Rather than present a long listing of activities common to most settings, we will briefly examine some of the unique features of employee recreation.

ATHLETICS—PHYSICAL ACTIVITIES—SPORTS

As noted previously, since the turn of the century industry has been a strong supporter of competitive athletics. Such major companies as Goodyear, Phillips Petroleum, Firestone and Caterpillar have committed thousands of dollars to the development of nationally recognized basketball teams. Within the past decade, however, nearly all firms have discontinued high-power competitive teams in favor of somewhat lower-keyed employee athletic leagues. This attitude was underscored when William DeCarlo of Xerox Corporation said "Xerox thinks there is nothing to be gained by paying out substantial sums of money so that a handful of men can spend company time playing ball in fancy uniforms."[17]

One of the more recent trends in physical programming has been management's endorsement and financial support of employee fitness programs. Since the Kennedy Administration created the President's Council on Fitness, there has been a growing commitment in this area. Under both YMCA and industrial sponsorship, a number of rather sophisticated programs have been developed, primarily stressing cardiovascular conditioning. This trend was underlined in 1973 when a national conference on Physical Fitness in Business and Industry was jointly sponsored by the President's Council on Physical Fitness and Sports and American Industry.[18] A former officer of NIRA noted that the rapid growth in fitness programs is partially due to the fact that improvement in an employee's fitness level can be measured. In addition, management has become personally active in many of the fitness activities. W.W. Keeler, chairman of Phillips Petroleum, confirms this executive support when he suggests that fitness programs are "a sound investment in employee health, morale and performance."[19]

SOCIAL AND EDUCATIONAL ACTIVITIES

It is in the area of social and educational programming that company identity obtains its greatest reinforcement. From an organizational viewpoint, most activities are offered (1) as a company-wide activity frequently involving instructions e.g., tennis classes, golf lessons; (2) within existing organizational units of the firm (departmental or divisional picnics, dances, awards banquets, etc.); and (3) under the structure of the employee club, regulated by its officers, bylaws, budgets, and so on. As with other areas of programming, the social and educational services continue to expand. Leadership courses, foreign language classes, stop-smoking and diet clinics, hunter safety and stock investment courses are typical offerings to be found in more and more industrial recreation programs.

Employee Clubs. Employee clubs have and continue to be one of the major forums for employee recreation. While some perceive a paternalistic role by management, it has been suggested that the formal structure of the club is the best medium for promoting a sense of belonging and company pride within the employee. The variety of employee clubs is as diverse as the leisure field itself, ranging from antique auto and bagpipe-playing clubs to skiing and table tennis. In many of the larger operations, the club structure may serve as many as several dozen diverse interests. Depending upon its resources, each club may be provided with meeting rooms, equipment, leadership and funding, and assisted with publicity and promotion. If the club format is intended to maintain an "esprit de corps," then it is working well, as evidenced by the growing number of employee special interests being offered under the formal structure of employee clubs.

Lunchtime Recreation. Having a somewhat captive audience, industry has assumed some responsibility for noon-hour recreation. Table games, playing cards, dart boards, television and table tennis are frequently provided in employee lounges and cafeterias. For the more active, handball, shuffleboard, badminton, volleyball and swimming may be offered. However, with an increasing number of employees electing a 30-minute lunch period, the term "lunch-hour" is fast becoming a misnomer, and as the lunch period shortens, even the most ardent participant will find it difficult to engage in such diversions. Because of this trend, the "noon-hour" may soon be receiving less attention by the industrial recreator.

COMMERCIAL ORIENTATION

One has only to chronologically scan copies of NIRA's publication *Recreation Management* to document the industry's increasing promotion of services and products normally associated with commercial enterprises. The irony or tradeoff of this extensive merchandising is that while the employee may gain financially, the sales may serve to dampen company-community relations, particularly if the local entrepreneur views such efforts as affecting profits.

The travel industry has developed a myriad of discounts, special packages and group rates for industry- and NIRA-affiliated companies. A survey conducted in 1976 cited over 80 major travel agencies, cruise lines, airlines, motel/hotel chains, and support services that are currently offering discounts to the employer.[20] For example, many of the nation's major amusement parks—Disneyland/Walt Disney World, Busch Gardens, Seven Flags over Texas, and others—have created various membership programs, thus presenting the company employee with reduced rates. The economic impact of such programs is indeed substantial. It was projected that if all member firms of NIRA "sponsored the Magic Kingdom Club program, NIRA alone could bring over $69 million to the Disneyland/Walt Disney World gates."[21]

An even more recent expansion has been in the merchandising of many unrelated products, ranging from athletic wearing apparel and watches to dictionaries and household smoke alarms. A traditional service of employee recreation has been the showing of full-length feature films. While this type of program has been offered for many years, most films were released to television networks well in advance of their release to private companies. A recent agreement between NIRA and Warner Brothers, however, now allows for many quality films to be released to NIRA's members within 18 months after they are distributed to theaters, and in some cases up to two years before television viewing.

RECREATION FOR RETIREES AND ALUMNI

Many firms are now beginning to realize that the company's responsibility to the retiree goes beyond the customary gold watch. Recognizing the trauma associated with retirement, industry is now attempting to provide the retiree or alumnus with various opportunities in company involvement, thus reducing the degree of disengagement.

Raytheon Company of Andover, Massachusetts, is an excellent example of a company's concern for the dedicated employee who has retired.[22] Before retiring, all employees are involved in a series of pre-retirement counseling programs. Once the inevitable day arrives, a series of special events are arranged to further honor the outgoing employee. For the alumni of Raytheon, there are annual reunion days, excursions, theater parties, and other special events. For those who have difficulty coping with enforced leisure or who have financial need, Raytheon attempts to locate volunteer or paid job placements. In order to assist the retiree in locating former work associates, Raytheon distributes directories which include current addresses of all alumni.

While the former employee is of prime concern in the offering of such services, there are other, more indirect company benefits to be accrued. Glenn Westover of Babcock and Wilcox notes that alumni days serve as a significant morale booster to the company's active employees by demonstrating that they too will be considered at time of retirement.[23] Johnson Wax, a family-owned company, views the retiree program as a very inexpensive vehicle for community relations; that is, "the referrals of grateful retirees help recruit applicants who are more likely to begin their careers at Johnson with a positive image of the company and its long-range concern for their welfare."[24]

ADMINISTRATION AND FINANCES

In many companies, employee associations have been delegated the responsibility for programming and operations; however, ultimate authority concerning capital expenditures, development, acquisition and so on is usually retained by management. In some firms, particularly smaller ones, all phases of the operations may remain within management's control. With the vast majority of companies using recreation personnel on a part-time basis only, more often than not someone in the department of personnel, industrial relations or employees services will be assigned the additional duty of employee recreation. It should be kept in mind that only a very small percentage of United States firms have established full-time positions in employee recreation.

As with administrative arrangements, financing of employee recreation takes many forms. In most instances there is joint financing by both company and employee. Management contributes by acquiring and deeding properties, developing facilities, underwriting maintenance costs and so on. The employees' financial commitment, which is usually administered through an employees' association, is usually directed toward programming, personnel, materials and supplies, and some equipment. The two major forms of employee funds come from fees and charges and from the employee association's membership dues. In nearly all recreation settings, today, fees and charges are accounting for a greater portion of annual revenues. Von Conterno, NIRA board member, is among those advocating the increasing of fees, particularly for specialized facilities.[25] He further suggests that other activities, such as employee travel, can provide revenues to offset other indirect costs. When one considers the large amounts of money involved in European and Asian charter trips, it is easy to see how only a ten-percent "markup" on the price of such trips can result in thousands of dollars in additional income. In addition, some product merchandising provides rebate programs against sales, thus providing the employee association with an additional source of income.

One of the major sources of income, somewhat unique to the work environment, involves receiving profits from the sale of vending machine products. Although the returns are dependent upon many factors, the potential income can be very substantial. Using a commercial vending firm, a large company of 20,000 or more employees can realize profits of several hundred dollars per day, which translates to well over one-quarter million dollars per year. For a few of the largest firms in the United States, vending income is reported to approach one-half million dollars annually!

A note of caution is offered to students interested in securing a full-time professional position in industrial recreation. While vacancies do occasionally occur, many of the positions are filled from within the company. Far too often it is the employee from within an existing department or an active member in the employees' recreation association who receives the full-time appointment. In response, the National Industrial Recreation Association, in 1969, published professional standards which called for undergraduate and graduate work in recreation for such positions as Recreation Specialist, Recreation Supervisor and Managers of Programs and/or Services. Admittedly adoption of the standards has not been overwhelming; however, some firms have responded. Thus, while employment opportunities are limited, employee recreation has sought to upgrade the delivery of services through the NIRA-sponsored certification program and a series of awards recognizing distinguished service, excellence of program and managerial excellence.

THE NATIONAL INDUSTRIAL RECREATION ASSOCIATION

As the national clearinghouse for guidance in matters of employee recreation, the National Industrial Recreation Association has dedicated itself to promoting recreation as a sound business policy. Its purpose has been to ensure that in American industry, an individual employeee and his family, regardless of income or station, be given an opportunity to use leisure fruitfully. Behind this goal is the belief that in a complete program of self-fulfillment through recreation the employee may become an increasingly greater asset to his company and to his community.[26]

Since its modest beginnings in 1941, under the leadership of Dr. Floyd Eastwood, the National Industrial Recreation Association has become the principal organization representing the needs and interests of employee recreation. For well over three decades, NIRA has, on a somewhat sporadic basis, experienced periods of membership growth. An analysis of the 1975 *NIRA Membership Directory* (1973–74 membership) identifies a total membership of approximately 700, including organizations, Allied, Associate, and Industrial Recreation Council members, and university and student members.[27] In 1964, NIRA reported an organizational membership alone of 650 companies;[28] at other times during the 1960's, a total membership of over 1,000 was reported, thus suggesting some fluctuation in membership rolls. From preliminary evidence, a recent surge in NIRA membership indicates the total will be in excess of 1,200 during 1976.

Organizationally, NIRA is divided into nine geographical regions. Regions 1 through 7 represent the United States, Region 8 includes all the provinces in the dominion of Canada and Region 9 represents international membership. Surprisingly, the 1975 NIRA Membership Directory shows that, in terms of location, the state of Arizona had the single greatest number of members, followed by Ohio, Illinois, California and New York.[29] With the exception of the Executive Director, all officers elected at large and the Board of Directors are selected from member firms of the National Industrial Recreation Association. Each of the nine regions is represented within the Board of Directors. In addition, there are over a dozen standing committees dealing with awards, conferences, elections, public relations, research, membership, finance and certification.

Although available services are dictated by the various categories of membership, NIRA does offer the following:

1. The journal *Recreation Management,* published ten times per year, which uses a "how to do it" approach in introducing new concepts, services, and products.

2. Program manuals, newsletters, and an annual membership directory.

3. Conferences and workshops, merchandise discounts, consultation and employment services, certification, awards and contests, coordination of student internships, and research facilities.

SUMMARY

Both the nature and quality of the industrial work experience has changed markedly since the late 1800's. In a service-oriented society where less than 2 percent of the nation's more than 80 million workers are on assembly lines, there is a growing tendency to refer to positions as occupations or careers rather than simply jobs or tasks. With industry no longer having to compensate for dehumanizing conditions, management has elected to broaden its base of innovative job enrichment programs through employee recreation services.

Continued growth can be expected both in the aggregate dollars committed and the sheer number of firms either initiating or improving upon employee recreation services. Admittedly, management's motivation does not always rest with a concern for the employee's welfare. Some firms may view employee recreation as a vehicle to improve company-community relations, thus assuring a more favorable position on taxes, ordinances and so on.[30] Still others may be forced into providing recreational facilities as a result of union demands. Whether the catalyst is external or whether it stems from a perceived social obligation, industrial recreation should be the beneficiary. Jackson Anderson, confirming this observation, stated that, "Top management through the country is convinced that this is one of the most important aspects of the total business picture."[31]

REFERENCES

1. Melvin Byers, "Telescoping the future," *Recreation Management,* 14:25–26, 1971.
2. Frederick Engels, *The Condition of the Working Class in England in 1844* (Translated by Florence Wischnewetsky) (London: Allen and Unwin, 1892).
3. National Industrial Recreation Association, *Management Speaks* (Chicago: National Industrial Recreation Association, 1976).

4. Jackson M. Anderson, *Industrial Recreation* (New York: McGraw-Hill, 1955).
5. Ibid.
6. National Industrial Recreation Association, op. cit.
7. Reginald Carter and Robert Wanzel, "Measuring Recreation's Effect on Productivity," *Recreation Management, 18*:42–47, 1975.
8. Stuart H. Clarke, "Job Enrichment and Productivity," *Recreation Management, 16*:28–30, 1973.
9. Don L. Neer, "Industry," *Annals of The American Academy of Political and Social Science, 313*:79–82, 1957.
10. National Industrial Recreation Association, op. cit.
11. Ibid.
12. Ibid.
13. Ibid.
14. Ibid
15. Robert W. Schott and Douglas Crapo, *Industrial Recreation: An Annotated Bibliography* (Chicago: National Recreation Association, 1973).
16. National Industrial Recreation Association, op. cit.
17. William B. DeCarlo, No Varsity Teams in this Industrial Recreation Program," *Parks and Recreation, 3*:33–34, 1968.
18. Frank Flick, "Pioneer Fitness Conference," *Recreation Management, 16*:10, 1973.
19. Ibid.
20. "Survey highlights NIRA discount market, *Recreation Management, 19*:46–48, 1976.
21. Ibid.
22. A. W. Porter, "The Retiree . . . Today and Tomorrow," *Recreation Management, 16*:8–9, 43, 1973.
23. "'Alumni Day' at Babcock & Wilcox," *Recreation Management, 19*:12–14, 1976.
24. "The Retiree Group Program at Johnson Way," *Recreation Management, 19*:20–22, 1976.
25. Von Conterno, "Low-Cost Programming," *Recreation Management, 16*:16–21, 1973.
26. National Industrial Recreation Association, op. cit.
27. National Industrial Recreation Association, *1975 Membership Directory* (Chicago: National Industrial Recreation Association, 1975).
28. "Employees at Play Are Big Business, *Business Week, 1806*:98–100, 1964.
29. National Industrial Recreation Association, 1975 Membership Directory (Chicago: National Industrial Recreation Association, 1975).
30. John Joyce, "Company-Community Relations Through Recreation," *Recreation Management, 11*: 39–44, 1968.
31. Jackson M. Anderson, Industrial Recreation in the Year 2000," *Recreation Management, 11*:12–15, 22, 1968.

QUESTIONS

1. What was the primary motivation for the earliest provisions of industrial recreation?

2. To what extent does research support the values of employee recreation?

3. What have been some of the unique provisions in recreation programs that serve to reinforce company identity among employees?

4. Discuss the major sources of financial support for employee recreation.

5. In terms of full-time professional positions, how would you assess the employment market for the student interested in pursuing a career in industrial recreation?

These Brownies at summer camp may be away from home for the first time.
(Hemlock (Pennsylvania) Council, Girl Scouts of America)

ABOUT THE AUTHOR

Patricia Farrell is a native of central Pennsylvania. She completed her baccalaureat and doctoral work at The Pennsylvania State University, and earned her master's degree from the University of Minnesota.

Her work experiences have been varied. Beginning as a recreation supervisor in a suburban Detroit community, she then worked as a program supervisor for a college student union, after which she served as an assistant recreation specialist and university professor in New England. Dr. Farrell than joined the faculty at Penn State and currently serves there as the program head for Recreation and Parks.

Her background includes involvement in scouting, settlement houses, church recreation, 4-H Clubs and Jewish community centers. For her own recreation, Dr. Farrell skies, golfs, plays badminton and is a sometime musician and actor.

chapter 9

RECREATION YOUTH-SERVING AGENCIES

The focus of most recreation, park, and leisure service delivery systems has been on serving youth. From the beginning of any societal organization, structuring experiences for the young, be these experiences in crafts, food procurement or defense, for example, was clearly the job of early "learning" for young people. The family unit was a survival group where children were quickly trained in the business of surviving and living.

HISTORICAL PERSPECTIVE

In the United States, the swing from the survival learning requirements for youth to the formalized character building experience structure developed in the late nineteenth century and matured in the early twentieth. Concern for young people has been the basis of educational philosophy in our democratic system: an educated person is considered more capable of making informed judgments which in turn enhance society as a whole. In addition to required formal education, youth programs in our churches have been fostered to teach young people certain ethical and moral principles.

It is not surprising, then, that various organizations developed whose purpose was to provide character building activities during the hours of a young person's day other than those taken up by school and church activity. In the late 1800's, most children were protected from work abuses by sweeping new legislation generally referred to as the Child Labor Laws. Better working conditions and pay scales and limitations on the number of hours that could be worked all had a significant impact on children's free time. Since this awareness level of our society had been raised, it was not a big step to carry a similar awareness into concern for what was happening to the young people when they were free to do as they pleased. Communities as a whole began to show a strong interest in providing a suitable environment for leisure-time activities. For many towns this was realized by the provision of park spaces and indoor gymnasiums.

The 50 years prior to the turn of the century marked the early beginnings of what we generally understand to be the youth serving agencies today. The first agency to take an important place in history was the Young Men's Christian Association, founded in England in the 1840's and organized in America in 1851 in Boston. The Young Women's Christian Association was also established in Boston in 1866. (New York City had similar groups prior to that date, but they were not using the YWCA title.) Both organizations grew quickly, and by 1875 the YMCA/YWCA's were common throughout the east coast, with approximately 35 and 28 associations respectively. The Christian atmosphere was fundamental to both organizations. Generally, the Y's were established to provide a good Christian environment for young people who had left home and gone into the cities to find employment. Not only were buildings provided for room and board, but the facility was generally designed to include the meeting rooms, a gymnasium and various social lounges.

Other important movements developed during this period. Settlement houses were established as a recreation service agency as early as 1887. The most notable example was Hull House, opened in 1889 in Chicago under the careful direction of Jane Addams. Hull House became a center for both social pleasure and talent development, providing not only supervised playground types of activities but also theatre, reading and debating activities, dances and parties, and many homemaking and trade arts programs. Pillsbury House in Minneapolis, the Neighborhood Guild or University Settlement in New York City, the Starr Center in Philadelphia and South End House in Boston were outstanding examples of the early settlement house, which provided recreation to young people as well as many other services.

Parallel to the development and growth of these multi-service organizations were movements with a specific focus. During the late 1880's, for example, the Amateur Athletic Union was established. Small ethnic group communities stabilized and began to foster all sorts of club organizations, usually focused on sports in addition to the usual social and drinking activities. Most notable among these were the turnverein societies, the New York Knickerbocker Clubs (baseball), the Kishwaukee Bicycle Club in Syracuse and the Westchester Polo Club. For the purpose of bringing formal competition with standardized rules and fair play to athletics, the AAU became the first national organization to sanction athletic competition in America. Regulations regarding classification by age group, standardized distances and weights, and the establishment of American records and record holder listings were now in the hands of a single official body. The appeal to youth was overwhelming.

Accompanying these developmental patterns was the continuing revision of public school curricula. Physical education, theatre, music and art became regular offerings in the large school systems. Emphasis began to shift from competition in spelling bees to competition on the playing fields. The private colleges and universities were in the early stages of developing varsity athletics. Traditionally the pattern for recreation services to youth has followed the school curriculum, and, as classroom activities became broader, interest developed on the part of non-school agencies to pick up and expand those recreational opportunities into the young person's free time.

PUBLIC SUPPORT

By late in the nineteenth century, public support for recreation activity had grown to such an extent that it became acceptable to use tax monies to finance it. The most common use of tax dollars was to support summer playground programs that provided structured opportunities during the non-school months. School sites were frequently used for such activities. Often land was scarce in the city and appeals were made to acquire additional land so that young people would have their place to play. Public involvement is mentioned here only to suggest to the reader the entry of yet another agency into this service area, occurring at approximately the same time as other agencies were developing recreation services for youth.

It is not the purpose of this chapter to cover private agency provision of recreation services, but it is important to note the beginnings of the youth camping movement at this time. Although camping was an important aspect of many of the youth-serving agencies, the private camps had a special place in youth services. It was not long, however, before the Y's and scout organizations began camps of their own to serve those who could not afford the more expensive private summer camps.

OTHER ORGANIZATIONS

During the last quarter of the nineteenth century and prior to World War I, a number of follow-up organizations in the style of the Y's came into being. Strong religious organizations for youth followed under the sponsorship of the National Jewish Welfare Board. Young men's and women's Hebrew associations were formed in the 1850–1870's, patterned on the Christian associations. Many of the Y's have become a part of the strong Jewish Community Center movement which followed World War I and which also included B'nai B'rith Youth organizations, established in the mid-1920's. In areas that were predominately Catholic, it was not unusual to find an established Catholic Youth Organization, whose purpose was similar to the Y organizations. The Church of Jesus Christ of Latter-day Saints established in 1875 its youth service branch, entitled MIA—Mutual Improvement Association, which incorporates young men's and young women's associations patterned on the YMCA/YWCA format.

The Boys' Clubs, although begun as separate entities, united in 1906, while Girls' Clubs never formally united until 1945. The organization of Woodcraft Indians (Rangers) was established in 1902, and was one of the forerunners to Lord Baden-Powell's Boy Scouts of America, founded in 1910. Juliette Gordon Low founded the Girl Scouts of America in 1912, in the model of Lady Baden-Powell's English Girl Guides.

The Smith-Lever Congressional Act paved the way for the incorporation of early rural youth into the present 4-H program, founded in 1916.

The Luther Gulicks established the Camp Fire Girls organization in 1910 and the younger Blue Birds group in 1913.

Other youth-serving agencies include American Youth Hostel, Inc., the

Salvation Army Youth Programs (founded in the early 1900's), the Pioneer Girls, the Christian Service Brigade and the Young Life and American Youth Foundations. These also had their early beginnings in religious organizations, but they have never gained the popularity of those mentioned earlier.

In summarizing the historical perspective of these recreation youth-serving agencies, it is interesting to note the developmental cycle in sponsorship for services. It is possible to predict this cycle with relative ease. First, a need is seen by a segment of society, or a current situation or new development produces secondary impacts requiring attention. The cycle begins with services to satisfy these needs. Usually the private business sector senses the market for an industry—especially when the need is satisfied by some elitist service or product, at high cost to the consumer. The next stage in the cycle involves the private foundations coming forward with target programs to serve this newly perceived need, usually on a small scale. The third entry into the cycle is the donation-supported agency. Finally, public taxes are brought in to support the service agency, since their mission is service for all and since the public pocketbook is larger than individual agencies or foundation support could ever be. However it is not uncommon for a tax-supported service to revert back into the private marketplace, as cutbacks are made in the public dollars set aside for recreation services.

DEFINITION OF THE FIELD OF SERVICE

Although each youth-serving agency has its own specific purpose, there is a distinct similarity among many of the organizations. To provide a forum for discussing these agencies, the following basic types may be identified: religious, outdoor and social service.

RELIGIOUS-ORIENTED RECREATION YOUTH-SERVING AGENCIES

One need only to reflect on the societal conditions at the time most of these organizations were founded (late nineteenth and early twentieth centuries) to appreciate the vision the founders of them had. Children and youth were involved in a transition period during which earlier technological changes were beginning to have an impact on free time and on working and living conditions. The first large immigration shifts, both from farm to city and from other countries to America, were taking place. The late 1800's were influenced by militants and progressives who stood firmly for reforming society. The Women's Christian Temperance Union, social welfare workers and churches were quick to point out the harmful effects that saloons and pool halls had on idle youth.

This concern for the way young people spent their free hours was quickly translated into the development of formal organizations which purported to provide wholesome, moral and character-building experiences that would prevent the evils of the adult world from tempting young people into partaking of sinful pleasures. Religious living was the foundation for most of this program activity. Learning to follow rules, being of service to others, expanding one's own skills, and leading a good life were the four major purposes of the new agencies.

The YMCA/YWCA, YMHA/YWHA, Catholic Youth Organization, Salvation Army, MIA of the Latter-day Saints, B'nai B'rith and Christian Service Brigade/Pioneer Girls are the youth groups most active today whose early foundations were church related or based on the furthering of religious teachings.

OUTDOOR-ORIENTED RECREATION YOUTH-SERVING AGENCIES

With today's emphasis on environment and ecology, it is important to note that the concerns of people almost a century ago regarding respect for the land and man's place in the total system were fundamental to early youth movements.

Character building, becoming a total person, and experiencing a positive transition into a mature and responsible life were the foundations on which these organizations grew. The natural environment became the laboratory. Outdoor living skills became the strategy through which young people built character and learned to become good responsible citizens. Reward systems of badges or tests broadened as the organizations matured.

As the scouting movement matured, the adult leadership could not resist reshaping the organizations. Although the scouting movement was open to all young boys and girls, the pattern of structure, programs, behavioral expectations and leadership almost forced the clientele and entire organization into a middle-class pattern. Requirements for badges were set in the pattern of how the middle class operated. Ceremonies and special occasions were formalized and filled with middle-class values. The leadership role model was in the tradition of the solid middle-class citizen in the community. The response from the children in the middle class was widespread, whereas the very rich and those of meager circumstance were not enticed into these organizations. Boy and Girl Scouts, Camp Fire Girls and the American Youth Hostel organization are among the agencies that have followed this middle-class pattern and enjoyed widespread popularity in this country.

SOCIAL SERVICE–ORIENTED RECREATION YOUTH-SERVING AGENCIES

These agencies, founded in the same period as the outdoor and religious groups, served a purpose that it might be fair to say was somewhat overlooked by the latter organizations—serving the disadvantaged and poorer children in the cities. While the Y's and scouts were appealing mostly to middle-class youngsters, the settlement houses and Boys' and Girls' Clubs were moving into the socially disadvantaged neighborhoods, providing programs highly focused on sports and other competitive activities. These programs gave young people a socially acceptable choice in the use of their free time. Roving youth looking for adventure and excitement who had been seen as troublemakers and potential delinquents now had another outlet. With sports as the main attraction, the programs in these clubs broadened to include crafts, homemaking skills, various hobbies and social activities.

Every large city had its assortment of settlement houses, many of which served all age groups within the neighborhood but had special programs for young people. The police departments also served young people through the establishment of clubs called the Police Athletic Leagues. These programs were highly competitive, historically in boxing and weightlifting and later in basketball.

SCOPE, AIMS AND SPECIFIC CHARACTERISTICS

The age groups for which most recreation youth-serving agencies were organized ranged between 6 and 18. Some organizations established junior groups, such as the Brownies, Cub Scouts, Gray-Y and Sunbeams. Thus early participation was possible through an organized structure with a wide variety of activities specific to age development and maturation. Some of these agencies, most notably the Y's, continued to attract people well beyond the school years and throughout adulthood.

The scope of program activity varied among the organizations, but always emphasized was the development of good citizenship. Sports, outdoor living skills, crafts, homemaking skills and social skills were the main focus of founders such as the Gulicks, the Baden-Powells and Jane Addams, but at the same time it was difficult for these founders to avoid including societal reform values in their organizing efforts. Character building became the major goal of all of these early organizations. Indeed, it appeared that a good bit of character needed to be built if one were to believe the social statements regarding youth in the nineteenth century. Therefore, any program that helped young people to be aware of the responsibilities of life or provided activities that literally kept young people from doing "bad deeds" was heralded as a positive influence on the nation's youth.

Except for the strictly denominational organizations, recreation youth-serving agencies as initially established were designed to attract all who were interested in participating. However, before too long, limited programs and rising costs resulted in the exclusion of some segments of the population from some organizations. Dues, uniform requirements, the need to purchase miscellaneous equipment and special fees cut off some children from full participation. Some agencies became privately supported, while others remained open to all youth. Unfortunately, often in the latter case financial support was mainly philanthropic, with leadership in the hands of volunteers or desperately low-salaried professionals. Thus a social status structure began to develop early in the history of the recreation youth-serving agencies.

Some youth organizations became quite distinctive, both physically and by reputation. Scouting was most prominent in displaying the physical trappings of membership. As membership increased, mass production became commonplace: the Scouts organization, based on a paramilitary model, lent itself easily to uniforms on which could be displayed all types of awards and badges, in addition to troop numbers, rank and class. The brown and green colors of scouting became national symbols for the all-American girl and boy. Other agencies developed similar items, but not to the extent that scouting did.

As more and more young people participated in the various youth-serving organizations, the reputation of the agency became increasingly well-known. Today there are people over fifty who are still able to recite the scout pledge or recall the name of a Y team leader. The youth who were being served were displaying the results of the "character building" program, and society as a whole was well pleased with these results.

Since most of the agencies were founded by social work professionals, the small peer group organizational pattern became a distinguishing mark. Scout troops tried to keep their size down to 12 to 15 members; activity groups in the Y's were of similar size, while church groups tended to be a little smaller. All of this was consistent with the early theory that living-skill development was best achieved through small social groups. Twelve to 15 was also the capacity size group which could be supervised by one or two leaders effectively and yet not give the participant the feeling of overprotection. This distinguishing point is mentioned only to contrast these services with other services available to youth. Public recreation agencies were charged with handling large crowds and soon became associated with providing mass activities only. Thus anyone wishing a small group recreative experience was more likely to seek out the youth-serving agencies.

VOLUNTARY LEADERSHIP

Perhaps the most distinguishing characteristic identified with the recreation youth-serving agencies was and is the use of voluntary leadership, which formed the backbone of these agencies. A minimum of paid leaders were employed to perform administrative tasks, while almost all of the face-to-face leadership was done by the volunteers themselves. Coaches, activity specialists, troop leaders and general chaperones were all part of the agency services. The Peace Corps volunteer of the 1880's was the college graduate dismayed with conditions of poverty and the lot in life of the urban poor. Thus did the Jane Addamses come forward to work in these neighborhoods among the poor. They brought with them some skills, but counted on indigenous leaders to provide additional breadth to the programs of the settlement houses.

The volunteer model appeared to be sound. It was impossible to pay the many leaders needed to serve the various programs. If a program helped children, then it was worthy of parents' time and effort. The middle-class adult, often a college graduate, sought opportunities to serve and become a part of something good and worthwhile. What could be better than building character? Thus the needs of both children and adults were met by the youth recreation movement. Volunteers were finding new experiences for their own lives as well as making a contribution to the lives of others.

FORMS OF ORGANIZATION AND OPERATIONAL TECHNIQUES

All of the agencies mentioned in this chapter are ones with national organizational structures. The international structure will not be discussed here. Readers interested in international agencies can contact any of the national offices for guidance on the worldwide scope of a specific organization.

The typical organizational configuration involved a central national office with a specialized professional staff. In the second level are the regional offices. These usually cover more than one state; in some instances as many as eight to ten states may be covered by one regional office. Each regional office has varying numbers of distinct units under its jurisdiction. There may be further refinements into area and group units.

The organization chart for the Girl Scouts of the United States of America is presented as a rather typical model of most youth-serving agencies.

The Girl Scouts has adapted this typical model to suit each of the various agencies within the organization. In youth agency work the chart often represents the different levels of professional staff. The Girl Scout model has been chosen to demonstrate the integration of professional staff with volunteer staff at all levels.

The national office is guided by a board of directors, all of whom are lay personnel. The board appoints an executive director who in turn employs professional staff for the central office. The functions of fund raising, public relations, publications, finance and so on are performed centrally. Six regional offices serve the country and are staffed professionally with directors and accompanying staff. Each regional office is responsible to the national office and serves as a liaison to its councils. The two main functions of the regional offices are training, for both professional staff and volunteers, and the development of program materials.

Councils represent the next level in the organizational structure. A varying number of councils report to a single regional office. There are currently 349 councils in the United States. Each council mirrors the national office in that a board of directors (lay men and women) serves each council and employs executive directors who staff council offices.

Between the troop leader and the council is a neighborhood association composed totally of volunteers. These associations are auxiliary agents, serving to stimulate programs, hear and advise on problems, seek and secure volunteers, and be a sounding board for face-to-face leaders who wish to bring any matter before the association.

Perhaps the best-known level of the Girl Scouts is the troop or group leader. These volunteers present the most visible level of leadership within the entire organization. It is to these leaders that much of the time and program materials development of the professional staff is devoted.

As stated previously, the recreation youth-serving agencies could not operate without the hours of service given by volunteers. In all agencies the role of the volunteer is of prime importance in meeting participant goals and objectives.

The preparation of volunteers to serve youth is a crucial assignment for the professional staff. Workbooks, guides, program materials, workshops and training sessions are but a few of the techniques used. A visit to any agency office will reward one with a rich variety of in-house guides and materials.

For organizations other than the outdoor-focused ones, a central building or buildings is essential to the operation of the program. Centers, camps, converted homes, store buildings and apartments have been the mainstay of agencies such as the Girls' and Boys' Clubs, PAL, Y Associations and settlement houses. The use of school buildings for these youth agencies has not been popular. Scout groups have had some success, but other agencies have been permitted only minimal use on a regular basis.

Constructing buildings and camps is an expensive endeavor but agencies managed, and the programs flourished or floundered depending on management and the fund raising capabilities of professional and volunteer staff. As

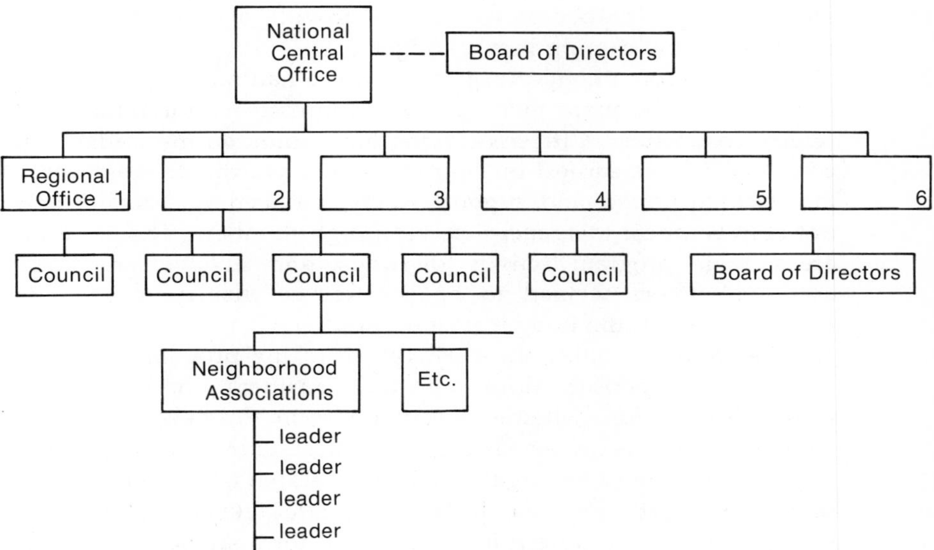

FIGURE 9–1 Organizational chart of the Girl Scouts of America.

the desire for more facilities rose, costs to participants followed suit. The feeling developed that better results could be achieved if, instead of having fund raising solicitation for each specific agency, all fund raising drives could be combined into one major effort—"all the begs in one ask it."

Red Feather campaigns to seek funds for all social services in the communities were popular as early as 1910. The recreation agencies that participated in these united efforts were a special group within the larger social agency services group. Scouts, Y's, Boys' and Girls' Clubs and PAL were popular recipients of Red Feather or United Way dollars for operational expenses. Capital building campaigns were usually considered outside of the regular Red Feather fund drives. It was not long before the recreation youth-serving agencies realized that volunteer support through a combination or united campaign was the best way to achieve a sound financial base. Attempts were made, through the governing boards of the Red Feather funds, to oversee recipient agencies and hear annual progress reports on program activities. Agencies were required to prepare and submit reports and justify past expenses as well as provide a rationale for the inevitable increases in the coming year's budget.

Competition among the agencies was a natural outgrowth of this process. More services to more members was impressive information for the budget review committees. Citizens serving long hours on the budget appropriation committees were earnest in their efforts to have the donated dollar have both far-reaching impact and support where the need was greatest. Boards could not deny support to agencies serving high numbers. Therefore broad service areas, wide program activity offerings, and involvement from numerous adult volunteers seemed to be the key to displaying the agency in an attractive way to the budget review teams.

The young people—the participants in the programs—rarely considered who was the sponsor. More important considerations were which programs were the most fun, whether a center was in the neighborhood, and where were the activities in which one was interested? It was not unusual to find programs for the same target groups of children on the same evenings, at the same times, yet sponsored by two separate agencies. Summer camps were serving the same children. It was possible for a single boy or girl in a single summer to attend one or two weeks of scout camp, return home and leave immediately for Y camp, and perhaps close the summer at church camp. Suffice it to say that many agencies were serving the child who was easy to serve. This group of young people was well provided with recreational program opportunities, while children who were not so easily identified were often missed or received only the barest amount of organized recreation. The Red Feather executive boards were aware of these duplications and voids, and worked hard to disperse funds in an equitable fashion.

CURRENT TRENDS

With the roots of recreation youth-serving agencies firmly based in the social reform periods of the mid-1800's, it is important to note the place of these agencies in today's leisure services arena. We have noted that many of these agencies served mainly the middle class, and this is still true to a great extent in the 1970's.

For a brief period during the 1960's, many community action programs brought organized recreational activities to children in the inner-city areas, most of whom were not being served by the Y's, Scouts, and Boys' and Girls' Clubs. Support for these center-city programs was hard to come by, as those who supported the greater part of the tax structure were generally moving to the suburbs. Federal government funding to the various community action programs began with a broad view of services, which later was restricted to such a degree that recreational programs were no longer eligible for funding requests.

Some agencies have made concerted efforts to keep abreast of the times by responding with program activities appropriate to the young person of the 1970's and 1980's. This has usually taken the form of programs with an educational focus—drug programs, environmental projects, health and sex education, and service projects for elderly, disabled and institutionalized persons.

Perhaps one of the most important trends in the recreation field today is the growth of organizations with a specific activity focus. In the model of Little League baseball, private industry has become interested in sponsoring nationwide sports such as football, soccer, tennis and bowling. Because of the financial opportunities afforded by these companies, these sports have become increasingly popular ones for assorted sponsors to implement. Some of the traditional recreation agencies have picked up on these programs, but mostly sponsorship has been in the hands of the local branch of the company, the public (city or county) recreation agency, service clubs or special interest groups. The attractiveness of these special activities to young people has again brought forward the competitiveness among the agencies for their participation.

In addition to commercial sponsorships, another important trend has developed which siphons away participants from the traditional youth-serving agencies. School districts have been forced through recent federal legislation to program activities equally for boys and girls. For many schools, this regulation has meant great expansion of the intramural and varsity sports programs offered. It has also meant that public recreation departments are faced with the choice of organizing either separate teams for boys and girls or sex-integrated activities. In periods of tight money, co-recreation teams appear to be the most popular choice in response to this dilemma. The Y's have been responding to this concept for years, so that in many of our cities we find the family Y with no women or men designation.

The recreation youth-services arena is reaching a crossroads today. Decisions in the near future will have a solid impact on the place of youth-serving agencies in the total societal picture. Youth services in recreation have proceeded through one full cycle: private, foundation, donation support and tax support. By 1910 one such cycle had been completed, and recreation services to youth continued to be supported through all four sources well past the second world war.

The post-war growth and rural-urban shifts gave us an opportunity to see the cycle begin again. The suburbs had no Boys' Clubs or Y's. Scout troops were the mainstay in these areas. Private clubs—for swimming, tennis, golf and other sports—filled recreation needs in the suburbs. As attendance at these clubs rose, support for the inner-city agencies declined. With the 1960's came new "foundation" support as the federal government created special programs targeted at specific groups. Model cities, youth conservation corps and many other programs helped areas that were unable to financially help themselves, by offering some minimal recreation activities.

The early 1970's saw a rise in support to the United Way. Record goals were met as communities put forth their best for their sons and daughters. Because school and city taxes set priorities unfavorable to expanded recreation services, the donation-supported agencies are experiencing renewed interest in membership and program participation. It is hoped that in the future the swing to less federal control of dollars and increased revenue sharing to our towns, cities and counties might be directed to recreation services. Perhaps the cycle model is a myth, yet the data tend to support it.

What does this mean for the youth-serving agencies? Step four of the cycle appears to be in the distant future. The times are right for agency services. The availability of young people with skills and talents unneeded in today's labor market is staggering. Jobs are not available in the areas in which so many college graduates are prepared. Perhaps the young progressive, in the model of Jane Addams and President Kennedy's Peace Corps volunteer, will seek experiences in youth work, volunteering his or her talents to helping young boys and girls in the late twentieth century realize their full growth potential. What appears to be on the horizon is a return to less expensive ways of providing recreational activity, with an emphasis on people-to-people relationships rather than on sophisticated facilities that only result in young people having had it all and done it all by age 13.

Perhaps most important is for agencies to continually examine their goals and objectives, so that they can respond to changing trends in recreation and in society at large, and thus provide new life experiences for their members. Life enrichment, human relations and an international focus are the major new trends of the 1970's. For most agencies, however, the guiding purposes remain those of the past: development of good citizenship through a democratic group experience; discovery of a set of true values; the building of character and instillment of healthy attitudes toward life; service to others; development of young boys and girls to their fullest capacity; and development of pride for oneself and for one's country. After Watergate, character building appears to be a valuable and needed commodity.

REFERENCES

1. Hedley S. Dimock, *Character Education in the Summer Camp II:* Report of Institute held at the YMCA College, Chicago (New York: Association Press, April, 1931).
2. John C. Farrell, *Beloved Lady: A History of Jane Addams' Ideas on Reform and Peace* (Baltimore: Johns Hopkins University Press, 1967).
3. David Gray and Donald A. Pelegrino, *Reflections on the Recreation and Park Movement* (Dubuque, Iowa: William C. Brown Co., 1973).
4. Robert F. Hanson and Reynold E. Carlson, *Organizations for Children and Youth* (Englewood Cliffs, N.J.: Prentice-Hall, 1972).
5. Robert A. Woods and Albert J. Kennedy, *Handbook of Settlements* (New York: Arno Press and The New York Times, 1970). (Reprint of New York Charities Publication Committee, 1911.)
6. *Book of the Campfire Girls* (New York: Camp Fire Girls, Inc., 1968).
7. *Fieldbook of the Boy Scouts of America* (New Brunswick, N.J., 1976 printing, copyright 1967).
8. *Girl Scout Handbook* (New York: Girl Scouts of the United States of America, 1959).
9. *Handicapped Girls and Girl Scouting: A Guide for Leaders* (New York: Girl Scouts of the United States of America, 1968).

QUESTIONS

1. Was the growth in services to youth in the late nineteenth century a recognition of the fact that recreation is a basic need in people's lives? Or was it simply society's need to control young people?

2. What organizational structure might be successful in serving less-privileged youth? Are the models described in this chapter a possible foundation on which some special services for youth might be built which would endure?

3. Some people have claimed that volunteers generally serve themselves and their own needs rather than the clientele to whom they are assigned. Do we have any evidence to the contrary?

4. Are youth-serving agencies, through their services and programs, making any contribution to society today? What indicators might we research to help provide the answer to this question?

At what age do people realize that voluntary learning is the most important kind? (U.S. Bureau of Outdoor Recreation)

ABOUT THE AUTHOR

Gordon Clay Godbey is Associate Dean for Continuing Education and Commonwealth Campuses, and Professor, College of Education, at Pennsylvania State University. He joined the staff at Penn State in July, 1962, after serving 11 years as Director of University Extension, University of Delaware.

Professor Godbey was born in Troy, Kentucky, and attended the public schools of Lincoln County, Kentucky, at Hustonville and Stanford. He graduated with honors from the Spencerian Commercial School, Louisville, in 1936. He was then employed in banking, and attended evening classes at the University of Louisville from 1936 to 1938. In 1938 he entered the University of Kentucky, where he received an A.B. degree in 1941 (major in English, minors in history and political science). He served in training with the War Department, Signal Corps, during World War II. Following the war, he was appointed principal of Lee County, Kentucky, High School. He entered business in Cincinnati for three years, resigning to return to the University of Kentucky as Assistant in University Extension. There he was granted an M.A. degree in 1947. From 1950 to 1951 he was a Grant Fellow at Harvard University, which subsequently awarded him the Ed.D. degree. Dr. Godbey held three awards from the Fund for Adult Education, which provided him the opportunity of studying adult education in a number of urban areas. From these studies he developed a thesis on volunteer workers in adult education. In addition to professional publications, Dr. Godbey has published poetry, literary and professional book reviews, and professional articles.

He has taught in a number of institutions, including the Universities of Maine, Cincinnati, British Columbia, Delaware, Kentucky, and, as already noted, the Pennsylvania State University. He has been widely active as a speaker and lecturer on human development through education, adult education and the social significance of education.

Dr. Godbey is a former President of both the Association for Field Services in Teacher Education and the Pennsylvania Association for Adult Education (in which he has also served as Editor of the quarterly "Newsletter" for two years). Dr. Godbey's university responsibilities include teaching courses in professional adult education and coordinating continuing education and in-service work, including foreign-based programs of the College of Education.

chapter 10

LEISURE SERVICE ORGANIZATIONS—ADULT EDUCATION

In 1965 there was published by the Aldine Publishing Company of Chicago a book of over 600 pages with the title *Volunteers for Learning,* and the descriptive sub-title "A Study of the Educational Pursuits of America's Adults."[1] The authors were John W.C. Johnstone and Ramon J. Rivera, and their work of over three years was financially supported by the Carnegie Corporation of New York. Professional and other support came from a large number of University of Chicago graduate students and staff of the National Opinion Research Center, which held the copyright. The book, out of print since 1970, is considered monumental, and is a collector's item among professional adult educators.

What so impressed those who read the 20 chapters of this book was the verification by capable scholars of the great size of the total enterprise called adult education in the U.S.A.

Johnstone and Rivera revealed that education of adults had become a major and significant part of contemporary American life. Three out of five adult Americans reported engaging in some aspect of adult education since completion of their more formal schooling.

By 1965 more than 25 million adult Americans each year undertook some form of continued education.[2] (It must be remembered that this figure is smaller than estimates by other authors, who go below age 21 for most of their subjects [Johnstone and Rivera used age 21 and older].) It was evident that if the trends the researchers saw in 1965 were continued, adult education would soon become a larger component of American education than the schooling of children and youth, *including college*.

Volunteers for Learning included 218 tables and five charts that thoroughly examined who the students were, what they were studying, how they felt about the experience of adult education, how often they took courses, and how their studies related to their work. They also reported data on the degree of public awareness of opportunities for adult education and the use of television and other means of instruction. Never before had a nation subjected such a large educational activity to such scrutiny in the short time of less than three years.

Who Is An Adult? What Is An Educational Activity?

Before we can discuss adult education usefully, we must do what the Johnstone and Rivera team did—settle on working definitions. We may not accept precisely the same limits, but minor differences in terminology need not bother people, so long as each communicator knows what is meant by others in the communication process.

From the first time anyone felt it necessary to distinguish between the education of children and the education of adults, the general term "adult education" has been used. Other terms have been used for this kind of education, but they usually have a special and restricted meaning. For example, "continuing education" is commonly used to refer only to adult education that is carried on by colleges and universities for their part-time students. "Cooperative extension" commonly means adult education carried on by a nationwide system involving land-grant colleges and universities, the U.S. Department of Agriculture, and a structure of specially trained people who teach, demonstrate to and advise farmers and others who work in varied aspects of agriculture. Lifetime or lifelong learning is another term often heard, especially in foreign countries, and increasingly in the United States. In 1976 the Pennsylvania Department of Education established the first Bureau of Lifelong Learning in the nation. "In-service education" commonly refers to on-the-job training and education, frequently for professionals and technicians, and especially for teachers. There are other terms, which will be discussed later, but for our purposes the words "adult education" will cover it all.

In general, a definition seems best which emphasizes the rationale of the activity in question as opposed to the motives of those who engage in it. For instance, taking lessons in fly tieing or fly fishing is an educational activity, but going fishing is not. Studying drama would be educational, but acting a part in a play would not.

The following educational activities are identifiable as instruction: lectures, classes, seminars, job training and educational TV. The specified purpose of the activity in question is to give knowledge and understanding, to develop a skill and/or to generate feeling or sensitivity.

The literature of adult education, which is growing rapidly, is filled with attempts to pin down what the term means, and more particularly what the various authors want it to mean. A casual inquiry among the general public will undoubtedly uncover a variety of definitions of adult education, each colored by the experiences of those interrogated. The farmer frequently defines adult education as related to agricultural extension; his wife, as a function of the home demonstration services. To the shift worker in a factory, adult education may be training on the job, as he learns about using new equipment or procedures. For the high school teacher, adult education may be further study in English, history or chemistry, or courses in how to teach and guide young people. Or adult education may be the experience of learning how to make pottery—preparing the clay, throwing it on the potter's wheel, handling the greenware, glazing and firing it in the kiln. And this experience could happen to the farmer, the farmer's wife or the teacher. For hundreds of thousands of Americans, adult education means learning to read and write the American language, to use simple numbers, to cope with the life processes that require literacy, and perhaps to earn a high school graduation certificate. Historically, adult education in the United States has meant citizenship or naturalization education for thousands of immigrants.

SPONSORS

Adult education has for generations been conducted by persons trained in specialties other than adult education itself. Typically, these persons are working in institutions that were established for some primary purpose other than adult education. Because of this situation, it is difficult to define the exact boundaries of adult education. The difficulty is increased when it becomes apparent that no single institution dominates the adult education enterprise. When one attempts to find the boundaries of adult education by inspecting records of membership in certain national professional organizations, the confusion only increases. Unlike law or medicine, adult education scatters even its best-known professionals and practitioners among several national groups.

Perhaps the diffusion of programs, funds, leadership and facilities for adult education can be attributed to the American spirit, which has permitted no single power to describe, prescribe and enforce patterns of adult education. Our national tendency to form organizations readily has been noted by both foreign and domestic observers. About 140 years ago, Alexis de Tocqueville, a visiting Frenchman, commented that Americans of all ages, conditions and dispositions form associations. The Americans, he said, use associations to head movements the way the French or English use government or royalty.

Associations or organizations can be classified, and to understand their role in adult education this is useful. The major groupings are religious (church and synagogue); colleges and universities; business and industry; community organizations; elementary and secondary schools; proprietary, for-profit schools; government (civil); military; prisons; and libraries and museums.

The state and local governments provide many opportunities for continued learning by adults, at times using federal funds (which come, of course, from local sources and are national only because of having been taken into Washington). Major programs dealing with adult literacy, or competency to cope with minimal but necessary life situations, generally operate in the states through local agencies, such as the public schools. Precise data are unavailable, but it is clear that several million adult Americans cannot read and understand such things as directions for assembling simple things for home or work, tax forms and work applications. Many adults cannot easily make change, determine whether a large package of food is a better buy than a smaller one or figure out whether their paycheck is accurate.

Public school programs for adults are widespread today, as the school system has increasingly developed to teach parents as well as children.

Another agency of the government that has long had a major educational role in the lives of millions of Americans is the Armed Forces. The civilian recruit, either draftee or volunteer, has much to learn about soldiering, sailing or flying. In addition to martial skills, many need to learn simple hygiene, safety, national history, civil law and so on. And as warfare has become more technical, even the lowest ranks of military men and women must learn skills, information and attitudes foreign to their civilian lives. Increasingly, especially since the Viet Nam war, the recruiting advertising of the Armed Forces has stressed continuing education. And in addition to required learning, the military person is urged to spend leisure hours in educational pursuits, to ease the eventual return to civilian life.

It was mentioned earlier that most of the institutions that provide adult education have some other activity as their primary function. In the case of the public schools, for example, the education of children and youth is the main activity, and a program for adults is "tacked on" later. Some agencies are created to serve the entire community, and as part of that service offer adult education, as is the case with the Y.M.C.A. Some agencies, such as hospitals, are not educational, but add an adult education component for a limited clientele. There are, to be sure, some organizations created solely for educating adults. In this group are schools operated to make a profit from teaching people to repair TV and radio sets, to make people beautiful (or at least well-groomed), to drive trucks or earth-moving equipment, to draw and paint, and so on.

Some non-profit organizations were begun long ago to educate adults, and have existed for years with only slight modification to their programs; two examples are Chautauqua and Cooper Union.

In 1874 John Heyle Vincent, a bishop of the Methodist Church, founded a residential summer normal school for Sunday-school teachers. Out of this organization grew the Chautauqua Literary and Scientific Circle, which went beyond the original religious content and backing, and even gave college degrees for a few years. It still operates a summer program in the arts, humanities and religion at Lake Chautauqua, although it is much reduced from the time (1875) when President Ulysses S. Grant attracted some 50,000 people to hear his presentation there.[3]

In 1859 Peter Cooper, a wealthy inventor, manufacturer and philanthropist, established The Cooper Union for the Advancement of Science and Art. Over the years, this organization has sponsored both informal and degree training and has been the scene of some well-known, important discussions. Abraham Lincoln's speech at Cooper Union is often credited with bringing him to prominence and making possible his nomination for, and election to, the Presidency of the United States.[3]

PROPRIETARY SCHOOLS

These schools, established for profit, form a large segment of American adult education. Generally they are not licensed by the states to give degrees, although in some cases they are. Most of the proprietary schools are designed to teach a salable skill. The list of specialties handled by the commercial or proprietary schools includes business or secretarial; construction; building trades; bus and truck driving; earth-moving equipment operations; radio and TV repairing; barbering; lighting for stage and studio; commercial and fine art; beauty salon work; police and investigative work; hotel and motel management; computer-allied work, and many more.

Estimates vary on the number of proprietary schools, and many come and go in a short time. There are probably nine or ten thousand at any given time.

Correspondence schools are a special form of proprietary school. Many universities use correspondence (which includes, besides just writing, using audiotapes, movies, slides, TV, and so on) as part of their continuing education service.

ADULT EDUCATION CENTERS

Both resident and non-resident centers for adults to use in continuing their education are an important if scattered part of the American educational scene. Some have historically carried dual roles as social service agencies or union headquarters. Most have been agents of personal and cultural change, wittingly or unwittingly. Some have been for blacks only; others to unite blacks and whites in economic, political and other actions. Perhaps no other residential adult education and cultural center stands so prominently in our history as does the Chautauqua school, located on a lake in western New York State. For more than 100 years it has been an example of how an idea can affect the lives of many thousands of people. The Highlander folk school celebrated in the book *Unearthing Seeds of Fire*[4] is another example of a school that stirred controversy with its ideas and their translation into action.

HOSPITALS

In early times hospitals cared for seriously ill people, but for many years they have had an important added function—education. Some of their programs are for their staff—nurses, technicians and physicians. Other programs are aimed at giving patients the information and skills needed to prevent illness or care for conditions beyond normal health. Other hospital-based programs are for the general public. The hospital thus becomes yet another agent of the community network for education.

Special hospitals dealing with a limited number of ailments or a limited clientele also play a part in community adult education, although a more restricted one than the general hospital. Mental hospitals are an example of this group.

LIBRARIES FOR LEARNING

The contemporary library in a progressive community is a strong member of the adult education team. Although most good library-based adult education programs really are the result of one person's advocacy and effort, it is the policy of state and national librarian associations to promote, support and sponsor adult education beyond the mere circulation and care of books. In some cases librarians cooperate with teachers of adult basic education by providing reading material uniquely suited to adults who read poorly but are trying to improve their abilities.

For more than a quarter century, there have been libraries that have lent educational movies, conducted discussion groups on varied topics, provided lecture series, engaged in educational broadcasting and conducted classes on many topics. But in each case where these exciting, constructive things were made available, there was a dedicated, active individual hard at it, ensuring that in that community the library did a generous share of the adult education needed for fullest living.

PRISONS

Persons imprisoned by society can serve themselves educationally while serving time. Although adult education in some form is provided in nearly all of the larger prisons, it is sadly lacking in most local jails. This condition exists not just because jail prisoners tend to stay shorter terms than prison inmates but largely from a desire to punish—not improve—the offender. The added cost of adult education provides the perfect excuse to let people stultify and learn only greater criminal skills and hatred for "the outside."

VOLUNTARY AND INVOLUNTARY ADULT EDUCATION

The typical participant in adult education has the option of not being there. Unlike children, who are required by law in all states to attend school until their mid- or late teen years (16 is the most common age limit), adults usually are not required to further their education. Perhaps some feel, as did one person who refused to enroll in a learning group, that they have a "God-given right to ignorance"!

What is frequently the case is that the individual person desires to be his or her own guide, instructor and examiner in regard to further learning. Many adults want to be at once the student and the teacher—a rather risky process for all but those truly dedicated, resourceful and skilled in the arts of learning and teaching. One risk is, of course, that of a biased curriculum and course of study. Another is the lack of peer adult students from whom we learn so much. But for better or worse, our democratic system maintains that adults are capable of choice, and that, for their best interests and the best interests of our nation, adults must be free to choose what, if anything, they will study, and when, how and for how long they will study it.

It may come as a surprise to the reader that there are in the United States some forms of involuntary, or mandated, adult or continuing education. In this kind of situation the "students" do not freely elect to attend the program, but rather are responding to external pressures to attend. They do, of course, have the option to refuse, but often this is at a price they will not prudently pay. The course content may range from literacy education to postdoctoral work in medicine, law or accounting. The pressure may be applied by the state, which can require certain continued learning (or at least class attendance) in order to retain one's license to practice one's profession or trade. The pressure may come from a professional group that disciplines its membership. The military recruit has no choice when it comes to taking a prescribed training program, and in many states the traffic-law offender may be required to attend a safe-driver school as part of his "rehabilitation." There have been laws considered and a few passed in some states requiring recipients of public welfare monies to attend adult literacy classes or to get through a high school degree equivalency program.

In some quarters, even the mention of required or mandatory adult education causes concern. To some people, the thought of mandatory programs of any kind conjures up visions of indoctrination, propaganda and even mind control. Even the reward-prompted adult education program is viewed with skepticism by many people, who feel that the individual person operating without pressure is the one best fitted to select a program of lifelong education for himself.

THE SOCIAL SETTING FOR ADULT EDUCATION

All of our societal functions take place in a setting which is peculiar to our nation, and which conditions efforts at recreation, adult education, work and other activities. One must be aware of this setting and of how it is changing before there can be any real understanding of adult education.

The issues and problems that confront us, and the demographic data that indicate trends and changes in our society, are basic to the education of us all, whether we are involved in formal education or in some informal educational enterprise. There are six characteristics of our population that generally affect adult education: educational level; heterogeneity; marriage practices; mobility; mortality; and urbanization. These factors will not be examined further at this time, but it is necessary to keep them in mind as we examine the present and future status of adult education.

The drop from the peak years (1970–1971) of enrollment in elementary and secondary schools (51.3 million students) is expected to reach bottom and level off at approximately 44.5 million students by 1983. During the early

1970's, slightly less than 50 percent of all high school graduates were going to college, but for the first time in the history of higher education there were more adults as part-time students than there were full-time students in colleges and universities. Within just over a decade (1974–1985) the number of people aged 65 and older is seen by a UNESCO study* as increasing from some 24 million to 270 million! Compared to a global population increase of approximately 11 per cent in that period of time, increase in the older part of the population is 24 percent. In the United States, the lengthening life expectancy and reduced birthrate is pushing the median age upward. By the turn of the century it is expected to be just under 35 years, placing the United States in the "old" group of nations. Our older population is growing at more than twice the rate of the population as a whole.

WHY ADULTS STUDY

The reasons people give for becoming involved in adult education are varied. People often state their reasons by referring to what they hope they will gain from the experience. Three goals that rank high are improving job skills, finding a more desirable job, or becoming better informed. Other reasons are meeting interesting people, escaping activity considered dull and unattractive, or just "making a more exciting scene."

IS ADULT EDUCATION A LEISURE SERVICE?

The answer to this question is, sometimes yes, sometimes no. It depends on how one defines the terms "education" and "leisure." If we define leisure as being time during which the individual has control over what he or she chooses to do, then it will be easier to determine whether adult education is indeed a leisure activity or not. In the case of a woman who is employed during the typical 40-hour work week, and in connection with her work is asked, ordered or strongly urged to take a course in computer science on a part-time basis, this bit of adult education does not classify as "leisure activity." If, however, the same woman decides on her own that she would like to know how to knit, and enrolls for classes in knitting run by the local school district, or by the neighborhood yarn shop, then her knitting lessons do classify as a leisure activity.

It would be easy to cite many similar examples, but in each case the criterion that determines whether the adult education activity is leisure or not is the same—freedom of choice. If the person engaged in the adult education activity could *freely choose* whether or not to engage in the education, then it classifies as leisure. Men who enter the armed forces as "rookies" with no previous training must undergo considerable adult education, albeit of a restricted and somewhat unusual type. Once sworn into the service, they have no choice (without penalty) about taking the training. This is not leisure. The public school teacher who gets a raise if she or he

---

*"UNESCO Adult Education—Information Notes" Nos. 1&2, 1975.

takes continuing education of a certain kind, but gets no raise if the continuing education is not taken, does not have a choice without penalty; this is therefore a compelling situation that cannot qualify as a leisure activity. However, another teacher who is at the top of the pay scale and can get no salary increase for taking the course, may decide that she would enjoy learning more about her profession, and will voluntarily take the course on her own time, perhaps at her own expense. This is leisure activity. Thus the same educational experience can be a leisure activity for one person but not for another.

ADULT EDUCATION CURRICULA

A number of studies have been made on what subjects adults study. For more than 10 years, different investigators have been reporting that the largest category under "Adult Education" is job-related studies of some kind. Jobs vary, of course, and included under this comprehensive heading could be courses in such varying subjects as postdoctoral medicine, astrophysics, carpentry, beauty culture, secretarial work, and health occupations. The second largest group in some studies, and third largest in others, is leisure activities, sports and hobbies. Although it may seem curious for people to work in order to learn to play, that is precisely what millions of Americans do. They study to improve their skill in sports, crafts, hobbies, music and the like.

Another large category, again involving millions of Americans, is the general field of religion, morals and ethics. Even when we exclude from this category those persons whose jobs are religion-related, there is still a huge number left. Many commentators on our society feel that the immense popularity of this aspect of adult education speaks to what they describe as the inherent religiosity of the human species.

Another large category of adult education subjects is home and family living. This includes the family; relations between and among family members; physical health and fitness; home decorative arts; and the like.

A final broad category is that of current events, public affairs and citizenship. Following the tumult of the 1960's and the disgrace of our national government in the early 1970's, many citizens felt a renewed concern for participation in government at all levels. Many native-born citizens discovered that they really did not know how the government operated, or was "supposed to" operate. They found new meaning for the term "participatory democracy," and this required continual study as well as continual action by virtually every citizen.

Some authors consider all adult education experiences under two headings: *vocational* and *recreational*. Under vocational they may list courses in the professional, technical, managerial and operative fields. These may apply to health work, business and industry, teaching and other service work, such as barbering, building maintenance or auto repair. The recreational category is generally subdivided according to content—foreign languages, the arts, athletics, crafts, and so on. Adult basic (literacy) education, and "G.E.D." or high school diploma programs for adults form a third category. While it might be reasonable to consider the uses of the latter programs only in terms of either their vocational importance or their personal (recreational) values, they are so important to so many people that they usually rate a separate category.

In a recent study, this author found that one school district in a small city (30,000 people) was offering 136 sections of 79 different topics in a calendar year. Courses were being given in such varied subjects as Chinese cooking, cake decorating, foreign languages, arts and crafts, stock market investing, understanding Black America, physical fitness for both men and women, refinishing antique furniture and local history. In a city of 45,000, a public library offered such courses as Witchcraft in America, Belly Dancing, Author of the Month, Reading for Speed and Understanding, Colonial America, Household Arts, and Local Birds.

A large state university annually serving well over 125,000 adults in programs lasting longer than one day, but not for college credit, presented a bewildering variety of topics. There was virtually something for everyone. Programs on bee keeping, horseshoeing, hay processing and tax problems for farmers were only a few of those offered in agriculture. A wide variety of courses were also available for people operating stores or performing services. Courses dealing with dying and death were offered for members of the clergy, para-medical people, physicians and families. Other courses dealt with liability and accountability of public officials.

Non-school organizations such as the League of Women Voters carry on programs to inform the public of the positions that various political candidates for office have taken on important issues. The League also instructs people on mechanics of voting and sponsors "Meet the Candidates" nights.

INFLUENCE OF SPONSOR, CONTENT, AND CLIENTS ON ADULT EDUCATION COURSES

It is convenient to look at the adult education enterprise from the point of the sponsor. What agency, organization or institution is providing or supporting the adult education experiences in question? The sponsor can make a difference in the content and/or presentation of a particular course. A lecture series on American economic history sponsored by the U.S. Chamber of Commerce might be considerably different from one sponsored by the Socialist Workers' Party, and a course on the role of organized labor in the United States might have an entirely different slant if sponsored by the A.F.L.–C.I.O. rather than the American Association of Manufacturers. A course in contemporary religion taught by a team of Zen Buddhists would differ greatly from one taught by the Maryknoll Fathers. In addition to subject matter, the sponsor affects the organization pattern, method of administration, fiscal policy and other essentials of the adult education program.

Similarly, the content itself of the adult education program affects organization, administration and financing. Basic courses for illiterate adults represent one extreme in the scale, and postdoctoral work in medicine or astrophysics the other. Certain concessions must be made to the requirements of the content of the course. For example, a welding class can hardly be held in a library reading room. The course on care of autistic children needs live subjects for familiarizing the students with the actual conditions to be dealt with. Watercoloring classes require brushes, easels, colors and cleanup materials, as well as space to store the work until the next class. Some classes call for pre-course testing to screen out those who have interest but lack prerequisite ability or training.

The costs of different adult learning experiences also vary greatly. Content governs, at least in part, who teaches the course, what instructional materials are needed, where the class can meet, the length of each meeting, and other issues.

The students themselves also have their effect on the adult education experience. The sponsor of the course may have to accommodate persons with hearing loss, persons with reduced vision, and those handicapped in other ways. Availability of transportation for students may determine whether the class can be held at all. The working conditions and hours of adult students often determine when the class can be scheduled. Persons on shift work may have to have class hours varied from month to month or even from week to week. Some students are available only on weekends; others never on weekends. Flexibility is a requisite ingredient of adult education, and it must be evident in regard to sponsor, to content, and to the needs of the clients.

CLASSIFICATIONS OF INSTITUTIONS

It may be obvious by now that organizations providing adult education fit into three general groups. First is the adult education organization that exists primarily to promote and provide further education for adults. Some of these organizations are public, some private. A second group of organizations providing adults with opportunities for further education are those whose primary purpose is the education of children and youth, but who add on evening classes to further educate the adults of the school district. A final category consists of agencies whose members are not concerned at all about adult education as such, but who use adult education for their own ends—whether it be selling ideas or things.

FOUR QUESTIONS

Now that we have had a thorough review of adult education, we should consider four questions that have bearing on how we look at adult education, what we understand about it, and where our inquiry will take us after finishing this book. Treatment of these questions will not be very long, since they are a bit more complex than our limited space will accommodate. But they must be considered, if only for a moment. The questions are

1. Why does adult education occur?
2. Who decides whether adult education will occur in a given situation?
3. How does it actually happen?
4. What are the results of adult education's having taken place?

The remainder of this chapter will deal primarily with question 2, although there will naturally be all sorts of interrelated issues connecting this question to the other three.

AGENCIES OF ADULT EDUCATION

If we were talking about professional baseball, the "agencies" would be the leagues that contain the several teams, with all the commissioners, broadcasters, writers, cereal manufacturers and others related to the sport. The agencies of transportation would be more complex, but would include the railroads, the airlines, the federal agencies that control rail, air, highway and waterway travel and transportation, the motor car and truck manfacturers and the aviation industry. But adult education? Where should we begin?

Earlier the sponsors of adult education were mentioned. Let us list several again, since they are really the agencies that we must examine. Higher education is one class of sponsor—colleges, universities and other forms of post-secondary schooling. If we stick to the more common definition of higher education, we will be dealing primarily with the extension or continuing education departments of colleges and universities. This usually includes two-year and four-year colleges, and universities.

If we use the term post-secondary educational institutions, we include those just mentioned and a number of others: vocational-technical schools and institutes; special military schools; religious training organizations (although seminaries usually belong in the higher education grouping); agricultural educational programs; industry-based training programs; and so on. If we include proprietary or profit-seeking organizations, we greatly enlarge the list, adding schools of beauty culture, schools for training operators of earth-moving equipment or trucks, correspondence schools, art schools, modeling schools, schools for training airline personnel, computer schools and so on.

Aside from colleges and proprietary schools, there are many other types of agencies that provide adult education services. In the broad area of health services, we must include hospitals, with their training programs for nurses, physicians (in-service), para-professionals of many kinds, food handlers, laboratory technicians and even patients There are also voluntary agencies about health, often usually concentrating on only one area of health care, such as heart problems, birth defects, tuberculosis, multiple sclerosis and so on. And within the government, at national, state and local levels, there are many programs to educate adults about aspects of improving their health. While the national government has for years pursued the policy of supporting the production of tobacco, it has at the same time also supported educational programs advocating the end of its use!

Many religious organizations sponsor programs for adult education, on the regional, state or local level. Some of these agencies have a multi-purpose program, combining worship with education. There are also ancillary religious organizations, an example being the YMCA, which has endured and flourished as an adjunct Christian service, worship and educational agency. Religions are also studied in a variety of non-sectarian contexts, but not with a religious agency as sponsor.

Voluntary agencies with many different interests abound in the American adult education scene, giving it a richness unmatched elsewhere. For the person wishing to learn, there is great choice. Even those with somewhat limited interests are likely to find some organization offering courses of study in their field of interest, unless it is indeed esoteric. The League of Women Voters conducts studies of current issues, of candidates' records and platforms, and of the political processes. The American Association of University Women conducts courses on a variety of topics, including foreign countries, plays, books, political matters and the arts. Service clubs such as the Rotary Club, the Association for Business and Professional Women, the Kiwanis Club, the Lions and the Optimists' Club have some educative function, although at individual meetings it may be hard to find.

ORGANIZATIONS FOR ADULT EDUCATORS

We have taken a very brief look at adult education, examining the clients (adult learners), the content or curriculum, and the sponsors or organizations that provide and arrange the educational experiences. Still to be discussed are those persons who teach, organize and administer the programs. They constitute a professional group in themselves, and have their organizations just as other professionals do.

Organizations for professional adult educators are found at local, state, regional, national and international levels. At the meetings of these groups there is discussion for ideas that affect whether programs are offered in certain places and on certain topics, who teaches, how money is obtained and divided, what media will be used to present programs, and many other related matters.

Among these oranizations at the local level are adult education councils or boards. These may meet monthly, quarterly, semi-annually or only annually. They usually represent the interests of a city, a county or some other geographical division.

State organizations may include chapters of the national organizations, or they may not have any affiliation outside the state itself. They typically have one major annual meeting with programs spread out over one to four days. They usually publish newsletters, often quarterly. Many carry on lobbying in their state legislature.

National organizations include The Adult Education Association of the U.S.A., The National Association of Public Continuing and Adult Educators, and The National University Extension Association. The first two are largely for individual persons and the last one mainly for institutions, although it does accept membership from individuals as well. These large organizations lobby at the national level for action favorable to adult and continuing education, and sometimes "inspire" the bills that may become laws. They also publish important journals, books and other material relating to certain aspects of adult education.

The Coalition of Adult Education Organizations is a national council whose membership is made up of only representatives of other adult education organizations. Its role is largely to coordinate, publicize, lobby for and otherwise further the general broad interests of all citizens in their adult education. There are 21 constituent national organizations forming the Coalition.

At the international level, the work of UNESCO in adult education has been of consequence, and promises to continue so. It must, of course, be quite limited, playing a leadership role and stimulating member states to at least consider the education of their adult populations. The International Council for Adult Education is a young organization trying to unite many diverse nations that have a common need for, and interest in, adult education. It may eventually do at the international level some of the things that the Coalition of Adult Education Organizations seeks to do in the United States. There is, of course, no world government to collect and dispense funds or pass legislation for all members, but other important matters do affect the member nations in common.

Finally, there are many ways for adults to learn on their own, especially in this nation. There are many sources of help, ranging from the local library, garden club or health clinic to more formal institutions such as colleges and universities. There is as yet no generally applied pressure on an individual person to seek to learn or to make a move toward those who want to help. Typically those who have the most learning want more, and typically they are the ones who can best afford it. If as a nation we desire to reduce the distance between the educational bottom and top; if we, as did John Dewey, want education (rather than violence and force) to produce change, we have much yet to do to improve the practices in adult education. If we are to enrich many lives through adult education, as its advocates fervently believe it can, we must put enough dollars into it to try it out fairly. Like all major social changes, these things can come about only when you start and continue your own personal part of the action.

REFERENCES

1. John W. C. Johnstone and Ramon J. Rivera, *Volunteers for Learning* (Chicago; Aldine Publishing Co., 1965).
2. Johnstone, op. cit., p. 34.
3. C. Hartley Grattan, *American Ideas About Adult Education, 1710–1951* (New York: Columbia University Press, 1959), pp. 48–74.
4. Frank Adams, *Unearthing Seeds of Fire* (Winston-Salem: John F. Blair Publisher, 1975).

QUESTIONS

1. How do you explain the large and growing number of adult Americans who involve themselves in learning situations every year?

2. List the major different agencies and organizations in your area that sponsor some kind of adult education.

3. What is your position on mandated or required adult or continuing education, as opposed to voluntary participation? What are the basic issues as you see them?

4. If the funds for adult or continuing education were limited, would you favor a greater part going to basic education for illiterates, semi-literates, and high-school-

level education, or would you prefer to put most of the funds into advanced professional and technical education? Give your reasons.

5. How do you evaluate the worth and desirability of non-vocational adult education—that which is designed especially to enrich life and make it more enjoyable and happier through understanding of and participation in the arts of music, theatre, painting, sculpture, poetry, literature, gardening and so on.

The school can serve as a focal point for mobilizing unused resources, including human resources, to deal with community problems. (U.S. Bureau of Outdoor Recreation)

ABOUT THE AUTHOR

Sarah Ratcliff Godbey is a member of the National Community Education Association and the State College Area Community Education Fact-Finding Task Force. She has given 19 years of service to the Park and Recreation Boards, and presently serves as Chairman of the Patton Township Recreation Advisory Commission. From 1975 to 1977 she was President of the State College Branch of the American Association of University Women. As Vice-President for Programs in 1974, she wrote the handbook—"Community Services and Resources"—for the Pennsylvania Division Project, "Community-School Involvement—A Way to Strengthen Education."

Mrs. Godbey is a graduate of the University of Kentucky, where she majored in political science and journalism. While a student at the university, she was a member of the Debate Team, the Women's Tennis Team, and Theta Sigma Phi and Kappa Delta Phi honorary sororities. She was also Secretary of the State Debating League at the University of Kentucky Academic Extension Department, and she organized the first Kentucky Junior Legislature for High School Students. After graduation she taught journalism to high—I.Q. students, and later became the first white woman to teach in an all-black school, in Newark, Delaware. She was Regional Chairman for the State College (Pennsylvania) Arts Festival for three years.

While a graduate student she married Gordon Clay Godbey, who is presently professor and Associate Dean of the College of Education at Penn State University. After completing 24 hours on her master's degree, she became pregnant, and subsequently had three giant (non-economy-sized) sons and one (right-sized) daughter. She thoroughly enjoyed playing the "mother role," nursed four babies, and found homemaking intellectually challenging. At the same time she satisfied her ego by giving lectures and demonstrations on gift wrapping, writing feature articles for trade journals and newspapers, and reviewing books (she prefers non-fiction and humorous) for newspapers, journals and women's organizations. She also collects decorative eggs (in keeping with her mother hen syndrome) and unusual Christmas ornaments.

Her interests are (in descending order): husband, children, grandchildren, art, decorating, architecture (especially restoration and low-income housing), ecology, gardening, accounting (including income tax), lecturing, consumer problems, gourmet cooking, and shadows.

chapter 11

COMMUNITY EDUCATION

The definitions and delivery systems of "community education" are as varied as the homes we live in. To understand the community-designed, tailor-made delivery system that coordinates all of the educational, recreational, social and cultural services within a defined geographical area, we must first explore the concept.

Ideally, community education is a systematic process "which attempts to bring resources and needs together for effective problem-solving by people on their own behalf." It holds that education should be made relevant to people of all ages, that the people should be involved in *all* of the decisions that affect them within their community. In its purest sense, community education concerns itself with the same involvements democracy has long proffered—shared power and a process of commitment and flexibility that makes provision for changing times.

Less ideally, as community education is practiced in many areas of the United States, it is sometimes more appropriately termed "community-school involvement"—indicating a hand-in-hand working relationship between a community and its schools. Dedicated to developing a sense of "common-unity" among all citizens within an area, the school opens its doors during hours, days and months when public school buildings have traditionally been closed. The school must be willing to reorganize its power structure and parts of its budget to enable new ideas, new cooperative relationships and a new "citizen-designed" thrust to enter into its program and facilities. School goals must be externally oriented. As school extension into the community develops, the possibility exists to approach the ideal—a school might follow its paths of learning and feedback into (and from) every existant agency, shop and factory.

The National Community Education Association maintains that community education is a philosophy that "pervades all segments of education programming and directs the thrust of each of them towards the needs of the community. The community school serves as a catalytic agent by providing leadership to mobilize Community resources to solve identified community problems . . . affects all children, youth and adults directly and helps to create an atmosphere and environment which sees its schools as an integral part of community life." The often discussed question of whether community education is a concept or a true philosophy is less important than the matter of how soon its potential benefits can be made available to more and more people.

BENEFITS

When a school, an agency, a service organization or one or more dedicated individuals decides to implement community education in a given community, the following special benefits may accrue:

1. Avoidance of duplication of effort and funds.
2. Maximum use of all local services, facilities and resources.
3. Better utilization of the resources already available that are needed to serve recreational and leisure-time interests.
4. Establishment of an unrestricted communications system.
5. Mobilization of local human and insitutional resources.
6. Establishment of a framework for continuous community problem-solving.
7. Coming together of people to work out common concerns, resulting in a stronger sense of community.
8. More efficient integration of funds, both private and public, for the delivery of needed services.
9. Provision of alternative activities that combat vandalism, juvenile delinquency and crime.
10. Improved human relationships among people from different cultural backgrounds, resulting from increased social interaction.
11. Increased understanding of political procedures, processes and issues.
12. Increased opportunities for people from varied occupations and social strata to assume leadership.

13. Around-the-clock year-round learning.
14. Up-to-date inventories of community resources.
15. Programs of remedial and supplemental educational needs.
16. Supplementary and alternative educational opportunities for adults and children, to extend their skills and interests.
17. Development of "outreach" centers to bring those individuals least likely to participate into community education activities.
18. Provision of outlets for legitimate protest and discontent.
19. Development of employment and vocational opportunities.

HISTORICAL BACKGROUND

The concept of "community" as we have it today was probably conceived by the ancient Greeks, although it is possible that it had developed in even earlier civilizations. It has been documented that early Greek thinkers—Plato, Socrates and Aristotle—upheld ideas promoted by the best of today's community education theories (e.g., Plato's belief that not only the mind but the whole soul learns). Education's need to produce a student or citizen more concerned with what he *is* than with what he *has* has been the thesis of well-known nineteenth and twentieth century writers. Henry Barnard, the first United States Commissioner of Education; Horace Mann, an early proponent of public education; John Dewey, a philosopher and educator; and Margaret Mead, a cultural anthropologist, are just a few of those who believed in the oneness of living and learning.

In 1929, after the collapse of the stock market, the disastrous economic conditions forced people "to apply their knowledge and inventiveness to the resources they could find in their immediate vicinities. The local community became, abruptly, the setting for a dramatic human struggle to survive."[2] Understandably people turned to their schools, to use the buildings and equipment their taxes had paid for and to seek solutions to community problems of unemployment and retraining. Schools searched for innovative ways to solve community problems. The searching took administrators, teachers and pupils out into the community to learn more about it, and thus their involvement grew.

In 1936, Frank J. Manley, a public school director of health and physical education in Flint, Michigan, appalled by the dangers surrounding children playing in the streets while nearby school playgrounds were closed and empty, sought to remedy the situation by soliciting help and funds from Charles Steward Mott, a businessman-philanthropist. Together they organized a program of supervised after-hour recreation in a number of Flint schools. The concept grew and grew as the entire community become involved—Manley and Mott had established the modern model for community education. Soon concerned citizens and educators were travelling to Flint to study how community education worked. Their need for detailed information grew, and to serve this need, the Charles Stewart Mott Foundation was established to provide information, research and training. Soon Regional University Training Centers were established and supported by the Foundation as more and more colleges and universities gained interest in the concept.

ORGANIZATIONAL BACKING

The proliferation of the community education concept since the formation of the Mott Foundation and its resultant adoption in some form by communities and individual schools has been extraordinary. Statistics are soon outdated; however, Larry E. Decker predicts that in "1978 there will be 2,600 school districts with 7,864 community schools; 4,632 trained community school directors; 2,502 masters and Ph.D. interns trained."[3]

Schools, agencies or individuals promoting the community education movement have numerous organizations supporting them by word, deed and funding. A *partial* list includes the following:

United States Jaycees
Big Brothers of America
National Congress of Parents and Teachers
National Community Education Association
National Recreation and Park Association
American Association for Health, Physical Education and Recreation
Society of State Directors of Health, Physical Education and Recreation
American Association of School Administrators
National Association for Public Continuing and Adult Education
National Association of Elementary Principals
National Association of Secondary School Principals
Association of Supervision and Curriculum Development
National School Boards Association
National Education Association
International Association of Community Educators, Inc.

In addition, numerous state and regional organizations are pursuing state and federal commitment and funding, and providing many needed services, such as dissemination of helpful up-to-date information.

IMPLEMENTATION OF COMMUNITY EDUCATION PROGRAMS

Plans for implementing community education must suit the unique requirements of each community. The job is easier to accomplish in small communities than in large cities. Many small towns center their organizations around local schools and depend largely on local resources. In large cities, some ambitious programs have failed as a result of the drying up of the "soft" money source they were overly dependent on. Careful initial planning has no substitute. Reading about community education as it has developed in other areas may be helpful; however, no one requirement surpasses detailed, specific information about your area, its people, resources, services and power structure.

SURVEYING THE STATUS QUO

The first step is to make a detailed survey of the status quo, in order to identify overlapping areas of responsibility and voids in community services and resources. Because communities are so diverse, there can be no universal detailed formula for such a survey; however, basic information is needed with regard to the following:

Four-Walled Facilities. A complete mapping must be made of all schools, churches, recreational shelters, shopping centers, health centers, governmental buildings, correctional and specialty institutions, service and ethnic clubs, hobby groups, museums, libraries, philanthropic organizations, warehouses, factories, newspaper and printing plants, bus stations, day-care centers, and so on. (In every community there are many public facilities that go unused a portion of the day or week. All such underutilized spaces should be used to capacity.)

Natural Facilities. A similar inventory must be made of all accessible parks, vacant lots, wooded areas, estates, swamps, caves, rocky areas, streams, beaches, zoos, camps, retreats, bird and/or wildlife sanctuaries, farms, gardens, and so forth.

Human Resources—Citizens and Organizations. People in each community have untapped skills, talents, and services to share with others, either on an individual basis or through existing organizations. Discover who these talented people are by distributing a questionnaire. No one "best" method of distribution exists. It could be done by a Volunteer Services Organization, through the schools in each elementary school district, by a special house-to-house canvass in designated areas through a highly publicized campaign in newspapers, by radio and television, or through the efforts of a highly motivated service organization. The questionnaire should include an inventory of hobbies, collections, travels, occupations, foreign language capabilities, artistic abilities, scientific, inventive and construction capabilities, business acumen, and social and leadership qualities.

CHOOSING LIAISON PERSONNEL

The person serving as the liaison between the community and the organization implementing community education may have emanated from any of many community interests. The title given this special person, the job description or list of qualifications needed are contingent upon community needs. He or she may be

—A (paid or unpaid) Director of Community Education or Director of Volunteer Services on the school superintendent's staff

—A Director of Leisure-Time Services from the local Parks and Recreation Department

—A Community Council Leader hired by the school board or the community, or recruited as an unpaid volunteer

—An ombudsman (or several) appointed by the school system or leisure services organization to work with neighborhood councils, a committee representing geographical elementary school areas, community volunteer services or some other representational group

FEEDBACK FROM THE COMMUNITY TO LIAISON PERSONNEL

Information concerning community needs and opportunities might be directed to liaison personnel by the following means:

Advisory or Neighborhood Councils. These represent a cross-section of civic, religious and ethnic organizations, and are composed of businessmen, safety and health department representatives, park and recreation department representatives, homeroom mothers, teachers, clergy, students and other concerned citizens.

Meetings in Schools or Community Buildings.

Telephone Surveying and Answering Service. Information is received from the community through such a service, staffed by volunteer corps registrants; members of one or more service organizations; retirees, (for early afternoon service); and college or high school students (for late afternoon or evening duty).

COMMUNITY SERVICES AND RESOURCES CHECK LISTS

Most of the tradesmen, professional people, factories, businesses and organizations within your community can serve as useful learning resources if the proper questions are asked to elicit definitive information on observable skills and processes. The following check lists can be used as a basic inventory of your community's present services and resources. Use and adaptation of the unusual and needed ones will broaden the scope of your community's offerings.

Some Service-Oriented Groups*

____ Girl Scouts
____ Boy Scouts
____ Camp Fire Girls
____ Big Brother
____ Goodwill Industries
____ Salvation Army
____ Legal Aid Society
____ Teen-age Job Corps
____ Teen-age Parents
____ Ministerium or Council of Churches
____ Civil Defense
____ Helping Hand
____ Planned Parenthood
____ Aid for Girls
____ League of Women Voters
____ Travelers Aid
____ Meals on Wheels
____ Golden Age
____ Senior Citizens
____ Grange
____ American Association of University Women
____ Council of Human Services
____ International Hospitality Council
____ Rotary
____ Kiwanis
____ Lions
____ Optimists
____ Soroptimists
____ Chamber of Commerce
____ Merchant's Associations
____ Women's Clubs
____ Jr. Women's Club
____ Business and Professional Women
____ Homemaker Club and Services
____ County Agricultural Extension Services
____ Y.M.C.A.
____ Y.W.C.A.
____ Y.M.H.A.
____ Y.W.H.A.
____ Veterans' Organizations
____ Crisis Centers
____ FISH
____ A FRIEND
____ Altrusa

*The names of some of these organizations may vary from one locale to another. Two names less familiar to several persons who have used the check list are FISH, an organization composed of local people who serve emergency needs of specific groups in the community (e.g., providing transportation for any medical need of the elderly) and A FRIEND, a 24-hour telephone answering service providing professional counseling and appropriate referral for any problem.

Learning Resources*

- ____ Libraries
- ____ Landmarks
- ____ Historical Societies
- ____ Museums
- ____ Galleries
- ____ Restorations
- ____ Monuments
- ____ Fairs
- ____ Arenas
- ____ Festivals
- ____ Churches
- ____ Stadiums
- ____ Race Tracks
- ____ Gymnasiums
- ____ Gardens
- ____ Greenhouses
- ____ Arboretums
- ____ Aviaries
- ____ Parks
- ____ Forests
- ____ Canals
- ____ Rivers
- ____ Planning Offices—city or town; regional
- ____ Specialty Farms—dairy, egg, cattle, berry, wild animal, tree, fruit, nut, horse, truck gardening
- ____ Professional Offices—doctor, lawyer, dentist, C.P.A.
- ____ Product Testing Organizations
- ____ Lighthouses
- ____ Ships
- ____ Boats
- ____ Dry Docks
- ____ Marinas
- ____ Dams
- ____ Water Works
- ____ Landfills
- ____ Police Departments
- ____ Fire Departments
- ____ International Houses
- ____ Ward Leaders
- ____ Oceanography Headquarters
- ____ Governmental Agencies—local, state, national, international
- ____ Rehearsals of bands, choral groups, symphonies, ensembles
- ____ Community Theaters
- ____ Science Centers and Houses
- ____ Food Distribution Centers
- ____ Caverns
- ____ Caves
- ____ Zoos
- ____ Game Preserves
- ____ Bird Sanctuaries
- ____ Factories
- ____ Foundries
- ____ Refineries
- ____ Junkyards
- ____ Theaters
- ____ Opera Houses
- ____ Artist's Studios
- ____ Planetariums
- ____ Hospitals
- ____ Medical Centers
- ____ Clinics
- ____ Laboratories—x-ray, diagnostic, human, animal, experimental
- ____ Post Offices
- ____ Courts
- ____ Farmers' Markets
- ____ Roadside Markets
- ____ Garbage Disposal Plants
- ____ Fish Farms and Hatcheries
- ____ Weather Forecasting Stations
- ____ Mining Facilities
- ____ Mills
- ____ Dredging Operations
- ____ Quarries
- ____ Construction Sites
- ____ Printing Plants
- ____ Radio Stations
- ____ Television Stations
- ____ Emergency Communication Centers
- ____ Moving and Express Services
- ____ Public Transportation Centers
- ____ Airports
- ____ Bus Terminals
- ____ Subways
- ____ Shopping Centers
- ____ Department Stores
- ____ Bakeries
- ____ Fish Markets
- ____ Cable Street and Trolley Cars Headquarters
- ____ Computerized and Automatic Establishments
- ____ Railway Stations, Dispatcher's Offices, Yards, Round Houses
- ____ Soil Testing Laboratories
- ____ One-Man Service Offices—weaver, cobbler, etc.
- ____ ____________ (other)

---

*NOTE: Any organization or person possessing a body of knowledge, whether esoteric or not, and capable of dispensing that knowledge is a *learning resource.* Further, any observable process is a learning resource. The learning resources listed here are ones that provide "real life" environments and experiences.

ONE IDEA BREEDS ANOTHER

Imaginative and creative leisure-time programs and services can enhance the quality of life of individuals and serve as a regenerator of society. If, as Woodrow Wilson said "Originality is simply a fresh pair of eyes," then viewing the ideas of others may create a spark that will translate into fulfillment of the leisure needs of the people in your community.

The following list of unusual and creative leisure-time activities or organizations is intended to be catalytic. (The possibilities for one of these ideas to breed another before or after attempted adaptation are considerable.)

Junior Museum—Family organization providing experiences in natural sciences, art and nature (held in schools during the summer and on selected weekends during the other sessions).

Coffee Counseling Drop-Ins—Understanding and helpful conversations with troubled youths and adults.

Foxfire or other Oral History Gathering Group—High school students (making use of tape recorders, cameras and their own curiosity) interview the grandparent generation to record what this country was like when today's golden-agers were teenagers.

Wishes, Lies and Dreams, and Other Unstructured Children's Poetry Writing Sessions—Classes (of the Kenneth Koch variety) taking full advantage of children's uninhibited innocence aided by concerned guidance.

Youth Court—Court composed of supervised and trained high school students (who pass Youth Court Bar Examination) serving as judges, advocates and juries. Young offenders and their parents may elect to have a Youth Court hearing and trial instead of Juvenile Court.

"There But For . . ."—Breakfast-group meeting one morning each week. Each member sponsors another who is trying to rediscover reality; especially useful for those who are trying to readjust to society—alcoholics, divorcees, widows, drug-users, parolees and so on.

Dial-A-Story—Library-centered telephone and tape-playing service offered to local children requesting a favorite story from a published list of those available.

Friendship File—A careful matching of the information filled in on questionnaires completed by high school juniors and seniors who have recently moved to an area with those completed by juniors and seniors who have lived in the area five years or more. A kind of forced (but needed) friendship. The matching is based on economic background, spare-time activities and educational interests.

Family Outing Club—Offers a variety of park and playground experiences for father and son, mother and daughter, or the entire family—accenting fun, safety, companionship and outdoor life. (Usually includes hiking, mountaineering, bicycling, canoeing and sailing.)

Land Resource Laboratory—Three or more acres set aside for a wildlife conservation site completely designed and improved by junior high or high school students in consultation with Game Commissions, Bird Clubs, Environmental Groups and other organizations. Students set up nature trails, teaching stations, specimen plant and tree identifications, weather stations and outdoor classrooms.

One World—An organization of national ethnic groups and international visitors, featuring cultural programs, language classes, orientation seminars, trips to local points of interest and training for host families.

Children's Workshops—An arts hideaway for the young set, featuring experimental art works, movies, slide shows, things to touch, see and hear, and other activities.

Age Mixer—A Saturday morning set-up for pupils to meet with one or more members of the local Golden Age Club or Modern Maturity chapter. Older residents share their specialized knowledge and time to teach photography, chess, automotive engineering and other areas of interest.

Bicycle Polo—Using collapsible bicycles, at noontime a group of business executives are off to the green of the local park to use croquet mallets for a game of "wheeled" polo.

Dial–A–Friend—Telephone project for daily contact with a person who lives alone. A friendly gesture, with caller and receiver changing roles on a mutually decided timetable.

Drag Club—Provides a safe outlet for a potentially dangerous pastime, with supervision under the guidance of a professional race car driver/mechanic and a member of the local law enforcement agency.

Adventure—An outdoor get-together for junior high school pupils to determine ecological relationships in natural settings.

Teen Consumers—Using the "buddy" system, teenagers tabulate and circulate price and other helpful information about merchandise most frequently purchased by teenagers, food sold at teen hang-outs and so on. The list is regularly updated. Monthly programs include audience-participation talks and discussions by adult consumer advocates.

Choreographed Unicyclists—Easy to intricate patterns of motion are taught to individuals who ride unicycles. A group always in demand for entertainment at special events.

Nutritional Consultation Pool—A volunteer phoning service staffed by registered dietitians qualified to prescribe diets and consult on a variety of nutritional problems, including diabetes, overweight, underweight, ulcerative colitis, hypoglycemia, vegetarian diets and the nutritional needs of pregnant women.

Seniors Serving—Participation by senior citizens in meaningful community activities, helping to boost their self-esteem. Activities may include bandage rolling, mailing brochures for fund-raising, volunteering services for health organizations, making stuffed toys for hospitalized children, or establishing a "phone" friendship with another senior citizen who may live alone, be chronically ill or reside in a nursing home.

Learning Exchange—A central clearinghouse established for individuals who wish to barter their special knowledge or ability in exchange for another kind of knowledge or skill. The Exchange is sometimes established on a pay basis (collecting a small percentage for overhead).

Citizens' Lobby—Citizens zero in on needed state and national legislation. The lobby is usually composed of neighbors, friends and coworkers who use the telephone and mail service to inform each other and to inform legislators of their needs and opinions.

Hobby Horse Groups—The kindergarten set does interpretative dancing to action-demanding music and scenarios.

Green Circle—A human relations program for elementary school pupils designed to change attitudes, develop brotherly love and reinforce the need for consideration of all people.

Single File—A new version of the singles club—dedicated to improving public outdoor areas.

"No Words" Workshop—Children, age 4 and up, explore ways to "talk" with adults without using words. Working as a pair, the child and adult increase their awareness of each other's body messages, play games, solve movement problems and learn more about their own relationship.

The Saturday Thing—Offering a smorgasbord of unstructured activities to high school students each Saturday, this program goes beyond the usual recreation programs. Using paid professional teachers, this substitute for weekend tedium offers a generous choice of activities.

Alternative Ideas—Meetings are concerned with examining in detail society's current life-styles and ideas.

Tel-Med Library—Audio-tape health information library made available to the public by telephone.

Youth Service Bureau—Helps to prevent juvenile delinquency and other anti-social behavior by meeting the expressed needs of youth. Community resources are fully utilized and new ones designed when needed.

Village Crafts—A sharing of craft talents and setting up of markets that often place special emphasis on historic local designs and wares.

Free Learning Center Library—Programs, rooms, stacks and facilities tailor-made to fit the needs of a specific neighborhood.

"Once Upon A Time . . ."—Kindergarten through second grade. Children act out stories read to them by adults. Because masks sometimes frighten children in this age group, the use of paper animal or human heads painted on wooden paddles is recommended.

"Hand in Hand"—Nature walks for pre-schoolers through 6th grade. Through this outdoor activity, children are taught the wonders of backyards and parks, the intricacy and need for bird banding, how to grow house plants, how to plant trees, and so on.

Second-Shift Serendipities—Educational and activity offerings for those who cannot take advantage of the myriad opportunities open to those who work from nine to five. Crafts and open discussion courses have been particularly successful.

LOOKING AHEAD

Ideally, community education requires synergistic action, meaning that, through combining their efforts, people can have a greater effect than if they act separately. It is especially necessary that the human services within each community join forces for the common good. If not, community education may wind up involving only the schools, with minimal input from the people to be served. School buildings may be open longer hours, duplication of effort may disappear, and a few highly creative classes may be held; however, the full potential of community education as envisioned by many of today's hopeful citizens will not be realized.

Leisure services organizations are making a strong stand for inclusion in the community school involvement movement. They are really seeking to become more than just expanded recreation programs. Robert M. Artz believes, "The time is now for every park and recreation department to take the initiative and build an effective partnership with the educational agencies in the community to insure that the new community school education program is truly a cooperative program which provides the best and most coordinated services possible for the most reasonable tax-payer expense."[5]

Progressive leaders in the community must band together to bring about the cooperative changes needed for genuine humanistic progress through community education. If they fail, the only hope for many communities is the dedicated and persistent *individual* who perceives "a better way."

REFERENCES

1. Harold E. Moore, "Strategies for Making Community Education Work," *The Community School and Its Administration,* November, 1971, p. 3.
2. Maurice F. Seay, et al., *Community Education: A Developing Concept.* (Midland, Michigan: Pendell Publishing Co., 1974.)
3. Larry E. Decker, "Community Education—Purpose, Function, Growth, Potential," *Leisure Today/ American Association for Health, Physical Education and Recreation,* JOHPER, April, 1974.
4. Sarah R. Godbey, *Community Services and Resources Handbook,* American Association of University Women, Pennsylvania Division Project, 1974.
5. Robert M. Artz, "Community School Movement: A Progress Report," *Parks and Recreation, 10*:37, October, 1975.

QUESTIONS

1. Trace how a given program of community school involvement might be developed into one that would fit the community education concept.

2. Detail the planning required to develop a broad-based program of community education in your home town.

3. Define *learning resources* and enumerate five that you recall from childhood.

4. Name ways in which community education might further the broad principles of democracy.

5. List factors that might retard the development of community education in a metropolitan area.

Sometimes it is difficult to determine where the leisure resources of a community begin and end. (U.S. Bureau of Outdoor Recreation)

chapter 12

DETERMINING A COMMUNITY'S LEISURE RESOURCES

In this chapter we will examine (a) the relationship of leisure resources to participation, and (b) the methods by which various kinds of leisure service agencies determine the existing scope of leisure opportunity and leisure activity within a given community or for a given clientele. Attention will be given to collecting data not only for given kinds of leisure service agencies, but also for a given community. By community, we mean not only a "concentrated settlement of people within a limited territorial area," but also "a number of people who share common traditions or interests."[1] Thus, wilderness hikers, employees of Aerojet, mentally retarded adults, or residents of Trenton, New Jersey, may all be considered as members of a group making up a particular community.

THE RELATIONSHIP OF LEISURE RESOURCES TO PARTICIPATION

In examining the state of leisure or recreation resources, it is imperative to understand that the *supply* of a given leisure opportunity directly influences *participation.* Simple availability is such a key determinant of usage that it even overshadows socioeconomic variables in importance. For instance, one important reason why driving for pleasure and watching television are quantitatively important forms of leisure experience is that we have television in 97 per cent of our homes and most families own a car. By the same token, people don't water ski too much in Washington, D.C., because there aren't any lakes. If lakes were supplied, however, water skiing might become a popular sport in that area. It is central to understand that no supplier of recreation or leisure resources is a passive reactor to "demand." Suppliers of recreation *create* participation, and they do so by making some activity or experience available.

Sheer availability will often profoundly influence usage of facilities and desire to participate in a particular activity. The citizen who votes against a bond issue for a new park, for instance, will nevertheless often use the park if it is established. What leisure facilities are supplied to the potential user will greatly influence the usage rate, which will often then be interpreted as "demand," which then will result in the provision of more of the same facility. The same may be said of programs sponsored by a leisure service agency. Offering classes in pottery making at a state hospital will influence many patients to undertake an activity they had never previously considered. Similarly, if an industrial recreation organization sponsors trips to historic areas, some people will go who would not have undertaken such an activity on their own. While this line of reasoning represents an oversimplification, it is an important planning consideration, because it demonstrates that the supplier of leisure resources cannot be passive. There is no alternative but to promote future participation in certain activities by providing facilities for them at the present. It seems quite likely, for instance, that if, instead of a Bureau of Outdoor Recreation, Congress had created a Bureau of *Indoor* Recreation that had made funds available for indoor sports and social recreation, there would now be an increased "demand" for such activities and funds to sponsor them. (And a number of people would now be wondering why the agency couldn't provide funds for outdoor basketball courts as well as indoor!) Because the supply of leisure resources is such an important determinant of how people spend their time, ascertaining what resources should exist is an important planning consideration.

THE SCOPE OF LEISURE SERVICES

As Christiansen has pointed out, the provision of recreation by public agencies is not a monopolistic function.[2] Indeed, from a user standpoint, private and commercial agencies and the family provide the majority of leisure experiences in most people's lives. While some government services, such as highway construction, are almost monopolistic, leisure services are provided by a vast array of organizations. Not only is there no monopoly on leisure services, but the numerous agencies sponsoring leisure activities and facilities are often highly interdependent—their actions affect each other, and some organizations depend upon others in order to function at all. The success of a commercial golf driving range, for instance, may be dependent upon a nearby public golf course to promote sufficient interest in the game. Publicly sponsored ballet lessons might drive a commercially operated studio out of business, or it might have the opposite effect and actually enhance its operation, depending upon the coordination of services between the two. Commercial resorts may create a need for more public campgrounds, to which government park authorities must respond. Because of this interdependence, many types of leisure service agencies benefit from obtaining an accurate inventory of what leisure services are available to people in a particular geographic area.

Because it is often advocated that public agencies play a coordinating role with regard to leisure opportunities in a given community, it might be expected that they would be extensively involved in inventorying leisure services within their communities. So far, however, there has been little systematic attempt to establish leisure resource information retrievable systems. A 1972 study by Hovis and Wagner of 65 municipal recreation and park departments in cities having populations of 250,000 or more found that 84 percent of such agencies did not operate any such system.[3] In spite of this, a number of different techniques have been attempted by different kinds of agencies to inventory the leisure services available in a given community. The principal methods used to date are as follows:

Telephone Book Analysis. A rough idea of the range of leisure services within a community may be obtained from checking the telephone directory.

In Memphis, Tennessee, for instance, the following entries were found in the yellow pages of the phone directory:[4]

- Amusement Places (13)
- Antique Dealers (70)
- Aquarium Supply Locations (3)
- Art Galleries and Dealers (12)
- Art Goods Stores (5)
- Bicycle Dealers (12)
- Billiard Parlors (14)
- Boat Builders and Dealers (44)
- Book Dealers (37)
- Bowling Facilities (8)
- Camp Grounds (13)
- Ceramics Suppliers (13)
- Churches (700)
- Concert Bureaus (2)
- Camping Equipment Stores (9)
- Cocktail Lounges (18)
- Fishing Supply, Bait and Tackle Shops (14)
- Fraternal Organizations (30)
- Gift Shops (63)
- Golf Courses, Public (7)
- Gun and Gunsmith Stores (17)
- Gymnasiums
- Motion Picture Theatres (28)
- Motorcycle Dealers (31)
- Museums, Public and Commercial (8)
- Music Instruction Businesses (22)
- Musical Instrument and Sheet Music Dealers (37)
- Night Clubs (33)
- Nurseries and Landscapers (21)
- Pet Shops (12)
- Radio Stations (15)
- Restaurants (600)
- Seed and Plant Bulb Suppliers (8)
- Skating Arenas, Roller and Ice (6)
- Swimming Pool Contractors and Dealers (18)
- Swimming Pool and Supplies Businesses (24)
- Taverns (68)
- Tourist Attractions (15)
- Universities and Colleges (13)

Questionnaires. Questionnaires may be administered to all organizations believed to offer leisure services throughout the community. Such organizations may be identified through a number of sources, including the telephone book, lists supplied by planning councils or social agencies within the community, or information shared by personnel from different leisure service agencies. On the questionnaire, agencies are usually asked to provide detailed information about their facilities, activities, staff, and so forth.

Brochure Analysis. By collecting brochures from identified leisure service organizations, it is possible to obtain much of the same information as would be obtained through the use of a questionnaire, with much less bother to agency personnel.

Use of Previous Surveys or Questionnaires. In many instances, agencies can be identified by referring to previous studies of leisure behavior patterns and preferences, in which people have been asked to identify the sponsors of various leisure activities.

Direct Observations. Watson and Hovis utilized the following procedure for assessing the supply of recreation services in Seattle, Washington.[3]

> **1. Determined boundaries to be included in the pilot study area via discussion with Recreation Division staff.**
>
> **2. Obtained 800′ map, supplied by Seattle Department of Parks and Recreation.**
>
> **3. Obtained census tract boundaries from the Department of Community Development.**

4. Plotted the boundaries of each census tract on the map.

5. Developed a preliminary inventory of potential recreation agencies located in each of the census tracts, utilizing the Seattle Telephone Directory, the Ballard Services Directory, the Seattle Social Services Directory, and verbal suggestions from Recreation Division staff members.

6. Employed three recreation resource analysts to conduct the agency interviews. All three were selected on the basis of their background related to recreation, their maturity and their recreation course work. After completing the inventory, but prior to starting the interviews, one of the analysts moved, and a substitute had to be hired.

7. Held a staff meeting to discuss the physical inventory process.

8. Allocated census tracts to three geographic areas, assigned one staff member to each district and began street-by-street canvass to determine the accuracy and completeness of preliminary inventory.

In step eight, the researchers drove all major arteries, all streets in commercial and industrial zones and approximately every other street in residential zones, checking off identified agencies and adding new ones as they were identified. This street-by-street canvassing resulted in many additions (93) and deletions (51) to the original list. It was concluded that simply searching printed sources such as the telephone book was an insufficient method for determining specific community recreation agencies.

In any such inventorying process, it is desirable to obtain various kinds of information, including the following:

1. Agency's name, address, phone number.
2. Agency's objectives, goals, purpose, organizational chart.
3. Agency's areas and facilities (i.e., those which they own, administer, or use) and their location, capacity, safety, security, hours of operation and restrictions on use.
4. Agency's programs: type of program, skill level, age groups, characteristics of intended participants, type of supervision or leadership (if any), program duration, when and where offered, fees or other membership requirements.

Any such inventorying process is an involved undertaking. A study in Nashville, Tennessee, that inventoried only those agencies that were a part of the metropolitan Nashville government or received part of their funding from the government, identified agencies, types of leisure services provided to Nashville citizens, and the qualities, resources and impact associated with each. Table 12–1* shows only the Arts and Crafts opportunities available from government agencies.

Most attempts at inventorying existing leisure resources do not make such qualitative judgments about what is being categorized. Another method of inventorying leisure resources which *does* take such considerations into account is the Recreation Experience Components Concept developed by

---

*Source: Christene McLean and Dennis Hermanson, *Leisure Services: A Measure of Program Performance* (Nashville: The Urban Conservatory of Metropolitan Nashville–University Center, July, 1974).

Christiansen. This concept is based upon the principle of "reasonable" availability of recreation opportunity:

> **. . . which means that within each planning area of a community each recreation experience opportunity is a *component* of the total standard for that unit. Since not all opportunities under the total system are controlled by one agency, these may be located in various places within the physical boundaries of the study unit. Therefore, no "standard" neighborhood park is expected to meet the requirements of the proposed standards. Under the new concept, the public park may have several of the components which provide recreational opportunities; the park by itself is not a component of the system. It is only a location.[2]**

For planning purposes, recreation activities are categorized into physical recreation, social recreation, cognitive recreation and environment-related recreation, with activity clusters (groups of activities offering similar experiences) included within each category. Both quantitative and qualitative indexes are developed for application at the regional, town, inter-neighborhood and sub-neighborhood level. Rather than being a simple set of standards, component standards are a series of criteria, "one for each demographic planning unit, all based upon the concept of providing opportunities for four basic recreation experiences. At each planning level, certain activity clusters offer alternatives to the way that the basic experience is provided. Some activity clusters are very significant in small demographic units and insignificant in large units."[2]

In evaluating the recreation opportunities within a geographic area, as illustrated in Table 12–2, those aspects of each site that could affect the quality of the leisure experience are listed under Humanistic and Support Considerations. This listing, when combined with a cataloging of the types of Recreation Experiences available in the area, gives a more complete picture of potential recreation opportunities. Such information might be useful to administrators of a community school, to YWCA board members, to those providing counseling to parolees from a state prison and to many others concerned with providing recreation for the public.

THE DISTRIBUTION OF LEISURE SERVICES

In addition to determining what leisure resources are available within a community, it is also important to study the distribution of these resources geographically. The mere existence of a given recreation resource in a community does not insure that all members of the community will be able to use it. If, for example, there are four swimming pools in a community but all of them are located in one neighborhood, in a section that is not served by public transportation, the pools may not realistically be considered part of the "supply" for residents outside that area. A community might have 1,000 acres of play area for youth, but use most of the space for baseball diamonds, which are used primarily by males, thereby denying recreational space to the other half of the population. Recreation staff may seem adequate for a given community until it is discovered that a certain area is being poorly served because very few workers have been assigned to it. Because of such situations, an important component of establishing what the "supply" of leisure services is

TABLE 12–1 Metro Agencies Providing ART AND CRAFT Recreation Opportunities (1973)

Quality	Participant *Adult Education* *Metro Schools*	*Parks & Recreation* *Parks Board*	Spectator *Parthenon* *Parks Board*	*Centennial Arts Center* *Parks Board*
Accessibility a. Geog.	Numerous school locations	17 Comm. Ctrs. (Adult art) 26 Comm. Ctrs. & 52 locations in schools (children's art)	One central location	One central location
b. Distance			Serves County Residents & tourists	Serves city
c. Hours	Nights & Saturday	Days & evenings	6 days a week	Open every day
Capacity a. Phys. Space			Frequently filled but not crowded; 17,980 sq. ft.	1300 sq. ft. Has a waiting list for classes
b.,# Staff		10 FT & 16 PT	5 FT & 3–5 PT	4 PT staff
Safety/ Security	No user accidents 1973 Depends on school system security provisions	Not recorded separate from accidents in location Estimate: None Depends on location security	3 accidents (persons fell or fainted). No incidents in facility. 19 incidents in Centennial Park.	No accidents No crimes reported
Supervision or Competence of Instructors			1–3 persons necessary	Instructors required to have college degree in art.
Variety		Adults: art, crafts, ceramics, weaving, macrame Children & Teens: art, crafts, ceramics, sewing, puppets	Permanent collections, annual shows, individual artist shows, pre-Columbian room	Pottery, painting, batik, weaving, beads, etc.

Citizen Perception				
Resources				
Manpower and Operating Costs Fees	$218,773 (Total for *all* classes, inc. G.E.D.) $15–17; G.E.D. free	July–Dec.: $31,884 (Art, crafts, sewing, ceramics) Adults $10; children free	July–Dec.: $20,105 (87% to salaries) No admission	July–Dec., 1973: $15,000 salaries); Pottery $4,694 $15/class; spectators free
% Client Support	96% (Total estimated costs for all classes; Metro subsidizes 4%)	Est.: $35,050 (or $17,525 for 6 mos.): 50%	None	
Impact				
Attendance			Est. 1973: 800,000 visitors* May, June, July, Aug.: 400,000 Sept., Oct., Nov., Mar., April: 270,000 Dec., Jan., Feb.: 134,000 Av. per mo. 67,000	1973: 10,458 spectators exhibits
Users:,#	(Total 4300 includes G.E.D. & other "non-recreational" classes.)	Estimates based on average class attendance: 13, 811		Participants: 855 Adults: 675; Teens & children:180
Characteristics	Adults	Adults: 3505 (25%) Teens: 1491 (11%) Children: 8815 (64%)	All populations visit	
Citizen Perception				

*All figures are estimates computed from head counts and guest book registration.

TABLE 12–2 Evaluation of Recreation Opportunities, Pleasant Gap (Community) Inter-Valley Region, 1970 Population – 1,773

- ☐ Existing
- (dotted) Proposed
- x Recreation Experience or Humanistic Consideration Provided or Proposed at Site
- / Specific Facility Existing or Proposed to Provide Experience at Site
- o Service for Specific Facility Necessary and Provided by Site Facility
- (hatched) Provision Not Recommended in Standards
- – Provision Not Recommended due to Specific Local Considerations

SUMMARY EVALUATION

- a Adequate
- e Expand
- i Inadequate
- n Need

SITE / Facility	RECREATION EXPERIENCES – Physical Recreation – Outdoor: Juvenile Low Organized Games & Free Play	Hard Surface Court Games	Recreational Turf Games	Specialized Individual & Dual Sports	Older Youth & Adult Field Turf Sports	Organized Competitive Team Turf Sports	Physical Recreation – Indoor: Juvenile through Adult Games & Sports	Organized Competitive Team Sports	Social Activites – Outdoor: Participant Involvement	Spectator Involvement	Social Activites – Indoor: Participant Involvement	Spectator Involvement	Environment Related Activities – Outdoor: Water Activities	Winter Activities	Outdoor Education	Unstructured Quiet Activities	Outing Sports & Activities	Environment Related Activities – Indoor	Cultural Educational & Creative Aesthetic Activities – Outdoor	Cultural Educational & Creative Aesthetic Activities – Indoor	HUMANISTIC & SUPPORT CONSIDERATIONS: Drinking Water	Sanitary Facilities	Refuse Control	Protection from Weather and Climate	Activity Lighting	Safety & Security Lighting	Staffing: Safety Supervision	Staffing: Facility Maintenance	Staffing: Activity Leadership & Programming	Transportation/Circulation	Communications	Special Considerations	LAND AREA (ACRES) 3 Actual (3) Approx.
PLEASANT GAP ELE. SCHOOL	x	x	x	x	x		x				x	x								x	x	x	x	x	–	x	x	x x	x	x	x		4.4
Play Apparatus	/																				o	o	o	o			o	o o	o	o			
Hard Surface Court Area		/		/																	o	o	o	o	–	o	o	o o	o	o	o		
Turf Area			/		/																o	o	o	o			o	o o	o	o			
Multi-Purpose Room W/Stage							/				/	/								/													
Meeting Room											/																						
LITTLE LEAGUE BALLFIELD					x	x				x											x	x	x	x	–	–	x	x	x	x	x		1.5
Ballfield					/	/				/											o	o	o	o	–	–	o	o	o	o			
PLEASANT GAP FIRE CO. CARNIVAL AREA			x						x	x									x			x	x				x	x	–	x	x		6
Turf Field Area			/																		–	o	o	–			o	o	–	o			
Carnival Area									/	/									/		x	o	o	x	x	–	o	o	–	o	o		
PLEASANT GAP COMM. BALLFIELD					x	x				x											x	x	x	x	–	–	x	x	x	x	x		5
Ballfield					/	/				/											o	o	o	o	–	–	o	o	o	o	o		
AMERICAN LEGION POST #867											x																						
Meeting Room											/																						
LOGAN GRANGE #109											x																						
Meeting Room											/																						
UNITED METHODIST CHURCH											x	x																					
Meeting Room											/																						
Banquet Facilities											/	/																					
PLEASANT GAP FIRE HALL											x	x																					
Meeting Room											/																						
Banquet Facilities											/	/																					
INDIVIDUAL BACKYARDS	x		x						x				x						x		x	x	x	x			x	x		x	–		?
Play Apparatus	/																				o	o	o	o			o	o	–	o			
Turf Area			/																		o	o	o	o			o	o	–	o			
Water Activities													/								o	o	o	o	–	–	o	o	–	o	–		
SUMMARY EVALUATION	a e	a	a	i e	a	a	a		a	a	a	a	a	i n	i n	i n	i n		a	a													

Source: Monty Christiansen, "Application of a Recreation-Experience Components Concept for Comprehensive Recreation Planning," *Leisure Tap,* Bureau of Recreation and Conservation Technical Assistance Publication, Vol. 1, No. 2, June, 1975.

TABLE 12–3 Differences in the Distribution of D.C. Department of Recreation Services: Anacostia and West of Rock Creek Park

Measures of Service	Residents		Visits	
	Individual	Children-Youth (0-19)	Individual	Children-Youth (0-19)
<u>Expenditures</u>				
Capital (1960-1973)	Anacostia (3.7:1)[a]	Anacostia (1.9:1)	Anacostia (1.9:1)	Anacostia (1.3:1)
Operating (all operations)[b]	Anacostia (2.3:1)	No Difference (1:1)	No Difference (1:1)	West of the Park (1.4:1)
Operating (community-based facilities)[c]	Anacostia (1.5:1)	West of the Park (1.4:1)	West of the Park (1.3:1)	West of the Park (1.9:1)
<u>Quantity of Opportunities</u>[d]				
Acreage of Recreation Centers	Anacostia (1.6:1)	West of the Park (1.3:1)	West of the Park (1.3:1)	West of the Park (1.8:1)
Number of Facilities	Anacostia (1.3:1)	West of the Park (1.7:1)	West of the Park (1.5:1)	West of the Park (2.4:1)
Days of Operation	Anacostia (1.6:1)	West of the Park (1.3:1)	West of the Park (1.3:1)	West of the Park (1.8:1)
<u>Quality of Opportunities</u>				
Accessibility (Within 1/2 mile)	Anacostia (1.3:1)	Not Available	Not Applicable	Not Applicable
Other Quality Variables (e.g., cleanliness, amount of space, hours of operation)	No Difference	No Difference	Not Applicable	Not Applicable

[a]These numbers are the ratios between service provided in the two areas. The first number in the ratio refers to the area listed.

[b]Total cost of operating all D. C. Department of Recreation Facilities and programs.

[c]Estimated cost of operating community-based facilities and programs.

[d]Quantity of opportunities per visit, or utilization rate, may reflect more opportunities provided, or it may indicate lower citizen interest in taking advantage of the opportunities provided.

Source: Donald Fisk and Cynthia Lancer, *Equality of Distribution of Recreation Services: A Case Study of Washington, D.C.* (Washington, D.C.: The Urban Institute, 1974).

TABLE 12–4 D.C. Department of Recreation Operating Expenditures Per Resident and Per Child-Youth (FY 1973)

Area	Operating Expenditures[a]	Per Resident	Per Child-Youth (0–19)
Anacostia	$4,707,544	$23	$52
West of the Park	$1,085,553	$10	$53

[a]U.S. Congress, Senate Subcommittee of the Committee on Appropriations, "District of Columbia Appropriations for Fiscal Year 1974: Hearings on H.R. 8658," 93rd Cong., 1st sess., 23 May 1973, pt. 1, p. 1118.

in a given community, is to determine its geographic distribution. Sometimes this is done by calculating supply figures for different planning areas for a community.

A number of measures of supply can be determined for different geographic regions within a community. Supply can be measured by the amount of money spent in capital and operating budgets; by the number of facilities, areas or acres of land set aside for recreation; by the number of full- and part-time staff; by the number of programs; and so forth. In a study for the Urban Institute, Fisk examined the equality of distribution of recreation resources within the Anacostia Area and west of Rock Creek Park in Washington, D.C.[5] As is seen in Table 12–3, the distribution measures used dealt with monetary expenditures, quantity of opportunity and quality of opportunity. Distribution was calculated in terms of both total residents and children-youth.

The distribution of resources is not at all a simple thing to calculate. For instance, look at the differences between the areas shown in Tables 12–4 and 12–5, depending on whether the supply was being calculated per 1,000 residents, per 1,000 children-youth, per visit, per user, and so on. In some cases, the figures in such tables would reveal a clear-cut pattern of inequality of distribution, but in this study they reveal no definite pattern at all.

For many commercial leisure services, determining the distribution of some specific leisure resource, such as indoor tennis facilities, is a crucial consideration in planning future development. Such information must then be combined with data concerning the location of actual and potential users of the resource, along with demographic information about such users, in order to make judgments about the financial feasibility of the undertaking.

TABLE 12–5 D.C. Department of Recreation Full-Time Equivalent Staff Per Facility, Per Residents, and Per Children-Youth (1972)

Area	Number of Full-Time Equivalent Staff[a]	Per Facility	Per 10,000 Residents	Per 10,000 Children-Youth (0–19)
Anacostia	168	4	8	18
West of the Park	45	3	4	22

[a]Affidavit of Joseph H. Cole, *Burner* v. *Washington*, undated, C. A. No. 242-71 (D.D.C.), Recreation Exhibit No. 14. The list of facilities can be found in Table A-2 in the Appendix. Estimates were made for the number of staff at Capitol View, Baptist, Ketcham, Forest Hills, Montrose, Wilson and Deal, since these figures were not provided in the affidavit. These figures do not include staff for the Roving Leader Program.

In summary, determining the leisure resources of a community and their distribution is an essential step toward understanding the recreation needs and desires of the community. Since leisure service organizations are highly interdependent, such information is relevant to the operation of public, private and commercial leisure service organizations. In many instances, however, such information is not collected and used in the decision-making process or, in instances where it is collected, collection is often limited to services provided by only one type of leisure service agency, e.g., public. The collection of *all* relevant data makes it easier to view leisure services as a system and thus to plan wisely, and help others plan wisely, for that system.

REFERENCES

1. George A. Theodorson and Achilles G. Theodorson, *Modern Dictionary of Sociology* (New York: Thomas Y. Crowell Co., 1969), pp. 63–64.
2. Monty Christiansen, *The Application of A Recreation Experience Components Concept for Comprehensive Recreation Planning* (Harrisburg: Bureau of Recreation and Conservation, 1974).
3. Watson B. Hovis and Fredrick W. Wagner, *Leisure Information Retrieval System City-Wide Recreation Project.* (Seattle: Leisure Services, Inc., 1972), pp. 17–18.
4. Christene McLean and Dennis Hermanson, *Leisure Services: A Measure of Program Performance* (Nashville: The Urban Observatory of Metropolitan Nashville–University Center, July, 1974).
5. Donald Fisk and Cynthia Lancer, *Equality of Distribution of Recreation Services: A Case Study of Washington, D.C.* (Washington, D.C.: The Urban Institute, 1974), pp. 12, 40.

QUESTIONS

1. What alternative methods can be used to identify the leisure resources of a community?

2. Should public recreation and park agencies take the initiative in coordinating an effort to identify the leisure resources in their community? Why or why not?

3. Of what significance is knowing the geographical distribution of leisure resources within a community?

4. Discuss the relationship between supply of recreation facilities and participation.

Are these bathers satisfied with conditions at their beach?
How would you find out?
(U.S. Bureau of Outdoor Recreation)

chapter 13

DETERMINING LEISURE PARTICIPATION PATTERNS AND ATTITUDES

INTRODUCTION

The methods by which current leisure activity participation patterns can be determined will be examined in this chapter, with particular attention given to the survey research process and agencies' use of these methods. The measurement of the attitudes and opinions of people toward leisure and leisure services will also be considered.

It is important, first of all, to know in what leisure activities people are currently engaging, since ultimately the decisions made by leisure service agencies are in some way shaped by current leisure patterns. There is no standard method of measurement used to record participation in leisure activities. Instead, a broad range of indicators may be used to determine the extent of participation in various leisure activities. These indicators include attendance; membership counts; license counts; aerial photography; self-reported participation through surveys and questionnaires; monetary spending; automobile counts; examination of equipment, areas and facilities to estimate amount of usage; percentage of potential users currently taking advantage of areas or facilities; percentage of a facility's capacity attained; staff estimates of users; attendance counts using a formula for estimation of attendance; registration or enrollment in classes or programs; sign-out lists for equipment; and records of permits issued.

Naturally, some leisure activities are more easily "counted" than others. If you go to a movie, for instance, you buy a ticket which serves as a fairly reliable indicator of how you spent two or three hours of your time. (A few people, of course, sneak in, or leave before the movie is over.) Other forms of participation, however, such as taking a walk in the park, are less easily counted. Table 13–1 shows some attendance figures taken for various leisure service programs in the Nashville, Tennessee, metropolitan area, and includes suggested procedures for improving their accuracy.

In some instances where entrance to a recreation facility is unrestricted or uncontrolled, a formula is devised to standardize the attendance estimating procedures. At many public and private recreation centers, for instance, leaders are instructed to count the participants at what they consider to be the peak attendance period, and to then multiply that attendance figure by 1.5. This is usually done once in the morning and once in the afternoon, and, if an evening program is operating, once in the evening. The multiplication factor is an attempt to recognize that, for instance, children and youth come to and go from playgrounds or recreation centers both before and after attendance is taken.

Many on-site count estimates are taken by estimating the attendance to capacity. If it is known, for instance, that an auditorium can hold 2,200 people, or that there are 125 picnic tables in a given park, it is possible to estimate the

TABLE 13–1 Reported Attendance Figures, Reliability, and Suggestions for Improvement

Program	1973 (or 72–73) Attendance	Reliability Rating	Suggested Procedure for Improving the Measure or Estimate of Attendance
Adult Education (classes)	4300 persons × # classes = attendance	Estimate	Record revenues
Centennial Arts		Registration Head Count × # weeks	Weekly head count
(classes)	10 wks × 855 = 8550		
(spectators)	10,458		
Community Centers (P & R)	Sept.–Nov.: 32,578 persons × # visits = 458,865	Estimate from survey Directors' records	Accurate daily head counts every 3 hours
Cumberland Museum	99,533	Head count and estimates	Daily head counts, registration, or random sample head counts
Library	126,258 card holders	May either over- or under-estimate library use	Head counts, mechanical gate counters (40% of Nashville population who said they used library, multiplied by # of times used per year)
WPLN	22,500 listener audience size	Estimate	Citizen survey–16% of Nashville households in county = 23,562, multiplied by number of times listened to station per year
Municipal Audit (music events only)	245,844	Projected estimate from gate receipts	Gate receipts
Nashville Symphony	157,000 admissions	Count or estimate	
PR			
Dance	966 × 41 weeks = 35,506	Estimate	Weekly head counts
Arts & Crafts	13,811	Estimate	
Music	175	Estimate	
Golf	183,985	Golf rounds receipts	Receipts, incl. membership play
Swimming	58,853	Ticket receipts	Receipts
Parthenon	800,000	Estimate	Reliable use of head counts & formulas
Schools:			
Music	57,000 participants × # classes, etc. = AH.	Estimate	
Athletics	7709 participants × # games = 94,895		
Spectators	Not known		Gate receipts for admission events

*Source: Christine McLean and Dennis Hermanson, *Leisure Services–The Measurement of Program Performance* (Nashville: The Urban Observatory of Metropolitan Nashville–University Center, July, 1974).

total attendance by relating the fraction of empty seats or tables to the capacity number.

Licenses, permits, memberships, entrance fees and registrations also can provide valuable information about participation in leisure services.

SURVEYS OF LEISURE ACTIVITY

One way of determining the present leisure patterns of a community or other group of individuals is to conduct a survey of the leisure activity patterns of those served by the agency in question. In some cases, the survey should also include information concerning the leisure preferences or attitudes of those surveyed. Federal and state agencies dealing with recreation, parks and other leisure services often undertake such surveys themselves, or encourage local governments or other groups to undertake them as a condition of funding certain programs or facilities.

Often, a survey of leisure activity at the community level will be of interest to a number of organizations within the community, including social planning councils, planning commissions, municipal recreation and park agencies, schools, voluntary and youth-serving agencies, organizations with ethnic interests, such as the NAACP, and others. For this reason, it may make sense to have joint involvement in planning the survey and carrying it out. In some cases, a committee may be formed composed of representatives of these agencies. The committee may undertake the study itself, or it may seek the assistance of those with research training and experience in taking surveys on leisure behavior. The use of consultants for this purpose has many advantages. As Chubb points out, studies are often undertaken by those who have little training in research techniques or statistics: "Frequently, staff have been given such assignments in addition to their normal duties and they are able to spend little or no time on investigation of methods used elsewhere."[1] In an extraordinary number of cases, citizen groups or committees of agency representatives will "reinvent the wheel" rather than identify existing recreation survey instruments and modify them for their own purpose. Also, many such councils mistakenly believe that the findings of survey research will automatically make decisions for them, when in reality such surveys can do no more than provide a better information base for the committee, which must still interpret and make value judgments before the plan can be completed. Many leisure planning questions are actually made more complicated by the taking of surveys, since often additional information is introduced which is irrelevant or impossible to easily interpret. For the most part, however, surveys improve the quality of the planning decisions made, and provide certain kinds of information that would not be otherwise available.

LEISURE ACTIVITY PATTERNS

There are several methods that may be used to determine the activities in which people participate, as outlined below:

1. Respondents may be asked to recall all their activities over a short period of time (e.g., one to three days) using a "yesterday" interview (see p. 250) or other time-budget approach. Information from these time budgets is then coded by the researcher in accordance with the needs of the study.

2. Respondents may be asked to fill out a check list that attempts to list all leisure activities commonly undertaken by the public (see Table 13–2).

TABLE 13–2 Recreation Resources Inventory Program Activity Code

10) 101) Amusements
102) 1021) Carnivals
Rides
Shows

10) 101) Arts & Crafts
102) 1021) Arts & Crafts in General
Astrology
Astronomy
Basketry
Boat Building
Carving
Ceramics
Decoupage
Drawing
Furniture
Interior Decorating
Jewelry
Leathercraft
Macramé
Metal Work
Models
Needlecraft
Painting
Photography
Photography Lab
Pottery
Printing
Refinishing
Scrap Craft
Sculpture
Silk Screen
Sketching
Textiles
Tie Dying
Upholstery
Weaving
Woodwork

10) 101) Dance
102) 1021) Ballet
Baton
Creative
Folk
International
Jazz
Modern
Primitive
Rhythms & Movement
Round
Social
Square
Tap

10) 101) Drama
102) 1021) Acting
Adult Theatre
Children's Theatre
Costume Design
Creative
Directing
Puppetry
Set Design
Storytelling

10) 101) Games & Sports
102) 1021) Archery
Badminton
Baseball
Basketball
Billiards (including pool)
Billiards (Ladies)
Billiards Tournament
Boating
Bowling
Boxing
Calisthenics
Canoeing
Conditioning
Cricket
Croquet
Cross Country
Curling
Cycling (Bicycle, Motorcycle)
Darts
Drag Racing
Exercising
Fencing
Field Hockey
Firearm Safety
Fishing
Floor Hockey
Football
Games & Sports in General
Golf
Golf Driving
Grandmother's Pool
Gymnastics
Handball
Handicapped Swim Program
Horseback Riding
Horseshoes
Hunting
Ice Hockey
Ice Skating
Informal Games
Jogging
Judo
Karate
Lacrosse
Model Boating
Polo (horse)
Power Boat Racing
Putting
Racketball
Roller Skating
Rowing (crew)
Rugby
Sailing
Scuba & Skin Diving
Self Defense
Shooting
Shuffleboard
Shuffleboard Tournament
Skeet Shooting
Sledding
Slow Pitch Softball
Snow Skiing
Snowmobiling
Soccer

TABLE 13–2 Recreation Resources Inventory Program Activity Code—Continued

Softball (fast)
Springboard Diving
Squash
Stunts
Surfing
Swimming
Table Tennis
Tennis
Track & Field
Trail Biking
Trampoline
Tumbling
Volleyball
Wading
Water Polo
Water Skiing
Weight Training
Whiffle Ball
Wrestling
Yoga

10) 101) Hobbies
102) 1021) Animals
Archeology
Coins
Cooking
Crochet
Flower Arranging
Gardening
Magic
Marine Biology
Rocks/Lapidary
Science
Sewing
Stamps

10) 101) Music
102) 1021) Band
Choral
Group Singing
Instruments
Listening
Music in General
Orchestra
Solo Singing

10) 101) Outdoor Recreation
102) 1021) Conservation Clubs
Day Camping
Driving Car
Hiking
Mountain Climbing
Nature Experiments
Nature Games
Nature Talks & Exhibits
Nature Walks
Outdoor Arts & Crafts
Overnight Camping
Picnics
Residential Camping
Scenery & Observation
Spelunking
Survival Training
Tours & Travel
Walking

10) 101) Reading, Writing, Speaking
102) 1021) Book Review
Creative Writing
Debating
Discussion Groups
Newspaper Writing
Public Speaking
Reading
Sensitivity Training
Technical Writing

10) 101) Social Recreation & Miscellaneous
102) 1021) Co-recreation Sports
Dining
Family Recreation
Games (Table)
Novelty Events
Parties
Preschool & Tiny Tot Programs (general)
Senior Adult Programs (general)
Scholarship Programs
Teen Programs (general)

10) 101) Spectating
102) 1021) Concerts
Exhibits (Art, Auto, etc.)
Lectures
Motion Pictures
Plays
Television

10) 191) Special Events
102) 1021) Banquets
Clinics
Concerts
Contests
Dances
Entertainment
Father & Son Program
Festivals
Meets
Outings, Excursions, Field Trips
Parades
Regattas
Shows
Tournaments
Vocational Training
Water Day
Water Pageant

10) 101) Voluntary Service
102) 1021) Activity Leaders
Board Members
Clerical Helpers
Club Leaders
Committee Workers
Counselors
Food Programs
Fund Raising
Officials
Special Events Assistants
Volunteers

Source: Watson B. Hovis and Fredrick W. Wagner, *Leisure Information Retrieval System—City Wide Recreation Project.* Seattle, Leisure Services, Inc., 1972, pp. 17–18.

3. A listing of broad types of recreation and leisure experiences (drama, music, sports) may be provided, on which respondents indicate their areas of interest.

4. Respondents may be given a highly specific listing of activities that are typically offered by the agencies undertaking the survey, and asked to check off those in which they participate (see Table 13–3). None of these alternatives is inherently correct. The best choice will depend upon the purpose for determining participation rates. Surprisingly, many such studies are undertaken without a very specific statement of why leisure patterns are being determined. If, for example, the leisure service agency wishes to provide a basis for more effectively coordinating its future offerings with other agencies, it is necessary to use a broad, inclusive listing. However, if the agency wants to determine the relative usage of certain types of recreation facilities or participation in programs (and cannot do so through registration, attendance counts, etc.) it should use a highly specific listing which also includes questions about locations of participation. If respondents are being asked their opinion about the desirability of future leisure activities or services, the agency must make sure that the listing does not include activities that it is not possible for them to provide, unless the study is being undertaken as a broad planning base for a number of organizations. In any case, the determination of study purpose is crucial to the proper selection of activity categorization.

FREQUENCY OF PARTICIPATION IN LEISURE ACTIVITIES

The frequency with which an individual participates in a given leisure activity is an important variable in determining leisure behavior. A person who undertakes five adult education courses within a year, for instance, will affect the agency differently from a person who participates in only one. In many park and recreation agencies, only a minority of the population uses the services, but that segment of the population uses them intensively. Further, people who participate in an activity frequently may have to be planned for differently from those who participate only occasionally. A ski slope for people who ski only a few times a year will be quite different from one for those who ski once a week or more.

In seeking to determine how often people participate in given recreational activities, a number of alternative methods may be used, ranging from actually specifying the amount of time spent to requiring only a very crude indication of frequency of usage. Determining which approach makes sense will involve answering the following questions:

1. How specific a level of information concerning frequency can be utilized in terms of the study's purposes?
2. How accurate will people be in the recall of their participation rates?
3. How much will it cost to collect the information?

While frequency-of-participation categories will vary from study to study, there is always some doubt as to how best to describe such frequency. Respondents may not be able to remember how many times they went swimming during a year, but may accurately estimate whether they swam (a) never, (b) less than once a month, (c) one, two or three times a month, or (d) once a week or more. Determining the most accurate frequency measure is often a complex process. In many areas, for instance, swimming might be done more than once a week in warm weather, but not at all during the winter months. Such situations have prompted some researchers to ask respondents to describe fre-

TABLE 13–3 Sample Questionnaire Form for Participation in Activities

New Programs and Facilities

In this section, we would like to know what new recreation programs and facilities would meet the needs of the citizens of Washtenaw County.

Listed below are possible programs and facilities that could be developed. For each one, please indicate how important you feel the development of such a program or facility is for Washtenaw County. Put a check (✔) in the appropriate column.

	1 Very Important	2 Moderately Important	3 Not At All Important
A. Beaches	☐	☐	☐
B. Day camps	☐	☐	☐
C. Nature center	☐	☐	☐
D. Fishing	☐	☐	☐
E. Senior citizen programs	☐	☐	☐
F. Tennis courts	☐	☐	☐
G. Community gardens	☐	☐	☐
H. Tournaments for organized sports	☐	☐	☐
I. Purchase and preserve lands with woods, hills, lakes, etc.	☐	☐	☐
J. Tobogganing/Sledding	☐	☐	☐
K. Ice skating	☐	☐	☐
L. Roller skating	☐	☐	☐
M. Sailing	☐	☐	☐
N. Organized outings (to see Detroit Tigers, Art Institute, Detroit Zoo, etc.)	☐	☐	☐
O. Trails for horseback riding or hiking, or bicycling or cross-country skiing	☐	☐	☐
P. Trails for snowmobiles	☐	☐	☐
Q. Camping	☐	☐	☐
R. Picnicking	☐	☐	☐
S. Indoor swimming	☐	☐	☐
T. Outdoor swimming	☐	☐	☐
U. Clinics for cross-country skiing, tennis, sailing, etc.	☐	☐	☐
V. Nature trails	☐	☐	☐
W. Canoeing	☐	☐	☐
X. Golf	☐	☐	☐
Y. Playgrounds for children	☐	☐	☐
Z. Quiet places to be alone out-of-doors	☐	☐	☐
AA. Other (specify) ______________ ______________	☐	☐	☐

Indicate the programs or facilities that you would *most like* to see developed.

a. First choice ______________

b. Second choice ______________

c. Third choice ______________

If the county is to develop more recreation facilities and programs, millage support will be necessary. If there were an election today, would you vote for a ½ mill levy?

☐ Yes
☐ No
☐ Uncertain
→ SEE TABLE

This table tells you how much a ½ mill levy would cost per year.

Market value of your house	Assessed value of your house	Cost to you of a ½ mill levy
$20,000	$10,000	$5.00
$30,000	$15,000	$7.50
$40,000	$20,000	$10.00
$60,000	$30,000	$15.00

Would you vote for a ¼ mill levy? This would cost you one-half the amount in the above table.

☐ Yes
☐ No
☐ Uncertain

Source: Jerome Johnston, *Recreation Behaviors and Attitudes of Residents of Washtenaw County, Michigan* (Ann Arbor, Michigan: Survey Research Center, Summer, 1974), pp. 12–13.

quency either in terms such as "occasionally," or in specific time increments such as those listed above.

LEISURE ATTITUDES AND OPINIONS

In addition to questions concerning leisure activity patterns, many surveys undertaken by leisure service agencies use a number of questions dealing with the attitudes and opinions of respondents. Occasionally, surveys are devoted exclusively to such questions.

Attitude and opinion questions usually fall into one of the following categories:

1. General questions asking the general public to rate the overall services of the agency.
2. Questions asking the respondent to rank or otherwise identify leisure activities in which they would like to participate in the future.
3. Questions asking users of a specific facility or participants in a given program to rate it in regard to a number of operational issues.
4. Questions asking non-participants and non-users to identify reasons for non-use.
5. Questions asking the general public to rate or react to contemplated future actions of the agency.

With questions dealing with respondents' overall satisfaction with any particular agency, it is difficult to use the results of a single administration of the question as an absolute indicator of general public satisfaction, since there is no information with which to compare the findings. Although it is worth knowing that 15 percent of the respondents are not satisfied with the agency's services, it means considerably more to know that four years ago 30 percent of the respondents were dissatisfied but now only 15 percent are.

Another important factor in analyzing such questions is to know as much as possible about the characteristics of those who are dissatisfied. Are members of one particular neighborhood significantly more displeased than any other group of respondents? Are new residents less satisfied than those who have lived longer in the community? Such information is helpful in that it makes it possible to identify a target group for further investigation as to causes of dissatisfaction.

Questions asking respondents what they would like to do during their leisure time in the future or what facilities they would like to see developed must be structured as carefully as possible, since they are very difficult to interpret. As Burton warns, "Simply to ask people about which activities they would like to take up is inadequate, since experience has shown that most people will determine these without any consideration of the impact that this will have upon the amount of money and time which they will have available for recreation."[2] Among some of the difficulties associated with using these questions are the following: (a) Many people tend to let their imagination run free when answering such questions. (b) Since leisure activities have different statuses, respondents sometimes are more likely to respond with high status leisure activities. (c) The respondent may forget that sponsoring such activities or developing such facilities will cost him money, either as a taxpayer or as a direct participant. Therefore, in any questions of this type, an attempt should be made whenever possible to put a price tag on such programs and facilities.

Many attitudinal questions are designed to allow users of a specific recreation facility or program to rate their satisfaction with it. Some of the subjects that respondents are most often asked to rate are leadership, supervision, cost, safety, lighting, maintenance or cleanliness, parking, equipment or supplies, hours of operation, program time or scheduling, degree of crowdedness, distance or time needed to get to facility, attractiveness, policy on officiating, policies at the facility or program (such as required dress, use of alcoholic beverages), and regulations for non-members or non-residents. Usually, an "open-ended" question is also asked, to allow respondents to volunteer additional likes or dislikes. While many respondents will not respond to open-ended questions, those who do are likely to feel strongly about what they write.

Questions asking about reasons for non-use of certain leisure services are usually administered to the membership or population at large. In many cases, such questions deal with many of the topics above, such as hours of operation, and so on. Again, with attitude or opinion questions, it is essential to include an open-ended question that allows the respondent to mention aspects of non-usage which prestructured questions do not cover.

In some instances, leisure service agencies include questions asking for opinions concerning either contemplated future agency actions or a range of possible actions. In such instances, questions should be as highly specific as possible, and whenever possible should include some reference to costs involved.

METHODS OF SURVEYING LEISURE BEHAVIOR AND ATTITUDES

Use of Time Budgets in Leisure Research

The time budget is a method of collecting information concerning leisure activity. It can be used for descriptive or analytic purposes. Special attention is devoted to it here because it represents a possible alternative to other survey research techniques in regard to leisure research. "A time budget is a log or diary of the sequence and duration of activities engaged in by an individual over a specified period, most typically the 24-hour day."[3] A time budget or structured diary measures what an individual does during all of some specified period of time; most typically a single day. Time budgets have a number of advantages for research concerning leisure time and its use, since they theoretically record *all* of an individual's activities, both work and leisure, so that duration, sequencing, location of activity and sometimes those with whom the activity is undertaken are recorded, thus giving a more complete picture of what an individual does. It might be said that for the researcher the significance of the sum of all activities may be greater than their separate parts.

Time budget data are broad, but shallow. They are often used as a frame of reference for more intensive inquiry, since they determine broad usage patterns and limits. While time budgets increasingly try to tell where and with whom various activities take place, the data per se do not reveal the function of the activity undertaken or its meaning to the individual. Thus information regarding "life style" and style of leisure participation is usually not determined through time budget studies. However, time budget data *are* useful in practical policy planning and also hold at least some interest for social theory.[3]

Time budgets have been used extensively by researchers from many countries. The first large-scale time budget was undertaken in Moscow in 1924 as part of a drive toward rational economic planning. The studies were resumed in the late 1950's. The Soviet Union has even held scientific conferences concerned with establishing uniform codes and standards for time budgets. Perhaps the largest study ever undertaken using a time budget was one involving a sample of 170,000 respondents in Japan during 1960–61 to aid in the scheduling of radio and television programs. Perhaps the three best known time budget studies undertaken in the United States are: (1) *Leisure—A Suburban Study,* undertaken by Lundberg and associates; (2) *A Nationwide Study of Living Habits,* undertaken by A. J. Ward, Inc., in 1954; and (3) the U.S. portion of the multi-national time budget study, directed by A. Szalai.

Methods. Basically, there are three main methods for eliciting the data from respondents using time budgets:

1. *Diary Method*—the respondent writes down his own log of activities on the basis of instructions and forms provided him.
2. *Yesterday Interview*—the respondent reconstructs his previous day's sequence of activities orally, through probing from an interviewer, and estimates the time spent on each.
3. *Direct Observation*—a second party observes and records the individual's activities.[3]

While past research has depended upon the diary method, the increasing tendency is to combine the diary method with the yesterday interview. For example, a subject may be asked to keep a diary for a 24-hour period, and then to use this diary as an initial skeleton for more detailed discussion in a yesterday interview. "Even a sketchy diary will put stringent limits on the respondent's imagination as far as time durations are concerned, yet the interviewing can serve to bring the account of activities on the part of a poorly educated subject to a level of detail that a well-educated subject may be able to capture by himself."[3] There is also an increasing tendency to expand the information collected by a time budget to include such information as where and with whom activity takes place, desire for more or less activity, whether the activity is routine or unusual, and whether it is initiated by the person himself or others. Such extensive interest has led to modification of the basic time budget approach, as in the "household activity system" developed by Chapin and Hightower.[4] Pre-testing for the 12-nation time budget study found that the following procedure was the most effective:

> **(1) During the day 'T−1' (i.e., the day preceding the one during which the respondent kept records) an interviewer visited the home of the respondent, conducted a short interview about the preceding day (without making this educational interview part of the research record), and then instructed the respondent how to use the forms for self reporting. (2) The respondent would fill out his forms for the day 'T'either at the evening of this day, or sometime during the next day. (3) Later, during the day 'T+1' (i.e., the day following the one for which the respondent's self-record was kept), the interviewer would return and conduct a 'yesterday interview,' if at all possible based upon the self-record of the respondent; this interview would follow the self-report chronologically, probing whether there were additional activities to record. The principal function of this 'yesterday interview' was therefore a check on the completeness in recording incidental activities. In addition . . . in every tenth case a so-called 'fresh interview' was required, i.e., the interviewer had to carry out a 'yesterday interview' relating to the day 'T−2' when he first met the respondent, without preparing him in any way (for) this exercise.[5]**

Time budgets may either have the respondent record his activities at some predetermined interval of time (although the actual recording is usually done at the end of the day) or let the respondent fill in activities according to the time each one began and ended.

Non-Response. Because time budget studies place a burden on the respondent that exceeds that placed upon him by the interview, researchers conducting them often run into the problem of high refusal rates. Therefore, quite a few time budget studies have had to be conducted using a "captive audience." Furthermore, in many cases non-respondents are not randomly distributed throughout the population. Burton, however, found that a time budget study undertaken in two areas of Britain obtained an overall response of 59 percent, which was identical to the response obtained from the same population using a self-administered questionnaire.[6] In regard to non-respondents, it was found that while they were representative of the population with respect to sex and marital status, those under 30 were less likely to be non-respondents than those over 30. However, Converse reports that it has been recently demonstrated that it is possible to keep non-response within tolerable limits (20 percent).[3] To achieve such success, however, is complicated and expensive and requires elaborate plans and inducements.

Difficulties in Interpretation of Data. Because determining how people spend their time is one of those areas in which reliability and validity of data are extremely variable even with the most detailed collections of data, there is, as Scheuch observes, "little in tables of time budget data that enables a social scientist to make even an inspired guess about the accuracy of the information."[5] In pre-testing for the 12-nation time budget study, it was found that activities that were routinized, provided they took up longer periods of time, could be relatively easily determined even if the interviewer's performance was faulty. Such activities included sleep, work outside the home and major meals. Activities that involved a change of location or interaction partner could be determined mostly by using a yesterday interview. Additionally, among the most stable data in time budgets are the incidences of all activities connected with equipment or appliances. These latter characteristics would appear to make recall of outdoor recreation activities comparatively easy, since they usually involve a change of location and the use of equipment.

A major difficulty in recording outdoor recreation activities through the use of the time budget is that of determining how often the activity occurs. "In general, for such studies, the unit of observation should ideally correspond to the length of the time span during which an activity occurs cyclically."[5] Since many large time budget studies have used a single day as the length of recorded activity, many outdoor recreation and other leisure activities that are important to the participant are omitted.

Categorization. Time budget entries must be grouped into categories for purposes of analysis. Often such a categorization is made using a small number of categories, one of which relates to recreation or leisure. Chapin, for instance, used six activity classification categories: (1) income-related activities, (2) family-related activities, (3) recreation and relaxation activities, (4) religious activities and organizational participation, (5) socializing activities, and (6) subsistence activities. A total of 30 activities are then subsumed under these categories.

Problems. A number of problems exist in the categorization process. First, in some cases it is necessary for the coder to assume the motivation of the respondent in order to categorize a given activity. Attending a party at the house of a fellow employee, for instance, might be classified as either socializing or work-related in terms of motivation to act. A second difficulty is that the larger the number of categories, the more complex and expensive the coding procedure becomes, but the smaller the number of categories, the less difference is observed among respondents. Another problem in the categorization process is that more than one activity may be undertaken at the same time. A person may, for instance, watch television while eating his dinner. Either the researcher must be willing to let the respondent omit one of the activities or he must use a more complex recording system incorporating a primary and secondary activity recording system. Even when the primary-secondary recording system is used, however, problems remain of interpreting which activity is central in meaning to the individual. In the 12-nation time budget study, primary activity was defined as "any act that was determined by a person's location, and/or his interaction partner plus the common sense notion for the beginning and the end of an activity."[5] In practice, a primary activity was the activity mentioned first by the respondent. A secondary activity was defined as "an activity performed concurrently with primary activities."[5] Generally, according to Scheuch, primary activities represent the rough organization of the day as a consequence of the organization of society and the combination of duties which result from a person's roles, while secondary activities represent the preferences of an individual.

The categorizing of activities for purposes of coding and analysis presents at least two problems: the determination of categories of activity and the transcribing of written or verbal reports into these categories. In designing categories of activity for analysis, many developers of time budget studies have used a hierarchical system in which the following levels of activity are used: (1) major category of activity, e.g., work; (2) basic activity groups within major categories, e.g., water-based activities; and (3) particular activities, e.g., swimming.

Co-Participants. When time budget data have been obtained concerning those with whom activities are undertaken, several different categorizations have been used. The 12-nation time budget study used the following: (1) all alone, (2) alone in a crowd, (3) spouse and children, (4) spouse but not children, (5) children but not spouse, (6) other household adults, (7) friends and relatives, (8) colleagues, (9) organization members, (10) neighbors, (11) formal contacts, and (12) others.[5]

Location. While many time budget studies have collected data concerning the location of an activity, usually such information specifies only whether the activity was done at home or away from home. From the standpoint of planning leisure services, more detailed locational information would be quite useful. The 12-nation time budget study did, however, obtain information on the location of the primary activity, and coded this information according to the following scheme: (1) one's own house or residence; (2) workplace (if outside home); (3) somebody else's dwelling; (4) outdoors, in streets (traffic); (5) inside a building where one offers or receives public or private services (e.g., doctor's office, shop, bank); (6) establishment for leisure, cultural, sport, etc., activities—indoors; (7) establishment for leisure, cultural, sport, etc., activities—outdoors; (8) eating and drinking locales (excluding the canteen or dining room of workplace, coded as #2 above); (9) others; and (10) no answer.[5] Obviously a more complete coding scheme in relation to location will increase the usefulness of time budget data to recreation planners.

Conclusions. Burton, at the conclusion of his use of the time budget for a study in Britain, concluded that the methodological problems associated with its use could be successfully overcome, although the method is more complex and laborious than the interview or questionnaire. He believed the particular value of the time budget to be the picture it gives of relationships between recreation and other activities, particularly in regard to length of time spent on these recreational pursuits and their distribution throughout a day or longer period. "These latter factors cannot be covered easily in an interview or self-administered survey. Yet, they have considerable implications for recreation planning."[2] Length of time spent in an activity, Burton says, has a direct impact on the length of time that people are willing to travel to get to it. Although most time spent in leisure activity takes place around the home in our society, certain types of recreation or leisure activity do involve travel, and the amount of time required for traveling may be a crucial factor in determining whether or not to participate. Burton believes that if "the data shown here were representative of a wider population, conclusions might be drawn about the optimum management policies for various kinds of leisure facilities . . . about optimum pricing policies for such facilities, and about the location and siting of additional facilities."[2]

Converse, similarly, concludes that the time budget can provide information that cannot be obtained using other methods of data collection, such as (1) exact timing of activities; (2) frequency of changing to a different activity; and (3) patterns in the sequence of activities.[3]

Perhaps the question to be raised is the relative importance of obtaining such information for the purposes of various kinds of leisure research. From a standpoint of recreation planning, the exact timing of activities is probably information which cannot be used in the planning process, because it is too precise to be of benefit to existing planning methodologies. Leisure behavior patterns are subject to a myriad of influences that limit precise future prediction from past behavior. The same thing may be said about information concerning the frequency of changing activities and patterns in the sequence of activities. As knowledge for its own sake or for theory development, such information may be important, but for practical planning purposes it will probably be only minimally utilized.

Bishop argues that what many time budget studies ultimately concern themselves with in terms of data are summary data.[6] He quotes Converse: "Many studies (that use time diaries) begin and end with examination of the summary duration of time allotted to the various activities in the code, expressed as an average across respondents."[3] Based upon research with undergraduate students, Bishop has undertaken comparisons that indicate "that the use of time diaries might be an unnecessary expense and effort in some studies that are aimed at the collection of summary information about activity participation."[6] Such evidence was most conclusive in regard to frequency of participation. While such a study can by no means be considered generalizable, it does emphasize the importance of the researcher's knowing what level of analysis of data is important and useful in a given study before determining if the time budget is appropriate.

The time budget may be useful in varying degrees to different types of leisure service agencies. For many public agencies, securing the participation of citizens may be difficult or even impossible, whereas for membership organizations or institutions, such as companies that sponsor recreation programs, participation is more easily guaranteed.

The Use of the Personal Interview in Leisure Research

In one sense it is incorrect to discuss the personal interview separately from the time budget as it relates to leisure research, since many time budget studies do utilize a personal interview, the yesterday interview, as a part of their study design. The personal interview has been used widely in leisure research to collect information concerning a broad range of topics, including range and frequency of participation in leisure activities, the leisure patterns of the family unit and leisure roles within the family, work-leisure interrelationships, attitudes toward leisure, evaluation of leisure services provided by various leisure service agencies, and desired future leisure activities.

Advantages. A major advantage of the personal interview is that it is comparatively flexible. The trained interviewer can make sure that the respondent understands what is being sought, probe responses, use visual aids to help focus attention and establish a rapport with the respondent to help secure his cooperation.

The personal interview also asks comparatively little of the respondent. He need not write (or be able to write). He need not commit himself to doing anything in the future, such as filling out time logs or questionnaires. Many respondents "feel important" because of the interviewer's attention.

An additional advantage of the personal interview is that it can be used to collect diverse kinds of information at one time, such as participation rates and attitudes, which the time budget cannot.

Problems. While the personal interview sometimes has problems in terms of non-response, these problems are often not as severe as those encountered with the time budget and mailed questionnaire methods. One problem in the actual administration of the personal interview is that lack of adequate training of interviewers results in variation in data. In studies in which respondents are encouraged to elaborate responses, some interviewers obtain more detailed data than others. Such interviewer-produced bias can only be controlled if the selection and preparation of interviewers are given primary importance. The author has found the use of students or untrained staff members in any large-scale interviewing to be an untenable practice, based upon several bad experiences.

From the standpoint of leisure research, a major problem has been that it is not possible to compare the results of various surveys concerning leisure usage, because each instrument has been developed separately. With the time budget, it is possible to make comparisons over many years, even if recorded activities have been coded into different categories, simply by recoding them. Also, in many cases, the time budget coding systems are quite similar from one study to the other.

As discussed previously, it is generally assumed that time budgets are superior to the personal interview in their ability to determine information about the precise timing of activities, frequency of changing activities, and activity patterns. While this does represent an advantage in giving a better picture of the respondent in terms of work-leisure relationships, the cycle of usual activities, and so on, this advantage must be weighed against the

TABLE 13–4 Estimated Time Requirements for a Recreation Citizen Survey (Sample Size of 800)

Task	Time Required			
	Initial Survey		Subsequent Survey[1]	
	Calendar Time[2]	*Man Weeks*	*Calendar Time*[2]	*Man Weeks*
1. Select topic, specify accuracy and estimate cost	2	2	3 (tasks 1–3)	2 (tasks 1–3)
2. Design output and select survey method	3	3		
3. Design and pretest questionnaire	5	2		
4. Design sampling plan, select sample and prepare material	6	20	7	16
5. Recruit and train interviewers	2	1	1	1
6. Select best interviewers	1	1	1	1
7. Conduct survey	3	7	3	6
8. Edit, code, key punch and tabulate data	3	8	3	5
9. Analyze and interpret findings[3]	10	14	3	5
TOTAL	20	58	15	36

[1]It is assumed that essentially the same questions are used for subsequent surveys with only minor changes.

[2]Some tasks are carried on concurrently.

[3]Includes computer program preparation for initial survey.

Source: The Urban Institute, *Measuring the Effectiveness of Local Government Recreation Services* (Washington, D.C., The Urban Institute, 1972), pp. 51–52.

interview's ability to collect diverse types of information concerning attitude about activities undertaken and to probe or seek elaboration of information about activities and attitudes toward them.

With a large research budget, including money for inducements, the most complete approach in studying leisure behavior might be the use of the time budget with a subsequent yesterday interview followed by attitudinal questions concerning leisure activity. However, since this is not always economically feasible, and since the problem of non-response might still be present even if it were, the personal interview would seem to represent the more feasible technique for data collection. Table 13–4 shows the steps and estimated time requirements for conducting a Recreation Citizen Survey for 800 people. The time requirements are rough approximations which may be altered by many circumstances, such as the number of people included in designing the survey and their degree of expertise, the degree of consensus on the survey's purpose, and the other duties of those involved.

Use of the Telephone Interview in Leisure Research

While the telephone interview has sometimes been suspect among social scientists, there is recent evidence of its usefulness for leisure research studies. A study by Field, supported in part by the National Park Service, indicates that the telephone interview is quite satisfactory for studies dealing with leisure or outdoor activities.[7] In a study involving a sample of those aged 18 and older in Northern California, Western Oregon and Western Washington, Field found it possible to control female response bias, obtain an 88 percent completion rate in interviews lasting an average of 20 minutes, and reduce costs considerably, since the telephone interview costs were $11 per interview compared to $35 to $50 for personal interviews. Information was obtained in four data sets from respondents, one containing 40 outdoor recreation activities. While it is true that interviews could not be obtained from the approximately 7 percent of the population who do not have telephones, it is also a fact that most alternative methods lose some respondents as well—questionnaires and time budgets usually lose people who can't write or read, personal interviews lose transients, and so on.

The Urban Institute also developed a successful format to utilize the telephone interview in a study of citizen evaluations of local recreation services in Washington, D.C., and Rockville, Illinois.[8] For a very complete report of methodology, see *Measuring the Effectiveness of Local Government Recreation Services.*[8] A recent study of outdoor recreation participation and citizen attitudes in Pennsylvania, funded by the Land and Water Conservation Fund Act, utilized the telephone interview and reported success in interviews lasting up to one hour in length. Data were obtained about all individuals aged five or over in a household. There appear, however, to be some methodological questions left unanswered in the information released to date.

Use of the Mailed Questionnaire in Leisure Research

The mailed questionnaire has been widely used for a number of purposes relating to recreation and leisure, among them the determination of leisure patterns and leisure attitudes and preferences. The mailed questionnaire has the primary advantage of gathering a large amount of data in a short period of time and at a lower cost than the alternative methods. In addition, the mailed questionnaire does not require skilled staff to serve as data collectors. Finally, there is no variation in interview procedures to cause bias in responses.

The mailed questionnaire, however, has at least two important disadvantages. Since no one is present to administer the questionnaire to the respondent, there is not as great a chance to probe or to make sure that the respondent understands what information is being sought. An additional difficulty is that the mailed questionnaire, since it requires the respondent to read questions and respond in writing, rather than merely answer questions verbally, is likely to have a significant rate of non-response. Further, those who are more likely to respond to mail questionnaires are generally in higher income and education categories compared with non-respondents. This may mean that some of the answers given are not representative of the population at large. In some cases, individuals in higher education and income levels may have different leisure patterns and attitudes from the population at large. Backpacking in wilderness areas, for instance, is undertaken mostly by those in upper education levels, so that a mailed questionnaire that received a disproportionate return from those with high education levels might overestimate the population's participation in this activity. Through careful analysis of the characteristics of respondents, it is possible to determine how closely the returns approximate the population at large, and hence what inferences can be drawn from them.

CONCLUSION

In conclusion, research concerning people's leisure activity patterns and attitudes proceeds from no one standard method of measurement. The importance of such research, however, is great, since it may potentially give an accurate picture of the characteristics of participation of a cross section of the population and their attitudes and opinions toward leisure services.

REFERENCES

1. Michael Chubb, "Recreation Behavior Studies: Empirical Indicators of Change," in Betty van der Smissen, ed., *Indicators of Change in the Recreation Environment—A National Research Symposium* (University Park, Pennsylvania, 1975), pp. 129–174.
2. Thomas L. Burton and P. A. Noad, *Recreation Research Methods—A Review of Recent Studies* (Birmingham, England: Centre for Urban and Regional Studies, 1908), pp. 3, 182, 184.
3. Phillip E. Converse, "Time Budgets," in *International Encyclopedia of the Social Sciences* (New York: Macmillan, 1968), pp. 42, 43, 45, 47.
4. F. S. Chapin, Jr., and H. C. Hightower, "Household Activity Patterns and Land Use," *Journal of American Institute of Planners, 31*:222–231, 315; 1965.
5. Erwin K. Scheuch, "The Time-Budget Interview," in Alexander Szalai, ed., *The Use of Time—Daily Activities of Urban and Suburban Populations in Twelve Countries* (The Hague, Netherlands: Mouton, 1972), pp. 74, 75, 76–77, 786, 795.
6. Doyle Bishop, Claudine Jeanrenand and Kenneth Lawson, "Comparison of a Time Diary and Recall Questionnaire for Surveying Leisure Activities," *Journal of Leisure Research #7*, Winter, 1975, pp. 73–80.
7. Donald Field, "The Telephone Interview in Leisure Research," *Journal of Leisure Research*, 6:51–59, Winter, 1973.
8. *Measuring the Effectiveness of Local Government Recreation Services*—Appendices (Washington, D.C.: The Urban Institute, 1972), p. 51.

QUESTIONS

1. What, in your opinion, would be the ideal way to determine the leisure activity patterns of those in a community of 20,000 for public recreation and park planning purposes?

2. What are the advantages and disadvantages of the time budget in measuring the leisure activities of the public?

3. What are some typical attitude and opinion questions that might be asked the public by a public recreation and park agency?

4. Why is it often difficult to compare one recreation survey with another?

5. What are some of the major steps in undertaking a recreation survey?

Recreation standards are often used to provide a guide for the public acquisition of parkland.
(U.S. Bureau of Outdoor Recreation)

chapter 14

THE USE OF STANDARDS

INTRODUCTION

This chapter will examine the use of standards by leisure service agencies, their advantages and disadvantages, and the process by which they are developed.

Many leisure service agencies use standards as a method of planning and evaluating their services. A *standard* is a desired state of affairs expressed in quantitative terms. Standards are used by nearly all of our societal institutions as a means of providing a guide for very complex issues, such as how long a child should be compelled to attend public school, how fast people should be allowed to drive their cars, how many police are needed to make our cities safe, and so on. Naturally, any such standards are somewhat subjective, since the questions involved are complex, subject to debate and not capable of being completely answered in strictly scientific terms.

In the administration of leisure services, a major question remains concerning what areas require the setting of standards. What are the relevant aspects of the recreation or leisure service supply that can be meaningfully quantified as a determinant of success? If we take the definition of recreation given by Gray and Greben, that it "is an emotional condition within an individual human being that flows from a feeling of well-being and self-satisfaction,"[1] it may be that standards will provide us with very little in the way of an indicator of success, unless they can be established in psychological terms. It is difficult, however, to set standards based on emotions; therefore they deal rather with the "input"—the characteristics in quantitative terms of what an agency offers its clientele. Gold, in Table 14–1, identifies the several types of recreation standards commonly used:

The standards shown in Table 14–1 deal with a wide range of concerns, but all of them are concerned with the mix of facilities, programs or leisure service personnel distributed among the population in question. The standards thus provide an index for both planning and evaluation, and in fact have been widely used in the past to quantitatively judge the adequacy of leisure services, particularly in the public sector. Often such standards are used in establishing a park system or system of recreation facilities believed to be interrelated (see Table 14–2).

Standards have not usually been determined through a process of scientific investigation, with the exception of some standards that deal with the actual construction of recreation facilities such as the ones listed in Table 14–2. These standards often are based on a physical necessity which is easily demonstrable.

Other standards, such as those dealing with needed park acreage per thousand residents or distance of facilities from the homes of residents, represent someone's vision of the ideal or the necessary. Henry Curtis, for instance, one of the first in the United States to undertake recreation surveys, stated that, while it had not been determined what constituted adequate

TABLE 14–1 A Classification of Selected Types of Recreation Standards

General Orientation	Specific Type	Measurement Units	Illustrative Examples
Recreation use	Population ratio Recreation demand Percentage of area	Area/population Area/user group Area/planning unit	1 acre neighborhood park/1,000 pop. 1 acre playground/600 children 10% of planning unit area
Recreation development	Facility to site Facility placement Facility to activity Facility size	Units/acre Distance bet. units Units/user group Area/facility	16 picnic tables/acre Picnic tables 50 ft. apart 1 softball diamond/10,000 pop. 3–5 acre neighborhood playground
Carrying capacity	User to resource User to time	Users/site Users/time/site	400 people/mile of trail/hr. 50 people/mile of trail/hr.
Recreation program	Activity to population Leadership requirements	Activity/population Leaders/activity	1 arboretum/10,000 pop. 2 leaders/100 children
Recreation management	Supervision to users Maintenance to site	Staff/population Degree/area	1 supervisor/1000 users 1 laborer/10 acres playground

Source: Seymour Gold, *Urban Recreation Planning* (Philadelphia: Lea and Febiger, 1973), p. 51.

TABLE 14–2 Criteria for Leisure Facilities: Florida Design Standards and Quantities for Parks, Recreation and Open Space

PARK FACILITY	SIZE	AREA PER 1,000 POPULATION	SERVICE AREA	LOCATION	USUAL FACILITIES	RESPONSIBILITY
Regional Park	Minimum of 250 acres to several thousand	20 acres	30 minute to 1 hour driving time	Where appropriate sites can be obtained incorporating natural features, one area for each 100,000 persons is desirable on the periphery of an urbanized area.	Beaches, bays, water resources, rustic areas, camping, nature study, bridle paths, picnicing and other facilities not requiring intensive development.	Usually the responsibility of a county, regional or state
Neighborhood Park	Minimum of 5 acres to 15 acres	2 acres	Square mile area, population ranging from 2,000 - 10,000	Adjacent to Elementary School when feasible.	Play apparatus areas for pre-school and older children, recreation building, sports fields, paved multipurpose courts, senior citizens area, picnic area, open or free play area, landscaping.	Usually the responsibility of a city or county
District (Community) Park	Minimum of 20 acres	2 acres	One to three miles radius	A community park is a "ride to" park designed to serve the residents of a group of neighborhoods, servicing four neighborhood parks, making up a community. Accessible by bike routes as well as vehicle traffic. Where possible adjacent to a Jr. or Sr. high school.	All the facilities found in a neighborhood park, plus facilities to service the entire family. Pools, center, lighted softball-baseball fields, lighted tennis courts, play areas, picnic area, passive and active recreation areas, multi-purpose hard court, and large building.	The responsibility of local, municipal, or county governments.
Urban-District Park	100 acre minimum, 250 to 1,000 acres desirable	5 acres	30-40 minutes driving time	Most desirable within large urban area but may be located on the periphery.	Playground apparatus area, restrooms, concessions, wooded areas with nature, hiking, and riding trails, nature center, ampitheater or center for the performing arts, areas for boating and swimming, picnic areas with shelters, day or overnight camping areas, and some unlighted, sand lot level sports areas.	Usually urban or county.
SPECIAL FACILITIES						
Golf Course	Minimum of 50 acres for 9-hole course or 100 acres for 180 hole course	2 acres	Within 20 miles of the population center	Where appropriate population demand and availability of required acreage are desirable.	Golf course, club house, parking, service drive, natural areas.	Public (city/county) or private.
Tennis Court	Ideal size is 2 acres.	One court for every 2,000 persons.	Within walking distance or short drive	Located in playfields or community parks.	Courts, parking, clubhouse	Local communities or private
Athletic field	Minimum size 8 acres	0.1 acre - or 1 field for 80,000 people	15-20 minute drive maximum	Within urban area	Track, gymnasium, exercise facilities	City Government or private
Swimming Pool	1 to 2 acre site	1 pool for every 7,500 people - 27 sq. ft. of water surface for each swimmer	Within walking distance or short drive	Usually in neighborhood centers, or in neighborhood parks.	Swimming pool, deck (2-3½ times more deck surface than water surface), lockers, showers, and food counter.	City/community or private operation

OPEN SPACE LAND	STANDARD
Total Gross Acres - 40,407,594	2,000 Gross Acres / 1,000 Population
Total Net Acres of Developable Land Area - 30,905,913	500 Net Acres / 1,000 Population
Urban Area Open Space	100 Acres / 1,000 Population

Source: *Criteria for Leisure Facilities,* prepared jointly by the Florida Recreation and Parks Association and the Florida Planning and Zoning Association, Tallahassee, Florida, January, 1975.

facilities for play, "we know that they must be within walking distance of the children if they are to be attended."[3] It should, of course, be noted that Curtis made this observation in 1910, when transportation was more limited than it is today, but even today, some recreation and park agencies follow the same general standard because it represents an ideal. The Philadelphia Department of Recreation, for instance, has established a series of neighborhood swimming pools within walking distance of users. Children wear their bathing suits and sneakers to the swimming facility rather than changing into their suits after they arrive.

REASONS FOR HAVING STANDARDS

While it may appear that standards are a simplistic, sometimes irrelevant way of dealing with complex, multi-dimensional issues, they continue to survive for a number of reasons, among them the following:

1. A standard makes concrete what is often intangible. How much park acreage should a city have? No one really knows, just as no one knows with any certainty at what age their children should begin school or how much money should be spent for police protection. Nevertheless, decisions must be made in these areas, and standards provide a rule of thumb. While they *do not* excuse the decision-makers from seeking information concerning felt, expressed and comparative needs, they often provide a starting point for action. As Meyer and Brightbill stated in 1956:

> **. . . standards provide the framework for providing recreation areas and facilities. Some recreation area standards are based upon population (i.e., one acre of parks for each 100 population) and some are based upon geography (i.e., 10 per cent of the area of a community). These standards could conceivably conflict if the average density of the population were not exactly ten persons per acre. Yet it is surprising how many American towns or cities approximate this figure. Standards must be applied with common sense and good judgment. They must be weighted and applied carefully in terms of the needs, conditions, resources, and characteristics of the particular community. Obviously standards cannot always remain fixed in their application. Communities vary in climate, topography and natural resources and scenic attractions, in size and open space, and in density, population and distribution of population, in social and economic status and in relationship to other communities, and in other ways. All these matters must be considered when using standards. If standards are worthwhile, they must be not only idealistic, but also realistic and flexible.[4]**

2. Standards represent a political tool for advocates of recreation and parks to utilize in an effort to increase provision of leisure services. It is sometimes pointed out with alarm that those who have established recreation and park standards are not neutral but are advocates of recreation and parks and are therefore biased in their favor. While this is true, it is a fairly typical situation. Advocates of public health, for instance, often set or seek to set sanitation standards. Standards are sometimes a way of calling attention to leisure services in such a way that further investigation or consideration will take place. Applying standards invites further attention and examination.

3. Standards are easily understood and therefore provide a simple way of giving information to the public or to lay boards or committees concerning the issue of leisure services. The question of what constitutes adequate provision of recreation and parks can be answered with such a complex array of information that practically no one can digest it. Information concerning standards, if it is accurately presented, may provide a basis for large numbers of citizens to react.

DISADVANTAGES OF STANDARDS

The use of standards as they presently exist has been severely criticized on a number of grounds. Some of the principle criticisms are the following:

1. *Standards represent an extension of the life style of their designer, which may not be applicable or desired by the community or user group in question.* To say, for instance, that there should be one tennis court for every 2,000 residents makes prior assumptions about the leisure skills and interests of the residents which may not be true. Let us look at what such a standard means if taken literally.

Let us assume that there are 10,000 people in a wealthy suburban community. Of the 10,000, 10 percent are incapable of playing tennis, either because they are too young or because of a physical or emotional problem. Another 25 percent simply are not interested in tennis and have no desire to play. Of the remaining 6,500 residents, 500 are tennis "nuts" and play an average of three times a week for an average of two hours at a time; 1,000 play twice a week for 1½ hours each time; 1,000 play once a week for 1½ hours each time; 1,000 play twice a month for one hour; 2,000 play once a month for one hour; and 1,000 play three times a year for one hour. That would require courts for 445,000 playing hours per year. Let us further assume that commercial and private tennis facilities account for 345,000 of those hours, leaving 100,000 player hours per year for the public courts. If the community met the standard for tennis courts, they would have five courts, which, if playable for ten hours a day and if doubles and singles were played for equal amounts of time, would provide 54,750 hours of time per year, or only about one half of the needed time. However, of those wishing to use the courts, 75 percent wish to use them on weekends. During the weekdays, then, there will be 39,105 hours of player court time available and only 25,000 hours of desired use. Thus, the courts will be idle for considerable periods of time on weekdays. Let us further assume, however, that 50 percent of the weekday users wish to use the courts from 3 to 6 P.M. This would mean that there would be room for only 11,732 potential users while 12,500 people wished to use them, and thus the courts would be overcrowded.

Weekends would be very crowded, as may be seen in Table 14–3. Further, one of the courts might be used more than the others or at certain times of the year or day or week more than others. Peoples' reaction to crowded courts on weekends might be to go at other times of the week, to quit playing, to join a private tennis club, to encourage the school or recreation and parks department to build more tennis courts, or to drive to another community to play. The addition of five more tennis courts in the community might alleviate the weekend crowding, result in more interest in tennis and thus continue the

TABLE 14–3 "Need" for Public Tennis Courts in Anytown, U.S.A.

Standard = 1 court per 2,000 people
5 courts per 10,000 town residents

Player Hours Per Year if Standard Is Met

10 hours per day, equal time for singles and doubles = 30 player hours per day per court.

Five courts × 30 player hours equals 150 player hours per day, or 54,750 player hours per year.

Actual Desired Playing Patterns

6,500 of 10,000 residents play tennis. Five hundred people play three times per week for two hours each time	=	156,000 hrs/year
1,000 people play two times per week for 1½ hours each time	=	156,000 hrs/year
1,000 people play one time per week for 1½ hours each time	=	78,000 hrs/year
1,000 people play two times per month for 1 hour each time	=	24,000 hrs/year
2,000 play once a month for one hour	=	24,000 hrs/year
1,000 people play three times per year for one hour each time	=	3,000 hrs/year
		445,000 player hours per year

445,000
−345,000 player hours spent at commercial and private clubs
100,000 player hours desired on public courts
−75% of player hours desired on weekends
75,000 on public courts

Results

15,642 actual player hours available on weekends
22,500 player hours desired between 3:00 P.M. and 6:00 P.M. on weekends
4,692 actual hours available between 3:00 P.M. and 6:00 P.M.
25,000 player hours desired on weekdays
39,105 actual player hours available on weekdays
12,500 player hours desired between 3:00 P.M. and 6:00 P.M. on weekdays
11,732 player hours available on weekdays between 3:00 P.M. and 6:00 P.M.

Conclusions

Standard is adequate for weekdays except for 3:00 P.M. to 6:00 P.M.

Standard is completely inadequate for weekends, particularly for 3:00 P.M. to 6:00 P.M.

weekend crowding, or cause some of the club players to quit their tennis clubs and begin to use public courts again.

Thus, even from this simplified example it may be seen that a facility standard is forced to make some assumptions about the life style of a community which may be false or drastically oversimplified.

2. *Standards don't allow for citizen participation.* As traditionally utilized, standards do not provide an opportunity for citizens to make their attitudes and opinions known before the standards are applied. In the example just described, if citizens had been consulted about the desirable number of tennis courts in their community, they might have recognized the strong interest in tennis in the community and set the standard higher. In a heterogeneous society, it cannot be assumed that there is some norm for recreation and leisure behavior that will be satisfied by providing certain levels of staff, areas and facilities.

3. *Standards give no consideration to quality.* While the exact number of staff or acres available per thousand residents is useful information to have, it does not easily translate into "meaningful" information. Suppose the acreage is mosquito-infested swampland or that the staff are unqualified political appointees with little interest in recreation or leisure. Since recreation and leisure activity is relatively freely chosen as opposed to forced or obligated, the *quality* of the program or environment offered may be central in determining whether or not people will be attracted to the activity. A study by the Maryland National Capital Park and Planning Commission, for instance, found that quality, flavor and style are all important in determining whether an individual will freely choose an activity.[5] These factors may also be important in determining whether leisure, in the sense of being a state of mind and a condition of the soul, comes closer to being realized. Unfortunately, standards don't provide for such qualitative factors.

4. *Standards often deal with the provision of recreation and park areas and facilities within the public sector only, rather than within* all *sectors, public, private and commercial.* As Christiansen has pointed out, the provision of recreation *opportunity* should be the object to be measured in judging the acceptability of a recreation system.[6] Furthermore, in determining the level of this provision, the *entire* leisure service delivery system—public, private and commercial—should be examined, since the recreation opportunity can conceivably be provided by any of these agencies and be satisfactory to the user.

One of the most innovative and promising tools for comprehensive recreation planning is the Recreation Experience Components Concept developed by Christiansen. This concept is based upon the principle of "reasonable" availability of recreation opportunity:

> **. . . which means that within each planning area of a community each recreation experience opportunity is a *component* of the total standard for that unit. Since not all opportunities under the total system are controlled by one agency, these may be located in various places within the physical boundaries of the study unit. Therefore, no "standard" neighborhood park is expected to meet the requirements of the proposed standards. Under the new concept, the public park may have several of the components which provide recreational opportunities; the park by itself is not a component of the system. It is only a location.[6]**

In Christiansen's system, recreation activities are categorized for planning purposes into physical recreation, social recreation, cognitive recreation and environment-related recreation. There are further subdivisions of activity clusters (groups of activities offering similar experiences) within each category. Both quantitative and qualitative indexes are developed for application at the regional, town, interneighborhood and subneighborhood level. Rather than being a simple set of standards, component standards are a series of standards, "one for each demographic planning unit, all based upon the concept of providing opportunities for four basic recreation experiences. At each planning level, certain activity clusters offer alternatives to the way that the basic experience is provided. Some activity clusters are very significant in small demographic units and insignificant in large units."[6] Although still in its early stages of development, this instrument could have a profound effect upon recreation and park planning, because of its systemic approach, which integrates all types of leisure service agencies in conceptualizing recreation opportunity, and its recognition that the site of a recreation experience is the means of the experience but not the end. The experience is the end product for the user.

While such judgments may be premature, there do appear to be drawbacks to the components system. For one thing, the instrument would be extremely time-consuming to implement. It would also demand a major change in the thinking of many recreation and park administrators, forcing them to conceive of their agency's having much more of a coordinating role than most presently do. Finally, the technique makes assumptions about the interchangeability of recreation experiences that cannot be proved (or disproved) by the empirical evidence available at the present time.

5. *Standards establishing service areas for certain types of recreation and park facilities have often been demonstrated not to correspond to actual usage patterns or even to be close to them.* The following brief review of the literature by Van Doren[7] shows their lack of precision:

> **In Baltimore County, Bangs and Mahler[8] tested the optimum size, shape, and service depth of recreation spaces, finding that open space was not used by persons living more than 400 feet from a park. Mitchell[9] in Columbus, Ohio, tested the range of a recreation playground service or good as well as the spatial gradient of the good. Using accepted standards of 1/4 mile to 1/2 mile distances around a playground, he found that the range was .3 of a mile. Accepted recreation standards were also tested in Stillwater, Oklahoma, by Crum[10] and found to be unrealistic. Actual users of parks did not conform to theoretical or standard radii. A study of accessibility to urban playgrounds in Baltimore by Dee and Liebman[11] emphasized the importance of a minimum number of street crossings between school and playground. . . . Hodges and Van Doren[12] were able to verify in Dallas that the rule of thumb standards of accepted service radii were not operational.**

From this review, it is obvious that a dilemma exists in regard to estimating service radii. Figure 14–1 shows the variation in rates of visitation per capita to recreation centers in Dallas, Texas. Obviously, the use of existing standards for service radii do not take into account such variation.

6. *There is little assurance that meeting certain standards will be related to success in behavioral terms.* If a recreation and park or other leisure service agency is

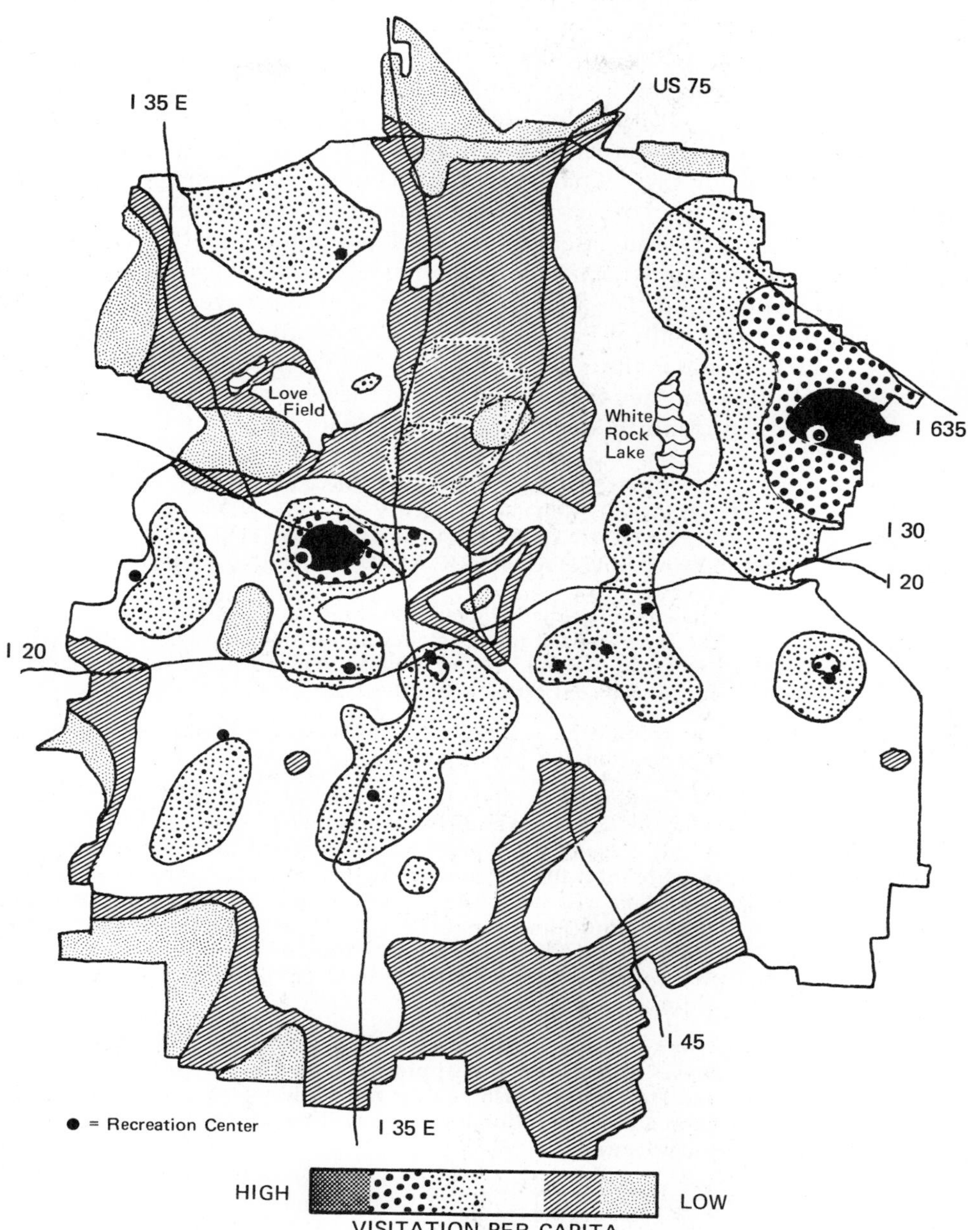

SCHEMATIC OF THE URBAN RECREATION SURFACE - DALLAS, TEXAS

Per capita visitation service areas of fourteen recreation centers. Note the uneven density surfaces with two major areas of high visitation. Interstate highways provide few barriers to access. A "spillover effect" is provided the residents of two political enclaves, University Park and Highland Park.

FIGURE 14–1 (From *Indicators of Change in the Recreation Environment—A National Research Symposium,* compiled by Betty van der Smissen, Penn State HPER Series No. 6, College of Health, Physical Education and Recreation, The Pennsylvania State University, 1975.)

charged with combating juvenile delinquency, improving physical fitness, lessening social disorganization and pathological behavior, or otherwise improving the "quality of life" in a community, is there any assurance that meeting standards will bring this about? Or could a city spend the money in alternative ways with better results in terms of behavior? Perhaps at this point these questions cannot be definitively answered. Standards therefore, as presently specified, must still be judged in the realm of belief.

In spite of these unanswered questions, recreation and park standards continue to be used as a recreation planning tool, as they do in other services of government. In some attempts to develop standards pertaining to recreation and parks, attempts have been made to systematically consider other concepts of recreation need. The following recommendations were made to a planning group charged with the development of standards for the Maryland National Capital Park and Planning Commission. The Commission previously used several standards in their planning process. The committee referred to consisted of both laymen commissioners and professional planners and recreationists.

PROCEDURES FOR THE DEVELOPMENT OF RECOMMENDATIONS OF NEW STANDARDS FOR PARKS, RECREATION AND OPEN SPACE FOR THE MARYLAND NATIONAL CAPITAL PARK AND PLANNING COMMISSION[13]

1. **The committee will review the compilation of policy statements and note areas of inconsistency and omission. Clarifications and additions to stated policy will be recommended as an integral part of the committee's report.**

2. **The committee will review a survey of the literature pertaining to recreation and park planning.**

3. **The committee will review the present classification of recreation and park areas and facilities utilized by the MNCPPC to see if this classification provides a sufficient range of leisure activity to meet the interests of citizens. In making this determination, data will be reviewed concerning the leisure preferences of users and non-users of MNCPPC facilities and programs. If additional kinds of recreation areas and facilities appear to be warranted, recommendations will be made concerning their acquisition and development.**

4. **The committee will review data concerning the number of presently existing and approved recreation areas and facilities and staff within each county and within each planning area or subregion. The following ratios will be calculated for committee consideration:**

   A. Within Each County
   Total Park Acreage
   Total Open Space Acreage
   Total Active Local Park Acreage
   Number of Acres of Regional Park per 1,000 Population
   Number of Acres of Stream Valley Park per 1,000 Population
   Number of Acres of Special Area Parks per 1,000 Population
   Number of Full-Time Staff per 1,000 Population

   B. Within Each Region
   Total Park Acreage
   Total Open Space Acreage
   Total Active Local Park Acreage
   Number of Neighborhood Playgrounds per 1,000 Population

Number of Recreation Centers per 1,000 Population
Number of Park Schools per 1,000 Population
Number of Youth and Community Centers per 1,000 Population
Number of Full-Time Staff per 1,000 Population

5. The committee will then review these ratios recalculated with projected 1984 or "ultimate" population figures.

6. The committee will decide if other public, quasi-public and private recreation areas, facilities and programs should be considered as a part of the supply for each county and planning unit or subregion for the purpose of long-range planning.
If "no," proceed to step seven.
If "yes," then the committee will determine what public, quasi-public and private recreation areas, facilities and programs should be included as a part of the supply for each county and planning unit or subregion for purposes of long-range planning. These will be included on the map and a formula will be developed to recalculate supply within each county and planning unit or subregion based upon supply. Future population projections will also be recalculated.

7. The committee will decide the role of usage rates in determining the development of standards. The committee may decide

   A. Usage rates are not relevant in designing standards.
   B. Usage rates should be quantified in some way, such as assigning ratings of "high, medium or low" to each planning unit or subregion and that these ratings should be used to weight the populations and projected populations in terms of generating ratios of facility to number of users.
   C. Usage rates should be the basis of standards, rather than population or other considerations

   If "A," proceed to step eight.
   If "B" or "C," collect all usage rates available, including attendance records, permits, questions from surveys, staff estimates, etc.
   Assign judgmental ratings to each planning unit or subregion. Determine the values of these ratings to weight the population to facility ratio.

8. The committee will decide if the socioeconomic composition of planning areas or subregions, such as population density, incidence of poverty, crime rate, percentage of children and youth, percentage of aged, etc., is relevant to establishing standards from the standpoint of priority of need for public recreation and park services.
If "no," proceed to step nine.
If "yes," then develop comparative need indicators and rate planning units according to priority of comparative need. These ratings could then be categorized as "high, medium or low" and used as a basis to reweight populations and projected populations for each planning unit or subregion in terms of population facility ratios.

9. The committee will seek expert input of governmental financial considerations and related fiscal policy.

10. The committee will determine (a) standards based upon either a continuation or revision of current standards using acreage, or (b) standards based upon number of specific units of "Active" local park facilities, such as playgrounds, youth and community

centers, urban parks, etc., and continued acreage standards for stream valley parks, regional parks and special parks. Standards will be specified for regions if deemed appropriate. For each standard developed, a minimum level of provision standards and a desirable level of provision standards will be specified. In specifying such standards, the committee will attempt to determine the implications for users in terms of service radii for each type of facility. No attempt will be made to establish standards for the entire county in terms of standard service radii, owing to the variation in population density evidenced throughout the two county areas. Developed standards will be compared to previously used standards in terms of cost implications, acquisition policies, etc.

11. **After the development of standards, the committee will develop guidelines for these areas and facilities. Such guidelines shall consist of two principal types.**
    - A. **Guidelines for the future operation of such areas and facilities.**
    - B. **Guidelines for the recreation programs and activities available at such areas and facilities.**
12. **Guidelines for future operations will deal with qualitative considerations such as safety, lighting, hours of operation, policy toward non-residents, etc. These guidelines will consist of two types:**
    - A. **County-wide guidelines, and**
    - B. **Planning area or subregion guidelines.**
13. **Guidelines for the recreation activities and experiences available at areas and facilities will deal with considerations such as the introduction of new activities and programs and opportunities for participation in them, changes in emphasis and priority in existing programs, programs for new segments of the population, new methods of programming, etc. These guidelines will consist of two types:**
    - A. **County-wide guidelines, and**
    - B. **Planning area or subregion guidelines**

As may be seen, certain values must be considered and stated in the development process. Without taking a position in relation to these values, the use of standards is arbitrary, and perhaps unjustified. In step seven, for instance, decision-makers are asked to judge whether or not standards should be modified according to the amount of use a given area or facility receives. Should one acre of parkland per 1,000 residents be supplied in areas where such land is rarely used? Should more be supplied in areas of intensive use? Judgments must be made about such issues before standards can be utilized.

REFERENCES

1. David E. Gray and Seymour Greben, "Future Perspectives," *Parks and Recreation,* July, 1974, p. 49.
2. Seymour Gold, *Urban Recreation Planning* (Philadelphia: Lea and Febiger, 1973), p. 151.
3. Henry Curtis, "Provisions and Responsibility for Playgrounds," *The Annals,* February, 1910, p. 125, cited by Seymour Gold.
4. Harold D. Meyer and Charles K. Brightbill, *Recreation Administration—A Guide to Its Practices* (New York: Prentice-Hall, 1956), pp. 276–277.
5. Institute for Urban Studies, *A Survey of Parks, Recreation, and Open Spaces in Prince George's and Montgomery Counties* (College Park: University of Maryland, 1975).

6. Monty Christiansen, *The Application of a Recreation Experience Components Concept for Comprehensive Recreation Planning* (Harrisburg: Bureau of Recreation and Conservation, Department of Community Affairs, Commonwealth of Pennsylvania, April, 1974), p. 1.
7. Carlton S. Van Doren, "Spatiality and Planning for Recreation," in *Indicators of Change in the Recreation Environment,* a National Research Symposium compiled by Betty van der Smissen (University Park: The Pennsylvania State University, 1975), p. 350.
8. Herbert P. Bangs, Jr., and Stuart Mahler, "Uses of Local Parks," *Journal of the American Institute of Planners,* Vol. XXXVI, No. 5, 1970.
9. L.S. Mitchell, "The Facility Index as a Measurement of Attendance of Recreation Sites," *The Professional Geographer,* Vol. XX, No. 4, July, 1965.
10. A.C. Crum, "Urban Park Planning: A Case Study of Stillwater Oklahoma," unpublished M.S. thesis, Oklahoma State University, p. 197.
11. Norbert Dee and Jon Leibman, "Optimal Location of Public Facilities," *Naval Research Logistics Quarterly,* Vol. 9, No. 4, 1972.
12. L. Hodges and Carlton S. Van Doren, "Synagraphic Mapping as a Tool in Locating and Evaluating the Spatial Distribution of Municipal Recreation Facilities," *Journal of Leisure Research,* Vol. VI, No. 4, 1972.
13. Robert Beuchner and Geoffrey Godbey, unpublished advisory paper prepared for the Maryland National Capital Park and Planning Commission, Silver Springs, Maryland, May, 1975.

QUESTIONS

1. What are the major reasons for the continued use of standards in the recreation and parks field?
2. Do the service radii specified in recreation standards conform to people's actual usage patterns in a precise way? Why or why not?
3. Should standards be "modified" when they are used in recreation and park planning? If so, how?
4. What, in your opinion, is the most serious disadvantage in the use of recreation and park standards?
5. Do standards address the "quality" of a recreation experience? If so, how?

Some people have a greater need for the recreation, park and leisure services of government than others. (U.S. Bureau of Outdoor Recreation)

chapter 15

COMPARATIVE NEEDS AND RESOURCES FOR LEISURE SERVICES

In this chapter, the rationale and methods for determining comparative need for recreation, park and leisure services will be examined. Particular attention will be devoted to conditions and statuses thought to be related to recreation need.

COMPARATIVE NEED–RESOURCE MODELS

One framework for making allocation decisions in leisure service agencies is the use of comparative need–resource models, which establish priorities for service within the population. This framework is based upon the assumption that people vary in their "need" for the leisure services of a given agency and that this variation can be systematically related to social or economic statuses or conditions. Traditionally, voluntary youth-oriented leisure service organizations tried to meet the needs of certain specialized clientele based upon a highly defined sense of mission. Public leisure service agencies, however, have traditionally stressed the *equality* of distribution of their services to all citizens within a given community or politically defined area. Although generally confining their attention to certain types of services, such as the provision of parks, playgrounds and organized athletics, public leisure service agency personnel held to the myth that they served all people equally. In reality, males have received more service than females, whites more than blacks, middle-class citizens more than lower-class citizens, non-handicapped citizens more than handicapped, and so on. Part of this situation was explainable in terms of the prevailing cultural norms. Recreation was something that had to be earned and re-earned through work, and those who were successful workers were believed to be entitled to recreation more than others. The enslavement of blacks and their subsequent segregation from white society led to a pattern of "separate but unequal" provision of leisure services. Jim Crow laws prevented blacks from using recreation facilities and programs utilized by whites. A Birmingham, Alabama, ordinance passed in 1930, for instance, made it unlawful for blacks and whites even to play dominoes or checkers together. Myrdal's famous study of race relations in the United States found provision of recreation services for blacks to be uniformly inferior:

> **. . . the visitor finds Negroes everywhere aware of the great damage done Negro youth by the lack of recreation outlets and of the urgency of providing playgrounds for the children. In almost every community visited during the course of the inquiry, these were among the first demands on the program of local Negro organizations.[1]**

In March, 1968, Kraus found that in the greater New York metropolitan area

> **. . . the facilities offered in Negro neighborhoods were usually of the most basic type—a playground, schoolyard or afternoon and evening center in a public school building. In contrast, the more attractive and diversified recreation centers in the majority of the communities studied—including the centers with varied sports and outdoor recreation opportunities—tended to be at a distance from the older center of the town—generally the Negro area—and in a predominantly white neighborhood.**[1]

The same type of situation can be documented with regard to provision of leisure services for women, handicapped citizens and others. The social changes of the last two decades, however, have brought about a re-examination not only of the "equality" with which leisure and other social services are provided but also of whether it makes sense to even *assume* "equality" of need. The civil rights movement dramatized the plight of blacks and other ethnic minorities. Womens' liberationists challenged the assumption that women should be passive, homebound and dependent upon males. The federal government's War on Poverty (although really just a small battle, since less than 1 per cent of the federal budget was spent on it) passed legislation that established model cities areas and other target population programs within which comparative judgments were made concerning social needs. As Dunn points out, however, the pendulum was swinging back toward "equal opportunity for all," spurred by enactment of general revenue sharing and the demise of federal anti-poverty programs.[2]

The same social forces have affected other leisure service agencies in different ways. The 4-H Clubs, for instance, have begun to offer their services to youth in low-income urban areas The Boy Scouts have made a similar attempt to recruit underprivileged youth, although with only partial success. The YMCA, on the other hand, appears to be expanding most rapidly into middle-class suburban areas. In state schools for the mentally retarded, it might be generalized that proportionately more services have been made available to higher functioning residents than to lower functioning ones.

It is often assumed that in the provision of public leisure services, preference *is* given to the poor, particularly the urban poor. Thus, in effect, it is assumed that a comparative need–resource model is already in operation, with low-income people, particularly minority groups, as the beneficiaries. However, in reality, this usually does *not* appear to be the case, and more often the reverse is actually true.

One reason for this has been the unequal distribution of monies from the Land and Water Conservation Fund (see box).

The Land and Water Conservation Fund Act, Public Law 88–578, established a fund to finance, with Federal dollars matched by State or local money, the acquisition and development of outdoor recreation areas and facilities. The fund—known as the Land and Water Conservation Fund—is administered by the Bureau of Outdoor Recreation. Projects eligible to receive fund monies must be in accord with a comprehensive statewide outdoor recreation plan prepared by each State and approved by the Bureau. Fund monies are also used to acquire Federal recreation lands for administration by the National Park Service, Fish and Wildlife Service, Bureau of Land Management, and the Forest Service.

THE LAND AND WATER CONSERVATION FUND ACT OF 1965, PUBLIC LAW 88–578, AS AMENDED

TITLE I—LAND AND WATER CONSERVATION PROVISIONS

Short Title and Statement of Purposes

SECTION 1. (a) Citation; Effective Date.—This Act may be cited as the "Land and Water Conservation Fund Act of 1965" and shall become effective on January 1, 1965.

(b) Purposes.—The purposes of this Act are to assist in preserving, developing, and assuring accessibility to all citizens of the United States of America of present and future generations and visitors who are lawfully present within the boundaries of the United States of America such quality and quantity of outdoor recreation resources as may be available and are necessary and desirable for individual active participation in such recreation and to strengthen the health and vitality of the citizens of the United States by (1) providing funds for and authorizing Federal assistance to the States in planning, acquisition, and development of needed land and water areas and facilities and (2) providing funds for the Federal acquisition and development of certain lands and other areas.*

**Administrative and Legislative Directives to the Bureau of Outdoor Recreation,* U.S. Department of Interior, B.O.R., January, 1975.

In assessing the distribution of funds expended for outdoor recreation through the Land and Water Conservation Fund, it may be said that most of the $1.1 billion distributed to the states has gone for the development of recreational facilities in rural and suburban areas.

> **In many states, the communities most successful in obtaining Fund grants are relatively wealthy and powerful suburban jurisdictions. Such communities frequently have matching funds readily available, and tend to be more successful than the cities in competitive grantsmanship. The suburbs are also major beneficiaries of new policy in a number of states in which the state park agency has assumed an interest in urban recreation. Often, this means that the state acquires and develops regional facilities in the suburbs.**[3]

State policies governing fund distribution have been a primary factor in a distribution pattern that has put urban areas at a disadvantage. Tables 15–1 and 15–2 show the distribution of Fund money to central cities and smaller cities in comparison with the rest of their respective states. As may be seen, the expenditure per person at the state level is considerably higher than the per capita expenditure within the city. Thus, the funding pattern systematically *reverses* the distribution that might take place if a comparative need–resource model were used at the state level for recreation need. As a report from the Center for Growth Alternatives concludes: "Inequitable distribution of money from the Land and Water Conservation Fund has been particularly prejudicial to the needs of impoverished residents of inner-city neighborhoods, where high density and paucity of private open space create special responsibilities."[3]

Naturally, while in some communities a greater effort is made to acquire

TABLE 15–1 Land and Water Conservation Fund (State Side) Grants to Central Cities to May 31, 1975

	Population in 1970	% Black	$ Total Fund Grants	$ City Per Capita	$ State Per Capita	$ City Grants FY 74 & 75
New York, N.Y.	7,895,563	21.1	13,716,113	1.74	3.77	713,000
Chicago, Ill.	3,369,357	32.7	2,546,412	.76	3.98	129,175
Los Angeles, Calif.	2,816,111	17.9	5,944,824	2.11	3.97	1,220,216
Philadelphia, Pa.	1,949,996	33.6	3,334,775	1.71	4.44	822,500
Detroit, Mich.	1,513,601	43.7	450,778	.30	3.98	103,500
Houston, Texas	1,232,802	25.7	515,791	.42	4.26	87,700
Baltimore, Md.	905,787	46.4	1,400,712	1.54	5.66	0
Dallas, Texas	844,401	24.9	1,428,621	1.69	4.26	103,100
Washington, D.C.	756,510	71.1	6,178,119	8.17	—	781,750
Cleveland, Ohio	750,879	38.3	120,582	.16	4.26	0
Indianapolis, Ind.	746,302	18.0	2,124,059	2.85	4.42	150,000
Milwaukee, Wisc.	717,372	14.7	695,915	.97	5.15	426,682
San Francisco, Calif.	715,674	13.4	815,787	1.14	3.97	0
San Diego, Calif.	697,027	7.6	1,587,559	2.28	3.97	85,935
San Antonio, Texas	654,153	7.6[a]	1,110,937	1.70	4.26	0
Boston, Mass.	641,071	16.3	4,005,420	6.25	5.19	2,940,698
Memphis, Tenn.	623,530	38.9	533,790	.86	4.98	0
St. Louis, Mo.	622,236	40.9	226,470	.36	5.63	0
New Orleans, La.	593,471	45.0	3,809,536	6.42	6.33	175,649
Phoenix, Ariz.	581,562	4.8	4,355,726	7.49	9.19	1,362,352
Columbus, Ohio	540,025	18.5	423,200	.78	4.26	239,710
Seattle, Wash.	530,831	7.1	230,437	.43	5.68	62,312
Jacksonville, Fla.	528,865	27.3	867,100	1.64	4.18	0
Pittsburgh, Pa.	520,117	4.8	1,558,166	3.00	4.44	113,000
Denver, Colo.	514,678	9.1	1,324,810	2.57	6.64	640,709
Kansas City, Mo.	507,330	22.1	465,056	.92	5.63	196,625
(United States)	203,212,877	11.1	1,094,022,669	5.38	—	275,512,052

[a]52.4% Spanish surname.

state or federal funds for recreation, this does not mean that the agency administering such funds is always powerless to insure a more equitable distribution. In Pennsylvania, for instance, the state Land and Water Conservation and Reclamation Act was passed in 1968, providing $125 million for planning and development of state-owned outdoor recreation areas, and $75 million for state grants-in-aid of up to 50 percent to political subdivisions to plan, acquire and develop municipal recreation areas. In March, 1974, the Department of Community Affairs announced its intention to institute, by regulation, a "fair share-funding curve," which would regulate the awarding of the remaining grant monies in such a way as to consider previous aid granted, median family income and statewide aid per capita. The following statement describes this process.

> **The funds remaining in the P–500 program are limited and are not sufficient to meet current local government requests. Therefore, the Department has developed new criteria for making its funding decisions in this final phase of the program. The Department is desirous that those municipalities which have not previously received the benefits of the program should now be accorded a higher priority.**
>
> **In regards the remaining funds, the Department recognizes at least three different philosophies that could direct the administration of the program: (1) Projects could be funded on a first come, first served**

TABLE 15–2 Land and Water Conservation Fund (State Side) Grants to Smaller Cities of Selected States to February 28, 1975

	Population in 1970	% Black	$ Total Fund Grants	$ City Per Capita	$ State Per Capita	$ City Grants FY 74 & 75
San Jose, Calif.	466,504	2.4	988,003	2.12	3.97	0
Oakland, Calif.	361,613	34.5	159,605	.44	3.97	0
Long Beach, Calif.	358,673	5.3	1,398,204	3.90	3.97	248,101
Sacramento, Calif.	254,364	10.7	313,643	1.23	3.97	35,283
Newark, N.J.	382,377	54.2	418,038	1.09	5.00	332,500
Jersey City, N.J.	260,532	21.1	169,500	.65	5.00	0
Paterson, N.J.	144,830	26.8	150,288	1.04	5.00	0
Elizabeth, N.J.	122,713	15.4	0	0	5.00	0
Trenton, N.J.	104,578	37.5	149,875	1.43	5.00	0
Camden, N.J.	102,551	39.1	0	0	5.00	0
Buffalo, N.Y.	462,783	20.4	418,786	.90	3.77	0
Rochester, N.Y.	296,233	16.7	136,950	.46	3.77	136,950
Yonkers, N.Y.	204,298	6.4	0		3.77	0
Syracuse, N.Y.	197,270	10.8	75,000	.38	3.77	75,000
Albany, N.Y.	115,876	12.0	656,820	5.67	3.77	486,971
Fort Worth, Texas	393,463	19.9	327,817	.83	4.26	130,352
El Paso, Texas	322,261	2.3[a]	82,560	.26	4.26	0
Austin, Texas	251,817	11.9	521,225	2.07	4.26	100,200
Corpus Christi, Texas	204,590	5.2[b]	263,097	1.29	4.26	0
Cincinnati, Ohio	452,550	27.6	3,619,810	8.00	4.26	1,283,462
Toledo, Ohio	384,051	13.8	960,927	2.50	4.26	25,000
Akron, Ohio	275,420	17.5	130,750	.47	4.26	0
Dayton, Ohio	243,459	30.5	200,000	.82	4.26	200,000

[a]58.1% Spanish surname
[b]40.6% Spanish surname

basis; that is, every project which is technically sound would be funded until the available monies ran out; (2) Funds could be dispersed on a straight per capita basis, irrespective of community differences in financial condition or social needs; (3) Funds could be dispersed on a varying scale based on differences in need of various local governments. The Department believes that the latter approach represents the most equitable direction for its decisions since it achieves its goal of assisting all, but those with the greatest need to a greater extent.

A. Limitations on Grant.

To achieve our goal of assisting those with the greatest need, a chart has been developed which uses two variables. Those variables have been plotted on a vertical and horizontal axis. The vertical axis represents P–500 aid per capita while the horizontal axis represents Median Family Income (M.F.I.).

P–500 aid per capita is defined as the amount of total funds from the P–500 and other recreational grant programs administered by the Department committed to a particular municipality, divided by the number of residents of that municipality. The Department has divided the total amount of funds available for the P–500 program by the total number of residents of the Commonwealth to determine a factor known as the Fair Share P–500 Aid Per Capita. That figure is $6.

Median Family Income (M.F.I.) is considered by the Department to be the best single indicator of social and economic need. The state Median Family Income is $9,558.

By interrelating the two components on the graph, a curve has been developed which is weighed to give greater assistance in response to greater need as evidenced by lower income. Along the curve the maximum P–500 aid per capita figure ascends as a municipality's Median Family Income decreases and descends as a municipality's Median Family Income increases.

To give a practical example of how the curve would be used to arrive at grant amounts for two different municipalities, the following example is provided:

Example:

	M.F.I.	*Per Capita Grant Ceiling*
Community A.	$10,500	$5.17
Community B.	9,000	7.11

Using the same example, with the addition of population for the municipalities, the maximum grant amount can easily be calculated.

Example:

	Per Capita Grant Ceiling	*Population*	*Grant Maximum*
Community A.	$5.17	10,000	$51,700
Community B.	7.11	10,000	71,100

After arriving at the maximum grant ceiling for the communities, the extent of previous aid received under the program would be calculated. If the grants exceed the remaining balance, no additional grants will be approved. If the grants previously received are less than the grant ceiling, the remaining balance may be committed.

Example:

	Grant Maximum	*Previous Aid Rec'd*	*Remaining Balance*
Community A.	$51,700	$60,000	-0-
Community B.	71,100	20,000	$51,100

The funding curve review process should not be construed to mean that every municipality which has *not* reached its maximum per capita grant ceiling becomes automatically entitled to the full amount permissible under the curve. Rather each project proposal must stand on its own merits, demonstrating that it warrants funding of the applicant to its maximum.

B. Exceptions to Funding Curve Limitations

There may be certain circumstances in which the funding curve process is not appropriate and in those circumstances it shall be within the discretion of the Secretary to make a grant which places the applicant above the maximum ceiling permitted by the curve. It is not possible to outline all the possible situations but the scope of permissible exceptions is illustrated by the following examples:

(a) land acquisition to perserve *unique* natural, historical or rare geological areas.

(b) a project undertaken by one government which will directly serve citizens of surrounding municipalities when those surrounding municipalities have not reached their maximum funding level.

(c) a seriously needed facility which is financially infeasible to construct with the funds available to the municipality under the funding curve.

(d) significant demonstration projects which may help develop techniques applicable to other areas of the State, particularly when those projects can be directly related to energy or natural resources conservation.

(e) projects which meet specific identified needs of disadvantaged citizens for which no alternate recreation facility is available.

In every case in which the funding of a project places the applicant above its maximum grant ceiling under the curve a report shall be prepared stating why on its merits the project has been approved and exactly what extenuating circumstances warranted the waiving of the funding curve. Such reports shall be signed by the director of the Bureau of Recreation and Conservation and the Secretary of Community Affairs.*

*From *Pennsylvania Bulletin,* Vol. 4, No. 13, Saturday, March 30, 1974, pp. 586–587.

As Tables 15–3 and 15–4 show, the percentage of funds within each region of the state matches the percentage of the state's population in that region very closely. Additonally, distribution of recreation funds by median family income shows a fairly equitable distribution.

Regions 1 (including Philadelphia) and 10 (including Pittsburgh and Allegheny County), the two largest regions, received the greatest amounts of state funds (see Fig. 15–1). However, interestingly, Region 10, with slightly less than one fourth of the state's population, received over one third of the $69 million available in state funds.

In determining whether a comparative approach should be taken to the public or private provision of leisure services, it is important to recognize that

TABLE 15–3 State Funding of P–70/P–500 Projects By Region

Region	Population (1,000's)	% of State Population	State Funds Received ($1,000's)	% of Total Funds
1	3,866	32.7%	$18,237	26.4%
2	766	6.5	5,320	7.7
3	874	7.4	6,023	8.7
4	157	1.3	373	.5
5	541	4.6	3,791	5.5
6	1,260	10.7	5,729	8.3
7	490	4.2	1,152	1.7
8	231	2.0	1,290	1.9
9	733	6.2	3,394	4.9
10	2,875	24.4	23,757	34.4
Total	11,794	100.0%	$69,066	100.0%

Source: Bureau of Recreation and Conservation, Department of Community Affairs, Commonwealth of Pennsylvania.

TABLE 15–4 Distribution of Recreation Funds by Median Family Income Ranges (State MFI = $9,558)

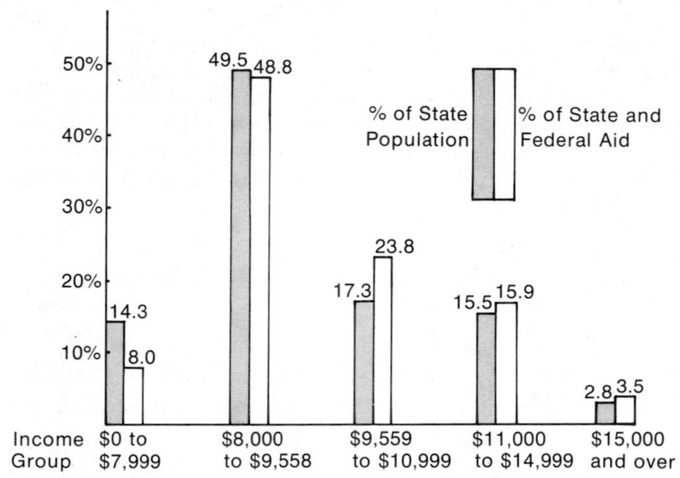

Source: Bureau of Recreation and Conservation, Department of Community Affairs, Commonwealth of Pennsylvania.

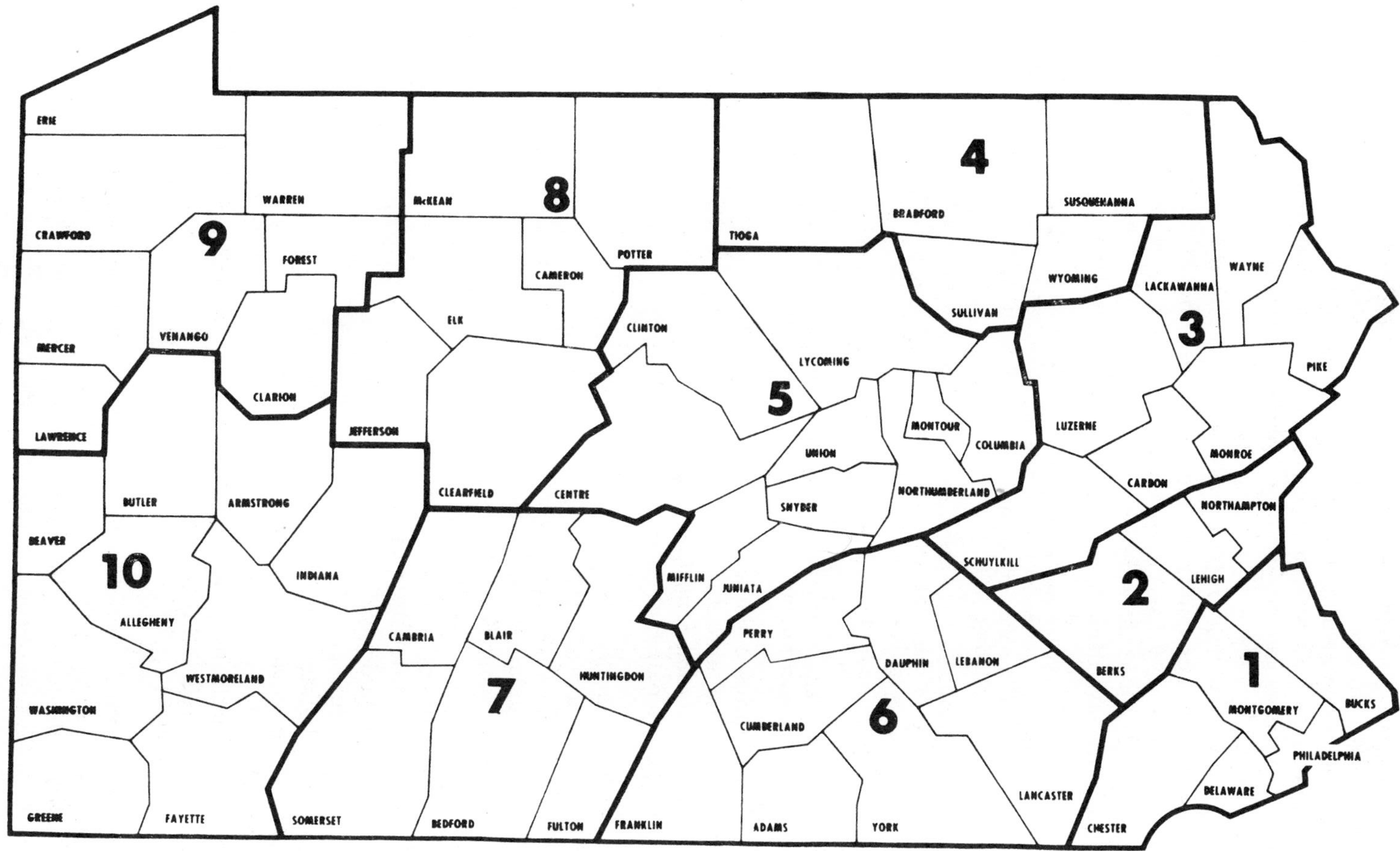

Figure 15–1 Uniform regions.

Source: *State Aid For Local Recreation Facilities*, Commonwealth of Pennsylvania, Department of Community Affairs, Office of State Planning and Development, August, 1972.

although it is difficult to measure need for recreation or leisure in an absolute physiological sense, it may be possible to determine *comparative* need for such leisure services by assuming that (1) people have some basic need and desire for recreation which, even though difficult to precisely determine, is a legitimate concern of government; (2) there are systematic differences in the opportunities that various citizens have to satisfy these desires; (3) the bases for these systematic differences can be identified; and (4) it is desirable to strive for equal opportunity.

Let us assume that propositions 1 and 2 have been accepted. If government accepts some responsibility for leisure services, should it then seek to identify target populations for service or should it seek to serve all people at an equal level of provision? A number of recreation and leisure service planning instruments have made the following assumptions concerning this question:

1. **There are measurable social characteristics and neighborhood recreation resources which indicate comparative need for recreation and youth services by areas, communities or neighborhoods in an urban setting.**
2. **All citizens have important basic needs for recreation services, but due to different socioeconomic characteristics and interests, their needs can be met in different ways.**
3. **Priorities in community-subsidized recreation services should go to those experiencing maximum social pressures from density of population, number of youth, low income and evidence of social disorganization.**[4]

Other studies have used a variety of leisure service need and resource indicators. One undertaken in Boston to determine the relative need for recreation, informal education and group work services used a jury judgment method to evaluate the following social indicators:[5]

a. *Population factors:*
   (1) total population
   (2) youth population, ages 7 to 17
   (3) population change between 1950 and 1960
b. *Social characteristics*
   (1) economic status
   (2) housing quality
   (3) educational status
   (4) child dependency
   (5) Negro population
   (6) delinquency
   (7) population density
c. *Special factors*
   (1) public housing projects
   (2) foreign-born whites
   (3) aged

After calculating service indicators dealing with facilities, professional and volunteer leadership, programmed activities, participation rates and finances expended, the following formula was used to determine areas of greatest need and existing services on a scattergram and profile chart.

Composite scores for both needs factors and existing services factors were developed and ranked in the following manner:

1. *Needs Factors*

The *average* of the three population factors' scores
plus
The *sum* of the seven selected social characteristics' scores
plus
The *average* of the three special factors' scores
equals
The *composite* score for NEEDS

2. *Existing Services Factors*

The *sum* of the Public Services' scores
plus
The *sum* of the Private Services' scores
equals
The *composite* scores for EXISTING SERVICES

These composite scores were then ranked from 1 to 5. The lower scores indicate less favorability, the higher scores higher favorability.

The Pennsylvania Need Index was developed in 1970 at The Pennsylvania State University by the Recreation and Park Department to rank order areas within the state in terms of need for outdoor recreation.[7] The Need Index was a part of the Pennsylvania State Comprehensive Outdoor Recreation Plan, and included the following factors:

1. *Population change between 1960 and 1970*
   a. A changing population indicates a changing need for services. More people need more services; a declining population indicates a re-evaluation of existing services.
   b. Recreation services increase proportionately as population increases.
2. *Median family income*
   a. Median family income is indicative of other social factors, notably education and occupation.
   b. Income is a real number for which no further judgment is required.
   c. Although income per se indicates nothing about the time required to earn that income, it does indicate the financial status for the study unit as a whole.
3. *Social disorganization*
   a. Juvenile delinquency is one measure of social disorganization—other indicators that measure social disorganization are statistics on suicide rates, on unwed mothers and on aid to dependent children, among others.
   b. The highest percentages of all recreation services are directed toward youth programs; therefore it is reasonable to focus on this as a possible index factor.
   c. Investigation of this factor does not necessarily mean directing attention at juvenile disorganization alone. Delinquency indicates the existence of much broader social problems than those of youth alone.
4. *Acreage*
   a. Acreage is one measure of the extent of recreation and park services provided under any particular governmental jurisdiction.
   b. An acreage factor is a valuable consideration only when something is said about this acreage in terms of quality or value.

TABLE 15–5 Need and Resource Variables Used in Ten Selected Studies Assessing Recreation Need

CITY	VARIABLES: NEED													RESOURCES					
	Foreign Born	Employment	Mortality	Dependency	Race	Education	Occupation	Pop. Stability	Housing	Income	Pop. Density	J. Delin-quency	Age	Costs	Programs	Attendance	Leadership	Facilities	Acreage
Los Angeles ('46)		X			X		X		X			X	X			X	X		X
Columbus, OH ('47)			X		X			X	X		X	X	X			X		X	X
Cleveland ('55)						X	X	X	X	X	X	X	X						
Boston ('62)	X			X	X	X		X	X	X	X	X	X	X	X	X	X	X	
New York ('63)								X		X		X				X	X	X	X
Richmond, VA ('63)				X		X	X		X	X	X	X	X			X		X	X
Los Angeles ('66)										X	X	X	X				X	X	X
Indianapolis ('66)						X	X				X					X		X	X
Cincinnati ('67)									X	X	X	X	X				X	X	X
Los Angeles ('69)										X	X	X	X				X	X	X
TOTAL	1	1	1	2	3	4	4	4	6	7	8	9	8	1	1	6	6	8	8

Source: Diana R. Dunn, "Recreation, Open Space and Social Organization," in *Indicators of Change in the Recreation Environment—A National Research Symposium,* compiled by Betty van der Smissen (Penn State HPER Series No. 6, College of Health, Physical Education and Recreation, The Pennsylvania State University, 1975), p. 276.

5. *Finance*
   a. Dollars spent through operational budgets are one measure of recreation and park service.
   b. By investigating the spending of school, city and selected recreation youth-serving quasi-public agencies, a general overview of non-commercial and non-private recreation services in the community can be assessed to a certain degree.
6. *Leadership*
   a. Leadership is an area of critical consideration of services within recreation and park agencies.
   b. Leaders contribute to different degrees of significance according to the time spent in their leadership capacity. Time is one measure of the leadership commitment to serving the specific target membership.

The Pennsylvania State Comprehensive Outdoor Recreation Plan recommended that this instrument be used in conjunction with other instruments in the planning process of any recreation and park services study.

In reviewing studies assessing comparative recreation need, Dunn found the need and resource variables used to be those shown in Tables 15–5 and 15–6.

INDICATORS OF RECREATION NEED

Let us look at the rationale for using various indicators of comparative recreation need. In doing so, it should be kept in mind that different indicators may be used in different situations depending on the socioeconomic make-up of the citizens or clients.

POVERTY

Poverty is often assumed to indicate heightened need for the services of both public and private leisure service agencies. There are a number of reasons for this. First, and perhaps most important, is the assumption that income in our society is a measure of independence, as is amount of education. Those with high incomes are regarded as better able to care for themselves than those with low incomes. This appears to be particularly true in urban areas, where the degree of human interdependence is higher than it is in rural or suburban areas. Poor people are less likely to own their own home, to have a large amount of play space in their living quarters, or to have a yard or other privately owned outside area nearby where their children can play. The poor are also less likely to own their own automobile or to have access to transportation needed to go to many recreation areas and facilities. Research by a number of leisure researchers indicates that the poor generally participate in fewer identifiable leisure activities than those in higher income brackets. They also are less likely to belong to voluntary associations. Finally, they are less likely to be employed at jobs which provide guaranteed vacations.

Partially because they lack access to so many recreation and leisure opportunities, poor people also lack leisure skills. Appreciation of many leisure activities is learned, and if there is no opportunity for that learning to take place, the range of activities in which the individual finds satisfaction will be very lim-

TABLE 15–6 Summary Chart: Ten Studies Assessing Recreation Need

City	Year	Total Population	Unit of Analysis					Methodological Approach
			#	Name	Range	Median	Mean	
Los Angeles, California	1946	2,376,500	65	Chest Areas		36,000	36,561	Ranked factors, separated into quartiles, added service and need factors and quartiled; graphed each unit of analysis showing the 2 measures
Columbus, Ohio	1947	360,000	59	Census Tracts	3,000-6,000		6,117	20 individual measures ranked averaged, then ranked into four indexes which were then averaged and ranked into a final Priority Index used as basis for recommendations
Cleveland, Ohio	1955		42	Social Planning Areas				Need factors ranked by quartiles and deciles into two indices: Area Characteristics & Social Problems. Results presented in line & bar graphs and tables
Boston, Massachusetts	1962	2,111,681	38	Social Planning Areas	33,309-87,409	55,000	55,571	Jury reviewed data; needs, and public and private service presented in independent scattergrams and profiles

City	Year	Total Population	Unit of Analysis					Methodological Approach
			#	Name	Range	Median	Mean	
New York, New York	1963	7,763,205	74	Neigh-bor-hoods	17,653-248,765		104,908	Three socioeconomic factors averaged and assigned quintiles; facility, participation and leadership quintiles also computed. 9 resource quintiles presented for each SES quintile, no city-wide rankings
Richmond, Virginia	1963		25					Weighted factors, ranked each assigned normalized T scores, multiplied times weight, and added total for each factor to obtain total score, ranked them
Los Angeles (south-central)	1966	579,199	12	Welfare Study Areas	10,174-89,280	51,195	5,409	Ranked factors, derived C-Scores; averaged these for Need and Resources Indexes; Difference = Need Priority
Indianapolis, Indiana	1966	990,000	83	Census Tracts		5,500	5,409	Lay-Professional Committee judgment and consensus
Cincinnati, Ohio	1967	500,000	35				14,285	Lay-Professional Consultant committee; data compared to city averages and 4 level intensity of priority scale
Los Angeles, California	1969	342,893	14	Cities	10,887-64,726	23,799	24,492	Same as Los Angeles 1966

Source: Diana R. Dunn, "Recreation, Open Space and Social Organization," in *Indicators of Change in the Recreation Environment—A National Research Symposium,* compiled by Betty van der Smissen (Penn State HPER Series No. 6, College of Health, Physical Education and Recreation, The Pennsylvania State University, 1975), pp. 273–274.

ited. Leisure is freedom, and handling freedom takes a tremendous amount of learning. Poor people, who are more likely to have dropped out of school and to be disadvantaged in other ways, thus are more likely to need the services of recreation, park and other leisure service organizations to help them acquire and/or improve their leisure skills.

In making this argument, no attempt is made to claim that people are necessarily more highly leisure-dependent *because* they are poor. That is, a person may not have much money but spend considerable time pursuing a number of leisure activities that are pleasing and meaningful to him, and which serve his leisure needs very well. The assumption made here is that, while this can happen, it usually does not, and therefore we may predict that the likelihood of high need for leisure services being associated with low income is greater than the likelihood of its being associated with higher income levels. This level of association, we assume, is great enough to be systematic. It might also be pointed out that government makes similar assumptions in other areas, for instance, in determining the need for food stamps and for health care.

In spite of this assumption, there is considerable evidence that many leisure service organizations provide more of their services to middle- and upper-income individuals than to the poor. The recent study of the Land and Water Conservation Fund, as previously mentioned, showed that funds were distributed in such a way that the urban poor often received much less in the way of services than the state average. Other evidence exists that also supports this generalization.

THE AGED

Another common assumption, that those who are old or retired have a greater need for organized leisure services than others in the population, is made for several reasons. First, we have already assumed that poor people have a greater need for such services, and retired people or those over 65 are more likely to be poor. A second reason concerns the physical problems associated with the aging process. Limitations are inevitably placed on what a person can and cannot do physically. The elderly must make adjustments in their leisure activity patterns. Assistance may be needed to do things which the individual could formerly do for himself. Some old people become institutionalized, which forces them to adjust their life style and to find new ways to pursue their leisure interests. Thirdly, retired people who are out of the labor force or who have given up their traditional work role of homemaker and parent find that leisure activity assumes a new importance. It is no longer something done for diversion or as a break from an established routine; often it *is* the established routine. Leisure activity often becomes a central source of meaning for old people. Because of this, their former leisure activities may need to be altered or changed to conform to the new meaning ascribed to them. So often literature concerning leisure services for older citizens shows two people playing checkers or cards. While such activities are worthwhile, they probably would not be satisfying as the major activity in the person's life. The need to be useful, to be needed, must be met in the leisure services provided for older people.

YOUTH

The percentage of youth within a given area, sometimes considered those residents aged 5 to 18, is often used as an indicator of comparative need for leisure services. Many public recreation and park agencies as well as voluntary agencies aim the bulk of their services at youth, although there has been some de-emphasizing of youth services in municipal recreation and park agencies during the last ten years. There are a number of reasons for considering the percentage of youth in the population in calculating comparative recreation or leisure service need. First, there is considerable evidence that people learn most of their leisure skills *before* they complete their schooling and enter the job market. Because of this, it is important that young people develop a wide range of leisure skills during their adolescence, to prepare them to use their leisure time in satisfying ways in later life. This is not meant to imply that there is no need to develop additional leisure skills in later life, but merely to recognize the fact that many adults tend to continue to do what they have been taught in their youth. There are, of course, some limitations in teaching leisure skills to youth. Many forms of leisure activity cannot be appreciated until maturity, and many forms of leisure skills taught to youth, such as football, are unlikely to be pursued in later life. Many lifetime sports, however, such as tennis, golf, archery, fishing, badminton and bowling can be enjoyed throughout one's lifetime. A crucial determinant of whether such activities will be engaged in during later life is the exposure a person was given to them during childhood and adolescence. The same may be said for the performing arts, hobbies and so on.

A second reason for considering youth as a relevant variable in determining comparative need for recreation and leisure services is that children's play and the leisure of adolescents represent periods during which the use of freedom is learned, and some guidance is necessary in this process. Many leisure service agencies and leisure services provided by the schools represent an alternative to compelled school activity in which youth begin to have some choice in what they select to do.

In many urban areas or areas where multiple unit housing is prevalent, there is little provision made for play or leisure activities. Because the mobility of young people is comparatively limited, they may have to play in the streets, in the parking lot of an apartment complex or in other undesirable places. Leisure service agencies play a major role in providing such areas as playgrounds, nature centers, afterschool drop-in centers and the like.

The changes in our ideas about raising children have accentuated the need for public and private agencies to play an ever-increasing part in serving young people. Currently about one half of the adult females in our society are in the labor force. While this percentage continues to rise, there has been no corresponding drop in the percentage of men in the labor force, with the result that greater responsibility for raising children is increasingly being turned over to various organizations, including leisure service organizations. Increasing divorce rates have also meant that many children and youth live in one-parent families, which often results in a decrease in the time spent in family recreation. Given these trends, the need for leisure services for youth will continue to grow.

JUVENILE DELINQUENCY

Combating juvenile delinquency has been a traditional mission of many voluntary youth serving agencies and also of public recreation and park departments. The relationship between crimes committed by youth and the provision of recreation or leisure services is obviously a complex one and not subject to sweeping generalizations. One thing that *is* clear, however, is that it is during their leisure time that juveniles are most likely to get into trouble with the law. Shoplifting, for instance, usually takes place after school by bored youths looking for kicks. Youth gangs often provide a source of identity and meaning for young men or women, who eventually come to believe that the mores of the gang are more important than the laws of society. Car theft is another impulsive act often committed by aimless teenagers. The potential for leisure service organizations to make an impact on such crime would appear to be great, since such organizations provide activity that would occupy an adolescent's time that might otherwise be spent in crime. Unfortunately, leisure service agencies sometimes actually discourage juvenile delinquents or youth who seem to be predisposed toward crime from using their facilities or participating in their programs, much as public schools increasingly deal with "incorrigible youth" by suspending them from school. Juvenile delinquents are often more difficult to deal with, and in some cases their presence may discourage others from participating in a program or using recreation facilities. Many leisure service agencies are judged according to how many people participate in their services, and therefore every attempt may be made to discourage those from participating whose presence will drive others away. However, when an organization *will* agree to work with juvenile delinquents, the positive impact can be great.

POPULATION DENSITY

Population density is assumed to be related to comparative need for leisure services, with higher population densities thought to have comparatively greater need for public leisure services. One of the reasons for this assumption is that high population density often is found in poverty areas, and poverty, as noted, is thought to be related to recreation need. In some instances, however, those living in high population densities are wealthy, living in luxury high-rise apartments. Dunn has argued that population density in itself may not indicate high recreation need in such areas, since the residents are wealthy and make little use of public recreation facilities.

It is very important to recognize that the leisure *preferences* of those living in high population densities is an important variable in determining what effect density will have on their comparative need. If the population involved is interested in participating in outdoor or land-based recreation activities, or in activities which take up large amounts of space, it is much more likely that they will not be able to satisfy their recreation needs as easily as if they were interested in activities that require relatively little space and take place indoors. Among the urban poor, however, leisure preferences are sometimes those which *do* require land or extensive space. A study of low-income urban residents in Milwaukee, for instance, found that fishing was among the most popular leisure activities of adults.[8]

RACE OR ETHNIC STATUS

Considering race as an indicator of comparative need for leisure services is a somewhat controversial assumption. There is no evidence that race per se should be an indicator of recreation or leisure need, or that any particular race has unique leisure needs. There is, however, evidence that blacks living in the United States are more likely than whites to be poor, to have a low education level, to live in high-density population areas and to have other of the characteristics previously noted as indicating greater need for leisure services. Other ethnic minorities with similar problems are also considered to have higher comparative recreation need.

CONCLUSIONS

In summary, accurate studies on comparative recreation need can assure that priorities for service will be identified within the population. While the processes for determining such need are still imperfect, they *can* result in a more precise notion of how resources *should* be distributed among the population, and why. On the negative side, it must be noted that comparative need–resource models are sometimes difficult to set into operation, and say nothing about exactly *what* leisure services should be distributed.

REFERENCES

1. Gunnar Myrdal, quoted by Richard Kraus in *Public Recreation and the Negro—A Study of Participation and Administrative Practices* (New York: Center for Urban Education; 1968), p. 10.
2. Diana Dunn, "Recreation, Open Space and Social Organization," in Betty van der Smissen, ed., *Indicators of Change in the Recreation Environment* (University Park, Pennsylvania; Pennsylvania State University, 1975), pp. 261, 273–274.
3. John M. Burdick, *Recreation in the Cities: Who Gains From Federal Aid?* (Washington, D.C.: Center for Growth Alternatives, 1975).
4. E. Staley, *An Instrument for Determining Comparative Priority of Need for Neighborhood Recreation Services in the City of Los Angeles* (Los Angeles: Recreation and Youth Services Planning Council, 1968), p. 1.
5. *Profile for Planning: An Approach to Measuring the Need for Leisure-Time Services in Metropolitan Boston* (Boston: United Community Services of Metropolitan Boston, 1963), p. 20.
6. *Assessment of Needs,* Vol. VI of the Commonwealth of Pennsylvania State Comprehensive Recreation Plan, Local Government Aspect, prepared by the Recreation and Parks Program of the Pennsylvania State University, 1970.
7. Diana Dunn, *Open Space and Recreation Opportunity in America's Inner Cities* (Washington, D.C.: U.S. Department of Housing and Urban Development, 1974).
8. *Characteristics and Recreational Participation Patterns of Low-Income Inner-City Residents* (Madison, Wisconsin: College of Agriculture and Life Sciences, University of Wisconsin, April, 1974), p. 49.

QUESTIONS

1. In your opinion, should public recreation and park agencies use comparative need–resource models? Why or why not?

2. What conditions or situations might indicate high comparative need for public recreation and park services in your community?

3. Can comparative need–resource models be used by therapeutic recreation agencies, recreation youth-serving agencies and employee recreation organizations? Why or why not?

4. From what you have read in previous chapters, do you believe that public recreation and park agencies originally served as "providers of last resort" for those who were underprivileged?

5. Does state government have the right, in your opinion, to establish "fair share-funding curves " as the state of Pennsylvania did? Why or why not?

Historically, both public and private recreation, park and leisure services evolved largely through the efforts of civic improvement groups, neighborhood improvement associations and other community action groups. (U.S. Bureau of Outdoor Recreation; reproduced from the collections of the Library of Congress)

chapter 16

CITIZEN OR PARTICIPANT INVOLVEMENT IN DECISION-MAKING

In this chapter, we will examine citizen participation in the decision-making process. While the primary emphasis in this discussion will be upon public agencies, it is believed that many of the issues raised have direct implication for the private and commercial sector.

The first section of this chapter will be concerned with an historical overview of citizen participation in the affairs of government, the costs and benefits of such participation, and levels of citizen participation. Next, research findings pertaining to citizen participation in public recreation and parks will be reviewed. Finally, an attempt will be made to develop a rationale for citizen involvement in the decision-making process of leisure service agencies and factors affecting the need for such participation.

HISTORY OF CITIZEN PARTICIPATION

DEMOCRACY IN ANCIENT GREECE

According to Aristotle's definition of primary government, citizens are those who help to make the laws of the state. The executive is meant to merely supplement those laws when they are inadequate or when they become too general.[1] In ancient Athens, the assembly *(ecclesia),* which consisted of all qualified voters, delivered the final vote on all legislative matters. Qualified voters were males 18 years of age or older who were born of Athenian parents. Slaves and women were excluded from the voting. The assembly met about three times a month to debate and decide by a show of hands the great issues of the day. Citizen participation was more than a right; it was a duty. If an insufficient number of citizens attended an assembly meeting, the Athenian police would herd in additional participants. Citizenship implied active cooperation in regard to all military and civilian functions. Most offices were chosen by drawing lots and were filled for a period of only one year.[2] Ironically, this extensive use of citizen participation was partially a result of the existence of slaves, who tended the houses and businesses while their masters were away.

While ancient Greece may have achieved an optimum in direct citizen participation, one cause of the failure of its society appears to have been its inability to go from a direct or highly participatory democracy to a representative democracy.[3]

DIRECT VS. REPRESENTATIVE DEMOCRACY

Modern attempts at democratic forms of government have usually been organized around the principle of representation, whereby government officials are elected to represent the interests of the residents of some geographic region who qualify as citizens rather than the principle of a direct democracy, in which all citizens vote on all issues.

A recent international conference on citizen participation sponsored by the International Union of Local Authorities identified some of the difficulties inherent in both direct democracy and representative democracy.[3]

Disadvantages of Direct Democracy. Direct democracy may create a vacuum of leadership by failing to suggest a role for the executive function and by failing to make legitimate any system for advancing policy initiatives. Direct democracy is also unstable. It may be destroyed by citizen disinterest, neglect and apathy, making it vulnerable to the desires of a powerful few. It may also be plagued by hyperactivity in which a kind of mob rule emerges, which in turn produces a repressive dictatorial takeover. As Bell points out, an increase in such participation leads to the "multiplication" of citizens' groups which, in effect, cancel each other out, creating a sense of impasse. Thus, increased participation in the democratic process may lead to an increased sense of frustration among citizens.[4] A direct form of democracy also fails to provide a system of rules or safeguards to protect the less vocal and forceful members of society from being dominated by the more aggressive members.

Perhaps the most important criticism of a direct democracy is that it simply can't be adapted to the realities of life in the twentieth century, which is characterized by mass societies involving communities of thousands of people. The New England Town Meeting approach to government simply isn't feasible as the number of citizens multiplies. The complexity of modern life also makes direct democracy more difficult. The highly technical nature of many government decisions means that citizens would have to have a tremendous amount of education in many diverse areas to understand the various issues and alternative courses of action.

Disadvantages of Representative Democracy. Representative democracy also has its disadvantages. First is the problem of legitimacy—how can a chosen representative reflect totally both the variety and intensity of feelings held by the population that he represents? Another problem of representative democracies is that representatives may seek only to sustain the current system and themselves in positions of power. They may also reflect only the preferences and values of a small segment of the population—often the business and banking interests, who may be totally insensitive to the mass of society, particularly the poor. Finally, a representative democracy may become immobilized and unable to respond when confronted with demands from a variety of divergent interests that are difficult to reconcile.

COMMUNITY ORGANIZATION

Although direct democracy may not be easily compatible with the rise of technology and specialization found in twentieth century post-industrial society, a number of methods, often lumped together under the term "community organization" have been used in this century to try to reconcile these two often conflicting concepts. Lindeman, in 1921, saw the essential problem of community organization as providing a working relationship between specialism and the democratic process. These two ideas were in conflict,

Lindeman said, because the democratic process is personified by a total community membership while specialization is characterized by a division of labor to produce individuals, organizations and institutions designed to do one thing effectively. Thus, he defined community organization as follows:

> **. . . that phase of social organization which constitutes a conscious effort on the part of a community to control its affairs democratically, and to secure the highest services from its specialists, organizations, agencies and institutions by means of recognized interrelations.**[5]

Other definitions have stressed a cooperative identification and working toward the solution of community problems. Ross, for example, defined community organization as

> **. . . a process by which a community identifies its needs or objectives, orders (or ranks) these needs or objectives, develops the confidence and will to work at these needs or objectives, finds the resources (internal and/or external) to deal with these needs or objectives, takes action in respect to them and in so doing extends and develops co-operative and collaborative attitudes and practices in the community.**[6]

According to Rothman, there are three basic models of community organization practice: locality development, social planning and social action.[7]

Locality development assumes that community change is most effectively pursued through broad participation of a wide cross section of people at the community level in determining goals and action toward these goals. It stresses democratic procedures, voluntary cooperation, self-help, development of indigenous leadership and educational objectives.

Social planning emphasizes a technical process of problem-solving with regard to such social problems as housing, recreation or mental health. Rational, deliberately planned and controlled change is its goal. Community participation may be high or low in this process, depending upon the particular problem. Social planning assumes that planners can skillfully guide complex change processes by exercising their technical abilities and manipulating large bureaucratic organizations.

Social action models assume that there is a disadvantaged segment of the population that needs to be organized, perhaps in alliance with others, to successfully make demands on the larger community for increased resources, social justice and other improvements in their living conditions. This requires large-scale societal and institutional change. Tables 16–1 and 16–2 present the major features of these three approaches as outlined by Rothman.

Recreation agencies have to some extent been involved in all three of these models of community organization. The involvement of recreation workers in settlement houses, agricultural extension projects, neighborhood and "roving" leader projects, and consultation regarding recreation and park development to communities may all be considered locality development. From a social planning standpoint, recreation planners, administrators and consultants in many types of recreation and park agencies collect and analyze data as a means of solving problems related to recreation. Additionally, such agencies often interact with planning councils and agencies at higher government levels in establishing policies based upon large amounts of data. The involvement of recreation agencies in social action models of community organization has come about in

TABLE 16–1 Three Models of Community Organization Practice According to Selected Practice Variables

	Model A (Locality Development)	Model B (Social Planning)	Model C (Social Action)
1. Goal categories of community action	Self-help; community capacity and integration (process goals)	Problem-solving with regard to substantive community problems (task goals)	Shifting of power relationships and resources; basic institutional change (task or process goals)
2. Assumptions concerning community structure and problem conditions	Community eclipsed, anomie; lack of relationships and democratic problem-solving capacities: static traditional community	Substantive social problems: mental and physical health, housing, recreation	Disadvantaged populations, social injustice, deprivation, inequity
3. Basic change strategy	Broad cross section of people involved in determining and solving their own problems	Fact-gathering about problems and decisions on the most rational course of action	Crystallization of issues and organization of people to take action against enemy targets
4. Characteristic change tactics and techniques	Consensus: communication among community groups and interests; group discussion	Consensus or conflict	Conflict or contest: confrontation, direct action, negotiation
5. Salient practitioner roles	Enabler-catalyst, coordinator; teacher of problem-solving skills and ethical values	Fact-gatherer and analyst, program implementer, facilitator	Activist-advocate: agitator, broker, negotiator, partisan
6. Medium of change	Manipulation of small task-oriented groups	Manipulation of formal organizations and of data	Manipulation of mass organizations and political processes
7. Orientation toward power structure(s)	Members of power structure as collaborators in a common venture	Power structure as employers and sponsors	Power structure as external target of action: oppressors to be coerced or overturned
8. Boundary definition of the community client system or constituency	Total geographic community	Total community or community segment (including "functional" community)	Community segment
9. Assumptions regarding interests of community subparts	Common interests or reconcilable differences	Interests reconcilable or in conflict	Conflicting interests which are not easily reconcilable: scarce resources
10. Conception of the public interest	Rationalist-unitary	Idealist-unitary	Realist-individualist
11. Conception of the client population or constituency	Citizens	Consumers	Victims
12. Conception of client role	Participants in interactional problem-solving process	Consumers or recipients	Employers, constituents, members

Source: Jack Rothman, "Three Models of Community Organization Practice," *Social Work Practice—1968* (New York: Columbia University Press, 1968).

TABLE 16–2 Some Personnel Aspects of Community Organization Models

	Model A (Locality Development)	Model B (Social Planning)	Model C (Social Action)
Agency type	Settlement houses, overseas community development: Peace	Welfare council, city planning board, federal bureaucracy	Alinsky, civil rights, black power, New Left, welfare rights, cause and social movement groups, trade unions
Practice positions	Village worker, neighborhood worker, consultant to community development team, agricultural extension worker	Planning division head, planner	Local organizer
Professional analogues	Adult educator, nonclinical group worker, group dynamics professional, agricultural extension worker	Demographer, social survey specialist, public administrator, hospital planning specialist	Labor organizer, civil rights worker, welfare rights organizer

Source: Rothman, "Three Models of Community Organization Practice," 1968. Copyright © National Conference on Social Welfare, Columbus, Ohio. Reprinted by permission of Columbia University Press.

recent years as a result of federal government programs such as the War on Poverty, minority and other social change movements and the environmental movement to which recreation and park agencies have reacted or been forced to react.

COSTS AND BENEFITS OF CITIZEN PARTICIPATION

Citizen or participant involvement in the affairs of both government and nongovernment organizations is characterized by a set of costs and benefits that may assume different dimensions in various situations. Perhaps the biggest benefit of citizen participation is that it represents a direct expression of our democratic ideal—it is literally democracy in action. Citizen participation can act as a check and balance against institutionalized sources of power. It can also provide a forum for the exchange of ideas and priorities in which people consider, debate and act upon issues that directly affect their lives. Our society assumes that the citizen should have some control over those decisions which directly affect their lives, and citizen participation provides this control. In doing so, it may help to alleviate much of the alienation and feelings of helplessness so often ascribed to post-industrial societies. Citizen participation reawakens individual feelings of identification with one's own environment and helps re-establish a sense of community.

Leadership development is another benefit of active citizen participation. The experience of individual citizens in community action projects may heighten their potential for future leadership roles in the community.

Through citizen participation, mistaken impressions held by government officials about citizen viewpoints may be corrected. A related benefit is the ability of citizens working together to "heat up" a cold issue or take the heat off a hot one, thus encouraging government or a private organization to re-evaluate the importance of an issue, reconsider it or delay consideration. The ability of citizen participation to make political bodies concentrate on specific issues encourages a trend toward issue politics. Politicians may be forced to take meaningful stands on specific issues rather than merely spout rhetoric.

Finally, citizen participation can help integrate the physical and social planning structures of government or private organizations, since citizen group interests and concerns frequently cut across both physical and social concerns.

In spite of these significant benefits, citizen participation is not without its difficulties. Perhaps the greatest is the belief that citizen participation actually undermines the representative democratic process established by the people. Those who take this view hold that there are already duly elected representatives of the people with a legal mandate to act in their behalf, and proliferation of citizen groups only weakens the existing democratic governmental apparatus.

Another problem is that citizen participation may sometimes be based more on passion than on logic, and may become an end in itself rather than a means to an end.[9] Citizens wrapped up in the involvement process may lose sight of their objectives. They may view citizen participation as a panacea for all of society's ills and become disillusioned when it doesn't produce the expected miracles. Citizen participation is a complicated process and differs in its effectiveness from situation to situation.

Another potential difficulty is that citizen participation may merely serve as an ego trip for a few who, carried away with their own needs, manipulate the many. Thus, citizen participation may become a duplicate in miniature of the very evil it seeks to oppose. A related problem is that citizen participation may reward those who are the most vocal rather than those whose needs are the greatest. Excessive citizen participation may make government so accustomed to a high degree of citizen advocacy and dissent that it learns to ignore it or successfully diffuse it.

A final dilemma of citizen participation is that the nature of the collective goods or benefits sought after is such that they apply to all members of the group. It is impossible to exclude anyone from the benefits. However, for this very reason, there is no incentive for each individual to make a payment of his own accord, since he will receive the benefit anyway once it is extended.[10] For a collective action to be fair, everyone must join in. If only a very few people exert the time and effort to campaign for a neighborhood park and are successful, everyone in the neighborhood will have the right to use the park. Therefore, if everyone doesn't put forth the effort to bring the park about, it is unfair to those who do.

While such a situation may be true, there is little reason to suppose that such "fairness" or equality of effort can be brought about in a democracy. Change is often brought about by a few, and it is their prerogative to shape such change according to their own vision. In sum, citizen participation, being a part of the political process, is still the art of the possible.

FACTORS IN THE DECISION-MAKING PROCESS

LEVELS OF CITIZEN PARTICIPATION

Citizen participation or the participation of members of a private organization in decision-making may be viewed as a continuum, with different levels of participation affecting the decision-making process in different ways. Arnstein identifies the levels of citizen participation, which she defines as citizen power, as manipulation, therapy, informing, consultation, placation, partnership, delegated power and citizen control.[11] At the *manipulation* level, citizens or members of private organizations merely serve to "rubber stamp" the desires of officials who educate, persuade and advise the citizen. Citizen participation as *therapy* occurs when government assumes that there is something wrong with citizens which will be relieved by allowing them to "let off steam" under the masquerade of participation in governmental planning and decision-making. *Information giving* is an important first step toward legitimate citizen participation, since citizens at least become aware of their rights, responsibilities and options. This one way communication may be done through pamphlets, posters, television, responses to inquiries and so on. If *consultation* takes place, the communication becomes two-way, in that citizens' opinions and ideas are solicited. This is often done through the use of public hearings, questionnaires, surveys, neighborhood meetings and other means. At the *placation* level of citizen participation, citizens begin to have some degree of influence, usually small, and government retains the right to judge the legitimacy of the advice. When *partnership* occurs, "power is in fact redistributed through negotiation between citizens and powerholders. They agree to share planning and decision-making responsibilities through such structures as joint policy boards, planning committees and mechanisms for resolving impasses."[11] Once ground rules are established, they are not subject to unilateral change. The level of *delegated power* occurs when citizens or members of a private organization achieve dominant decision-making authority over a particular plan or program, usually as a result of negotiation. Another model of delegated power is when citizens are given veto power over powerholders in situations where differences cannot be resolved. Finally, at the *citizen control* level, residents of an area are put in charge of the policy making and managerial aspects of a decision. No one, of course, ever has absolute control.

In terms of citizen participation in government planning, Aleshire identifies five models into which most forms of citizen participation fit.[8] These five models make the following assumptions:

Model One—Community problem-solving is a scientific pursuit and the citizen basically has nothing to contribute.

Model Two—The government technician can assume he is representing the best interests of the citizens and may proceed in a scientific fashion unless he hears otherwise. The citizen is the "shotgun behind the door."

Model Three—The citizen doesn't know what he wants but when his statements are interpreted correctly by social scientists, they will provide the key to solving his problems.

Model Four—The citizen can say "yes" or "no" to various proposals and can contribute a few bright ideas, but he can't make a significant contribution.

Model Five—Given the opportunity, citizens can work together and arrive at a consensus that will be the clearest and perhaps the only accurate perception of the needs and priorities for their community.

APPROACHES TO DECISION-MAKING

Vrooman identified five approaches by which citizens participate in decision-making: the community therapy approach, the social action approach, the information-communication-education approach, the advisory-consultation approach and the delegated authority and community control approach.[12] Organizations seeking change use more than one of these methods, but each of the methods seeks to influence social change.

Community Therapy. The community therapy approach has been the most common mechanism used to promote citizen participation in community development in Canada. It seeks to develop a feeling for and awareness of community through participation in problem-solving activity. The method assumes individual adjustment through participation in a "therapeutic" group situation. Canada's comprehensive community health programs have used the method with the basic objective of reducing the incidence of psychopathology, often including self-help projects as part of the therapy. While this method may reduce the isolation of those who cannot compete successfully in society and are thus isolated, there is a problem in that some involvement of this nature may actually be anti-therapeutic, that is, it may produce additional stress on the individual leading to further alienation. Another drawback is that the method is not applicable within the structure of formal organizations, since it concentrates on means and not on the accomplishment of external tasks.

Social Action. The social action approach is similar to the community therapy approach except that it assumes individual dysfunction is a two-way cause-and-effect relationship between social forces and the personality system. It emphasizes the negative effects of social institutions on the individual and tries to make agencies concentrate on the needs of the alienated individual rather than on changing the individual. The approach assumes that those who make and administer policy are responsive to public pressure, and thus attempts to focus public attention on the plight of the disadvantaged. One difficulty of this method is that of organizing the unaffiliated or the inarticulate and others who are unsuccessful at managing organizational form. Most large-scale attempts to change institutional structure have failed.

Information-Communication-Education. The information-communication-education approach tries to engage social institutions in changing policies by educating the public and government through the distribution of information. The widespread coverage of information campaigns by the media can be a potent force in bringing about change. In many cases, however, communication is not a two-way street; in other words, government gives out the information but receives little feedback.

Advisory-Consultation. The fourth approach by which citizens participate in decision-making is the advisory-consultation approach. In this process, citizens may serve on committees to advise the government or various government agencies, such as social planning councils, of their needs and desires. Advisory councils may serve a valuable function by providing a means of feedback concerning government plans and operations. In many instances, however, they become merely a rubber-stamp group, providing only the illusion of participation.

Delegated Authority and Community Control. The delegated authority and community control approach is similar to the high participation levels of

Arnstein's scale. Decision-making authority is either shared or is delegated to citizens. Under such conditions, programs become more directly accountable to those they are designed to serve. For the success of such an approach, a highly informed and motivated citizenry is required.

HOW VARIOUS LEVELS AND APPROACHES WORK

If we consider a government decision involving recreation from the standpoint of these levels and models, it becomes evident that the particular level or model of participation chosen may significantly influence the actual decision that is made. Let us suppose that a municipal recreation and park department is faced with the decision of whether or not to purchase two acres of land for a park in a residential section of a community. Let us further assume that funds are already available for the acquisition of that land. In such a situation, if citizen participation were only at the manipulation or therapy level, citizens might be given the chance to voice their opinions about the wisdom of purchasing land for a park, but the decision as to whether or not to acquire the land would be made completely apart from the citizens, or might have been made previously. Sometimes a neighborhood group concerned with recreation is given the opportunity to "blow off steam," in order to calm them down or dissipate their energy.

If the recreation and park department gave the citizens in the neighborhood (or the entire community) accurate and complete information about their intentions to purchase parkland, the options open to the department regarding purchasing alternate parkland, using the funds in another manner or not using the funds at all, citizens would be in a better position to understand the significance of the decision.

If citizens were involved in this decision at the consultation level, they would have to have the opportunity to react to the information presented to them concerning the possibility of acquiring a park site and to have this reaction heard and considered by officials of the department of recreation and parks. This might be accomplished by a public hearing, a survey or an informal neighborhood meeting.

At the placation level, a few citizens might be appointed to a special task force or committee to advise the recreation and park department concerning citizen reaction to the proposed park. For partnership to be achieved, a joint committee of residents and members of the department of recreation and parks would have to be established in such a manner that any decisions made concerning the acquisition of land or use of funds for other sources would have to be jointly approved before action could be taken.

If some planned responsibilities were delegated to a citizen group by the department of recreation and parks, the citizen group would have to have veto power over some phase of the decision. It might be decided, for instance, that the determination as to whether or not to purchase the land for a park would be made jointly but that the authority for the development of policy for citizen use of the park would rest with the citizen committee.

Finally, if there were complete citizen control, some group of citizens would be empowered to make the decision whether or not to purchase the parkland without the consent of the department of recreation and parks. The municipal agency would then carry out the decision or policy.

TABLE 16–3 Descriptive Dimensions Characterizing Various Public Involvement Mechanisms

	Descriptive Dimensions*				
	Focus				
Type of Public Involvement Mechanism	Scope (No. of people)	Speci-ficity	Degree of Two-way Communi-cation	Level of Citizen Activity Required	Agency Staff Time
Workshops	L	H	H	H	H
Public Hearings	M	L	L	H	M
Mass Media (including use of newspapers, radio and TV)	H	L	L	L	L
Task Forces	L	H	H	H	H
Agency Publications	H	M	L	L	M
Speeches and Presentations	M	M	M	L	M
Survey Questionnaire	M	H	L	M	M
Advisory Boards	L	H	H	H	H
Informal Contacts	L	H	H	M	M

*H = High degree
M = Medium degree
L = Low degree

TYPE OF INVOLVEMENT MECHANISM

The level of citizen participation in governmental decision-making determines, to a great extent, the type of public involvement mechanism used. As Table 16–3 shows, different public involvement mechanisms require varying numbers of people, degrees of two-way communication between citizens and government, levels of citizen activity and amounts of agency staff time. They also operate at different levels of specificity.[13]

As may be seen from Table 16–3, an advisory council, for example, requires a high degree of citizen activity, staff time and two-way communication, but involves comparatively few people. In subsequent chapters, several public involvement mechanisms used in public recreation and park agencies will be examined.

CITIZEN PARTICIPATION IN PUBLIC RECREATION DECISION-MAKING: SOME RESEARCH FINDINGS

There is a tradition of active citizen participation in the affairs of both public and private recreation and park agencies in the United States and Canada. In large part the organized recreation movement came about through the efforts of community action–styled organizations, often composed of influential citizens and social workers. In Canada, such groups included local chapters of the National Council of Women, neighborhood playground associations, service clubs and community associations.[14] Following World War I, a number of social, religious and civic groups began to assume responsibility for promoting neighborhood and community recreation programs. In the post-Depression years, the need for greater citizen interest and public support to continue municipal recreation programs initiated by federal "relief" type agencies led to the widespread formation of citizen advisory councils.[14]

During the 1960's, urban recreation and park administrators were pressured to examine their methods of involving citizens in the affairs of their departments. The quest for representative government during this period centered upon administrative agencies, which had grown quickly in size, function and authority. As human interdependence increased as a result of technological change, government complexity, abstractness, size and distance from citizens had increased, with resulting frustration for citizens who felt powerless to do anything about it. The major government impetus for citizen participation in the United States, particularly for the poor, came from the "War on Poverty." The Economic Opportunity Act of 1964 consisted of seven titles loosely tying together a wide range of old and new programs to combat poverty. Its most controversial features were contained in Title II-A, Section 202 (a) (3), which authorized the creation of Community Action Programs. These programs were to be "developed, conducted and administered with the maximum feasible participation of the residents of the areas and members of the groups served."[16] Ostensibly, the purpose of Title II was to stimulate local communities to take the initiative in developing programs and mobilizing support in a coordinated manner for a broad-based attack on poverty. Although the resource committed to the War on Poverty amounted to less than 1 percent of the federal budget, the program was highly publicized and created great expectations.[17] While "maximum feasible participation" became a rallying cry for many involved in the War on Poverty, studies by Moynihan, Kramer and Westby took the position that these programs failed because of the inability of Community Action Programs to make changes in the social structure.[16, 18, 19]

While the War on Poverty may not have realized its goals, the impetus toward participatory management in many administrative branches of government continues. This impetus has extended to many federal organizations involved in outdoor recreation, such as the U.S. Forest Service and the National Park Service. Research concerning citizen participation in urban recreation decision-making is not extensive, but it is possible to generalize the results of several studies that dealt directly and indirectly with the subject. While such findings are not conclusive or without significant exception, considerable consensus among studies' results was evidenced.

STUDIES OF CITIZEN PARTICIPATION

The studies from which generalizations are presented were undertaken for a number of purposes. One study sought to identify municipal recreation problems, examine various solutions and outline planning methods used and emerging citizen roles in 15 major cities, using documentary analysis and interviews.[20] A second study used interviews with officials in 60 communities thought to have "successful" recreation programs in order to provide guidelines for the management of outdoor recreation programs.[21] The participation of blacks in public recreation programs was examined in a third study.[22] Participation rates and administrative practices were determined in 24 suburban communities in New York, New Jersey and Connecticut, as well as the five boroughs of New York City, through interviews with recreation and park administrators, recreation supervisors and directors of school recreation programs. Another study focused upon the recreation problems of urban-impacted areas of California.[23] In one section of this study, a sample of residents of impacted areas were surveyed on their use of leisure, desire for more leisure participation, leisure needs and use of local parks, while in a second section a questionnaire was used to determine agency response to 10 operational problems. Representatives of six municipal recreation agencies in communities of over 100,000 population were interviewed concerning approaches to problem areas.

A local recreation and park survey was conducted by the National Recreation and Park Association, with the help of two federal agencies, to determine the geographic distribution of recreation and park agencies, managing authority, budget allocations, personnel and services provided.[24] A total of 1,119 agencies participated.

A study of the role of recreation advisory councils in Philadelphia's Department of Recreation was the sixth study reviewed.[25] It sought to determine the representativeness, effectiveness and level of participation in decision-making among citizens in a system of 70 local councils, as well as variations between poverty area councils and those outside poverty areas. Interviews with recreation officials and citizen council members, direct observation of meetings, a questionnaire and documentary analysis were used to collect the data.

A final study used in this review sought to determine the impact of problems such as physical blight, urban congestion, rises in crime, intergroup tensions and other contemporary urban problems upon municipal recreation and park departments; to identify creative and innovative solutions being brought to bear on such problems; and to formulate useful guidelines for municipal administrators and educators.[26] The study utilized extensive interviews with administrators and other officials and direct observation of recreation facilities and programs in eight large cities. Then, based on the findings, a nationwide questionnaire survey was carried out among cities having populations of 150,000 or more.

Major Findings

The following represent the major thrust of these research findings:

1. As of 1970, most local recreation and park agencies (91 percent) had a citizen board or commission: 45 percent were policy-making, 39 percent were advisory and 7 percent were of another type. In 70 percent of the local recreation agencies with boards and commissions, members were appointed, in 18 percent of the cases they were elected and in 12 percent of the cases they were chosen in some other manner.

2. An increased demand for recreation services and participation in recreation planning has come about as an outgrowth of minority group demands for social justice. Recreation administrators in two thirds of the cities with populations of 150,000 or more reported that they experienced strong demands or confrontations from socially disadvantaged residents, especially minority group members. Such demands chiefly concerned new recreation facilities or expanded programs in inner-city neighborhoods. To a lesser degree, however, they included demands that minority group members be hired in certain neighborhoods, that insensitive staff members be replaced and that local people be permitted to take over the operation of recreation facilities.

3. Urban recreation resource allocation systems are hypersensitive to citizen group inputs that threaten confrontation or harm to departmental image.

Often, local recreation and park agencies seek meaningful citizen participation as a result of confrontation. The squeaky wheel gets the oil.

4. While demand for participation in recreation decision-making is increasing in poverty areas, there is still generally less input into the decision-making process in poverty areas than in non-poverty areas. Poor urban dwellers are frequently less vocal and persistent in requests for recreation services than are other citizens. Additionally, the urban poor who represent their neighborhoods to recreation and park agencies are sometimes less willing to use confrontation tactics than are middle class representatives. The poor are not as skilled as their middle class counterparts at mobilizing political support to achieve their desires.

Recreation advisory councils frequently are handicapped in their activities by a lack of clear definition of function. This is particularly true in poverty areas. There are also class differences in the perception of an advisory council's role. In the Philadelphia study,[25] council presidents in poverty areas were likely to perceive their role as that of a "helper," whereas council presidents in middle class areas perceived it as that of a "consultant" or "lobby."

5. Recreation advisory councils in poverty areas are often forced to perform a different function from that of non-poverty area councils. Whereas in middle class areas the council may be primarily concerned with improving, expanding and altering existing services, in poverty areas the council may find that it is forced to focus all its energies on protecting the status quo; on seeking to protect the recreation programs and facilities from forces in the neighborhood that would destroy them, such as youth gangs, drug addicts and community apathy and fear. Performance of this "holding function" by the poverty area council often prevents them from lobbying for change, while failure to perform this holding function risks the council's becoming inoperative.

6. Urban recreation councils are often composed of individuals of similar socioeconomic background who live in close proximity to each other. They are thus a poor integrating device. In the Philadelphia study, racial integration was practically nonexistent within a council.[25] In poverty areas, over 90 percent of the council members were women. Both in poverty areas and outside them, council members frequently lived on the same street.

7. Urban recreation agencies often have trouble securing the participation of poor citizens in the decision-making process on a continuing basis. Citizen councils in poverty areas are frequently smaller, experience higher turnover rates and function for fewer man-hours than their middle class counterparts.

8. Urban recreation agencies often have trouble recognizing the legitimacy of one ad hoc neighborhood organization over another. A multiplicity of groups and organizations frequently claim to represent the community in matters pertaining to recreation. Determining who speaks for the bulk of the citizens in an area may be almost impossible.

9. Some citizens' groups originally organized on a volunteer basis for advisory purposes usurp the identity of the recreation agency by assuming administrative duties. Such behavior causes administrative distrust of citizen councils.

10. In recreation programs directly funded by the federal government for disadvantaged citizens, citizen representatives have played a significant role in decision-making. Municipal recreation agencies and anti-poverty agencies, however, have maintained only superficial relationships.

11. Black inner-city neighborhoods that have received federal funds to

operate their own recreation facilities and programs tend not to feel a need to support and work through the public recreation and park agency. Instead, they often fight for their own programs, which are locally managed, are free of the civil service structure and may provide jobs for neighborhood residents.

12. Some municipal recreation and park departments have given considerable attention to the task of developing effective neighborhood recreation advisory councils. Often, successful attempts have been made at establishing a network of councils that will perform a number of functions, including fund raising, recruiting volunteer leadership, assisting with transportation, making staff aware of local traditions and needs, helping to evaluate existing programs and investigating complaints from individuals in the neighborhood and suggesting solutions for them.

Such councils may organize, coach and manage athletic teams, elect chairpersons to different recreation program areas, own extensive equipment, publish a newspaper and serve as an invaluable aid to the municipal recreation and park agency.

13. Urban recreation and park departments have achieved little true decentralization. Participation of neighborhood people in decision-making has generally been superficial. Although urban recreation and park administrators may express a willingness to involve the community at the policy level, they are in reality often reluctant to have this happen.

In spite of this, many municipal recreation and park administrators perceive of their agencies as having successfully involved citizens in the decision-making process. In a self-evaluation survey, administrators of 40 local recreation agencies providing leisure services in the urban-impacted areas of California ranked their success in involving citizens in decision-making second highest among 10 operational problems.[23]

Even where the desire to decentralize exists, a number of problems stand in the way in addition to those of community apathy and not recognizing the legitimacy of neighborhood groups. Civil service specifications often make it impossible to create new job titles, upgrade job descriptions or hire indigenous leaders within poverty area neighborhoods. Labor union resistance to decentralization, which is viewed as a threat to the security of civil employees, makes it difficult to bring about personnel changes needed to further such plans.

Another problem is that most recreation and park administrators would have to assign higher levels of responsibility to their area or district supervisors, allowing them to act very much as if they were chief administrators of smaller cities if decentralization were to be achieved. Currently, district supervisors in urban recreation and park departments very often act as mere message carriers from recreation center employees and advisory councils to the municipal recreation hierarchy, and have no real power to implement action. Frequently they are saddled by a host of routine, bookkeeping and "busywork" activities. While theoretically they may be community organizers, coordinators, catalysts and "idea generators," in reality their time is taken up with reports, scheduling, requisitioning supplies and the like. Some district supervisors, recognizing their powerlessness, encourage citizen councils to bypass them and go directly to the department administrative chief with their concerns.

Decentralizing by giving increased authority to district supervisors would also require additional funds to "beef up" district services. Under present conditions, the financial problems of urban governments make it unlikely that such funds would be forthcoming.

Implications

The preceding findings imply a need for urban recreation agencies to identify new modes of citizen participation. Such modes must systematically involve citizens in meaningful levels of participation in governmental decision-making; not just information giving and consultation, but also negotiation, shared policy and decision-making, joint planning, delegation of planned responsibility and even neighborhood control.[27]

Given the nature of the findings concerning the participation of the poor, the urban recreation agency may have to assume more of an initiating role, providing both incentives and training for participation. The citizen participant must have extensive information and understanding about community resources and political machinery, as well as realistic notions of what possible alternatives exist in regard to departmental decisions. The citizen, in short, must be confided in.

Agency assumption of an initiating role in involving citizens in departmental decision-making may well have an effect on departmental susceptibility to confrontation tactics, since such tactics often result from lack of agency-citizen communication and reactionary agency decision-making on a crisis basis.

Where local advisory council systems are utilized, urban recreation agencies must seek new ways of recognizing their legitimacy. One way of doing this would be to give the council closer communication with those recreation officials who have the authority to make recreation resource allocation decisions. This might be accomplished by establishing frequent, systematic contact with the recreation department hierarchy or by giving district supervisors more authority to make policy and allocate recreation resources within their respective districts in the city. Another way of recognizing council legitimacy would be to allow major variation in council organization, methods of operation and even purpose. Such variation already exists in many cases, particularly in regard to poverty area and non-poverty area councils, and it must be recognized and encouraged. This means that the organization representing the neighborhood to the agency may be multi-purpose, may be indigenous to the community or may even have been formed by another agency of government. It may be extremely homogeneous in terms of membership and not "representative" of the community in the pluralistic sense.

Perhaps another implication is the need for experimentation. There is little experience among recreation agencies concerning the decentralization process. No one really knows if it can succeed. It is time to find out.

MAJOR RECOMMENDATIONS

In closing, it seems worthwhile to note the conclusions of a study of citizen participation in the decision-making of the United States Forest Service. As a result of examining citizen involvement in a variety of situations, the following recommendations were made:

> 1. *Clarify objectives.* The objectives of public involvement for any specific issue should be clearly articulated, and then communicated

both internally and to the public. These objectives should govern the resulting collection, analysis and evaluation of public input.

2. *Decentralize responsibility for public involvement.* Public input must be a decision-making factor at all levels of the organization—district, forest, regional and national. Planning and conducting public participation must directly involve the administrative level that will be responsible for implementing the decision. This is necessary to secure adequate input of local views and to facilitate the involvement of citizens and agency people most directly affected. Other administrative levels also may need to participate in order to achieve adequate national and/or regional perspective.

3. *Develop a comprehensive plan.* A comprehensive plan is required for major public-involvement efforts. Do not proceed to the public regarding an issue until all organizational levels have a common understanding of objectives. Avoid "piecemeal" instructions. Completely open and reciprocal vertical communication within the organization is essential.

4. *Allow adequate time.* Because the public plays a key role in all land-management decision-making, it should be involved early in the decision process and be given adequate time to respond.

5. *Broaden public input.* The views of all potentially affected interests must be secured.

Public input most often comes from the local population that is directly affected. Without minimizing the importance of local input, there is also a need to consult the broader regional and national populations—particularly the masses of city dwellers—who have a stake in National Forest decisions.

The Forest Service should strengthen efforts to inform the national and regional publics of issues that concern them. Publicity to stimulate public involvement should extend beyond the apparent areas of interest.

The Forest Service should examine its present use of public information resources. It should explore the feasibility of expanding its use of all mass media and of increasing its efforts to educate and inform media editors. The Forest Service should consider sponsoring its own publication to inform a broad public on issues and to solicit their views.

6. *Provide a full range of alternatives.* The Forest Service should present the public with an array of alternatives indicating no preferences. These alternatives should cover the full range of possibilities (legally and with regard to resource capability). Five or six alternatives would not be excessive in most cases, although there can be no single guideline.

7. *Use a variety of collection techniques.* The kind of techniques used to secure public involvement should be based on specific objectives for the particular issue at hand. Varied opportunities for input should be provided. Public meetings do not equal public involvement but are only one of a possible set of tools.

8. *Encourage primary input.* A position should be established and communicated to the public that all input is desired and will be considered. But more importance will be placed on primary input such as personal letters and statements than on endorsement of views through secondary input such as petitions, form letters or newspaper coupons.

9. *Strengthen analysis with systematic methods.* Forest Service analysis of public input must be strengthened by use of systematic methods. Public input is too important in the decision process—and

the danger of misperception is too great—to rely on subjective, informal analysis procedures. And systematic analysis will facilitate the use of public input in decision-making.

10. *Analyze all input.* Analysis must describe all public input, including emotional statements and general opinions as well as the more specific comments and detailed management proposals. All input expresses opinions and values; thus, all of it has implications important to the decision-maker.

11. *Separate analysis from evaluation.* Analysis must be kept apart from evaluation. Analysis is merely the description of the nature, content and extent of public comment. Evaluation is the interpretation of its meaning and its integration with other factors with regard to a decision.

12. *Recognize line officers' responsibility for evaluation.* Line officers at each level must be responsible for evaluating the implications that public input holds for their recommendations or decisions. This responsibility cannot be delegated. And officers must substantiate their judgments in a logical and defensible manner.

Evaluation should be recognized as a subjective part of professional resource decision-making. It requires sensitivity, perception and judgment as well as technical ability. This should serve as a criterion in educating, recruiting, training and promoting line officers.

13. *Develop consistent procedures.* The public deserves assurance that its input will be treated with reasonable consistency from one forest or region to another. There is particular need for greater uniformity in the analysis and evaluation of public input. Procedural guidelines must be developed and communicated both internally and to the public.

14. *Provide full disclosure at all levels.* To protect the credibility of public involvement and to make it effective, recommendations or decisions based on public input should be disclosed in full as they are developed at all levels of the organization.

Public involvement must be visible and traceable whenever it is used in developing a recommendation or decision. How public input was used and its relationship to other decision-making factors must be clear.

15. *Give feedback to the public.* As part of the public involvement in any issue, keep the public up to date on progress in the decision-making process.

Make sure the public is told what input resulted and how it was used. When the Forest Service is unable to comply with some public recommendations, explain why.

Citizens deserve personal, individualized replies when they write to ask questions or in any way indicate they expect response. In all cases, feedback about the decision should be sent to everyone who provided input.

16. *Seek the expertise needed.* The importance of public involvement requires that all pertinent Forest Service resources, including research, be focused on developing philosophy, concepts, techniques and skills to meet the challenge. Where necessary, outside expertise should be consulted. Good intentions are not enough. An honest but inept effort can backfire and alienate the very public it sought to involve.

17. *Provide comprehensive training.* A broad program of training covering all stages of public involvement should be implemented quickly. All line and staff officers in the Forest Service down to the

district level should be taught the philosophy and concepts underlying public participation—issue definition, collection, analysis, evaluation and decision implementation. Those line and staff officers who will implement public involvement need training in specific techniques and procedures.

A RATIONALE FOR CITIZEN PARTICIPATION

In presenting a rationale for citizen participation in the decision-making process of leisure service agencies, let us start from an existential standpoint: existence precedes essence. There is no model of decision-making that is inherently correct or good; only after the specific environment and context in which decisions are to be made are established can the best methods for making them be determined. The degree to which decision-making should be a democratic process is situationally determined. In times of war, for instance, democratic countries suspend some democratic processes by necessity. A "town meeting" is functional in some situations, but not in large urban areas.

With regard to the decision-making of leisure service agencies, there are several components that must be examined before an ideal method for making decisions can be determined. One important variable is degree of population homogeneity. The more "alike" a population is with regard to life style, socioeconomic characteristics and political outlook, the less it would appear that an administrator of recreation and park services would need to involve citizens in the decision-making process at the higher levels. This is based on the assumption that it is easier to identify the leisure patterns of a homogeneous population, that the conflict level with regard to recreation needs and desires will be less and that there will be more predictability concerning the leisure behavior of the population than in a highly heterogeneous population.

A second variable is the education and information level of the general population. Inputs into decision-making aren't meaningful unless there is some minimum knowledgeability on the part of those participating. When people vote in elections in which they don't know the candidates, for instance, the act of voting becomes almost meaningless. One major unsolved dilemma in urban recreation decision-making is that in situations where variation in the population is extreme and conflict levels high, there is also wide disparity in the education level of the population. While a high level of participation is needed based upon heterogeneity, a low level is seemingly logical based upon education level for some parts of the community. While recreation agencies and other services of government talk about "educating the public" in regard to their operations, such education is extremely limited. Based upon the two criteria listed so far, an almost inherent dilemma is established.

The desire for and expectation of participation in decision-making are variables that cannot be overlooked. Different cultures and subcultures have varying levels of trust in government and expectations about what their participation rights are. The decision-making process established for recreation agencies must roughly correspond to the expectations of citizens concerning their role in it. When changes in this expectation level occur, the agencies must readjust their decision-making process.

A final, perhaps overriding variable, is the nature of the subject matter about which a decision is to be made. As stated earlier, leisure and recreation activity are highly personalized and diffuse concepts, even by definition. Because of this, the need for citizen input in decision-making may be greater in communities where leisure patterns are more complex.

While the previously mentioned variables are important in determining the level and nature of citizen involvement in recreation decision-making, a number of factors indicate that citizens should play a greater role in decision-making in recreation and parks than in other functions of government. Among such factors are the following:

1. Parks and recreation are a "threshold experience." Perhaps more than any other function of government, public park and recreation agencies serve to provide the citizen with an introductory or threshold experience in the affairs of government. Participation in the decision-making process of a recreation and park agency may serve as a springboard for citizen involvement in the affairs of other agencies and other functions of government.

2. Parks and recreation as a public and private organizational service evolved largely through the effects of civic improvement groups, neighborhood improvement associations, social clubs and other community action type groups, which turned partial responsibility for operating recreation services over to local government only after the burden of operating the programs and facilities became too large a task for volunteers. These precedents developed expectations about the roles citizens should play in regard to the functioning of a park and recreation agency which still continue today.

3. The influence of technology upon recreation and park departments has been comparatively low compared to many other functions of government. Many of the operations of a recreation and park department are easily understandable by large segments of the population. While there are many technical competencies needed to administer such a department of government, the citizen sees the recreation *services* rather than their management. All citizens feel they know something about these recreation services, because they have experienced recreation activity and thus know something about it. While this may be said of other functions of government, there are quite possibly more citizen "experts" in the recreation field, because nearly everyone has some leisure interests that overlap with the offerings of a recreation and park agency.

Because citizens feel they can understand the operation of a recreation agency and its functions, they are more likely to serve as volunteers or in some other capacity which assists the agency. This involvement often becomes a springboard for participation in the agency's decision-making process.

4. Public visibility of recreation and park services is higher than that of many other functions of government, so citizens are in a better position to judge. Parents, for instance, get feedback from children who participate in recreation services and sometimes come and observe the children or participate themselves. Recreation leaders and supervisors working with children and youth are observed, analyzed and judged by youth and their parents. Areas and facilities administered and maintained by the department are frequently distributed throughout the community in many different neighborhoods. Residents know about the physical condition of such facilities, how well they are

maintained, who uses them, when they are used, how and for what purposes. In many neighborhoods, in both poverty and non-poverty areas, housewives know more about the day-to-day usage of the facility than does the park and recreation administrator.

5. Recreation and leisure activity is a direct expression of the culture of the community. As such, it must be continually redefined. To deny significant citizen input is a negation of the concept of recreation and leisure, especially the aspect of "freely chosen" activity. While both private and public park and recreation agencies are limited in the manner in which they deal with leisure activity, their offerings reflect activities as diverse as sport, dance, theatre, free play, picnics, and music, all of which directly reflect the mores and folkways of the community. Because of this situation, a high level of participation by diverse segments of the population in agency decision-making is needed to insure that the mode, style and content of activities are in keeping with and reflective of the specific community in question.

In urban areas, which are often multi-cultural, park and recreation officials are faced with the difficult task of providing recreation services to groups within the community whose culture is different from their own. Even with the best of intentions, most park and recreation administrators, although they know something about the various cultural and ethnic groups within their community, are bound by their own culture in decisions they make concerning recreation. This situation is problematic for both public and private agencies. A park manager or a Boy Scout executive, for instance, may believe that camping is a valuable, character-building experience, but his belief may not be shared by some groups within his community. Many urban poor, for instance, may not see sleeping outside on the ground as a pleasurable activity. It is the citizen's right not to be interested.

People today are in some ways less tolerant of enforced regimentation during their leisure time, or of being told what to do or how to do it in recreation settings. A recreation leader in this society increasingly takes the role of a community organizer or enabler in regard to recreation rather than directly leading some pre-determined program. The concept that recreation is a fixed number of activities which can be provided to the public like so many miles of concrete highway is badly out of date. Recreation must literally be defined by citizens at many levels before any agency of government can deal with it successfully. When this process of definition is not continuous, park and recreation agencies suffer from trying to deal with yesterday's culture.

6. The hardware-software mix of a recreation and park department is such that change can occur in a relatively short period of time. While all recreation and park agencies have hardware such as physical areas and facilities and building and maintenance equipment which they administer, the emphasis today appears to be more upon the utilization of existing hardware or physical resources in the community. At the same time, the software functions of recreation and park agencies, which consist largely of the programming of these areas and facilities and of other areas and facilities which the department does not "own" are increasing in importance. Software components, such as program selection and planning, publicity, leadership and supervision, evaluation and so forth, are relatively susceptible to rapid change. The hidden costs in many aspects of programming are not so great that changes in direction

or emphasis are prevented; that is, they don't involve many capital expenditures or long-term expenditures for relatively permanent things. This changeability makes the recreation agency more attractive to citizens in terms of their participation in decision-making, since in the recreation field they have a greater opportunity to produce change from short-term involvement or a lower level of commitment than in the affairs of most other functions of government.

7. In past decades, many of the services offered by private and public park and recreation agencies served merely to provide refreshment or a short break from work. The activity involved was of short duration and served the end of merely preparing the individual to work again. As leisure potential in our society has increased as a result of increasing industrialization, leisure activity has occupied a much more important place, often playing an important role in the self-definition of individuals. To the extent that individuals in a post-industrial society define who they are in terms of what they do, and to the extent that these activities are recreational in nature, it becomes increasingly important that public leisure service agencies involve citizens in their decisions.

8. The tendency of government to use recreation as a means of social control must be understood and, in some cases, countered by citizens when they believe it is not in their best interests. It is particularly important that those citizens who are the target of this social control participate in the decisions made by the agency. In some cases, park and recreation agencies may try to mollify some potentially disruptive group by providing recreation facilities for them. Since it is much simpler to provide leisure activities than to deal with more complex problems such as unemployment or inadequate housing, a dangerous temptation may be to offer recreation instead of more concrete solutions to societal problems.

CONCLUSIONS

It should not be assumed, of course, that all decisions made by recreation and park agencies will be made in agreement with what some group or groups of citizens favor. Indeed, citizen input on many decisions will be sharply divided. On a decision such as whether to build an indoor hockey arena in a park, for instance, citizens may divide into "conservationists" versus "hockey nuts," one group favoring keeping the park in a natural state and stopping the encroachment of open parkland while the other group pushes for an arena to meet the increased demand for ice hockey in the community.

Although the recreation and park agency professionals are not always given a clear indication of what the prevalent sentiment is on a particular issue, as in the above example, they do gain a better understanding of (1) what specific individuals or groups share an opinion, (2) the basis for the opinion or belief, and (3) the intensity of the opinion or belief.

Often, citizen participation in recreation decision-making will not simplify a decision that must be made; it may make the decision much more complicated. What may often improve, however, is the quality of the decision.

REFERENCES

1. Aristotle, *The Politics,* Book III, Chapters 1 and 16.
2. Steven Harvey, "Direct Democracy in Athens Required All-Citizen Activity," Los Angeles Times, October 30, 1972.
3. J. M. Banovetz, "Public Participation in Local Government," *Studies in Comparative Local Government,* Vol. 6, No. 1, Summer, 1972, pp. 54–60.
4. Daniel Bell, "The End of Scarcity," *Saturday Review of the Society,* Vol. 1, No. 4, May 1973, pp. 49–53.
5. Edward C. Lindeman, *The Community* (New York: Association Press, 1921), p. 173.
6. Murray G. Ross, *Community Organization: Theory and Principles* (New York: Harper and Brothers, 1955), p. 39.
7. Jack Rothman, "Three Models of Community Organization Practice," *Social Work Practice — 1968* (New York: Columbia University Press, 1968).
8. Robert Aleshire, "Planning and Citizen Participation: Costs, Benefits and Approaches," *Urban Affairs Quarterly,* June, 1970, pp. 369–70, 379.
9. David Critchley, "Citizen Participation — Opiate or Opportunity?" *Canadian Welfare,* Vol. 47, May–June, 1971. p. 13.
10. Mancur Olsen, *The Logic of Collective Action,* quoted by Daniel Bell in "The End of Scarcity," *Saturday Review of the Society,* Vol. 1, No. 4, May, 1973, pp. 49–53.
11. Sherry Arnstein, "A Ladder of Citizen Participation," *American Institute of Planners' Journal,* June, 1969. pp. 217, 221.
12. Paul C. Vrooman, "The Power Dilemma in Citizen Participation," *Canadian Welfare,* Vol. 48, May–June, 1972. pp. 3–7, 31.
13. K. P. Warner, cited by Alex Semeniuk in "Citizen Involvement and Planning," *Recreation Canada.* Vol. 31, No. 2, 1973, p. 28.
14. Elsie Marie McFarland, *The Development of Public Recreation In Canada* (Ottawa: Canadian Parks/Recreation Association, 1970), pp. 18–46.
15. George Butler, *Introduction to Community Recreation* (New York: McGraw-Hill, 1959), pp. 68–91.
16. Ralph M. Kramer, *Participation of the Poor: Comparative Community Case Studies in the War on Poverty* (Englewood Cliffs: Prentice-Hall, 1969), p. 1.
17. Edgar S. Cahn and Jean C. Cahn, "The War on Poverty: A Civilian Perspective," *Yale Law Review,* Vol. 73, July, 1964, pp. 1317–52.
18. Daniel P. Moynihan, *Maximum Feasible Misunderstanding: Community Action in the War on Poverty* (New York: The Free Press, 1969).
19. David Westby, *People, Politics and the War on Poverty* (University Park, Pennsylvania: Institute of Public Administration, 1971).
20. National League of Cities, *Recreation in the Nation's Cities: Problems and Approaches* (Washington, D. C.: National League of Cities, 1968).
21. National Association of Counties Research Foundation, *Outdoor Recreation,* Vol. 10, *Citizen Support* (Washington, D. C.: NAC, 1968).
22. Richard Kraus, *Public Recreation and the Negro: A Study of Participation and Administrative Practices* (New York: Center for Urban Education, 1968).
23. State of California, *Recreation in the Urban Impacted Areas of California* (Sacramento: Department of Recreation and Parks, 1970), p. 55.
24. "Local Recreation and Parks," *Parks and Recreation,* Vol. VI, August, 1971.
25. Geoffrey Godbey, *The Role of Advisory Councils in Philadelphia's Department of Recreation* (University Park, Pennsylvania: Doctoral Dissertation, 1972), pp. 43–47, 55–61.
26. Richard Kraus, *Urban Parks and Recreation: Challenge of the 1970's* (New York: Community Council of Greater New York, 1972).
27. From a scale devised by H. B. C. Spiegel and S. D. Mitternthal, *Neighborhood Power and Control—Implications for Planning* (New York: Institute of Urban Environment, 1968), p. 2.
28. John Hendee, et al., *Public Involvement and the Forest Service* (Washington, D.C.: U.S. Forest Service, 1973), pp. xi–xv.

QUESTIONS

1. What are the major problems associated with a direct democracy?
2. What level of citizen participation in local recreation and parks would be appropriate in your community? Why?
3. Discuss some major findings of research on citizen participation in decision-making regarding urban recreation and parks.

4. Was the material treated in this chapter of any relevance to private and commercial leisure service organizations? Why or why not?
5. On what grounds can it be argued that the area of public recreation and parks is different from other government services in terms of its need for a high level of citizen involvement?

Involving recreation participants in decision-making may ultimately affect the quality of the recreation experience directly. (Bureau of Reclamation, Department of the Interior; photo by Lyle C. Axthelm)

chapter 17

TECHNIQUES FOR CITIZEN OR PARTICIPANT INVOLVEMENT IN DECISION-MAKING

In this chapter, we shall examine some of the techniques by which citizens or consumers of recreation and park or leisure service agencies influence the actions of such organizations. Citizen or participant action groups will be considered first; their use of pressure and confrontation tactics will be discussed, as well as the steps such groups go through to solve problems.

Citizen or participant advisory councils will be considered next—their creation, advantages and disadvantages, and use by leisure service agencies. Particular attention will be given to the formation of such councils and the selection of members, the need for training of council members, and the characteristics of the various types of councils that exist.

Finally, the rationale for a process by which government and other organizations decentralize services will be considered.

CITIZEN OR PARTICIPANT ACTION GROUPS

Many citizens or participant groups form to bring about change in regard to recreation and parks within their own community or neighborhood. In many instances such groups have no formal relationship with the governmental power structure and no prescribed way of being brought into the governmental decision-making process. Such groups are often referred to as *ad hoc,* and are likely to be formed during periods of confrontation between a governmental or private agency and the residents of a particular neighborhood. They usually promote or campaign for a point of view on some particular issue. Ad hoc citizen or participant groups may campaign for a playground for their neighborhood, protest the dismissal of a valued recreation agency employee, question the proposed location of a park, seek to change a YMCA membership policy, or campaign for the inclusion of programs for the physically handicapped.

Ad hoc citizen or participant action committees have the advantage of being free of all government ties and obligations. They may meet when desired and take any action which seems appropriate. Also, as previously mentioned, there is evidence that municipal recreation and park agencies sometimes pay inordinate attention to communication and "demands" which originate from outside the citizen councils and boards that officially represent the community to the agency.

Often, however, such ad hoc committees have difficulty in establishing and carrying out long-range plans. As a study of ad hoc citizen action groups within the city of Toronto determined, such groups have considerable difficulty surviving after the direct threat of neighborhood was resolved in one way or another. Council members often tended to have short-term goals and were very active only during periods of specific threat to the neighborhood.[1] The study also found that the general goals differed between councils in stable neighborhoods and those in less affluent ones. Councils in stable neighborhoods were interested in the preservation and improvement of the residential quality of the neighborhood, while groups from less affluent areas emphasized the more general problems of rehabilitation in their neighborhoods.

Ad hoc citizen action groups are also subject to co-optation by a recreation and park agency. That is, a leader of such a group may be successfully recruited into the policy-making structure of the organization in order to get him or her off the organization's back. According to Etzioni, "Co-optation is often used in order to create a semblance of communication from clients to those in control, without actually providing for effective communication. Thus, although co-optation is theoretically a mechanism for consumer influence, it is frequently not applied so as to realize its potential."[2]

Some political theorists believe that it is best for government to keep a hands-off policy concerning ad hoc citizen action groups, since government support, particularly financial support, may lead to the indigenous citizen group becoming dependent upon government or subconsciously starting to adopt the viewpoint of government. On the other hand, some ad hoc groups, after having received support from government and after having improved their information base concerning their area of interest, have become effective ongoing citizen councils.

Since many ad hoc citizen groups have a relatively short life span, some agencies of government may go along with the group on the assumption that the group will burn itself out before the agency is required to take action or address itself to the group's concern. On an issue such as the need for more swimming facilities in some area of the community, a recreation or park agency may propose that the matter be studied in detail, believing that the demand for swimming will disappear as the weather grows cooler. Inner-city residents have claimed for years that obvious situations of comparative recreation deprivation had to be "researched" by recreation agencies, sometimes at the exclusion of action.

Many problems around which ad hoc citizen or participant action groups organize, however, really do require research, or at least some systematic information gathering before decisions can be acted upon intelligently. Just because a citizen group organizes to lobby for more swimming facilities for its neighborhood does not necessarily mean that its neighborhood has the greatest comparative need for additional swimming facilities. It may merely mean that they have citizens who are willing to organize. It is difficult to determine when an agency of government is genuinely trying to research a problem and when it is trying to stall. At the extremes are inaction or action based only on the whim of a vocal minority.

PRESSURE TACTICS

Pressure tactics have been defined as "the persistent use of the existing communication channels in a perfectly legal manner."[3] Since there is evidence that bureaucracies respond favorably to organized pressure, pressure tactics represent the logical and legitimate use of the media of communication to remind decision-makers of citizen concerns. Continual inquiries by telephone, telegram, letter or direct visitation may serve to remind the decision-makers that the group concerned will not go away or lose interest in their subject of concern. Citizens interested in the use of a local school for evening recreation programs, for instance, might launch a letter or telephone campaign to local politicians and school and recreation officials to remind them that, since the school is paid for with taxes which they contribute, taxpayers want a say in the policies of the school. Such a campaign is often a reflection of faith in the decision-makers involved that they will respond when they understand the depth of feeling involved. Sometimes, when this faith produces no results, it is lost altogether, and confrontation tactics result.

Since pressure tactics still reflect the faith that decision-makers will be responsive, they often involve questioning rather than demanding. Why aren't the schools open for public use during the evening? When will they be? What can be done to bring this about? How do you stand on the issue of recreational use of the schools during evening hours? Why?

Another form of pressure tactic is the use of the petition. Petitions seek to give added impetus to an issue by demonstrating the number of people who are willing to go on record regarding it. Departments of recreation and parks are petitioned on a number of issues. Sometimes, such petitions are used when there is a difference in interpretation between the agency and a group of citizens concerning local opinion on some issue. A citizen handbook produced by Places for People suggests the following in preparing and presenting petitions:[3]

A. *Steps before petitioning:*
1. Know exactly what it is you want done.
2. Organize thoroughly and make sure everyone wants the same thing.
3. Call other interested persons, explain the situation. Organize these people around your central steering committee.
4. Use flyers, questionnaires, posters, telephone, etc., to get the people in your community informed about the situation. Anticipate apathy.
5. Make sure people stay informed even if they seem apathetic at first. They may just be waiting to see if you are really serious or if you will fall apart the minute you meet a little resistance.
6. Examine your group carefully for signs of politicking. If other people suspect that you are in it for yourself rather than out of concern for the community, they will avoid you like the plague.
7. Find out what data the planners have been using to make decisions about your community.
8. Get the information and data from the other sources mentioned in this handbook.
9. Divide the information into that which supports your case and that which could hurt it. Prepare valid reasoned arguments against the information which might hurt you. If you cannot refute the evidence you can dig up yourselves, then you will not be able to support your case when they bring in even more damaging information to use against your position in committee.
10. Present the information to a general meeting in your community, show that you are concerned, ask for their support in specific ways.
11. Get an appointment and present your case to the Director or Commissioner of the Department involved. Request specific action and enclose a copy of the brief and petition along with your proposal in writing.
12. Wait for a month to six weeks to give his department a chance to investigate thoroughly.

13. Request an explanation of the present status of your request, pressure for a commitment; if none is forthcoming, contact your alderman and ask for assistance in taking your case to council or committee.

B. *Petition format:*
   1. State the name of the organization and where it is based.
   2. State the objective of the petition, i.e., support of the enclosed brief, which outlines community needs and proposal to meet those needs.
   3. Have at least 150 names, i.e., signature, occupation and address.

C. *Committee presentation:*
   1. Attend at least one committee meeting prior to your presentation so you understand exactly what the situation is. Presume that they know nothing about your area or your problems, since they have not corrected the situation previously.
   3. Presentations to standing committees of council are heard on nights of the week other than council nights, so check in advance to determine when and where the meetings are held.
   4. Do not allow them to convince you that you can just send in the brief and petition; insist that you be allowed to come to the meeting to give a short (15 minutes maximum) presentation.
   5. A copy of the signed petition and accompanying materials must be forwarded to the Secretary of the Committee at least a week before you wish to make your presentation.
   6. When you go to make your presentation, have as many people come with you as is possible, considering the size of the room and any regulations they might have concerning attendance.
   7. Your name will be called out when your presentation time comes up.
   8. You will be asked to come forward and stand at a lectern or table.
   9. Re-state your name and address; then read your presentation slowly with a firm clear voice.
   10. Be prepared for questions; you should have already prepared answers for the most obvious problems related to your request.
   11. Also be prepared for no questions; in getting to the committee, you don't have a guarantee that they will listen; keep cool.

CONFRONTATION, PROTEST AND DISRUPTION

Citizens or participants influence decisions made by public and private recreation and park agencies through the use of confrontation tactics, protest and disruption. Such tactics nearly always emanate from a citizens' group rather than from an individual and may be used to (1) serve as an expression of frustration with departmental policy or its operations, (2) serve to publicize a belief which may be only indirectly related to recreation and parks or (3) serve as a pragmatic technique to obtain desired recreation and parks resources or policy changes. In regard to the first and third purposes, such tactics may represent an escalation of efforts to obtain a goal when it isn't obtained through established governmental channels. A group of citizens interested in obtaining a swimming pool for their neighborhood, for instance, may grow tired of appealing to the recreation and parks board and decide instead to "disrupt" its next meeting. A group of mothers may picket a playground in an attempt to get an undesirable staff member transferred or fired. A young gang may vandalize a recreation center to force its renovation or closure. In regard to the second purpose, citizens might demonstrate against municipal hiring practices by demanding that an indigenous leader from the neighborhood be employed by the recreation and park department at a nearby center. Citizens may, because of religious beliefs, protest the opening of recreation centers, parks, or athletic facilities on Sundays or Saturdays.

While such tactics do not always succeed, large centralized municipal bureaucracies (and other bureaucracies also) seem particularly susceptible to them. Additionally, protest tactics very often serve to force an issue into the open when previous tactics had failed to obtain any response.

Sometimes a demonstration serves to tip the scales on some issue which has not been decided and where there has not been an indicator of intensity of community sentiment. Residents of a neighborhood in Oakville, Ontario, for instance, which for years had desired a neighborhood swimming pool, appeared at a city council meeting wearing bathing suits on the night when the council was to vote whether or not to appropriate funds. The sight of hundreds of citizens sitting silently in the gallery in bathing suits may have been a powerful factor in the council's decision, which was to appropriate funds for the pool.

Since the operations of governmental recreation and park agencies are highly visible by the public, such agencies are often particularly susceptible to confrontation tactics. Hence, the extent and distribution of recreation services easily become subject to controversy. One factor underlying civil rights and racial demonstration and rioting, as Kraus and others have noted, has been the continuing deprivation of public recreation services to residents of the ghettos.[4] Lack of organized recreation programs and inadequate recreation facilities ranked fifth among the grievances of riot area residents, according to the Kerner Commission report.[5]

Subsequent attempts to keep ghetto areas riot-free have often involved "cool money" supplied to cities on short notice in late spring by federal government agencies. The existence and amount of such funding often correlates highly with the amount of civil disobedience observed in areas in question. Thus, protest, demonstration and confrontation tactics play a central role in the decision to spend such funds to provide, for example, portable swimming pools, playstreets or the hiring of local residents for summer jobs in recreation.

It should not be assumed, however, that the use of confrontation tactics is primarily a tool of low-income groups. As the study of recreation advisory councils in Philadelphia discussed in Chapter 16 demonstrates, middle class citizens were more willing to engage in confrontation tactics than were their counterparts in poverty areas. Additionally, middle class recreation advisory councils were "more skilled at the manipulation of individuals in positions of power and (were) frequently able to do so with low visability."[6] In a number of cases, it was found that while recreation advisory councils in poverty areas were conservative and worked within the established structure, middle class councils were likely to make a great number of inputs into the decision-making process, including the use of veiled threats, confrontation and tactics that successfully shortcut the layers of bureaucracy.

In many cases, public and private recreation and park agencies actually encourage citizens to influence the decision-making process from outside the established procedures. This happens when the agency responds positively in terms of resource allocation to communication that does not come from established channels and which threatens negative reprisal or was actually made after negative reprisal. Administrators in recreation and park agencies, sometimes out of political necessity, appear to be more concerned with resource demands that come from outside the system rather than from within it. Perhaps the most important implication in this situation is that recreation and park agencies may function in such a way as to encourage or "teach" the citizen *not* to use the system which it itself maintains.

STEPS IN THE ACTION PROCESS

Many different kinds of citizen or participant groups undergo a common series of steps to arrive at a point of action, regardless of what tactics they eventually decide to use. While there is disagreement about the classification and division of these steps, the series presented by Edward Lindeman provides a good framework for analyzing community action groups involved in recreation undertakings.[7] Let us take the example of a citizen who believes there is a need for a recreation center within his community.

1. *Consciousness of Need:* Some person, either within or without the community, expresses the need which is later represented by the definite project.

   In this step, a citizen might become convinced that there was nothing for teenagers to do in the neighborhood and that this could lead to their getting into trouble unless something was done. His perception of need is for establishing a recreation center; somewhere that teenagers can go. The citizen tells his neighbors.

2. *Spreading the Consciousness of Need:* A leader, within some institution or group within the community, convinces his or her group, or a portion of the group, of the reality of the need.

   One of the neighbors discusses the recreation center idea with the president of a neighborhood organization, P.T.A. or other organization within the neighborhood, who agrees to bring the matter up at an upcoming meeting. At the meeting, there is considerable support for the idea of establishing a recreation center, although the discussion is based more on the idea than on the implementation of the idea. A committee is appointed to investigate the establishment of a recreation center.

3. *Projection of Consciousness of Need:* The group interested attempts to project the consciousness of need upon the leadership of the community; the consciousness of need becomes more general.

   The committee appoints members to contact the Mayor, the Superintendent of Schools, the head of the community's social planning council, the newspaper editor and a few other community leaders to discuss the need for a neighborhood recreation center with them and to get their advice. The newspaper editor, while expressing concern about the cost of such a project, agrees to write an edition supporting the idea "in principle." The committee undertakes a questionnaire of residents in the neighborhood to get their reaction to the establishment of a recreation center, although respondents are not asked about their willingness to help bear the cost of such a center. Most of the 40 percent of the citizens who return the questionnaire are positive, although several write in that older citizens have just as great a need for such a center as do teenagers.

4. *Emotional Impulse to Meet the Need Quickly:* Some influential assistance is enlisted, in the attempt to arrive at a quick means of meeting the need.

   Having become convinced of the need for a recreation center, the committee reports back to the neighborhood association and recommends that some immediate action be taken in order to secure a location for the recreation center. The committee suggests that the availability of a local church basement be investigated. It is also suggested that the community director of recreation and parks be contacted for help. A special meeting is arranged between members of the committee, the neighborhood association president, the director of recreation, representatives of the local church, a representative of the Mayor and the principal of a school.

5. *Presentation of Other Solutions:* Other means of meeting the need are presented.

   At the meeting, a number of different methods of developing a center are proposed. It is variously proposed that a section of the elementary school be used, that a vacant lot be purchased and the municipality build a recreation center on it, and that a large house in the vicinity be purchased and used as a recreation center. The recreation director expresses the view that old citizens in the neighborhood have a need for some organized program, but some of the committee members feel that there will be problems if both teenagers and senior citizens use the same facility on a daily basis.

6. *Conflict of Solutions:* Various groups lend their support to one or the other of the various solutions presented.

   A second meeting of the group is called at which various alternatives are debated. Sites for a recreation center and prospective clientele and programs are discussed. A number of differences of opinion arise as to how much of a formally structured program should be established as opposed to a "drop-in" approach. The Mayor's representative feels that most of the program should be structured, while others feel it should not. A local Golden Age Club representative attends the meeting and supports the idea of giving some center space to senior citizens, although no recreation programs need be provided.

7. *Investigation:* It appears to be increasingly customary to pause at this point, and to investigate the project with expert assistance. (This step, however, is usually omitted and the following one takes its place.)

   It is decided to attempt to get cost estimates for each of the proposed recreation center sites and to examine the experience of a nearby community which established a teenage drop-in program two years ago. Another meeting is scheduled. At this meeting, testimony is given by the chairman of the teen-age drop-in program in a neighboring community. Other committee members provide data concerning the availability of building lots and a large old house in the area. The president of the P.T.A. and the school principal present a preliminary report on the possibility of school usage, which indicates that the school would be available only two days a week and that maintenance, staff and related costs would have to be borne by some group other than the school. One member of the committee argues forcefully that the group has to get additional reaction from neighborhood residents, since the questionnaire was not even completed by a majority of households. It is decided to hold a public hearing at the school to solicit the opinion of neighborhood residents.

8. *Open Discussion of Issue:* A public mass meeting or gathering of some sort is held, at which the project is presented, and the groups with most influence attempt to secure adoption of their plan.

   At the mass meeting, a presentation is made by various committee members concerning alternative sites for a neighborhood recreation center, as well as who might use it. A dispute develops between several citizens at the meeting and the president of the P.T.A. over the use of school facilities for such a purpose. In further discussion, several neighborhood residents strongly object to building a new recreation center, because of existing taxes and the additional financial burden that a major center would create. Further discussion centers around who the recreation center should be for. Some people feel the center should be for everyone in the neighborhood. Two other senior citizens suggest that they have a greater need for a recreation facility than do teenagers. Several residents express a fear that without adequate supervision, the center will become a meeting place for "undesirables." A further issue raised is whether residents outside the neighborhood should be allowed to use the center. The Director of Recreation says that if municipal funds are used in the development of a center, it must be open to all community residents. It is decided that another meeting of the committee is necessary.

   At this meeting, it is learned that the large house in the area is available for a price of $60,000. The Director of Recreation suggests that this site might be a good compromise location between a costly new center and the use of school facilities. The president of the Neighborhood Association concurs, and suggests that his organization might be persuaded to undertake a fund-raising campaign to bear part of the cost of purchase price. He agrees to check with his organization and report back. The other committee members are generally favorable. While there is still considerable debate about whom the facility is intended for and the degree of structure needed in the program, there is little disagreement voiced about the purchase of the house.

9. *Integration of Solutions:* The various solutions presented are tested, with an effort to retain something out of each in the practicable solution which is not emerging.

   Plans are made to purchase the house under an agreement whereby the municipal department of recreation will fund $40,000 of the cost and the neighborhood association will provide the other $20,000. A recreation center committee is established.

ADVISORY COUNCILS

An advisory council or board is a group of citizens, members, clients or participants who serve an organization through an established, ongoing relationship in order to represent the interests of the organization's clientele. An advisory council has no executive or legislative powers. It may recommend courses of action, but it has no power to make decisions arising from these recommendations or to set action in motion to implement them. Such a council may investigate, promote, criticize, recommend, question, help, publicize, consult or otherwise contribute to the decisions and programs of an organization, but it doesn't have the final authority to make or implement action.

CREATION OF ADVISORY COUNCILS

Advisory councils are created in a number of ways. In some instances, an advisory council comes into being because of some legislation specifically intended to create it. The fact of enactment through special legislation may give great impetus and prestige to an advisory council.

Provision may also be made for an advisory council in legislative acts that deal with much broader subjects, where the council serves as an aid in carrying out the objectives of the legislation. While such legislation does assure the creation of an advisory council, it may not specifically state the council's duties or powers.

Permissive legislation is the vehicle by which many governmental advisory bodies come into existence. In such instances, the legislation *permits* the establishment of an advisory council but does not *require* it. When a government decides to implement the provision for an advisory council, it must take further action to actually bring the board into being.

Some advisory councils have their legal status in a statute that authorizes the formation of a special purpose agency. For instance, recreation agencies at the federal, provincial, state, regional, county or municipal level may be created in such a way that an advisory council is formally attached to them. Such legislation may also be permissive, leaving it to the agency's discretion whether or not to form a council.

At the municipal and neighborhood level, many advisory councils have no legal status and have been created by agreement with some agency of government. Such councils may be recognized in departmental policy statements, but not in law.

ADVANTAGES AND DISADVANTAGES OF ADVISORY COUNCILS

The use of advisory councils has a number of potential advantages and disadvantages which must be carefully examined in considering their use. The *advantages* of an advisory council were characterized by Schaller as follows: (a) provides a channel of communication between professional administrators and the general public, (b) assists planners in formulating planning goals, (c) serves as a sounding board for preliminary ideas and proposals, (d) overcomes public apathy and ignorance toward necessary public projects, (e) becomes a visible and responsible pressure group upon a recalcitrant administration, (f) releases funds for specific projects not available from government, and (g) overcomes disinterest induced by fragmentation of local government, by drawing residents from many political subdivisions.

Disadvantages of the use of advisory councils include (a) their possible failure to be representative on a social, racial and economic basis; (b) imposition of membership requirements that drive potential members away; (c) existence of a void between committee members and the general public greater than that between the government and the governed; (d) manipulation of the committee by a department head or administrator, which may cause a "rubber stamp" group; (e) the possibility that group may be completely dependent upon professional administrators for information; (f) the chance that the existence of advisory committee may allow elected officials to escape responsibility for decision-making in controversial issues; and (g) the danger that the existence of an advisory committee may lend respectability to highly partisan proposals.[8]

A number of these problems would seem to indicate that the advisory council technique might be untenable for effectively involving the poor in the affairs of urban recreation and park departments. The poor appear to be unskilled in many requisites for participation on advisory councils. They are often alienated and have little identification with local government structures. They are distrustful of bureaucracies and frequently do not understand their workings.[9] Their low socioeconomic status may put them at a disadvantage in bargaining. They are more susceptible to co-optation. "The orientation of the poor to the present and their inability to defer gratification"[9] may be problematic in planning for long-range goals. The female-based household, which is prevalent among the poor, may make regular attendance at council meetings difficult or impossible. It should be noted, however, that most methods for representing citizens in governmental decision-making are more easily utilized by the middle and upper classes than by the poor. Part of the challenge of representing the poor in the affairs of government is to determine methods that will allow them to more effectively use the existing methods of citizen participation, including advisory councils.

A study of advisory councils and boards in Canada undertaken by the Canadian Association of Adult Education stated that "Advisory boards vary widely in the efficiency of their internal organization, the quality of their performance, and the response they elicit from government."[12] The report stated three main criticisms leveled against advisory councils. First, advisory councils aren't part of a chain of command through which government should formulate policy. Although both in the United States and Canada there are established processes through which government makes policy, today a great number of councils, boards and committees, often with ill-defined goals and objectives, have been inserted into this process.

A second major criticism is that councils are sometimes merely "window-dressing," and that government is sometimes merely playing games when it creates advisory councils. The mass media carry so little information concerning the recommendations referred to governments by councils that knowledge of it simply never reaches the average citizen.

A final criticism is that advisory councils are sometimes not competent to advise. Some council members, although they may be upstanding citizens, may know very little about the subject in question. Their service on the council, therefore, may serve only to educate them—an insufficient defense of their appointment.

There is much evidence suggesting that the usefulness of advisory councils can be accurately judged only in the context of a specific situation. It simply isn't meaningful to say that all private and public recreation and park agencies should or should not utilize advisory councils until more is known about the folkways and mores of those involved, the specific purpose of the agency, the desired relationship between citizens' members, clients or participants and the agency itself, the political issues, the conflict level among those involved, the degree of homogeneity and so forth.

RECREATION ADVISORY COUNCILS

Advisory councils have played an important role in the functioning of public recreation and park agencies. A survey taken of 112 public recreation and park agencies in 1970 found that approximately four out of ten such agencies had an advisory board or council.[13] Additionally, many such agencies employed advisory councils at the district level within a city, at the neighborhood level, or to deal with specific issues, such as school-recreation agency coordination, the operation of particular recreation facilities or programs, or the recreation needs and interests of some subgroup within the community, e.g., the aged, ethnic minorities or the physically handicapped.

COUNCIL MODELS

Recreation and park advisory councils, boards and committees often assume radically different functions in different situations, even though the method of organization may be essentially the same. This variation may occur as a result of differing social conditions, characteristics of members, relation with government, political issues and other factors. The following typology is designed to illustrate the major roles that most recreation advisory councils undertake. In reality, of course, most recreation councils will to some degree be a composite of the following types:

Program Supporter This type of council is primarily concerned with creating interest in the recreation programs, raising funds to support them, and defending them from criticism. It also is involved in making minor improvements to areas and facilities. Of the four kinds of councils, the program supporter type plays the smallest role in implementing change. Meetings tend to be informal. Members tend to be active in the agencies' programs but are not often leaders in other community organizations. There are few intense arguments at council meetings, and quite frequently the meetings are followed by socialization and refreshments. The relationship between the recreation administrator and the council members is one of leader–subordinate. There is usually a high percentage of females and a low turnover rate. Council members are essentially concerned with preparing for special programs or fund-raising activities.

Special Interest – The special interest council is specifically interested in one type of program or one specific program or event. Though members of this council work hard in their special interest area and want fairly complete control of it (which they usually get), they otherwise play a small role in decision-making and implementing change. A very high percentage participate in the agencies' programs, but usually only in those concerning their special interest area. Owing to their lack of genuine interest in most of the other facets of the agencies' operation, the recreation administrator and the council have a leader–subordinate relationship, except in the council's special interest area, where the roles are reversed. The council members often turn to the recreation administrator for advice on matters not pertaining to their special interest, and they may "rubber-stamp" his suggestions. Socialization and fellowship are important functions of this type of council.

Community Welfare – This type of recreation advisory council is actually interested in the general welfare of the community in which they live. They are likely to deal with other government agencies in addition to the recreation and park agency, and to collect data or testimony as a basis for action. Many of their members are recognized community leaders and tend to be older than members of the other three council types mentioned here. The community welfare type of council spends a great deal of time at its meetings discussing subjects that do not pertain directly to the recreation program. They have a high degree of organizational structure.

Pressure Group – The pressure group type of council is concerned with the fulfillment of a number of specific demands, which take up more of their meeting time than anything else. Such councils are very likely to collect and utilize data to support their demands and viewpoints. They often appoint ad hoc committees to investigate hotly disputed issues. The pressure group maintains a formal relationship with the recreation administrator and seeks to deal with someone higher up the governmental chain of command whenever possible. In situations of extreme conflict, the pressure group may avoid the governmental chain of command completely and go directly to the mayor, city manager or the highest official in the government. The pressure group has the highest attendance rate of any council during times of conflict, but attendance may drop markedly when conflict is at a minimum. The pressure group seeks to maximize its influence and power.

Selecting Council Members

The basis upon which members are chosen to serve on a recreation or park advisory council, board or neighborhood committee will have a direct effect on what the group does, on its interests and attitudes, and on its methods of operation. For this reason, the selection method is extremely important, and sometimes is a decisive factor in the stand taken by such a group. A number of alternatives are available in regard to the selection of council or board members.

A first consideration is who should determine the method of selection. It may be argued that the recreation and park agency should specify the requirements for the board or committee or actually make the appointments, since it will be most likely to understand the role of the committee and the abilities needed to participate successfully. On the other hand, the recreation and park agency may choose to ignore those who differ in viewpoint or philosophy with them, or who represent a consitituency that is hostile to the recreation agency. The agency may also appoint members who will benefit them directly (such as those in a position to donate large amounts of money or land to the community), but who are not aware of issues in the community that directly effect recreation services. It appears that today there is an increased involvement in the organization of recreation and park councils and committees by departments of parks and recreation.

Council members may also be selected by the legislative body of the government or private agency, or by the executive; they may be volunteers or they may be elected. Of the local recreation and park agencies with boards or commissions, the NRPA study found that in 70 percent of the cases the agency appointed the members, in 18 percent the members were elected and in 12 percent they were chosen in some other way.[11]

A second consideration after *who* determines the method of council member is *what* the method of selection will be. One basis for selection frequently used is division by geographical area, leading to the creation of neighborhood recreation advisory councils or a city-wide council with representation from each geographic section of the community. Such council members represent citizens in their own geographic area or neighborhood to the recreation agency and express views which may be unique to that geographic area. Strong neighborhood recreation advisory councils help insure that the recreation agency is aware of diverse needs and desires of residents living in areas with different customs and socioeconomic conditions. They help to insure a balance of recreation and facilities within the community, and contribute to the shaping of the program to meet individual neighborhood situations. (Similarly, an employee recreation council may be made up of representatives from different sections or occupational divisions of a factory or office.) In the Philadelphia study, it was discovered that a recreation advisory council in one area of the city supported the department of recreation's position on volunteers, whereas another neighborhood council, which had had negative experiences with volunteers, tried to end the practice of recruiting volunteers. The local recreation staff concurred with the neighborhood council.[6]

Councils organized on a geographic basis by neighborhood have some unique advantages in that they are close physically to the programs and facilities in the neighborhood and may have good insights about neighborhood reaction to such services. They may actually participate in the recreation services themselves, or have children who do; hence, they have a strong motivation for improving their neighborhood recreation services. Traditionally, neighborhood recreation advisory councils have raised funds which augmented financial appropriations from recreation agencies. Such funds have made possible the creation of new programs, the purchase of unique recreation facilities and equipment, and the acquiring of materials needed for special events and celebrations that would otherwise not have occurred. There are two major difficulties in the use of recreation councils organized on a neighborhood basis. The first is that, like other neighborhood level citizen groups, neighborhood reaction councils typically reflect the desires of the immediate neighborhood only, sometimes to the detriment of the geographic community as a whole.

A second serious problem is that research indicates that neighborhoods in low socioeconomic areas are less likely to be able to secure citizen participation for ongoing councils, particularly sustained participation. Because of this, the creation of a system of neighborhood councils may put the poverty area at a further disadvantage in competing for the limited supply of public recreation services available to neighborhoods.

Another basis for organizing citizens, members, clients or participants is interest in a specific recreation activity or program. A recreation agency could establish formal relationships with organizations interested in some specific activity such as baseball, hockey, or symphonic music, or it could form a city-wide council composed of representatives of these special interest groups. In a hospital, informal advisory groups of patients could be formed who were interested in different activities offered by therapeutic recreation services. One advantage of this organizational method is that such groups are frequently highly knowledgeable about the activity involved and can communicate their needs and desires concerning this activity in a direct manner. Also, recreation special interest groups have shown a willingness to take high levels of responsibility in the organization of programs and services in which they are interested. Since some recreation and park agencies concentrate on providing only a limited number of recreation activities that have mass appeal, those knowledgeable about such activities can make a valuable contribution.

A major difficulty in organizing recreation councils on this basis is that members of special interest groups may not have a corresponding interest in other recreation activities in the community and may become merely a rubber-stamp group for the recreation agency if they are given responsibility for areas other than their specific recreation interest.

A third approach to organizing recreation councils is to select those in the community who are leaders by virtue of their position, such as a superintendent of schools, and who represent organizations and resources which the recreation agency needs or with which it will interact. Appointing a school superintendent or principal, for example, would seem logical, since the department of recreation may utilize school facilities, and vice versa. The owner of a large business may be able to use his influence to tap financial resources. A planner or social worker may be able to identify emerging trends in the community that have a direct implication for the recreation agency before the public or the agency itself becomes aware of them. Generally, such leaders are able to provide valuable information about prevailing community conditions and access to important resources in the community.

Unfortunately, in many instances, positional leaders in the community have similar socioeconomic characteristics and life styles. Because of this, a council composed of positional leaders may not consider the viewpoints of those in different socioeconomic levels with different life styles. They may, in short, "think alike" on many matters and thus lose the benefit of diversity.

TRAINING COUNCIL MEMBERS

Regardless of duties, there is often confusion over the council's specific role and its relationship with a recreation, park or leisure service agency. The council, on the one hand, is supposed to represent the attitudes and opinions of residents to the municipal recreation agency and to "interpret" these attitudes and opinions to professional recreation personnel. At the same time, the council is supposed to "support" the recreation agency by helping establish programs, raise funds, plan facilities and, in effect, defend the agency from criticism. The New York City Parks and Recreation Department statement on guidelines for community participation, for instance, presents a "Suggested Outline for Community Advisory Committees to support the Community-Based Recreation Program of the City." This support of the recreation agency's programs may be interpreted quite differently by the neighborhood residents and the recreation staff, particularly staff members who deal with the neighborhood in a face-to-face relationship. While many recreation staff understand that it is natural and even desirable for the neighborhood council to have differences of opinion with the recreation staff, some staff members may feel that the recreation council is being "disloyal" when it disagrees with the recreation agency. A recreation or park staff member may feel that the neighborhood council is "his" council and owes him loyalty by virtue of his position.

The recreation advisory council members, conversely, sometimes feel that they must automatically oppose or suspect the decisions made by the recreation agency, and thus they continually complain and protest. Such situations, besides reflecting a general distrust of "government" or "the public," also indicate a need for training of both the layman and the recreation staff for participation in shared decision-making.

Another reason for training is that research indicates that one major problem of many recreation advisory bodies is their lack of preparation for their duties. Difficulties are often created because the advisory council does not understand its role, its authority and responsibility, the goals and operational problems of the agency and existing neighborhood and community conditions. A council that undertakes its duties with a low information base may become a liability to the citizens it represents by creating unrealistic expectations or ignoring pressing community needs.

Artz suggests that the following techniques be used to educate citizen councils:[12]

1. Staff-citizen training sessions: The kit or manual should be distributed to council members before they begin service. Special sessions at the council meetings should be scheduled to review this material in depth with citizens and staff. This also gives holdover members an opportunity to review the total operation and evaluate all possible revision and updating.

2. Planned tours to see, firsthand, department operations, program activities and facilities.

3. Visits and meetings with other departments and citizens' organizations in the same field of work.

4. Citizens' training institutes and conferences at state, regional and national levels.

5. Selected readings of applicable literature and publications, such as NRPA's Parks and Recreation magazine and other technical bulletins developed by the Association for citizen involvement and training.

In addition, each council member should be given a departmental manual or some other form of written departmental information covering the agency's (1) legal provisions, (2) department policy statement on objectives and goals, (3) functions of the department, (4) administrative organization, (5) established departmental policies, (6) departmental operation information, and (7) recreation and park education information dealing with concepts and philosophy.

NEIGHBORHOOD OR SMALL UNIT RECREATION COUNCILS

In a number of urban areas in both the United States and Canada, municipal recreation and many recreation youth-serving agencies have been greatly affected by neighborhood recreation advisory councils. Such councils may serve to coordinate recreation resources in the area by dealing with a number of governmental, voluntary, youth-serving and commercial agencies, or they may be primarily involved with the recreation services of a particular recreation or park agency or recreation center, playground or park. Municipal recreation agencies that have sought to organize such neighborhood councils have used various rationales. In New York City, for instance, the mayor mandated that recreation department programs operate under a philosophy of participatory democracy.

In other types of recreation, park and leisure service agencies, the advisory council may also be organized on a small unit basis. In a large hospital, councils may be organized on a ward basis or on the basis of specific disability groups. Employee recreation programs may similarly divide into small advisory groups based upon different occupational groupings.

CREATING A NEIGHBORHOOD RECREATION ADVISORY COUNCIL

The initial steps taken to create a neighborhood recreation advisory council may actually determine its success or failure, depending on the structure, information and basic orientation that the council is given. Because of this, the manner in which the council is created must be carefully considered.

In cases where recreation advisory councils are going to be created by electing citizens at large from a neighborhood or small community, some recreation agencies initially hold a mass meeting open to the public. Any interested person can attend. In addition to publicizing the meeting, groups and organizations in the area, such as churches and synagogues, clubs, civic organizations and labor groups, might be invited to send representatives.

The first meeting begins with a discussion on why a recreation advisory council is needed. Additional discussion may focus on the duties and responsibilities of a council, which people might be good potential council members, the number of people who should serve and the length of service. It might be decided to secure advice from other citizen councils on a method of operation. The first meeting should also establish a regular meeting schedule, and a nominating committee should be elected to prepare a slate of people to stand for election as officers. A date should be set for the second meeting.

At the second meeting, the slate of officers would be presented, other nominations received from the floors, and officers and council members elected. In some instances, only officers may be elected; other council members would consist of volunteers. Some councils establish member qualifications, often based upon residence and/or attendance at some minimum percentage of the meetings. At this meeting or at subsequent ones, committees may be established within the council to deal with a variety of purposes.

DISTRICT RECREATION COUNCILS

A number of large recreation and park agencies serving urban areas have established district recreation advisory councils, which serve a geographical district of the city encompassing several neighborhoods on matters pertaining to recreation or the public recreation agency. In some urban communities, district recreation advisory councils are the middle link in an advisory council system functioning at neighborhood, district and city-wide levels. District councils usually work closely with the area or district supervisor of recreation, who oversees and coordinates the services of the public recreation agency in a geographic area of the city. The goals and duties of a district council vary from city to city but usually include the following:

1. To encourage closer cooperation between the member neighborhood recreation advisory councils in the district.
2. To keep abreast of important recreation developments and keep neighborhood councils informed of them.
3. To promote better understanding of the recreation needs of the district.
4. To bring together representatives of community organizations and neighborhood recreation advisory councils to deal with problems that are district-wide in scope and require united action.

Membership on a district recreation advisory council may be determined in several ways. In some cases, where local recreation advisory councils are active within the district, each local council may be asked to appoint a representative to the district council from their own council. Officers may then be elected by the group. In other instances, elections may be held in which any citizen residing in the district is eligible for office.

The district council concept sometimes represents an attempt to decentralize the recreation services to a community by recognizing that different geographic areas of a community are inhabited by people with varying recreation needs and desires, and that some mechanism must be used to identify and act on them.

RECREATION COORDINATING COUNCILS

In a number of municipalities, recreation coordinating councils have been organized to ensure that the communities' recreation sources are used efficiently, avoid duplication of services, work cooperatively toward solutions to recreation-related problems, conduct research and plan future recreation undertakings in the community. In some cases, recreation service agencies are first called together by some "neutral" organization, such as a community health and welfare council or a planning commission. In other instances, a recreation service agency within the community may be the organizer. Sometimes there is legislation to establish a recreation coordinating council.

The City of Philadelphia Home Rule Charter, for instance, set up a Recreation Coordinating Board to make recommendations from time to time to the Department of Recreation for the maximum coordination of all recreation activities conducted by the department, the Fairmount Park Commission and the Board of Education.[14] In other instances, recreation coordinating councils have included representation from a wide variety of organizations in the community, such as the Y's, Boy and Girl Scouts, Boys' Clubs and Girls' Clubs, Catholic Youth Organizations, Jewish Community Centers, settlement houses, museums and libraries.

The scope of duties for such councils is usually quite broad and may vary considerably from neighborhood to neighborhood. Artz mentioned the following list of duties of the recreation coordinating council:[12]

> **1. Serve as a community communications medium for all area organizations.**
>
> **2. Serve as a clearinghouse for citizen suggestions, reactions, opinions, interests and needs, and as a sounding board for recreation, park and cultural agencies.**
>
> **3. Serve in an advisory capacity to the appropriate local bodies providing recreation, park and cultural services, to insure the advancement of sound, coordinated and cooperative park, recreation and cultural planning and programming.**
>
> **4. Serve as a training ground for potential board and commission members.**
>
> **5. Help recruit citizen volunteers to assist in recreation, park and cultural services.**
>
> **6. Help interpret park, recreation and cultural policies, programs and plans to the community.**
>
> **7. Survey, study and evaluate total community needs, services and resources.**
>
> **8. Help provide effective public information and education programs on recreation, park and cultural needs, demands and values.**
>
> **9. Encourage individuals, citizen groups and organizations to give funds, properties, manpower and leadership for development and operation of park, recreation and cultural facilities.**
>
> **10. Enable civic and service organizations to accomplish results through cooperative and coordinated efforts with other organizations for projects they could not possibly accomplish alone.**

In many instances, recreation and park agencies have banded together to undertake research relating to the future recreation needs and interests of their clientele. In Niagara Falls, Ontario, for instance, a number of recreation and youth-serving organizations, including the Niagara Falls Boys' Club, the Boy Scouts, the Recreation Commission, the Social Planning Council, the Family YWCA and the Detached Worker Project, banded together to assist a number of organizations in Niagara Falls to develop programs and facilities that would provide relevant leisure-time opportunities for the citizens of this community, both now and in the future. Their research produced an inventory of existing recreation facilities, a study of the likes and dislikes of leisure service organization members, a household survey of leisure activity patterns in the community and reasons for non-participation in certain recreation activities.

Often recreation coordination councils serve as a basis for improving relations between recreation-related organizations. Because there are very few clear mandates for one particular recreation-related agency to offer a specific recreation service to the community, recreation-related agencies often find themselves competing with one another with regard to the programs they offer and the clientele they serve. With some integrating mechanism, such as a recreation coordinating council, such organizations can work toward cooperation and coordination of services.

Other kinds of recreation coordinating councils established in municipalities have tried to improve cooperation between the school system and the recreation agency; advise and coordinate the offerings of recreation-related agencies to various subpopulations in the community, such as the aged or minority groups; or advise the agency concerning a particular recreation event or program. A school-recreation committee is sometimes organized to encourage the cooperative development and efficient use of school and municipal recreation facilities that can serve the recreation and park functions of both agencies. Such committees may help alleviate conflicts and duplication of effort between public schools and recreation and park agencies.

The following findings of the Ontario Select Committee on the Utilization of Educational Facilities are perhaps representative of conditions existing in many other places:

> **We find the arrangements for the use of school facilities that have been developed between the municipal recreation authorities and the school board as unsatisfactory. These arrangements have excluded the community from the decision-making processes related to the provision of recreation services and to the use of facilities. They have tended to ignore the resources and interests in the community for recreation programs. They have also restricted use of school facilities by the community. The community must be totally involved in all the decisions that are made concerning the provision of recreation services. We are convinced that the role of municipal recreation authorities must change from one involving direct provision of recreation programs to one of coordinating and supporting the development of community resources for recreation.**[15]

Many school recreation coordinating councils have been established to try to deal with the problems just outlined.

The Denver City–School Coordinating Committee serves as an advisory committee to the mayor and the superintendent of public schools, and performs the following functions:[16]

> **1. Reviews the present recreation programs and make suggestions for expansion or elimination of activities.**
>
> **2. Studies proposed plans for new activities so that duplication of activities can be prevented.**
>
> **3. Considers the planning of new areas and facilities that are to be jointly used for recreation.**
>
> **4. Makes suggestions regarding the maximum use of present facilities without conflicts in scheduling.**

5. Considers any other points that affect joint policies, coordination, and cooperative efforts of the city and school programs.

6. Carries out other such functions as may be determined jointly by the mayor and the superintendent of schools.

The more specific phases of planning and programming are carried out by two subcommittees: the Planning Committee and the Program Committee. The Planning Committee is responsible for activities related to the acquisition of school and park sites, decisions on specific details of site development and determination of costs. The Program Committee reviews present recreation programs and suggests appropriate revisions, examines plans for new activities so that duplication may be avoided and suggests ways for obtaining maximum use of present facilities without conflict in scheduling.

CONCLUSIONS

In summary, the advisory council may serve a number of functions in the decision-making process of recreation and leisure services. To insure the success of advisory councils, there must be an interested citizenry, training for participation and a continuing agency commitment to the advisory council concept.

HEARINGS

A public or private hearing represents an opportunity for the members of a community or organization to be heard by government or "management" concerning issues that affect them. In a sense, the public hearing represents the attempt of a representative democracy to maintain the kind of dialogue that was possible in a participatory democracy.

PURPOSES OF HEARINGS

Hearings fulfill a number of distinct and diverse roles in the decision-making of government and organizations. Some of the purposes of hearings are:

1. Tokenism — an empty ritual.
2. To help determine a "yes or no" question of policy or development.
3. To select from a number of options in terms of policy for development.
4. To counter the voice of pressure groups.
5. To review and evaluate past policies and projects.
6. To develop policies, goals or objectives of government or other agencies.

Let us examine these purposes in some detail.

In many cases, a hearing represents merely tokenism. While the idea of public participation is one of the most often voiced ideals of public planning, its use in practice is somewhat less than ideal. The granting of a public forum or hearing is frequently done only as a measure of appeasement. Often, policy decisions have already been made and will be implemented regardless of the outcome of the hearing. Thus disregard of public opinion is usually based on the belief that (1) the public at large does not know what is best for them, (2) the solutions of the public are too costly, and (3) expert professional planning has already been done on the matter. Such tokenism is evident in the abundance of professional jargon that riddles most policies that are meant for the people. Public law, for example, is written by lawyers in such a way that often another lawyer is needed to decode statements for the average citizen. Tokenism is also evident in situations where agencies of government plan to continue a policy or implement some course of action unless the squawk from the public is so loud that they feel they can't get away with it.

In some instances, hearings deal with a single contemplated act, policy or issue. In these cases citizens, participants, clients or members present ideas and opinions only in terms of whether or not some contemplated action should be taken. Citizens might be asked, for instance, to testify on whether or not they believe a new school should be built in their community. In such a situation, testimony would be given which debated the pros and cons of (a) building a new school, (b) the need for it, (c) the cost of it, and (d) its costs and benefits. In such hearings, citizens judge a fully developed plan rather than participate in the actual development of the plan. Some critics of public hearings imply that by the time an issue is reduced to a "yes or no" situation, it is too late for effective citizen participation, in that their testimony has been limited to merely affirming or denying an idea that did not spring from them. In hearings dealing with a "yes or no" issue, there are many cases in which only citizens with extreme viewpoints are represented, while those with middle ground positions do not participate. The opposing viewpoints of such groups often are presented emotionally and with little opportunity or willingness to compromise.

In some hearings, citizens are presented with a number of alternative policies or courses of action. Testimony centers on which of these is most favorable. Usually, such options are put forth by the agency in question, and the ultimate choice is made by the agency, using a combination of feedback from the public hearing and their own best approach method. Hearings in which there are choices of options represent an advantage of the yes or no structure on a single proposal, because there is a chance that less emotional arguments will be made, and nuances of opinion have a better chance to be recognized.

Some hearings are held to review and evaluate past policies and projects. Such hearings represent a kind of citizen's or constituents report. Many public agencies undertake programs and policies which, once initiated, are never evaluated or questioned by citizens. Any ongoing evaluation is usually done by the agency itself rather than the citizens. Ideally, hearings regarding past policies and performance of government agencies should represent a kind of open forum, in which citizens and representatives of various interest groups may raise whatever questions and concerns they wish.

Let us examine the steps undertaken in the public hearing process established by Parks Canada, an organization that functions at the federal level. Naturally, the public hearing process is more complex in such cases than at the local level, since an attempt must be made to inform a cross section of people across the nation who may wish to participate.

STEPS IN THE PROCESS OF A CANADIAN NATIONAL PARKS PUBLIC HEARING

1. A need or desire for the change of the present condition is felt tc be needed. This need for change is usually developed from within the National Parks Branch. It is usually a result of overuse of an area, misuse of an area, etc.

2. If in principal there is an agreement among the staff, etc., that a change is needed, the next step would be to produce with an inventory of the area. This inventory would include such things as (1) natural features, the fauna and flora of the area, the geology of the area, etc.; (2) the man-made features, such as highways, rail lines, buildings, camp areas; (3) a look at the types of useages would be made: how many people, where do they go, what do they do, etc. (4) the past policies and useages will be studied: how has the area been managed in the past, were there any "special" cases to consider, such as grazing allowances, etc.; (5) what are the present policy directions; and (6) what may be some of the things that may influence the area in the future, such as growing population trends, more cars, etc.

3. After the inventory is completed, a type of synthetic process is then undertaken. All elements of the inventory are looked at and a provisional plan is drawn out. This process usually involves a combination of those who do the inventory (this could be done on contract) and the planning and administrative people in Ottawa. The Provincial Master Plan (P.M.P.) is then drawn up, and undergoes review, change, review, etc., until the point where it is considered acceptable to the administrative level of the national parks, the minister in charge of Indian and Northern Affairs, and perhaps even the cabinet as a whole.

4. The P.M.P. is then produced in a number of sections, such as (1) the booklet itself, which describes the park, the fauna and flora, etc., what changes are proposed and why; and (2) maps (large-scale) that show the area before and after the changes, as well as other features.

5. The sections then come back to Ottawa, where they are assembled into an Information Kit. This kit includes the booklet and the maps, and usually also a copy of the National Parks Act, the National Parks Policy, an Information page which gives dates, times and locations of the hearing, and a pre-paid post card for pre-registration of people to attend and speak.

6. As these kits are being put together in Ottawa, a press conference is usually announced to be held in a large city near the park that is being affected. For example, park hearings concerning the four mountain parks—Jasper, Banff, Yoho and Kootenay—were held in Calgary, Edmonton and Vancouver.

7. The information kits are sent out to a number of the elected officials of the province where the park is located, and to some of the federal members of the area.

8. Usually, after the press conference, the public in mass becomes aware of the public hearing and begins to send for information kits, or sends in a brief relating their position in regard to the proposed change.

9. As briefs are received in Ottawa, they are numbered and photocopied.

10. They are then read by staff members of public hearings staff. As they are read, sections, paragraphs, etc., are categorized as to what they say. The staff has a type of index system, in which general areas, say wildlife, are broken into specifics, e.g., "bears, black, management of," or "roads, icefields, widening."

11. These sections are taken from the article and grouped, so that all like sections are together. The name and brief number are usually put with the sections, in case someone would like to refer to the whole statement, or information leading up to the section.

12. This process of section classification is a time-consuming task. The actual hearing itself may have been held before all the sections have been classified.

13. The hearing itself is held (usually) at a minimum of 90 days after the first public announcement, in a city near the park or area involved.

14. While everyone registers at the start of the hearings, some people pre-register, using a post-card type system that is included in the information kit. This pre-registration list is used to gain some idea of the number and types of people who are likely to attend.

15. The hearings usually begin on weekday mornings, about 9 A.M.

16. The chairman, usually the senior assistant deputy minister to the minister, introduces the panel at the head table. The panel may include some or all of the assistant heads of the National Parks, the chief planner from Ottawa, the Regional Superintendent, the Park Superintendent, and a secretary from the public hearings.

17. After the introductory remarks, a presentation of the proposed changes is shown, using slides, and a talk is given by the chief planner or by someone else if he is not present.

18. The presentation complete, the chairman again takes the floor and reviews the rules of the hearing. Some of these in the past have been as follows: (1) everyone is allowed five minutes in which to speak, or longer if the panel agrees it is a worthwhile presentation; (2) there is a question period at the end of the day, but no questions are to be asked during the presentations; (3) break times will be set aside for lunch, dinner, etc.

19. Members of the public give their presentations.

20. These presentations are taped and later transcribed.

21. The transcribed presentations are read and categorized in the same manner as the briefs.

22. When all the briefs and oral presentations have been processed, the public hearings staff write what is called an Interim report. This report gives an outline of the major points of interest, and what was generally said about them. The names and addresses of those people who send briefs or spoke at the hearings are also included. The report is then sent to those people who spoke at or attended the hearing, or who sent in briefs.

23. A ad hoc task force, composed of experts in administration, operations, interpretation, etc., from the national parks, then take the information (briefs, and sectionalized data) and review it in terms of what was proposed by the primary master plan. In most cases changes will have been offered. For example, a campground for Jasper was cancelled because of strong opposition, and a project at Lake Louise was stopped because of public disagreement with it.

24. The report from this committee is then passed up through the channels of government, to the minister, and probably the cabinet.

25. If approval is not granted by the government hierarchy, the report is sent back to the committee for revisions.

26. If the revised report is approved, a final position paper is produced. It states the final and approved conditions or changes that have occurred. This report is also sent out to those people who attended or spoke at the hearing, and to those who wrote briefs.

27. The approved changes are then put on some type of implementation schedule, as funds allow. This step is usually carried out over a period of many years.

CENTRALIZATION VS. DECENTRALIZATION

The degree to which government should be centralized or decentralized has long been the subject of political debate. De Tocqueville wrote over 100 years ago that there were two ways of diminishing government authority: "The first is to weaken the supreme power in its very principle by forbidding or preventing society from acting in its own defense under certain circumstances."[18] This, according to de Tocqueville, had been the European method of establishing freedom. The second way of achieving decentralization was to distribute the exercise of society's power among many people, "each of whom is given the degree of power necessary for him to perform his duty."[18] This scheme, said de Tocqueville, could lead to anarchy but did not necessarily have to. Centralized power, he stated, excelled at preventing, not action: "Centralization easily succeeds, indeed, in subjecting the external actions of men to a certain uniformity, which we come at last to love for its own sake."[18]

Using classical administration theory, Etzioni says the question of the effect of centralization on the efficiency and effectiveness of an organization is:

> **Whenever there are two or more organizational units, with one (or more) of them superior to the others in decision-making authority, which decisions should be left to the lower ones and which should be made by the higher units? The more decision-making authority held by those lower in the authority structure (and larger in number), the less centralized the organization is.**[19]

The degree of decentralization, Etzioni maintains, is influenced by cultural norms, the educational level of unit heads (the higher the level of education, the greater the decentralization that the organization can tolerate), the personality of the leader and the availability of specialized service units (which may increase coordination among departments). Centralized organizations will promote less local experimentation and less flexibility among units. They are more likely to be capable of providing facilities that independent units could not afford, and to enforce labor standards more efficiently.

DECENTRALIZATION AND LOCAL GOVERNMENT

During the last few decades, individual alienation has increased dramatically within American society. Political alienation, distrust of government and a sense of political powerlessness is eroding many traditional government forms. Urban riots, low voter registration, vandalism, apathy to the plight of others and lack of willingness to interact with government are all parts of the larger societal problem. Proponents of decentralization believe it can decrease people's sense of alienation because "decentralization reduces organizational scale and makes government more responsive to neighborhood needs; the citizen is more active in relation to neighborhood institutions, receives better services, and somehow becomes less alienated." It has also been argued that decentralization will give government better responsiveness to neighborhood needs; develop community cohesion, thus focusing local concern on shared problems; and increase local democracy by developing local leaders and providing wider opportunities for citizens in decision-making.

Those opposing decentralization argue that it will not solve any problems in urban areas unless there is a massive commitment of resources to the city. It is also argued that decentralization will increase racial segregation and strife by further polarizing neighborhoods. It may shortcut due-process procedures and administrative impartiality, thus permitting widespread corruption and inefficient allocation of resources.

METHODS OF DECENTRALIZATION

There are many methods by which local governments or other local organizations can decentralize. Governmental forms increase in autonomy the more that certain structural elements are included. Such elements include actually placing government officials in neighborhood offices to find out what is going on, giving local people authority to administer central government programs, and systematically getting the opinion of local people on policy issues.

Decentralization of governmental services to the neighborhood level takes one of several forms. Outreach programs often involve opening neighborhood-based "storefront" facilities in an attempt to bring governmental services closer to people by distributing information and investigating grievances at a neighborhood level. The shifting of the authority of a bureaucracy occurs under administrative decentralization from a central office to local district-based ones, on the assumption that the district-based officials will have a greater knowledge about neighborhood needs and can widely use increased authority to provide better services. Political decentralization refers to situations in which municipal resources are transferred to a neighborhood-based political entity. In some large cities, for instance, school systems with a central board of education have been divided into districts, each with a local governing board. Model Cities programs were an example of an attempt to develop alternative institutions. While no decentralization of the municipal bureaucracy occurs in this situation, development of alternative institutions is undertaken for the same purpose.

DECENTRALIZING PUBLIC LEISURE SERVICES

Government involvement in recreation and leisure has been affected by the recent movement toward political decentralization, and government officials are trying to find meaningful ways to respond. Doing so requires recognizing changing societal aspirations and the emergence of a new political system in which there is a power vacuum with tradeoffs among many groups, great consideration for minority opinion, and no one person really in charge.

A number of factors within this new political system have caused administrators of recreation, park and leisure service agencies to consider decentralization. Perhaps foremost of these factors has been the increased recognition of the extreme heterogeneity of the urban populations. As variation in the recreation needs and desires among different sectors of the population is recognized, it becomes increasingly difficult to plan programs centrally and to justify not adapting decisions to fit different situations. It may, for instance, be a workable policy to turn certain children's programs entirely over to volunteers in one section of a community while in other areas it may be completely infeasible. Fees and charges may enhance the ability of recreation personnel in one part of a city to offer special programs or programs with unusually high costs. In another area, however, such fees and changes may be untenable. Even as basic a question as what to do when confronted with illegal or anti-social behavior in a recreation center may have different answers in different parts of the city. In some areas, for instance, calling the police would improve the situation, whereas in other parts of the city it would make the situation worse, and in the most crime-ridden areas of the city, the police might not even come.

In some cases, recognition of the failure of urban recreation agencies to provide services that meet the interests of diverse neighborhoods has not come about until people have actually stopped using the facilities. Gold, for instance, cites a number of studies which conclude that many neighborhood parks are being underused or not used at all. Such non-use of neighborhood parks has three explanations: "(1) those who do not use the park may have some significant physical, mental or cultural difference from those who do; (2) the park's image and facilities do not coincide with the leisure preferences and satisfactions of the majority of potential users; and (3) some physical environmental or institutional restraints encourage non use.[20] Such non-use of facilities and declining attendance at recreation agency programs has caused several attempted decentralization schemes.

Another impetus to decentralize has been the increased availability of employees whose educational preparation has been in recreation or a related area. Since decentralization often results in more authority being given to those further down the chain of command, it is important that leaders and supervisors who are competent at making wise decisions are chosen. It should be noted, however, that few such students seek employment in inner-city or poverty areas.

Attempts at Decentralization

Recreation, park and leisure service agencies have attempted decentralization using a number of techniques. Some large public leisure service agencies have undergone administrative decentralization by dividing their constituencies into service areas or districts corresponding to geographical areas of the city and then assigning district supervisors to each of these districts. Instead of being advisors and carriers of messages between the recreation district and the recreation agency hierarchy, district supervisors would be given increased authority to distribute recreation resources within their district and to determine policy. The advantage the district supervisor would have under decentralization would be the ability to perceive a need and act upon it with a minimum of delay, interference or consideration of the "macro" political consequences. In effect, a large recreation agency would be made into a number of small ones, corresponding, perhaps, to neighborhoods and socio-economic boundaries.

In a number of Canadian recreation agencies, the area or district recreation supervisor has become a "Social Animator" under decentralization schemes. The social animator seeks to work with a group of individuals who are similar in life style and values to bring about positive changes in their environment. The animator seeks to bring people together to exchange views and define a common situation. After some common awareness is established, the group sets goals and then attempts to reach them in an autonomous manner. The animator serves to bring the group together, train members in the methods used by committees, help the group identify its informational requirements after goals have been set and establish divisions of labor and sequencing of tasks. He or she also may play a role in supervising the performance of the individuals within the group and assessing the results of the group's efforts.

Through social animation, the group is helped to become self-sufficient. The goals the members of the group set for themselves are not those of the animator but rather their own.

Social animation has great potential in low-income areas of cities, where many citizens have lost the sense of being participants in the decisions that effect their lives. Although the technique originated in the Province of Quebec, it would seem to have great potential elsewhere.

As applied to the recreation field, the use of social animation means that the recreation professional does not approach citizens with a preconceived set of recreation services, but rather seeks to bring residents together to establish a reference point for recreation and leisure, literally conceptualizing these terms as they relate to the values and goals of the group. Recreation goals are then set, with the help of the professional, using the resources of the recreation agency as requested.

A somewhat related concept found in some large urban recreation agencies in the United States is that of the "roving leader." This is an outreach worker assigned to a specific community to stimulate youth to participate in wholesome recreation programs. The outreach service tries to help disadvantaged youth use free time constructively and assists them in the effective use of community resources in education, employment, health services and so on. The roving leader starts with the group at its own level and may spend weeks, even months, establishing a rapport with the group. This may involve "hanging out" with the group in bars, pool halls, playgrounds or their "home turf." "The final proof of the roving leader's success is when he is no longer needed."

The social animator and roving leader are varieties of detached workers, that is street workers, block organizers, community development field staff workers and so forth. They represent an extension of the detached agency principle into an occupational role. Many public recreation agencies evolved from detached agencies, which have traditionally been settlement houses and neighborhood, community and youth centers. These detached agencies have generally been small in scale, secular in character, either autonomous or, if related to a larger sponsoring body, relatively independent, with a high degree of discretion for determining their own programs. Such agencies are commonly situated as geographically close to their client constituencies as possible.

New types of detached agencies have been developing in recent years, and there has also been a marked increase in the use of detached workers by such agencies and the concept of constituent involvement well past the traditional view of constituents as being either "clients" of services or "participants" in pre-planned programs.

Another aspect of decentralization has been the trend toward "portable programs" that can be brought to people at the neighborhood level. Often such programs are designed to take a recreation facility or program to people who are unlikely to come to it. Portable pools, nature mobiles, traveling zoos, temporary play streets and other innovations are attempts at diffusing program opportunities through all neighborhoods. Similarly, the mini-park or vestpocket park movement has tried to provide small parks in areas where there is no space for a larger one.

The experiences of many large urban recreation agencies with portable programs, however, have often not been positive. While many of the services were theoretically decentralized, local citizens often had little say in their operation, nor were they extensively involved in the planning. In many cases, the portable programs have not produced a greater sense of community among neighborhood residents. The mini-park movement, for example, has not been highly successful in inner-city areas. Although the Department of Housing and Urban Development spent $875 million in urban open space development in 1970, much of which was earmarked for the inner cities, the results have not been highly satisfactory. After observing over 200 small neighborhood parks in urban areas, Clay reported:

> **We were constantly struck with how empty they were even on warm days and evenings when we expected them to be teeming. There are exceptions, of course, but from a cross-country survey they are indeed underused. Some, photographed two years ago in Brooklyn as examples of innovative ways to use modular wooden components, are now vanishing through vandalism and deterioration, reabsorbed by wind and rain. Far worse is a later crop built of heavy concrete and steel which may be around for as long as mothballed battleships. In some places, neighbors complain the minipark causes increased vandalism to nearby homes, brings "winos, peeping Toms, drug-users and lovers" and "ruins" the neighborhood. So inappropriately located was a $15,000 parklet in a midwestern city that it was torn down and the area paved over for a parking lot—costing a second $15,000. Recently, neighborhood groups in a large eastern city turned down eight out of twelve proposed vestpocket parks as being irrelevant to the needs of the people.**[21]

CONCLUSIONS

In conclusion, it should be mentioned that many of the so-called attempts at decentralizing public recreation agencies have not really been decentralization at all, since little authority or responsibility has actually been shifted to the neighborhood level. In short, we still do not know if the decentralization of public leisure services can succeed and under what conditions it is most likely to do so.

REFERENCES

1. Wilson Head, *Neighborhood Participation In Local Government* (Toronto Bureau of Municipal Research, 1970), pp. 1–15.
2. Amitai Etzioni, *Modern Organizations* (Englewood Cliffs: Prentice-Hall, 1964), p. 101.
3. *A Citizen's Guide to Participating in the Planning of Free-time Facilities,* Toronto, Ontario, Research Council on Leisure, 1973, pp. 14–15.
4. Richard Kraus, *Public Recreation and the Negro; A Study of Participation and Administrative Practices* (New York: Center for Urban Education, 1968).
5. *Report of the National Advisory Commission on Civil Disorders* (New York: Bantam Books, 1968), p. 150.
6. Geoffrey Godbey, *The Role of Advisory Councils in Philadelphia's Department of Recreation* (University Park: Doctoral Dissertation, 1972), pp. 6–88.
7. Edward Lindeman, quoted by Collie Verner *in* James A. Draper, ed., *Citizen Participation: Canada,* (Toronto: New Press, 1971), pp. 423–424.
8. Lyle E. Schaller, "Is the Citizen Advisory Council a Threat to Representative Government?" *Public Administration Review,* Vol. 24, September, 1974, p. 175.
9. Genevieve Carter, "The Challenge of Research," in *Recreation Research* (Washington, D.C.: American Association of Health, Physical Education and Recreation, 1966), p. 7.
10. Canadian Association of Adult Education, *Advisory Councils* (Toronto, 1971), p. 1.
11. "Local Parks and Recreation," *Parks and Recreation,* Vol. VI, 1971, p. 19.
12. Robert M. Artz, "Citizen Leadership," *Parks and Recreation,* 1971, Vol. V1, pp. 109–126.
13. Philadelphia Department of Recreation, *Community Organization for Recreation* (mimeographed), 1968, pp. 2–5.
14. *Philadelphia Model Cities Program* (mimeographed), 1970.
15. Select Committee on the Utilization of Educational Facilities, *Interim Report Number One,* June, 1973, p. 3.
16. Report of the City-School Coordinating Committee, revised October, 1965; retyped by the Recreation and Parks Department, Pennsylvania State University, University Park, Pennsylvania, July, 1967.
17. *Guide to Public Involvement in Decision-Making* (Washington, D.C.: U.S. Forest Service, 1974), p. 14.
18. Alexis de Tocqueville, *Democracy in America,* edited by Richard D. Heffner (New York: The New American Library, 1956), pp. 62, 63.
19. Etzioni, op. cit., p. 28.
20. Seymour Gold, "The Titanic Effect on Parks and Recreation," *Parks and Recreation,* Vol. X, 1975, pp. 23–25, 42–43.
21. Nanine Clay, "Miniparks—Diminishing Returns," Parks and Recreation, Vol. VI, 1971, p. 23.

QUESTIONS

1. What is the difference between pressure tactics and confrontation tactics?
2. How would you go about creating a local recreation and parks advisory committee in your home town?

3. What are some of the advantages and disadvantages of the use of advisory councils in the recreation and parks field?

4. Give some examples of situations in which it might be appropriate for a leisure service to hold a hearing.

5. What is "social animation"?

When freedom of choice is evident, recreation, park and leisure services become a part—an important part—of a continuing and ultimate celebration: the celebration of life.
(U.S. Bureau of Outdoor Recreation; photo by Ted Dingman)

chapter 18

EVALUATION AND SOME OTHER FINAL CONSIDERATIONS

This chapter will discuss the evaluation process in recreation, park and leisure service agencies, as well as some of the issues affecting the future of these agencies, such as professionalization, coordination among agencies and leisure provision as a secondary function of other organizations

EVALUATION BASED ON CONCEPTS OF NEED

In one sense, evaluation has already been dealt with in this book. Because evaluation depends on one's concept of recreation need, organizations will ultimately be evaluated in terms of how well they meet the recreation needs of those they serve or are supposed to serve. Basically, we have dealt with five concepts of recreation need, each of which implies certain methods of evaluation. General evaluative approaches springing from these concepts of need are as follows:

1. *Normative Need*—Since normative need implies that desirable minimum supplies of recreation resources can be prescribed through the use of standards, a primary method of evaluation would be determining the extent to which recreation standards are being met by a given agency.

2. *Felt Need*—Felt need assumes that people's attitudes and opinions are the basis for determining what recreation services should be provided; therefore evaluation would be undertaken by obtaining the attitudes and opinions of those served or eligible to be served toward what has been provided.

3. *Expressed Need*—Expressed need assumes that what people are currently doing during their leisure time is the surest indication of what they need or want. Therefore, evaluation would be based primarily upon the extent to which people participate in activities and utilize facilities provided by a particular leisure service organization.

4. *Comparative Need*—The assumption of comparative need is that certain subsections of the population, such as those at the poverty level, have a comparatively greater need for recreation services than do others in the population. In evaluating an organization's leisure services according to comparative need, the distribution of resources among the population would be the primary consideration.

5. *Created Need*—This is a leisure need which those served do not have until a leisure service organization creates an interest and appreciation for it. Evaluating agencies on the basis of created need would, like expressed need, rely primarily on participation and attendance figures.

Different types of recreation, park and leisure service organizations will use different evaluation measures. Commercial organizations, such as resorts, use financial profit as the ultimate evaluative measure, since participant counts and trends are directly related to financial success. It is also possible that agencies may rely on an evaluative concept that does not present a true picture; the Camp Fire Girls, for instance, may have a preconceived notion of what types of programs are desirable, and thus pay less attention to the actual felt needs of young girls. Recognizing that different organizations will be interested in different aspects of evaluation, the following basic types of evaluative measures may be undertaken.

EVALUATIVE MEASURES RELATING TO SIZE, SCOPE AND SUFFICIENCY

These measures are concerned with answering questions pertaining to the following areas:

Attendance

1. What was the total attendance for each service offered over a given period of time?
2. How many people attended each service offered over a given period of time? Why?
3. How many people did not attend the services who potentially could have? Why?

Variety and Availability

4. What is the total number of separate program services offered?
5. What percentage of the population lives within a given number of minutes or miles of the program or facility?
6. How many hours per day, days per week, weeks per year is the program or facility available?

Cost

7. What is the per capita cost of providing leisure services?

EVALUATIVE MEASURES RELATING TO QUALITY

These evaluative measures are concerned with answering the following questions:

Eligibility

1. Who is allowed to use the facility or participate in the program?
2. Must they possess certain equipment?
3. Must they register in advance?
4. What is the attitude of users and non-users toward fees and charges imposed as a condition of participation?

Safety

5. How many or what percentage of the participants have incurred an injury or illness as a result of their participation?
6. How often do criminal acts take place at recreation and park facilities?

Crowdedness and Maintenance

7. What percentage of participants or non-participants perceive the leisure service in question to be overcrowded?

8. What is the ratio between attendance and physical carrying capacity?

9. How long must interested people wait to participate in a given program or use a recreation facility?

10. How many or what percentage of non-users avoid a given program or facility because of the physical appearance of the facility or area or the conditions under which it is maintained?

11. How many or what percentage of users of a facility or area are satisfied with the maintenance of the area or facility?

Leadership and Supervision

12. How many or what percentage of non-users avoid a given program or facility because of perceived inadequate leadership or supervision?

13. How many or what percentage of leaders and supervisors meet appropriate certification standards?

EVALUATIVE MEASURES RELATING TO EFFECTS OF PARTICIPATION

These measures attempt to answer the following:

1. What changes occurred in the leisure skills or competencies of participants?

2. What were the economic consequences in terms of surrounding property values, business income generated in the surrounding area and jobs created?

3. What undesirable consequences occurred to the area in which the activity took place (e.g., traffic congestion; air, water and noise pollution; incidents of anti-social behavior; harm to property)?

4. What is the relationship between participation in leisure services and propensity to commit crimes?

5. What is the relationship between participation and the health and physical fitness of the participant?

These and other subjects of evaluation are relevant to a variety of recreation, park and leisure service organizations. All evaluation processes are necessarily dependent upon the goals and objectives of the organization in question. As some of the earlier chapters showed, many such organizations have only a very general, sometimes even vague, notion of what it is they seek to accomplish. While this situation is not much different from that in other types of organizations, such as education organizations, it does mean that evaluation processes will be diverse and often subject to different interpretations. This is viewed as a problem by many systems analysts, who seem to believe that it is possible for an organization concerned with leisure behavior to precisely state its goals in quantifiable terms. While it is true that many leisure service organizations, particularly those in the public sector, have *not* addressed themselves to sufficiently precise statements of goals and objectives and should be encouraged to do so, it must be recognized that leisure service organizations cannot always state goals and objectives in a precise and complete way. Such an approach is ultimately impossible, because leisure activity and behavior are not finite. In motivation, style, form, social grouping, duration, satisfaction level and other important aspects, leisure and recreation activity is ever-changing. As proof of this, we need merely to examine the cliché that what is leisure for one person is work for another, and vice versa. No listing or classification of different leisure activities ever seems satisfactory to us. It is either incomplete, or it doesn't accurately reflect the true motivation of the participant, or it doesn't capture the meaning or essence of the activity. A simple activity such as picnicking could involve infinite combinations of physical settings, social groupings, motivations, travel, types of food, related activities and so on. Because of this, and because leisure and recreation activity is constantly changing, recreation, park and leisure service organization cannot become too specific in setting their goals and objectives, because of the danger of limiting the activities, areas, facilities and clientele they are to deal with.

LEISURE SERVICES AS AN EMERGING PROFESSION

During the last 50 years, primarily because of the involvement of government and the growth of voluntary youth-serving agencies, recreation, park and leisure services have come a long way toward professionalization. Although its roots are in such diverse areas as social work, physical education, forestry, landscape architecture and public administration, recreation and park services today is a recognized occupational specialty possessing many of the characteristics of a true profession.

GRADUATE TRAINING IN LEISURE SERVICES

Since 1926, when the National Recreation Association began the National Recreation School for Professional Graduate Training, higher education opportunities in leisure services have multiplied. In 1940 there were still only ten undergraduate curricula in recreation and parks. By 1950 there were 38, by 1960 there were 66 and by 1970 there were 261 programs in existence. This rate of increase caused some alarm among many recreation and parks professionals, who feared that too many students were being prepared for the profession as it then existed.

In 1970, of the 144 baccalaureate programs in recreation and parks in the United States and Canada, 40 percent emphasized recreation program management. Fifteen percent emphasized park and/or natural resource management and 45 percent stressed recreation program and park management.[1] At the associate degree level, of the 70 curricula in existence, 59 percent stressed recreation program management, 31 percent emphasized recreation program and park management and 10 percent emphasized park and/or natural resource management. Of the 16,719 students majoring in recreation and parks in 1970, 20 percent were at the associate degree level, 69 percent at the baccalaureate level, 9 percent at the master's level and 2 percent at the doctoral level.

By 1973, Stein found that a huge increase in enrollment had taken place since 1970. As many as 27,694 undergraduates were enrolled in recreation and park curricula in the United States and Canada.[1] A total of 5780 students were enrolled in 122 associate degree programs, while 21,894 students were pursuing baccalaureate degrees. This represented a student increase of 65 percent over 1970. It should be noted, however, that the number of doctoral students declined slightly during this period. By 1975, an estimated 35,000 students were enrolled in various programs. Of these students, 23.5 percent were associate degree students, 68.3 percent were baccalaureate degree students, 7.5 percent were enrolled in Master's degree programs and 0.6 percent were pursuing the doctorate.[2]

Many such programs are beginning to deal with the issues of leisure in a broader context, recognizing the heightened importance of the role of leisure services in facilitating leisure activity and shaping leisure values in contemporary society. This has meant a closer relationship with other disciplines such as sociology, psychology, landscape architecture, political science and urban and regional planning. Furthermore, many curriculums have begun to develop course work relating to commercial recreation operations, and are therefore seeking to strengthen their ties with the field of business administration.

It is too early to judge the impact of professional education programs on recreation, park and leisure services. A recent study by Henkel and Godbey reported the percentages of employees in public recreation and park agencies who possessed advanced preparation in recreation and parks (see Tables 18–1 and 18–2).[3]

Students who graduated from recreation and park curricula still constitute a minority of employees in public recreation and parks. This situation undoubtedly parallels that in other employment areas such as therapeutic recreation and commercial recreation. It should be noted, however, that over half the chief executives in public recreation and parks have a college or university degree in recreation and parks. It is expected that the percentage of employees holding such degrees will continue to increase as the field of recreation and parks moves toward professionalization and university programs increase in quality and quantity.

LITERATURE, RESEARCH AND PROFESSIONAL ORGANIZATIONS

Just as higher education curricula related to leisure services have multiplied, so has the literature. During the 1960's, a number of books appeared dealing with leisure and its challenges in contemporary society. The establishment of the *Journal of Leisure Research* in 1969 gave impetus to leisure-related research, as did the publication of *Society and Leisure*, also begun in 1969 and issued quarterly by the European Centre for Leisure and Education in Prague, Czechoslovakia. The introduction of *Leisure Sciences: An Interdisciplinary Journal* in 1977 represented the second journal geared specifically to recreation and leisure-related research. Other publications—*Therapeutic Recreation Journal, Parks and Recreation, Leisure Today, Recreation Review, Review of Sport and Leisure, Recreation Canada, The Journal of Leisurability, Outdoor Recreation, Action* and many others—contribute to leisure service professionals' understanding of their work in its many contexts.

Currently, several educational and research institutes are involved in the study of leisure. The research, conferences and publications of these centers have contributed much to interdisciplinary interest in leisure. The following are among the better known centers: the Leisure Centre in Hamburg, University of Hamburg, Hamburg, Germany; the Leisure Research Group, Department of Sociology, University of Lund, Lund, Sweden; the European Centre

TABLE 18–1 Percentage of Employees at Each Educational Level by the Level of Government Agency

Political Unit	High School or Lower		Some Post High School		Associate Rec./Park		Associate Other		Bachelor Rec./Park		Bachelor Other		Master Rec/Park		Master Other		Total	
	#	%	#	%	#	%	#	%	#	%	#	%	#	%	#	%	#	%
Municipality	10,895	49.51	4,282	19.46	523	1.38	855	3.89	2,087	9.48	2,518	11.44	474	2.15	373	1.69	22,007	61.26
County	4,836	51.74	1,463	15.65	204	2.18	275	2.94	1,278	13.67	1,024	10.96	144	1.54	123	1.32	9,347	26.02
Special District	641	34.83	351	19.08	47	2.55	61	3.32	333	18.10	269	14.62	68	3.70	70	3.80	1,840	5.12
State	1,518	55.60	365	13.37	95	3.48	149	5.46	145	5.31	393	14.40	15	.55	50	1.83	2,730	7.60
Combined Total	17,890	49.80	6,461	17.99	869	2.42	1,340	3.73	3,843	10.70	4,204	11.70	701	1.95	616	1.71	35,924	100.00

Source: Donald D. Henkel and Geoffrey C. Godbey, *Parks, Recreation, and Leisure Services—Employment in the Public Sector: Status and Trends* (Arlington, Virginia: National Recreation and Park Association, 1977), p. 44.

TABLE 18–2 Percentage of Employees at Each Educational Level by Occupational Category

Occupational Category	High School or Lower		Some Post High School		Associate Rec./Parks		Associate Other		Bachelor Rec./Parks		Bachelor Other		Master Rec./Parks		Master Other		Total	
POSITION	#	%	#	%	#	%	#	%	#	%	#	%	#	%	#	%	#	%
1. CHIEF EXECUTIVE	68	4.46	111	7.28	29	1.90	40	2.62	468	30.69	347	22.75	303	19.87	159	10.43	1,525	4.24
2. ASST. DIR. PARKS & REC.	41	6.79	82	13.58	19	3.15	20	3.31	186	30.78	161	26.66	66	10.93	29	4.80	604	1.68
3. SUPERINTENDENT OF PARKS	174	27.70	145	23.09	30	4.78	32	5.10	101	16.08	103	16.40	23	3.66	20	3.19	628	1.75
4. SUPERINTENDENT OF REC.	23	4.90	29	6.18	19	4.05	9	1.92	194	41.36	104	22.18	64	13.65	27	5.76	469	1.30
5. DIVISION HEADS	151	18.78	165	20.52	9	1.12	37	4.60	118	14.68	235	29.23	27	3.36	62	7.71	804	2.24
6. RELATED PARK PROS.	55	5.72	92	9.56	8	.83	44	4.57	119	12.37	556	57.81	16	1.66	72	7.48	962	2.68
7. DIST. SUPERVISOR PARKS	115	28.89	131	32.91	14	3.52	25	6.28	47	11.81	60	15.08	2	.50	4	1.01	398	1.11
8. PARK MANAGERS	450	38.26	234	19.90	36	3.06	47	4.0	209	17.77	171	14.54	14	1.19	15	1.28	1,176	3.27
9. PARK POLICE	916	61.73	285	19.21	18	1.21	58	3.91	68	4.58	118	7.95	7	.47	14	.94	1,484	4.13
10. FOREMEN	2,045	67.42	676	22.29	67	2.21	104	3.43	47	1.55	85	2.80	3	.10	6	.20	3,033	8.44
11. SKILLED PARK PERSONNEL	10,511	77.44	2,375	17.50	115	.85	325	2.39	54	.40	185	1.36	1	.01	7	.05	13,573	37.79
12. DIST. SUPERVISOR REC.	34	10.86	28	8.95	8	2.56	9	2.88	105	33.54	88	28.11	23	7.35	18	5.75	313	.87
13. RECREATION SUPERVISOR	188	9.70	231	11.92	53	2.74	71	3.66	739	38.13	501	25.85	88	4.54	67	3.46	1,938	5.39
14. COMMUNITY CENTER DIR.	203	14.11	207	14.38	75	5.21	65	4.52	436	30.29	403	28.01	27	1.88	23	1.60	1,439	4.01
15. RECREATION FAC. SUPV.	238	32.08	164	22.10	20	2.70	32	4.31	115	15.50	145	19.54	7	.94	21	2.83	742	2.06
16. ACTIVITY SPECIALISTS	353	25.04	361	25.60	77	5.46	78	5.53	163	11.56	328	23.26	12	.85	38	2.70	1,410	3.92
17. REC. PROGRAM LEADERS	757	23.60	726	22.63	211	6.58	285	8.88	643	20.04	543	16.93	17	.53	26	.81	3,208	8.93
18. RECREATION AIDES	1,568	70.69	419	18.89	61	2.75	59	2.66	31	1.40	71	3.20	1	.05	8	.36	2,218	6.17
TOTALS	17,890	49.80	6,461	17.99	869	2.42	1,340	3.73	3,843	10.70	4,204	11.70	701	1.95	616	1.71	35,924	99.99

Source: Donald D. Henkel and Geoffrey C. Godbey, *Parks, Recreation, and Leisure Services—Employment in the Public Sector: Status and Trends* (Arlington, Virginia: National Recreation and Park Association, 1977), p. 47.

for Leisure and Education, Prague, Czechoslovakia; the Section on Leisure and Culture, Institute of Philosophy and Culture, Polish Academy of Science, Warsaw, Poland; the Centre of Sociological Studies, Study Group on Leisure and Popular Culture, Paris; the Leisure Research Center, Tokyo, Japan; the Recreation and Leisure Studies Center, Federal University of the Rio Grande, Brazil; and the Leisure Studies Program, University of South Florida, Tampa, Florida.

A number of professional organizations serve the leisure-service professional. The *National Recreation and Park Association* is a national organization of both laymen and professionals interested in expanding the recreation and park resources, programs and professional services of the American people through research, education and service undertakings. The NRPA, which was created in 1966 through the merger of the American Recreation Society, the American Institute of Park Executives, the American Association of Zoological Parks and Aquariums, the National Conference on State Parks and the National Recreation Association, is currently the nation's largest non-profit organization in the recreation and parks field, with over 17,000 members. Currently it has seven branches: the American Park and Recreation Society, the Armed Forces Recreation Society, the Commissioners-Board Members, the National Conference on State Parks, the National Student Recreation and Park Society, the National Therapeutic Recreation Society and the Society of Park and Recreation Educators.

The *World Leisure and Recreation Association,* located in New York City, seeks to coordinate and increase cooperation among the national and international organizations operating in the fields of play, recreation and leisure. It serves as a consultant to the United Nations and its agencies, arranges for international conferences and conducts exchange programs.

The *International Playground Association* promotes playgrounds and leisure-time facilities in every country through international exchange and cooperation, and coordinates the efforts of national and international agencies having similar aims. The organization also sponsors an international conference at least once every three years.

The *National Industrial Recreation Association,* located in Chicago, is interested in promoting industrial recreation as a sound management policy and in improving the caliber of these programs. It is a non-profit organization that tries to keep its members abreast of trends in industrial recreation through workshops, conferences and the publication of its magazine, *Recreation Management.*

The *National Association of County Park and Recreation Officials* is an affiliate of the National Association of Counties, designed to lend either support or opposition to federal government policies in the field of recreation and parks, and to stimulate interest in county recreation programs through education and information programs.

The *American Alliance of Health, Physical Education and Recreation* is a voluntary professional organization interested in improving the quality of American life through programs of health, physical education and recreation. AAHPER, which is affiliated with the National Education Association, is made up of career members with career interests in athletics, dance, outdoor education, recreation, safety education, school nursing and sports. The organization has taken a greater interest in the recreation and leisure movement during the last few years and currently publishes *Leisure Today,* as well as many other publications.

The *American Association of Zoological Parks and Aquariums* promotes the advancement of these facilities, both as educational and recreational institutions, through programs of professional registration, legislative support, workshops and publications.

In Canada, the *Canadian Parks and Recreation Association* is concerned with the "stimulation and advancement of National, Provincial, Regional and Municipal Parks, recreation and leisure services, facilities and programs in Canada." CPRA sponsors educational and research projects and publishes *Recreation Canada.*

Many other organizations serve the leisure-service professional when we define leisure service in the broader sense. Among these are the American Association of Museums, the American Library Association, the American Society of Landscape Architects, the American Society of Planning Officials, the International Association of Auditorium Managers and many others.

To date, there has been no widespread licensing of leisure service professionals as there has been with public school teachers, doctors or lawyers. Some state societies of recreation and parks professionals have established voluntary registration plans, but usually without examinations or other kinds of professional competency testing. Such plans have generally had little impact.

In 1973, however, the National Recreation and Park Association Board of Trustees approved a Model Registration Plan which differentiated between "professional" and "technician" levels of responsibility, established education as a requisite for professional recognition and gave definite advantage to those having recreation and park degrees.[4] This model plan stated conditions for national approval, specifying requirements that would have to be incorporated into new or existing state recreation and park societies or registration plans of branches of the National Recreation and Park Association. Some certification system seems a strong possibility within the near future.

In 1976, however, Professor Pat Delaney, Chairperson of the National Registration Board of the National Recreation and Park Association, reported the following:[5]

> **Registration continues to be voluntary in spite of several past and current efforts to develop mandatory licensing through state legislation.**
>
> **Few park and recreation job specifications require, or even suggest, registration, except for therapeutic recreation positions.**
>
> **Registration continues to be seen by some practitioners primarily as a status or image symbol, with little functional value.**
>
> **Park and recreation professionals remain divided on the merits of registration.**
>
> **No national examination process exists that is reliable and valid.**
>
> **Retention of one's registration status is based exclusively on the payment of renewal fees, as opposed to substantive criteria like continued education.**
>
> **It will be a few years before accreditation of park and recreation curricula will have an impact on registration standards.**
>
> **Only a third of all states have registration plans approved by the NRPA National Registration Board; a third of the states operate plans without NRPA recognition; and a third of the states are without registration programs.**

Obviously, this phase of professionalization has a long way to go, but the recent large-scale increase of students majoring in recreation and parks or leisure services at the university level would seem to indicate that registration-certification will stand a better chance for widespread implementation in the near future.

Leisure service professionals today work in many diverse settings, including municipal, state (provincial) and federal government agencies; voluntary youth-serving agencies such as the Young Women's Christian Association or Boys' Clubs; hospitals, correctional institutions and other institutions for special need populations; churches and synagogues; public schools; the armed forces; libraries and museums; industrial and other employee-based recreation services; travel and tourism agencies; private and commercial recreation enterprises, such as resorts; and recreation planning and consulting firms.

The roles assumed by leisure service professionals are many, including manager, administrator, supervisor, leader, community organizer, planner, consultant, educator and therapist. These roles are rapidly changing, and while it is difficult to generalize, in many cases changes have led to a broader concern with leisure resources, along with greater involvement in stimulating and coordinating the leisure resources of a community or institution through planning and citizen involvement rather than by direct leadership of specific activities.

No one can accurately predict the future roles of the leisure service professional, but Toffler's comments in *Future Shock* could be relevant.[6] Toffler believes that our economy has gone from the production of goods as a primary concern to the production of services, and will next go to the production of "experiences" for people, in which pre-programmed experiences or series of experiences of a leisure nature will be designed, using simulated or live environments. Education, he believes, will become a key experience industry. The leisure-service professional may well become an "experience maker" in the future, designing leisure environments and experiences based upon psychological need. In such a role, the leisure service professional would work with many organizations whose primary functions weren't recreation, park or leisure services.

Many other types of organizations provide recreation, park or leisure services as a secondary function. Government agencies concerned with housing, for instance, may be interested in improving play space for children in public housing. Airlines may provide vacation and touring packages. The many public and private agencies concerned with the management of land often become involved in recreation management after it has become apparent that people wish to use the land in question for recreative purposes.

It may be said that a number of types of organizations with primary purposes other than recreation are beginning to recognize the leisure element of their mission. Public schools show increasing interest in education for leisure and willingness to let facilities be used for a wide range of leisure activities. Shopping malls are sponsoring entertainment and contests and providing room for special interest groups to meet. Even cemeteries have been made available for a number of forms of outdoor recreation! So far there has been comparatively little interaction between such organizations and recreation, park and leisure service professionals. The trend, however, appears to be toward more involvement. Ultimately, the role of the recreation, park and leisure professionals with organizations whose primary mission is in another area may be equally important or even more important than their services to leisure-oriented organizations. The proliferation of college and university programs to train such professionals may accelerate this trend.

A CAUTIONARY FAREWELL

Much of what has been said in this book would seem to imply that it might be logical to organize recreation, park and leisure services into one unified system of agencies that would coordinate offerings, avoid duplication of services and allocate resources in a rational manner.

It is true that recreation, park and leisure service organizations are interdependent, need similar kinds of information, face common issues in terms of involving their clients in both their decision-making processes and in the social meaning of the activities and facilities they sponsor. In spite of this, it is the author's belief that a system of interlocking recreation, park and leisure service organizations would be disastrous for all concerned. There are a number of reasons for this. A first concern, as stated earlier, is that leisure activity is infinite. It cannot be completely systematized. Leisure research cannot ultimately explain or predict it. Because of this, it is important to have a mix of organizations offering leisure opportunities that provide *alternative* meanings, *alternative* styles, *alternative* social groups and *alternative* environments, and proceed from *alternative* goals and assumptions about what is worthwhile. Leisure and recreation are concepts in which individual choice is central, and individual choice cannot be protected if all choices are part of a system with one set of values, styles and decision-making processes.

A second danger that a conglomeration of recreation, park and leisure service agencies would bring about is the increased potential to use leisure as a means of social control. By concentrating power within a system of leisure service agencies, the individual citizen would have fewer alternatives and thus would be more subject to control by that system. Many countries with totalitarian governments recognize the importance of controlling leisure activity as a means of carrying out other objectives.

Recreation, park and leisure services provide one alternative or set of alternatives for the use of leisure. Most of an individual's leisure continues to be spent "around home" with friends and family, or by oneself. It is important that this aspect of leisure be protected; that the official organization of all kinds of leisure be avoided. Individuals need to be free *not* to join, *not* to participate, *not* to "get organized." Those who work in recreation, park and leisure service organizations must remember this.

When such freedom of choice is evident, the recreation, park and leisure services become a part—an important part—of a continuing and ultimate celebration: the celebration of life.

REFERENCES

1. T. Stein, "Recreation and Park Education in the United States and Canada—1973," *Parks and Recreation*, January, 1974, pp. 32–33.
2. T. Stein and R. Lancaster, "Professional Preparation," *Parks and Recreation*, July, 1976, p. 55.
3. D. Henkel and G. Godbey, *Parks, Recreation and Leisure Services: Employment in the Public*

Sector—Status and Trends (Arlington, Virginia, National Recreation and Park Association, 1977), pp. 44 and 47.
4. J. Sharpless, "Registration/Certification," *Parks and Recreation,* August, 1974, pp. 26–27, 46–47.
5. P. Delaney, "Registration/Certification," *Parks and Recreation,* July, 1976, p. 78.
6. A. Toffler, *Future Shock* (New York: Bantam Books, 1970), pp. 219–234.

QUESTIONS

1. Why is it difficult for some recreation, park and leisure service agencies to evaluate themselves?

2. What are some evaluation measures related to crowdedness? How might information be collected concerning each of these measures?

3. What evidence is there that recreation, park and leisure services is an emerging profession?

4. Do you believe a college or university degree in recreation and parks should be required of all those working in recreation, park and leisure services? Explain.

5. Do you agree that a single interlocking system of recreation, park and leisure services is not advisable?

INDEX

Page numbers that are *italicized* denote illustrations; (t) denotes tables.